*MARIA CHRISTINA, QUEEN REGENT.*

# SPAIN

IN

# THE NINETEENTH CENTURY

BY

## ELIZABETH WORMELEY LATIMER

AUTHOR OF "FRANCE IN THE NINETEENTH CENTURY," "RUSSIA
AND TURKEY IN THE NINETEENTH CENTURY," "ENGLAND
IN THE NINETEENTH CENTURY," "EUROPE IN AFRICA
IN THE NINETEENTH CENTURY," "ITALY IN
THE NINETEENTH CENTURY," ETC.

FIFTH EDITION

CHICAGO
A. C. McCLURG & CO.
1903

# NOTE.

THE present volume will be the last of this Nineteenth-Century series of Historical Narratives. I again disclaim, as I have done in several previous prefatory Notes, any right to be classed as an "historian," and deprecate being judged by the high standards properly applied to those who look beneath the surface of events, and elucidate the causes of history.

I would like to say, however, that I claim one merit for this book, — that there is no other, so far as I know, which supplies what it offers to my readers, namely, a general view of what has happened in Spain during the present century.

There are many excellent books, both of history and travel, which tell us about Spain in the days of her glory, — about Ferdinand and Isabella, the expulsion of the Moors, the Peninsular War, the Alhambra, Bull-fights, and the Cathedrals; but there seems to be nowhere a continuous history of the period about which I have been writing. I have had to dig out my facts, one by one, from contemporary sources; or, to use a more feminine simile, I have drawn my threads out of a tangled skein.

I trust my readers will not find the story too involved to be interesting. It has many picturesque peaks, but, like hills in Navarre and the Basque country, it has between

these peaks rugged paths, dense thickets, and miry morasses.
I have done my best; some one, no doubt, hereafter will do
better. Meantime I offer my readers what I do not think
they can at present find elsewhere without much patient
research and literary labor.

E. W. L.

BONNYWOOD,
HOWARD CO., MARYLAND.

# CONTENTS.

# LIST OF ILLUSTRATIONS.

# SPAIN

## IN THE NINETEENTH CENTURY.

———◆———

### CHAPTER I.

#### THE PRINCE OF THE PEACE.

THE history of Spain since she sank from wealth and greatness into a second-rate, impoverished power, is one continued tangle of revolutions. Revolution is interlocked with revolution, all seeming to end nowhere and in nothing.

It is not an agreeable history to write, nor even to read, because of its inextricable confusion, but it has several prominent points of great interest which rise like mountain peaks out of a dim chaos. It is these mountain peaks that I will endeavor to point out; the history between them lies without form and void, each event seeming to be the prelude to a revolution.

The story of Napoleon's connection with the affairs of Spain constitutes at once the most disreputable and the most disastrous chapter in the history of his career. To understand it we should know something of the Spanish character, and of the events that immediately preceded the nineteenth century. These may be best told briefly in a sketch of the career of Don Manuel Godoy, Prince of the Peace, Duke of Alcudia, Count of Evora Monte, Grandee of the First Class in Spain, Commander of the Knights of Malta, Knight of the Golden Fleece, Grand Cross of the order of Charles III., President of the Council of Castile, Generalissimo of the Spanish Armies, Colonel of the Household Troops, High Admiral of Spain, etc.

Before taking up the history of this unworthy favorite we will say a few words that may throw light on the character of the Spanish people.

It is with no wish to join a popular cry that I charge the Inquisition with the deterioration that has taken place in the Spanish character since the days of their great national heroes Gonsalvo de Cordova, and Don John of Austria. Popular opinion dwells only on the horrors of the Inquisition ; we hear little of its effects on the moral and intellectual character of Spaniards, or of the fatal division of classes which it produced, the result of which in modern times has been to induce the greater part of a brave but unfortunate people to rush recklessly from anarchical " liberty" into absolute despotism, and *vice versa.*

For seven centuries Spain had carried on a fierce war of religion, a contest which connected honor with orthodoxy in the minds of Spaniards, and associated all that is disgraceful and odious with dissent from the established creed.   " When Moorish wars ended, orthodoxy became the principle of that pretended superiority of nature which distinguishes the nobler from the inferior or degenerate castes."   All Spaniards with purity of descent were entitled to bear the epithet " Honorable."   The poorest peasant was prouder of his genuine and unpolluted Christian blood than the grandees of their proudest titles.   Indeed, the highest nobles and even the sovereigns had occasionally sullied their line by misalliances with misbelievers, and so entailed on their posterity the reproach of having some among their ancestors who, as the Spanish saying expressed it, " had stood upon their legs for baptism."

When, in the present century, revolutionists were trying to cast reproach on the nobility of Spain, a pamphlet was printed to show that many of the grandees had had one or more infidel ancestors, and these disclosures were so damaging to hereditary adherents of royalty that all the power of the government and the Inquisition was put forth for the suppression of the pamphlet, of which copies were secretly circulated from hand to hand.

Honor and disgrace are matters of opinion. No Spaniard, however liberal his political opinions might be, could
bear the discovery of mixed blood in his veins. The Cortes
in Cadiz refused citizenship to any man in Spain or in its
colonies whose descent was tainted by any drop of African
or Indian blood. We shall see the effect of this when we
come to consider the history of the Spanish colonies in
America.

The distinction between a heretic and a Mohammedan is,
almost to this day, too nice for the peasant class in Spain.
The Church condemned both alike; they belonged to the
same category, and it was the part of a faithful Christian to
hold both in abhorrence.

Disgrace entailed on his posterity from generation to generation was often felt to be the worst part of the punishment
of a heretic at an *auto da fé*. The "decree of infamy" was
harder to bear than the stake. Men who had suffered everything else with composure have been known to burst into
tears when that part of their sentence was read. In other
martyrdoms the sufferer had support and consolation in his
sense of dying with honor, but where was the bold spirit of
inquiry or love of truth which could induce a Castilian
possessor of a bright inheritance of honor, purchased by the
blood of his ancestors in wars with misbelievers, to swerve
from the religion for which those ancestors had bled, and
thereby sink, with his posterity, to the social status which
classed him among the remnant of execrated misbelievers?

At the close of the sixteenth century a strong spirit of
religious inquiry began to display itself among the learned,
who were chiefly of the priestly class in Spain; and churches
identical in creed with those in Protestant Germany —
though they took no distinctive name — sprang up at Valladolid and Seville. Soon all learning was discouraged by the
Inquisition, and viewed with suspicion, both by the ignorant
and in social circles. Whole libraries of valuable books and
manuscripts were committed to the flames; so also were all
Hebrew and Arabic writings. This policy was carried out
in Mexico by the monks who accompanied Cortez and his

followers, and we have thus lost valuable records of Aztec civilization. Yet Cardinal Ximenes, who is accused of having instigated this destruction of libraries and manuscripts, promoted the publication of the first Polyglot Bible, before fanatical fury had borne him away in its stream.

The Inquisition, first established in France to root out the heresy of the Albigenses, was in 1477 introduced into Spain by the pious Isabella, and its powers were enlarged under Charles V., her grandson. Many historians think that his unhappy mother, Joanna the Mad, was considered insane only because she had imbibed the new views of religion. She was imprisoned, and even tortured, by order of her son, with a view, it is believed, to make her renounce her heresy.

The wars waged by the Spaniards against Protestants in the Low Countries and in Germany intensified their hatred against those who might, by writing or by speech, spread heresy in their own most orthodox land.

On the accession of Philip II. a fierce persecution began in Old Castile and Andalusia against all those suspected of opinions not in conformity with the doctrines of the Church of Rome. The Protestants of Valladolid and Seville were rooted out, their churches were broken up, and on Trinity Sunday, 1559, an *auto da fé* was held at Valladolid with great pomp in honor of the presence of Don Carlos, Prince of the Asturias, who, with his aunt (the king's own sister), the grandees and ladies of their suites, together with the nobility and gentry in and around the city, occupied the great Square, which was fitted up as an amphitheatre.

Fourteen persons, men and women, were there condemned to die by fire; and sixteen others, condemned only to *infamy* and perpetual imprisonment, received their sentences. After a sermon had been preached to them, and their doom had been read, those condemned to the stake were handed over to the civil authority, and burned without the city.

The last of these executions by fire for heresy took place at Seville in 1783. In one of the earlier *autos da fé* in the same city two Englishmen were among the victims. From

the records of these atrocities Charles Kingsley drew his
pictures in " Westward Ho ! "

The great peril of knowledge — the danger that learning
might lead to suspicions of unorthodoxy — crushed the spirit
of mental independence among the leisure classes in Spain.
Religious dissent, as we have seen, entailed not only death
but degradation. Every advance in knowledge seemed to
imperil the honor of the nation. The study of the ancient
languages was discouraged, travel in foreign lands was condemned. Spanish books were under such strict censorship
that they were almost prohibited. Saint Theresa has recorded her feelings of despair when a sweeping decree of
the Holy Office snatched from her hands the books that
were her friends. " My grief," she says, " was exceedingly
great, for many amongst them were to me a constant source
of consolation. What could I do for reading, all Spanish
books being taken away, being ignorant of Latin? In this
distress the Lord said to me : ' Theresa, be of good cheer ;
I will give thee The Book of Life.' "

Studies that tended to promote investigation were dis-
continued in the universities, and science was pursued only
so far as it might serve to make a living. Students indeed
increased ; " but at the same time," says Jovellanos, " also
increased the decay of every kind of knowledge."

All this had its effect upon the national character. The
Spanish *hidalgos*, sons of the men who in the sixteenth century had been led by circumstances into fields of glory, sank
into sloth, sensuality, and ignorance.

Whilst in other countries the intellectual faculties of men
were expanding and brightening, in Spain all activity of
mind was thwarted ; and the country, degraded and exhausted, reached its lowest point during the reign of Charles
II., the last of the Austrian line.

Then came the War of Succession under Philip V., grandson of Louis XIV. ; and with the accession of these Bourbon
princes something was done to dispel the thick mist that had
settled on the minds of the Spanish people. The Inquisition
was astonished when the new sovereign declined to be pres-

ent at an *auto da fé* that the Holy Office was planning in
his honor.  It did not indeed discontinue such exhibitions,
but it felt that the court discouraged them.   Indeed Ferdinand VI. and his brother Charles III. (sons of Philip V.)
were free-thinkers of the philosophic school, and were inclined to limit the temporal powers of the Church as much
as possible.

The philosophers of the new French school sorely baffled
and perplexed the Inquisition.  As they believed in nothing,
they were always ready to give in their adhesion to any
creed.   As soon as their Catholicism was questioned they
made profession of the most orthodox beliefs.   Having no
convictions, it cost them nothing to conform.

Meantime, through French channels, a great deal of
modern revolutionary thought was finding its way into Spain.
As in France the first "liberals" were found in the ranks
of the aristocracy, so it was in Spain.  The peasantry were
the stanch adherents of their church and king, but after
the French Revolution broke out, its political catechisms
made their way into the maritime cities, and the middle and
commercial classes caught the infection.  In vain the doctrines of the Constituent Assembly were officially branded as
*heretical.*  That word had ceased to be a spell to conjure
with.  Yet the people were the same Spaniards who had
howled " Long live the faith! " round the flaming scaffolds of
Philip II.  It needed but a summons to defend the faith to
rouse the Spanish peasantry ; to maintain their national religion was a point of national honor.   " Long live the King !
Long live the Inquisition! " was a rallying cry even in the
first quarter of the present century.  A brave, independent,
faithful people, — fanatical, bloodthirsty, easily misled.

Don Manuel Godoy was born at Badajos May 12, 1767,
two years before Napoleon, Wellington, and other leading
men whose birth made illustrious the year 1769.  His family
was noble, but none of its members had ever distinguished
themselves, and at the time of Don Manuel's birth his parents
were very poor.  They gave him no advantages of education ;
probably their circumstances were such that they could not

afford to do so ; but they got him admitted at the age of seventeen as a private into the body-guard of Charles III., a corps in which all privates, like the *mousquetaires* of France, had been born gentlemen. In this he served until the death of the old king, Charles III. His ignorance, frivolity, and loose morals seemed likely to mar his chances of promotion, but withal he was a handsome lad, and knew how to make the most of his advantages. Maria Louisa, Princess of Naples, wife of Charles IV., then Prince of the Asturias, had shown a disposition to favor his elder brother, Don Luis Godoy, who was in consequence sent on distant service by the old King, her father-in-law, who in the last years of his life became alarmed by her irregularities. Don Manuel became the channel of communication between the Princess and her lover, and the charming songs he sang to his guitar soon raised him at a bound to her favor and to fortune. No sooner had the Princess become the Queen than her favorite adorned his handsome person with the finest clothes, and purchased the most beautiful Andalusian horses. Then he asked for promotion, next for honors, and before long for a title. He could ask and obtain anything from the fond Queen, and anything she wished for was at once granted by her infatuated husband. Charles cared for nothing but the chase. All his affairs, regal and domestic, were in his wife's hands.

Maria Louisa was a Bourbon of Naples. She was thirty-four when, in 1788, she bestowed her favors on Godoy, who was barely twenty-two. She had had several children : a daughter who had married the Prince of Parma and is known as the Queen of Etruria ; Ferdinand, Prince of the Asturias, and Don Carlos, subsequently leader of the Carlist party, who saw in him the legitimate successor to the Spanish throne. The Queen had one other son, Don Francisco de Paula ; but as he was born after her connection with Godoy, as in a moment of great excitement she acknowledged Godoy to be his father, and as she intrigued to have his elder brothers set aside, and to secure him the succession, doubts may be considered to exist concerning his legitimacy.

Maria Louisa undertook the education of her handsome favorite. She persuaded him to acquire some instruction in the primary branches of knowledge, she initiated him into national affairs, and above all she instructed him in the skilful management of court intrigues. In two years she had seated him in the Council of Castile, and made him Colonel of the Guards. He was vain, indolent, self-seeking, and dissipated, but it is so easy to rule a nation accustomed to subservience that he managed the affairs intrusted to him better than could have been expected. To be sure, in all things he was directed by the superior tact and experience of the Queen. A good many useful works were, however, begun in Spain under his administration, some of which survive to the present day.

The French Revolution broke into a flame, and at once created two parties in the Peninsula. The court at Madrid did not know which party to join. The sympathies of the King and Queen were naturally with Louis XVI., as a sovereign and as a Bourbon, but if Spain too openly espoused his cause, revolutionary France might pour troops over her Pyrenean frontier. Godoy hated war, chiefly because he disliked the trouble it entailed. To form an alliance with France would have been to encourage Spanish revolutionists; besides, England would at once have cut off communication between Spanish ports and the Spanish American provinces; but the policy that adopted the cause of royalty in France commended itself to the Queen, and consequently to her favorite. It was abandoned, however, in 1792, when Count Aranda, head of the French party in Spain, contrived to bring about a treaty of alliance with France, which secured for the revolutionary government, in its contest with the royalties of Europe, the neutrality of Spain.

This policy lasted only for eight months. Then Count Aranda was dismissed, and the favorite was made prime minister. King Charles had grown very fond of Godoy, who, instructed by the Queen, knew how to obtain great influence over him.

Godoy, on his elevation to power, was made Count of

Evora Monte and Duke of Alcudia, but he found it hard to choose which party to adhere to, and in his perplexity took a middle course, which was to his country the beginning of troubles. Both France and England were hated by the Spanish nation; both countries were eager to secure the alliance of Spain. Austria and Prussia were marching armies into France. Godoy would not join them, but offered his services as a peacemaker. These services were rejected by the National Convention. Then Godoy, willing to spend large sums of money to avert war and to save the life of the French king, offered bribes to members of the Convention, to induce them not to vote at the trial of Louis XVI. for the death penalty. But revolutionary fervor was stronger than avarice in the breasts of the "patriots" in the Assembly. Besides, if such a transaction had been discovered, or even suspected, it would have been death to all concerned.

When Louis had been executed, the Spanish court went into mourning, and several regiments were moved northward to the frontier. These things offended France, which declared war against Spain in March, 1793. Then Spain allied herself with England, and at first her armies in the northern provinces met with some success. Godoy was much elated when he heard of this, but the campaign of 1794 dispelled his transient dreams, and disappointed his expectations. French arms had the advantage, and Godoy was ready to accept peace. The only stipulation he endeavored to make was that the rulers of France should show kindness to the orphans in the Temple; and he was ready to cede to the French the Spanish half of Saint Domingo.

This treaty was signed at Basle, July 22, 1795, in spite of the refusal of the Convention to accede to the sole stipulation made on Godoy's part concerning the royal children.

In acknowledgment of Godoy's services on this occasion, he was made Knight of the Golden Fleece, Grandee of Spain of the First Class, and Prince of the Peace, receiving at the same time a large sum of money.

A treaty of alliance made by Spain with the Dutch in 1796 gave umbrage to England, and led to a war, which was aggressive on the part of Great Britain, defensive on that of Spain. Spain did not, however, take any steps to defend her American possessions ; that duty she left to France, her ally. England took the Island of Trinidad, and annihilated the commerce carried on from Spanish ports with the West Indies.

Instead of making vigorous preparations for the conduct of this war, Spain suffered her arsenals to remain despoiled and empty. The Spanish army was not paid, and the troops deserted. But the prime minister looked on all disasters with indifference.[1] He enjoyed the king's favor, he lulled him by false reports, and took care that no one should approach his person who would tell him the truth. The queen grew more infatuated than ever. Godoy had many mistresses ; the one in chief, or we may say " in permanent possession," was Doña Josefa Tudo. Godoy's relations with this lady were perfectly open. They were known and acknowledged even by the Queen. The minister held official interviews at Doña Tudo's house, where offices were bought and sold, and the pair had several children.

The second daughter of Don Luis, uncle to the King, who had displeased his father by refusing to become a priest, and marrying a lady not of royal birth, was a lovely, pure young girl, whose beauty caught the fancy of the Prince of the Peace. He dared to ask the Queen to solicit for him the Infanta's hand in marriage. This alliance would make him cousin to the King, and brother-in-law to the highest dignitary in the Spanish church, the Bishop of Toledo. The Queen seconded the ambition of her favorite. The marriage took place in the Royal Chapel, but few persons were present at the nuptials. The grandees of Spain who had been summoned refused to come, and the Archbishop of Toledo

---

[1] Godoy in 1836 published his Memoirs, which the "Biographie Universelle" describes as a tissue of lies. This judgment seems justified by a passage in the opening of his defence, in which he claims credit for great *purity of morals.* He says he won the favor of the Spanish people, spent immense sums in charity, and set on foot (which is true) many useful public works.

declined to perform the ceremony. Doña Tudo was made a countess in her own right, and was appointed one of *the Queen's ladies in waiting.* She did not, however, long lose her lover; Godoy returned to her a few months after his marriage.

In vain during the war of 1796 France tried to rouse her ally to action. She endeavored to induce Spain to invade Portugal, and then finding that Godoy would not fall into her views, the French Ambassador, Admiral Truguet, resolved to accomplish his ruin. All Spain was in sympathy with the French minister. The favorite, who had been created a Serene Highness on his marriage with the Infanta, was everywhere despised. The cabal at court against him was so strong that the Queen had to give way, and in 1798 Godoy retired, giving up his office of prime minister, and resigning his post as Colonel of the Guard. He soon, however, came back to the Council Board, and even in his absence carried on an active correspondence with the King and Queen.

By this time Bonaparte was First Consul of France, and his imperious will reached even to Madrid. The expedition to Portugal was undertaken, and Godoy was made generalissimo; but his troops never encountered an enemy, and made a speedy retreat.

Bonaparte was furious, but Portugal, being greatly obliged to Godoy for his forbearance, rewarded him liberally with sums of money.

By the treaty of Lunéville between the German Empire and the French Republic, signed in February, 1801, the kingdom of Etruria, which consisted of Tuscany and some smaller duchies, was given to the Duke of Parma, a Spanish Bourbon, who had married the eldest daughter of King Charles IV.

In 1799 the United States made preparations to attack New Orleans, being outraged by repeated violations of a treaty made the previous year, which secured to American citizens the free navigation of the Mississippi. This war was averted by a declaration from Spain that by a secret agreement she had ceded Louisiana to France. France failed, however, to secure possession of the province, the forces destined to occupy it being blockaded in Dutch ports by the English, and on April 13, 1803, Louisiana was made over to the United States, which, having paid fifteen million dollars as purchase money to the French government, entered into peaceable possession of it. The Spaniards considered themselves ill-used by this cession of a province contiguous to the possessions of a growing power in the West; and the transaction increased the unpopularity of Godoy, who now again was virtually restored to power. Millions of *reals* came from Mexico, but nothing was done, while war was raging around Spain, to put the country in a state of defence; the army, the navy, and the roads received none of the treasure, while Madrid and the court were engaged in celebrating two royal marriages, — that of Ferdinand, the Prince of the Asturias, with Maria Isabel, Princess of Naples, and that of the heir apparent of the kingdom of Naples with an infanta.

At last, when the brief Peace of Amiens was broken (1803), Spain became alarmed for her own safety. If she favored the interests of France, England might cut off her supplies from Mexico and her colonies in South America; if she refused to favor France, that power might again attack her on her northern frontier.

By endeavoring to propitiate England, Godoy exasperated Napoleon, who hastened to force a new treaty of alliance on Spain, by which a subsidy of seventy-two million francs was exacted to assist the Emperor in his proposed invasion of England. France might have demanded aid in men and ships from her ally, but the fighting qualities of the Spaniards Napoleon appears always to have despised.

Godoy at first endeavored to diminish the amount of the subsidy demanded from his country. Then Napoleon wrote a letter to King Charles, which he desired his ambassador to deliver with his own hand into those of the King. This letter contained disclosures very damaging to the Prince of the Peace, which the Emperor hoped would be his ruin. But Godoy was equal to the emergency. He had received information of the plot. He knew the contents of the letter, and the purpose for which it was intended. He consulted with the Queen, who understood how to deal with her husband, and when the letter was delivered to King Charles as he stood surrounded by his courtiers, he quietly returned it to the ambassador, saying: " Our affair has been arranged by a treaty, signed this very day at San Ildefonso, in such a manner as to suit the views of your Emperor. It is therefore unnecessary that I should read his letter. I even believe that he would prefer it should remain unread."

Napoleon's terms were all accepted. It was, however, agreed that should Spain declare war against England, payment of the subsidy should cease, and that, when peace was made with England, France should require her to give back Gibraltar to Spain, and to receive in exchange the island of Trinidad.

This danger having been escaped, Godoy set himself in all things to flatter and propitiate Napoleon. But a few months later the English, resenting the purchased neutrality of Spain, (more injurious to her interests than open hostility), seized four Spanish frigates laden with gold from Mexico, without a declaration of war. This forced Spain, greatly against her will, to commence hostilities against Great Britain.

On October 19, 1805, the allied squadrons, French and Spanish, put to sea, and two days later the naval power of Spain was destroyed in the battle of Trafalgar. Such French and Spanish ships as escaped destruction in that engagement ran into harbor at Cadiz, where they were closely blockaded by an English squadron.[1]

Spain, dreading that the loss of her fleet might entail that of her South American colonies, felt the disaster keenly.

---

[1] My father served in this fleet as flag-lieutenant to Admiral Purvis, who was in command. I am afraid to say how long the "Atlas" cruised before Cadiz without dropping an anchor. The result was much sickness on board. My father was invalided for six months and sent to England, Admiral Purvis promising to keep his place as flag-lieutenant vacant for him till his return.

Godoy appeared indifferent to it. He had never approved of despatching Spanish ships in company with the French to fight a great battle, and he felt that by the event his own opinion had been confirmed.

Napoleon was furious. The defeat of Villeneuve by an English fleet under Sir Robert Calder had already broken up his plans for the invasion of England, and he was more and more resolved to ruin Great Britain by what was called the Continental Blockade.

An alliance was signed in 1806 between England, Russia, Prussia, and Saxony against France. By secret treaties Spain and Portugal were to be compelled, when the time should serve, to join this alliance. Emboldened by a knowledge of this treaty, Godoy put forth a proclamation to the Spanish people, warning them that their country would soon be at war (he did not say with what power), and calling on them to make every exertion to raise men and supplies. Napoleon received news of this proclamation at Berlin in a moment of triumph, immediately after the battle of Jena, when all parties to the alliance seemed to him to be at his feet. He resolved to be revenged upon Godoy, and when the Corsican Emperor was bent upon revenge there was small hope for the offending party. In vain Godoy sent explanations of his conduct, and congratulations to the Emperor on the success of his arms. All idea that Spain might join the coalition was at once at an end, and Napoleon (already meditating the annexation of Spain to France, either as a province or a subject kingdom) exacted as reparation for Godoy's proclamation a contingent force from Spain of fourteen thousand men, whom he sent into Germany, and the co-operation of what remained of the Spanish fleet, which he despatched to Toulon. Portugal, which had failed to comply with his policy of a continental blockade, was to be punished by an invasion of French and Spanish troops, — the latter to be commanded by French generals, and treated, not as allies, but as auxiliaries.

Meantime Ferdinand, the Prince of the Asturias, who was hated by his mother, intrigued against her favorite, and being virtually banished from court, cast about how he might improve his position. He had a former tutor, the Canon Escoïquiz, to whom he was attached. This man had been exiled from court and was living at Toledo. Ferdinand wrote to him entreating his advice. Escoïquiz, impressed by the mighty power of Napoleon, and assured also of his hostility to the Prince of the Peace, advised him to apply secretly to the French Emperor, and to offer — as he was now a widower — to give his hand in marriage to some lady of the Bonaparte family, or at least of the Emperor's choice.

Then began a secret intrigue or understanding with De Beauharnais, nephew by marriage to the Empress Josephine. De Beauharnais was the French ambassador at Madrid; but he had been by no means instructed in the designs of his master.

On October 11, 1807, Ferdinand, the descendant of kings, addressed the following abject letter to the successful soldier : —

SIRE, — The fear of troubling your Imperial and Royal Majesty in the midst of those more important affairs which incessantly demand your attention, has hitherto prevented me from gratifying in a direct manner the warmest wish of my heart, — that of expressing, at least in writing, the sentiments of respect, esteem, and attachment which I entertain for a hero who has been sent by Providence to save Europe from the confusion with which it was threatened, to sustain its tottering thrones, and to restore to the nations tranquillity and happiness.

Your Imperial Majesty's virtues, your moderation, your generosity even towards your most unjust and implacable enemies, all induce me to hope that the expression of my sentiments will be received as the effusion of a heart impressed with the highest admiration and the most sincere friendship.

The situation in which I have been placed for some time, and which cannot have escaped the penetrating eye of your Imperial and Royal Majesty, has operated also as another obstacle which has checked the expression of my wishes; but animated by the hope that I shall find in your Imperial and

Royal Majesty's generosity the most powerful protection, I have resolved not only to testify the sentiments of my heart towards your august person, but to confide its inmost feelings to your breast as to that of a tender father.

I am peculiarly unfortunate in being obliged by circumstances to conceal as a crime an action so laudable and just in itself; but such are the unhappy consequences of the extreme good nature of one of the best of kings.

Entertaining as I do the greatest respect and filial love towards him to whom I owe my existence, and who is endowed with the most upright and generous heart, I should never have ventured to repeat to your Imperial and Royal Majesty a fact with which you are much better acquainted than I am, but that these very qualities, however estimable in themselves, are too often converted by artful and wicked persons into instruments for concealing the truth from the eyes of sovereigns, however congenial it may be to a character like that of my respectable father.

If those men who unfortunately surround him suffered him to become acquainted with your Imperial and Royal Majesty's real character, as I am, how ardently would he not desire to draw closer the ties which should unite our respective houses. And what means could be better calculated to attain this object than that of soliciting from your Imperial and Royal Majesty the honor of giving to me in marriage a princess of your august family? This is the unanimous wish of all my father's subjects; it will be his too, I doubt not, in spite of all the efforts of a few persons who oppose it, as soon as he shall know your Imperial and Royal Majesty's intentions. This is all my heart desires, but it is not what is calculated upon by the perfidious and selfish men who surround him, and they may on the first opportunity mislead him. Hence arise my apprehensions. . . . Written with my own hand and sealed with my seal at the Escurial, the 11th of October, 1807. Your Imperial and Royal Majesty's most affectionate servant and brother,

FERDINAND.

There were several other paragraphs in the letter, but this appears enough to show the lying, abject, treacherous spirit of the man who was the evil genius of Spain from the moment he penned this document, to his death twenty-six years after; nay, who left behind him, by his treachery, his curse on Spain, deluging her northern provinces with the blood of her sons.

In spite of all the precautions taken by Ferdinand and Escoïquiz, — interviews in secret places with Count de Beauharnais, the dropping of handkerchiefs as signals, and so on, — Godoy, whose spies were set about the French embassy, knew all that was going on. Before the Emperor received Ferdinand's letter, a courier had brought him one from King Charles, written with his own hand, but evidently the composition of Godoy, which informed him of events which had taken place, and cautioned him against the intrigues of his son.

Ferdinand, by the advice of Escoïquiz, had written (or, rather, copied from a manuscript drawn up for him by Escoïquiz) two documents. The King was in feeble health, and Escoïquiz suggested that if he died the Prince of the Peace, being colonel of the Household troops, and generalissimo, would certainly take advantage of his position to conceal the death until he had secured his own power by proclaiming a minor King of Spain, for whom he could act as regent till the youth attained his majority.

A paper was therefore drawn up, signed by Ferdinand as the King, but without date, appointing the Duke of Infantado colonel of the Household troops, and Cervallos, Orgaz, and others of his own friends, to offices of trust about his person. This paper was to be dated the moment news should be received of King Charles's death ; and the Duke of Infantado and the rest had received their orders. But Ferdinand and Escoïquiz were no match in astuteness for Godoy, who had already found out their secret relations with De Beauharnais. He had, as we have seen, apprised the King of his son's dealings with Napoleon, and he now proceeded to urge his arrest, representing the Prince as having plotted against the life of his father. Charles IV., painfully surprised by such a sudden and horrible revelation, and blinded more than ever by the confidence he reposed in Godoy, the declared enemy of his son, put himself, in compliance with that person's dictation and advice, at the head of his guard, proceeded to Ferdinand's apartment in the Escurial, and on October 29, 1807, arrested him, and had him conducted into a chamber which had been converted into a dungeon. There in the presence of his ministers, he demanded his son's sword, informed him that he was a prisoner, and then left him, guarded by sentinels, and surrounded by attendants who were entirely in the confidence of Godoy. All the Prince's papers were seized, and among them was found the compromising document concerning what should be done as soon as he received news that his father was no more. That father, in a fury of wrath and pain, wrote that very night a letter to the Emperor Napoleon:

SIRE AND BROTHER, — At the very moment when I am occupied in providing the means of co-operating with you for the destruction of our common enemy, when I believed that all the plots of the *ci-devant* Queen of Naples had been buried with her daughter,[1] I have discovered, with a feeling of horror that makes me shudder, that the most shocking spirit of intrigue has penetrated even into the bosom of my palace. Alas! my heart bleeds at attempting the recital of such a frightful crime. My eldest son, the presumptive heir to my throne, has formed the horrible design of dethroning me; he carried it even to the extent of meditating to take away the life of his mother. Such a frightful crime must be punished with the most exemplary rigor of the laws. The law which calls him to the succession shall be revoked; one of his brothers will be more worthy of taking his place in my heart and on the throne. I am at this moment endeavoring to find out his accomplices, in order to fathom the plan of this most atrocious conspiracy; and I shall not lose a moment in letting your Imperial and Royal Majesty know the result, entreating at the same time that you will aid me with your observations and your counsel. Also I pray God, my good brother, that He may take your Imperial and Royal Majesty into His holy and worthy keeping.   CHARLES.

SAN LORENZO, Oct. 29, 1807.

The Prince's captivity did not last many days. Having been assured by one of the King's ministers that nothing would save his life but a full and free confession, he spontan-

---

[1] The late wife of Prince Ferdinand.

KING CHARLES IV.

eously revealed all particulars concerning the events which had brought him to prison. He described the letter he had written to the Emperor, the part Escoïquiz had taken in the whole affair, and finally gave the names of all persons (including that of De Beauharnais) who had been his confidants or accomplices. All, including some on whom suspicion had not previously fallen, were immediately arrested.

Then Ferdinand was summoned before his father, his mother, the Prince of the Peace, the ministers, and the governor of the Council of Castile, who endeavored to prevail on him to confess the project of assassination and dethronement. This, as no such plot had existed, he steadily refused, and was remanded to prison. But personages about the court were sent to intimidate him ; and believing that his only chance of safety was to acknowledge everything laid to his charge, he signed a letter dictated to him, confessing himself guilty of a crime he had not contemplated. He wrote letters also to the King and Queen abjectly imploring their forgiveness, and entreating permission to throw himself at their feet. This favor was granted him, mainly through the intercession of Godoy, who was never cruel, nor disposed to push revenge to extremity. The so-called accomplices in the crime were subsequently tried, and acquitted by their judges, though the king condemned them to banishment from his court and capital.

Meantime the mighty autocrat whom both father and son were endeavoring to propitiate — approaching him as classical heroes might have approached an offended all-powerful divinity — had no idea of allying himself with the interests of either father or son. As far back as July 7, 1807, when he met the Emperor Alexander and the King of Prussia at Tilsit, and steps for a completely new arrangement for the balance of power in Europe were made, he had, according to his own statement to Escoïquiz at Bayonne, revealed to the Emperor Alexander his designs on Spain, which were formed at that period. Savary tells us that the Emperor Alexander was so completely dazzled by the French Emperor, during their almost familiar intercourse at Tilsit, that he was ready to be led by him even to the extent of forgetting the interests of his own country and friends. His approval of Napoleon's plans concerning Spain and Portugal was not only confidentially given to the Emperor, but in the secret articles of the treaty drawn up at Tilsit it was agreed that " the houses of Bourbon and Braganza in the Spanish Peninsula were to be replaced by princes of the family of Napoleon." The idea in the minds of the two Emperors seems to have been that they would govern Europe between them, Alexander in the East, Napoleon in the West. The final partition of the Turkish Empire was also discussed. " It is impossible," said the Emperor Napoleon to Alexander, " any longer to endure the presence of the Turks in Europe. You are at liberty to chase them into Asia. But observe only, I rely upon it that Constantinople is not to fall into the hands of any European power."

At St. Helena Napoleon is reported to have said: " All the Emperor Alexander's thoughts were directed to the conquest of Turkey. We have had many discussions about it, and at first I was pleased with his proposals, because I thought it would enlighten the world to drive those brutes the Turks out of Europe. But when I reflected on the consequences, and saw what a preponderating weight it would give to Russia, I refused to consent to it, especially as Alexander wanted to get Constantinople."

It was probably during these discussions that Alexander, willing to propitiate the autocrat, who might hinder or promote his scheme of possessing himself of Turkish territory, agreed without scruple to the dismemberment of the kingdoms in the Peninsula, weak powers since Spain had fallen from her high estate, — kingdoms disposed to be entirely subservient to France, faithful to her alliance, and unresentful of her oppressions.

In furtherance of the design communicated to his brother Emperor at Tilsit, Napoleon, October 27, 1808 (two days before the quarrel between Ferdinand and his father reached its height), caused a secret treaty to be drawn up at Fontainebleau, which was signed by Duroc upon Napoleon's

part, and by Isquierdo, a secret agent of the Prince of the
Peace, on that of his sovereign. The treaty was kept secret
even from the Spanish ambassador at Paris, and this is the
substance of its principal articles : —

The King of Etruria (formerly Duke of Parma, who had
married Maria Louisa, Infanta of Spain, daughter of Charles
IV.) was to be deprived of his Italian kingdom, and to receive in return the northern provinces of Portugal, the city
of Oporto, and the title of King of Northern Lusitania. To
Godoy were to be given the two southern provinces of Portugal, — Alentejo, and the tiny ancient kingdom of Algarve,
over which he was to reign with the title of Prince of the
Algarves. The central part of Portugal was to be occupied by French and Spanish troops until the peace, when
Charles IV. and Napoleon would settle what should become
of them.

There was a rider to this treaty, a convention signed by
the same parties on the same day, on the same table, by
which it was stipulated that French troops should have free
passage through Spanish territory on their way to effect the
conquest of Portugal.

Napoleon lost not a moment's time in marching his soldiers, whom he had already concentrated at Bayonne, over
the Spanish frontier. The main body, commanded by Junot,
proceeded through the northern provinces of Spain upon its
errand ; but two other bodies of French troops poured also
into Spain : one of which, under General Duchesne, took
peaceable possession of Catalonia, its cities, and its fortresses ; the other was divided into two *corps d'armée* one of
which was under Dupont, a distinguished general much
esteemed by Napoleon, while the other one, under Marshal
Moncey, took the road, not into Portugal, but directly to
Madrid.

The Spaniards offered no resistance whatever to the advance of the French soldiers, whose behavior was friendly
and orderly. Not a shot was fired, hardly was a remonstrance made. The Queen of Etruria and her son, who had
been dispossessed of their Italian realm, which was annexed

to Tuscany, arrived in Madrid *en attendant* the events in Portugal.

The behavior of the Spanish people as their country was thus overrun by the armies of a friendly power would be wholly unaccountable were it not for two circumstances : the first was the universal hatred of Godoy, to whom were attributed the disorders of the government, the humiliation of the monarchy, and the state of the finances ; the second was the absorption of all public interest in the quarrel that was taking place between father and son at the Escurial, Madrid, and Aranjuez.

Ferdinand was undoubtedly popular at this time with his people. Great sympathy was felt for him among all classes of Spaniards ; he was known to be the enemy of their enemy, the Prince of the Peace ; and on him their hopes were fixed for future reform.

Meantime Junot had received instructions to accelerate his march through Spain, and to reach Oporto before the royal family of Portugal and their court could set sail for their possessions in South America. Junot therefore hurried his troops by forced marches through mountain passes, where their sufferings from fatigue, hunger, and thirst were terrible, and he reached Oporto with a remnant of his troops only in time to see the sails of the slowest ship in the fleet bound to Brazil disappearing over the horizon.

This fleet of eight ships of the line, four frigates, three brigs, and a schooner, which transported to a distant quarter of the world the hopes and fortunes of the Portuguese monarchy, was escorted by an English squadron under Sir Sidney Smith. It arrived at Rio de Janeiro January 19, 1808, after a six weeks' prosperous voyage.

Junot's campaign in Portugal until the arrival of the English on the scene was a "walk over." In February, 1808, he issued a proclamation announcing to the people of all Portugal, that the house of Braganza had ceased to reign, that the government of their country was to be administered in the name of the Emperor of the French, that the administration of justice would be based upon the Code Napoleon, the taxes collected in the name and for the service of the French, while their own armies would be marched off for service under French commanders in foreign lands. The peasantry were heart-broken ; resistance seemed vain.

Godoy, who had forbidden opposition to the French as they poured into the Basque provinces, Navarre and Catalonia, believing that they entered Spain to subserve his personal advantage and make him sovereign of the principality of the Algarves, now had his eyes opened ; nor could he refuse to believe that he had been basely tricked, when Izquierdo, by order of Napoleon, arrived in Madrid to inform Charles IV. that, in consequence of the perilous state of affairs in Europe, the interest of France indispensably demanded the incorporation of the northern provinces of Spain with the French Empire. In return, King Charles was offered the whole of Portugal, no mention being made of Northern Lusitania, or the principality of the Algarves ; the one promised to the young King of Etruria, the other to Godoy. Meantime the Old Guard was on its march toward the Peninsula, and all France was in motion making preparations for a Spanish campaign.

"My apprehensions are great," wrote Godoy to Izquierdo. "The treaty no longer exists ; the kingdom is covered with French troops ; the entrances to Portugal are about to be occupied, Junot commands them all ; the French cabinet demands the surrender of our fleet ; our ships are about to join those of the Emperor ; all is intrigue and distrust ! What will be the result of these uncertainties ? "

The message sent by Izquierdo and the intelligence he brought with him to Madrid left no doubt that the lion who had played the fox was about to reassume his character of lion. Godoy and his King dared not run the risk of exasperating Napoleon by rejecting his demands for the cession of all Spain north of the Ebro, and it was rather a relief when another army reached Madrid from France, bringing a present of fourteen Percheron horses to the King, and a letter from Napoleon informing him that he had resolved to visit the Peninsula, not only that he might enjoy the satisfaction of becoming personally acquainted with his august ally, but also that he might terminate in a friendly manner, and without diplomatic forms, the negotiations relative to the political condition of Spain and Portugal.

It seems hard to believe that the government of the once proud and powerful Spanish people slavishly consented to the incorporation into France of the northern Spanish provinces, adding only a petition that the Emperor would look with magnanimity on the affairs of the King and Queen of Etruria.

Matters in Spain had now arrived at such a crisis, and escape from the imperious will of the master of western Europe seemed so hopeless, that Godoy advised his King and Queen to follow the example of the royal family of Portugal and escape to the American colonies. The consent of the royal pair was given. They were to set out apparently for Seville, but were to turn aside upon their route, reach Cadiz, and embark there. The secret, however, leaked out among the courtiers, and the Marquis of Caballero, minister of Grace and Justice, so earnestly opposed the plan that it was set aside for a time as premature, if not impracticable. This triumph of the advice of Caballero over that of Godoy was extremely agreeable to Prince Ferdinand and his party. But the views of the Prince of the Peace were not so easily frustrated. As military commander he had brought together large bodies of the household troops at Aranjuez, a country palace of the King in the province of Toledo on the borders of La Mancha where the court was then residing, and had stationed other regiments along the roads over which the royal party was to travel. At Cadiz lay several ships of war ready to put to sea on their Majesties' arrival. News of the King's probable departure spread among the peasantry, and they assembled, armed only with staves, to the number of some thousands. The presence of this multitude filled Godoy and his adherents with alarm. The project of the journey was resumed, and the night of departure fixed for March 17, 1808. The royal travellers were to start off without guards or attendants. But the mob had guessed rightly what was going on, for

Doña Tudo with her children and some *fourgons* full of baggage left Aranjuez in the afternoon.

Prince Ferdinand declined to accompany his family, stimulated by the marks of attachment to himself that he began to perceive among the people. The troops of the line, and many of the royal guard sided in feeling with the populace. At dusk a street tumult took place. A soldier who had seen a lady and gentleman issue from the apartments of the Prince of the Peace, attempted to look into the lady's face, supposing she might be Doña Tudo. This insult led to a street broil. A trumpeter sounded, by mistake, the signal for the guard to mount. The mob surrounded the palace, closed up every avenue by which its inmates might have quitted it, and then made an attack upon the house of Godoy. The King appeared upon a balcony, and promised that he would not leave his people. Then the multitude, satisfied with having searched and pillaged all the rooms of Godoy's house, and believing that he had escaped, quietly withdrew. The Prince of the Peace had long before prepared for such an emergency. Under some mats in a garret he had constructed for himself a hiding-place. He had snatched up a roll on his way to this retreat, but after thirty-six hours of concealment he became so parched with thirst that he resolved to risk all things to satisfy the craving. He came forth, therefore, and offering the first sentinel he met his jewelled watch and some gold pieces, asked him to procure him a glass of water. The soldier scorned the bribe, and shouted that he had found the traitor. At once Godoy was seized, dragged down the staircase, beaten, maltreated, and wounded in several parts of his body. A few more moments would have put an end to his existence, when Ferdinand appeared, having been urged to interfere by his father and mother. He brought with him some cavalry soldiers of the guard, and crying out that he would answer for the safe-keeping of Godoy till justice could be done on him, he prevailed on the excited crowd to yield up to him their victim. Dragged on foot between two mounted guards at a quick pace through a crowd of forty thousand infuriated people, who heaped upon him insults and maledictions, Godoy was at last got into the barracks and lodged in a small chamber,— it was the same that he had occupied when a private soldier of the guard, — and a *juge d'instruction* shortly afterwards came to interrogate him, and take down his replies.

What the feelings of the King and Queen were under these circumstances, and what view they wished the great "arbiter of their destiny" to take of what had occurred, we may see in the letters written by the Queen to her daughter the Queen of Etruria, letters which Napoleon considered so discreditable to her who wrote them, as well as to those of whom she wrote, that he caused them to be published in the "Moniteur," that his subjects might form their own judgment on the miserable son and parents whom it was his fixed intention to dethrone. There are several of these letters, all pleading earnestly for mercy or favor to be extended to the Prince of the Peace, who really seems from the time of his imprisonment to have shown himself more of a man than any other actor in this extraordinary drama. The abject flatteries addressed to Murat, the Grand Duke of Berg, who was invading Spain as Napoleon's lieutenant, fill women with a sense of shame for womanhood. "Will your Imperial Highness," writes the Queen, "obtain permission for us to spend our days in quiet, in some place suitable to the King's health, — which, as well as my own, is in a delicate state, — in order that with our only friend, — the friend of your Imperial Highness, — the poor Prince of the Peace, we may finish our days in tranquillity?"

This letter is dated March 23. On March 19 the King had signed his abdication, on the 20th, Ferdinand VII. had been everywhere proclaimed. The King subsequently protested that on March 21 he had signed a revocation of his act of abdication. If so it was a document of which it is evident the Queen had never heard.

Here is an extract from another letter addressed by Maria Louisa to her daughter, the Queen of Etruria, but intended through her to reach Napoleon. It is dated March 26, 1808.

MY DEAR DAUGHTER, — You will inform the Grand Duke of Berg of the situation of the King my husband, of mine, and that of the poor Prince of the Peace.

My son Ferdinand was at the head of the conspiracy. The troops were gained by him; he had a light held out at one of the windows as a signal for the commencement of the explosion. At the same moment the guards and persons who were at the head of the revolution fired two shots, which were said, but most untruly, to have proceeded from the guard of the Prince of the Peace. At the same instant the body guards, the Spanish infantry, and Walloons, were under arms; and thereupon, without any orders from their superior officers, they themselves — the guards — called together all the people; they of their own accord threatened whomsoever they wished. My son, whom the King and I sent for, to tell him that the King his father was too ill with his rheumatism to appear at the window, and that he ought to appear there in his stead to tranquillize the people, answered us with great decision that he would do no such thing, for that at the moment he came to us firing had commenced, and he did not wish to appear. The next day we asked him if he could not put a stop to the tumult, and tranquillize the people. He then said he would do so immediately. . . . Just as he had given his orders the poor Prince of the Peace was discovered. The King sent for his son, and desired him to seek out this unfortunate prince, the victim of his attachment to us, of his friendship for the French, and above all for the Grand Duke. He proceeded as his father had commanded, ordered that the Prince should not be touched, and accompanied him to the quarters of the body guards. He told him in a tone of command, as if he were the King, " I grant you your life." The Prince of the Peace, in spite of his wounds, thanked him, and asked if he was already King; for that was in contemplation, as the King, the Prince of the Peace, and I, intended, after seeing the Emperor, to arrange everything, and also the marriage, and then the King would abdicate in favor of his son. He replied, " No, not yet, but I shall be soon." My son commanded every thing without being King, and without knowing that he should be King. The orders that the King my husband gave were not attended to. My son acted and spoke in every respect as a King. Afterwards a tumult, more violent than the former, directed against the King's life and mine, was to have taken place on the 19th, the day of the abdication, which obliged us to take that step. From the moment of the abdication my son acted in every respect as a King, through contempt of his father, without having the least consideration for us. At the same moment he sent for all the persons who were in his favor, and who never have been our faithful subjects or friends; he did everything he could to annoy the King his father; he urged us to set out. He indicated Badajoz to us; he left us without the least consideration, highly satisfied to be what he is, and to think that we are going away.

As for the poor Prince of the Peace, my son did not wish he should be even thought of. He is with the guards, who have orders to give him no answers to his questions and have treated him with the greatest inhumanity.

My son brought about this conspiracy for the purpose of dethroning his father. Our lives have been far from safe. That of the Prince of the Peace is by no means secure. The King my husband and I expect from the Grand Duke that he will do everything in his power for us, who have always been faithful allies of the Emperor, and great friends of the Grand Duke; the Prince of the Peace entertains the same feelings, and has always entertained them, as would appear if he could express his sentiments; and even as he is, he does nothing but utter wishes for the presence in Madrid of his great friend the Grand Duke. We entreat of him to save the Prince, to save us, and to let us remain together always, that we may finish our days near each other; for it is our wish to end them tranquilly in a mild climate, sequestered from the world of intrigue, without authority, but with honor. Such are the King's wishes and mine; such also are the wishes of the Prince of the Peace, who was always desirous of being on good terms with my son. But my son, who has no generosity or frankness, never wished it; always declaring war against him and also against the King and me. His ambition is great. He looks upon his parents as if they bore no such relation to him. What will he do to others?

In a subsequent letter she says : —

"My son knows nothing, and it will be necessary to keep him in ignorance of all our proceedings. His character is false; nothing affects him; he is void of feeling, little disposed to clemency. He is led by evil counsellors; and ambition, which rules him, will prompt him to do anything. He makes promises, but he does not always perform them."

# CHAPTER II.

### THE LION IN THE SKIN OF A FOX.

THE expression at the head of this chapter is one that Napoleon applied to himself, at his headquarters during the campaign of 1807, when he was planning in his mind his treacheries toward Spain and her reigning princes. He then in a moment of confidence said to Talleyrand : " When it is expedient, I know how to change the skin of a lion for that of a fox."

Aranjuez was formerly the spring residence of the court of Spain, and perhaps the most beautiful of the four summer palaces belonging to the royal family. The gardens, as well as the interior of the palace, suffered barbarous devastation during the war of independence, but in the days when Aranjuez was the favorite retreat of Charles IV., they were superb. The beautiful town, situated on the banks of the Tagus, about twenty miles from Madrid, had been built in a semicircle, and during the stay of the court at the neighboring palace it was able to accommodate about twenty thousand persons. On the 19th of March, 1808, however, it was filled with thousands of Manchegan peasants keeping watch in the streets and in the garden walks all night to prevent the threatened departure of the royal family.

Prince Ferdinand, having saved the life of the Prince of the Peace, and seen him dragged to prison, swinging between the horses of two cavalry soldiers, and clinging to their saddles, heard himself saluted as King of Spain by the multitude, and found himself surrounded by many persons who the day before had been the flatterers of his enemy. The old King and Queen, alarmed for their own safety, but still more concerned for the life of their favorite, conceived that a speedy abdication alone might save him.   They cared little for power, they cared only for him they called their friend.   On the evening of the day when Godoy had been captured, rescued, and committed to prison, Charles IV. signed his abdication in favor of his " well-beloved son, the Prince of the Asturias," and the next day, with great popular enthusiasm, Ferdinand VII. was proclaimed.   He at once appointed men of high character and influence to be his ministers, and put forth proclamations full of gracious promises and enlightened sentiments.

The public celebrated his accession and evinced its loyalty by sacking and plundering in Madrid the houses of Godoy, his youngest brother, and his principal adherents.

On the 24th of March the new King was to make his public entry into Madrid, where all possible preparations were being made to receive him.

Charles IV., two days after signing his abdication, — acting we know not upon whose advice, — drew up and signed (or subsequently professed to have drawn up and signed) another paper, in which he declared that his abdication had not been voluntary, and that it therefore was null and void.

It is probable that the true date of this document was later than March 21.   The Queen's letters quoted in the last chapter, under date of March 23, give no indication that it was her husband's wish to resume his sceptre ; her letters breathe only their desire to retire, in company with their friend and favorite, into private life.

Meantime news of the events at Aranjuez reached Murat at Burgos.   He was on his way to Madrid, having been appointed the Emperor's lieutenant-general in Spain, and was accompanied by two armies, the one under Dupont, the other under Marshal Moncey.   He at once hurried forward, attended only by his staff and a large body of cavalry.   He made his entrance into Madrid almost unobserved, so occupied were the inhabitants with preparations to receive King Ferdinand upon the morrow.   Never was an invasion accomplished with so little stir, so little opposition.   The new ruler of Spain, by the grace of Napoleon, was in the capital with forty-five thousand Frenchmen at his back, when the inhabitants to the number of two hundred thousand were pouring out of the gates to welcome the prince of long descent whom they believed to be their lawful sovereign.

Murat, who had received the appeals forwarded to him from King Charles and his Queen, through the Queen of Etruria, and who knew Napoleon's ultimate intention of placing a member of his own family on the Spanish throne, was careful to make no admission that he looked upon Ferdinand as King of Spain. He denied him even the style and address of a sovereign ; he treated him with marked neglect and rudeness, not bestowing on him, when they met in the presence of the Queen of Etruria, the ordinary courtesies due from one gentleman to another.

The correspondence already quoted, together with some other letters, was forwarded to Napoleon, who in answer to the appeals of both parties for his counsel and protection, only replied that he had no concern in the domestic quarrels of the Spanish royal family, but that he would shortly visit their country, and endeavor to arrange satisfactory relations with father and son. At St. Helena, a dozen years later, he said, " I never excited the King of Spain against the Prince of the Asturias. I saw them envenomed against each other, and conceived the idea of deriving advantage to myself, and dispossessing both."

On March 2 7, he wrote accordingly to his brother Louis :

"The King of Spain has just abdicated, the Prince of the Peace has been imprisoned, insurrectionary movements have shown themselves at Madrid. At that instant our troops were still forty leagues distant, but on the 23d Murat must have entered that capital at the head of forty thousand men. The people demand me with loud cries to fix their destinies. Being convinced that I shall never be able to conclude a solid peace with England till I have accomplished a great movement on the Continent, I have resolved to put a French prince on the throne of Spain. In this state of affairs I have turned my eyes on *you* for the throne of Spain. Say at once what is your opinion on that subject. You must be aware that that plan is yet in embryo, and that, although I have one hundred thousand men in Spain, yet according to circumstances I may either advance directly to my object, in which case everything will be concluded in a fortnight, or be more circumspect in my advances, and the final result will appear only after several months' operations. Answer categorically. If I declare you King of Spain, I rely on you."

Louis did not accept the offer. He had felt, on the throne of Holland, the chains of servitude. He had chafed under the impossibility of doing what was expected of him as a Frenchman and a Bonaparte and fulfilling his duty to his subjects at the same time. Then Napoleon fixed his eyes upon his elder brother Joseph, already established on the throne of Naples, where he was acquiring popularity among his subjects, and laboring to do them good.

Napoleon sent for Izquierdo, Godoy's secret agent in Paris, and sounded him as to whether a prince of his family, or even himself, would be acceptable to the Spaniards if seated on their throne. The reply of Izquierdo showed that he knew his countrymen far better than Napoleon did with all his statecraft: "Sire, the Spaniards would accept your Majesty with pleasure, and even with enthusiasm, for their sovereign, but only in the event of your having previously renounced the crown of France."

In this uncertainty, — for Napoleon said openly that he could not understand the state of affairs at Madrid, and thought that they were turning out in a way he had never intended, — he sent Savary (the Duke of Rovigo) on a special mission, adding to the instructions given him, " If I cannot arrange matters as I wish with either the father or son, I will make a clean sweep of them both; I will reassemble the Cortes, and resume the designs of Louis XIV. I am fully prepared for all that; I am about to set out for Bayonne. I will go on to Madrid, but only if it is absolutely unavoidable."

Such being the Emperor's feeling, though he flattered both Charles and Ferdinand with the hope that he was coming to Madrid to settle their differences in person, a chief part of Savary's mission was to persuade Ferdinand to travel to Bayonne.

The Prince of the Peace, soon after Murat arrived in Madrid, had been transferred from Aranjuez to Puerto, thence to Villa Viciosa, whence on the peremptory demand of Murat he was delivered over to French soldiers, to the great indignation of the Spaniards. Tattered and torn, with his wounds only partly healed, he was supplied with clothes by the French, and sent, under a strong guard, to Bayonne, where Napoleon had an interview with him immediately on his arrival.

Ferdinand busied himself with making magnificent preparations for the expected visit of the Emperor Napoleon. He sent three grandees to the frontier to receive him, but these noblemen to their great surprise saw no evidence along their route that the Emperor had formed any design of undertaking such a journey. Savary next intimated to Ferdinand that it would be well if his brother Don Carlos, heir presumptive to the throne, were sent to escort the expected Emperor. This suggestion was also complied with; and indeed any demand it pleased the French to make was instantly attended to. For instance, the sword of Francis I., which had hung in the Royal Armory since the Battle of Pavia, was brought forth with great pomp and delivered over to Murat, who had made a request for it.

Ferdinand, in spite of his false confidence, as the days went on began to feel a little uneasy. He expressed his apprehensions in an interview with Savary, who replied that he would pledge his life for the performance of all the Emperor's promises, and that if in his first interview with Ferdinand he should only give him the title of Highness, it would be merely a matter of etiquette, since he would not long defer saluting him with the title of Majesty.

Thus reassured, Ferdinand set out for Burgos on the 10th of April, expecting there to meet the Emperor and to escort him to his capital. He left behind him a regency for the government of his kingdom during his absence, under the presidency of his uncle Don Antonio, but the people of

Madrid, already weary of the presence of the French troops, and distrustful of Napoleon, witnessed the departure of their King with fear and suspicion.

At Burgos Ferdinand found no Emperor awaiting him, nor anything to indicate that his presence was expected. There was not even a letter. Savary, boldly persevering in his former assertions, urged his dupe to push on to Vittoria. Ferdinand had grown suspicious, and might have turned back then and there but for the unalterable confidence in the promises of the Emperor of the French apparently felt by his confidants and advisers. At Vittoria, however, he told Savary that he would go no further without personal assurances from the Emperor, and he wrote to Napoleon urging his claims for consideration, and earnestly entreating that he might be relieved from the painful situation in which he found himself.

Savary, intrusted with this letter, went to meet the Emperor, who had that day arrived at Bayonne. As soon as Savary was gone, leaving behind him orders to the French in Vittoria to prevent Ferdinand from quitting that town till his return, Spaniards of position and influence sought interviews with Escoïquiz and the Duke del Infantado, and endeavored to open their eyes to the perilous position of their sovereign. The only argument that Ferdinand's advisers seemed able to advance for continued subservience to the commands of the Emperor was that it was *impossible* that a hero like Napoleon could conceive the idea of sullying his fame by an act of dishonor.

All efforts were useless. Ferdinand remained virtually a prisoner at Vittoria, with French guards posted round him, till on April 18th Savary returned, bringing a letter from Napoleon. This letter should have opened Ferdinand's eyes, for it was almost a declaration of the writer's intention to dethrone both parties. Ferdinand and his advisers — Escoïquiz and the Dukes of Infantado and San Carlos — still kept up their false confidence in the honor and word of the French hero.

When, on the morning of April 21, Ferdinand and his

suite prepared to set forward on their journey, the inhabitants of Vittoria crowded about him, entreating him not to leave his kingdom, and (for at that date he was a popular sovereign) some cut the traces of the mules that were harnessed to his carriage. But Ferdinand stood up and assured them that he had full confidence in the Emperor Napoleon, and would shortly be back in Vittoria, when he would have arranged all things for the prosperity and happiness of Spain as the close ally of France.

At Irun, the last stage of the journey before crossing the frontier, Ferdinand and his personal attendants were lodged in a detached house, a little out of the town. There a last remonstrance was made by its proprietor, who pledged his life that he could put the King secretly on board a boat which would carry him either to St. Sebastian or to one of several English ships then cruising in the offing.

On crossing the frontier, where no preparations had been made to receive him as a royal guest, Ferdinand was met by his brother Don Carlos, and by the two grandees he had despatched to the confines of his kingdom to escort the Emperor. Their report of the condition of affairs was alarming, but Ferdinand had now gone too far to recede. He entered Bayonne April 23, and immediately on his arrival received a visit from Napoleon. This visit was brief, and was merely an exchange of compliments. When it ended Duroc appeared upon the Emperor's part to invite the Prince to dinner. The repast was short, the guests preoccupied, and the next morning after an interview between Napoleon and the Spanish sovereign's chief advisers, Savary presented himself to notify to Ferdinand in Napoleon's name what had already been announced to the Spanish officials, — that the dynasty of the Bourbons no longer reigned in Spain, that it was about to be succeeded by a prince of the family of Napoleon, and that Ferdinand must renounce, for himself and for the princes of his family, all right to the crowns of Spain and the Indies.

Ferdinand stood petrified as he listened to this address. He seemed unable to find voice to answer it. When he recovered he spoke gravely and with dignity, saying that he now perceived his situation, and could no longer blind his eyes to the violence that had been committed against him ; but that in spite of this he was personally willing to submit in all things to the Emperor, but he could not sign away the rights of others.

In vain Napoleon tried to secure the adhesion of the Spanish confidants of Ferdinand. They were at last fully aroused. In vain he assured them that his only object in effecting the proposed change in the dynasty was to promote the welfare of Spain, by giving her institutions analogous to those adopted by other countries, and that they ought to favor so mild and bloodless a revolution, — when revolution in other countries had cost tears and blood. They urged that if a close alliance with Spain was necessary to France this might be best secured by confirming the rights of Ferdinand, a prince who had given every proof of devotion to Napoleon's views and wishes. And they pointed out the danger to which French troops in Spain might be exposed if the Spaniards suspected that the Emperor had played false with their young sovereign. They enlarged on the fierce hatred that the Spanish people felt for foreigners, and predicted a terrible war if Napoleon's policy were forced upon the nation.

In vain ; Napoleon despised the fighting qualities of the Spaniards ; he had seen them submit tamely to the march of his one hundred thousand soldiers through their country ; they had not resented the occupation of their principal fortresses, or of their capital. The Emperor of the French, bred up in the ideas of 1789, did not at all enter into the feelings with which the mass of the Spanish people would regard French interference with their church or with their King.

The crown of Etruria, the offer of which seems to have been tossed from one prince to another in these negotiations, was tendered as compensation to Ferdinand, should he, before eleven o'clock in the evening of April 29, cede his rights and those of his house to the throne of Spain. Ferdinand sent no answer, and the next morning, Escoiquiz having ventured to reopen the subject, was sternly told that it was " too late."

The next morning, April 30, King Charles and his Queen arrived at Bayonne. Their reception was in marked contrast to that of Ferdinand. With them came the Duchess of Alcudia, daughter of the Prince of the Peace, who on the arrival of the royal party quitted the house to which he had been conducted on his arrival in Bayonne on the 25th, and thenceforward formed part of the royal family. Meantime orders by Napoleon's desire had been sent to the Queen of Etruria, Don Antonio, and the boy Don Francisco, to hurry to Bayonne and join the other members of their house there. Don Antonio, who had been made regent of the kingdom and president of the council by Ferdinand before his departure, had been already summarily superseded by Murat.

The departure of these last members of the royal family was at first resisted by the council at Madrid; but its members gave way when Murat used a threat which had several times before been found useful by his countrymen, namely, that if they refused obedience they must take upon themselves the whole responsibility of an inevitable civil war.

On the morning of May 2 the royal carriages drew up at the door of the Palace at Madrid, and the Queen of Etruria, her young daughter, the Regent Don Antonio, and the young Infante Don Francisco prepared to depart. The Queen's carriage was allowed quietly to pass. The memoirs of Georges Sand give an interesting account of how as a child she journeyed with her mother to Madrid and met on their way the dusty, terrified, disordered party, of whom their landlady, to whom royal fugitives were no novelty, exclaimed, " Voilà encore une reine qui se sauve ! "

But when it came to the turn of Don Antonio and Don Francisco to depart, a rumor spread among the crowd that the boy was weeping in the rooms above, and refused to go away. An aide-de-camp of Murat made his appearance, and it was then asserted, and believed, that force was to be used. The French officer was violently assaulted, and was

saved only by the bravery of a captain in the Walloon
Guards, and the arrival of a party of French soldiers.  At
once Murat sent foot-soldiers with two cannon, who fired
with grape-shot on the crowd.  " But the roar of these
cannon," says Alison, "resounded from one end of the
Peninsula to the other ; in its ultimate effects it shook the
empire of Napoleon to its foundation ; it was literally the
beginning of the end."

Instantly all Madrid was in a tumult.  The people were
already dissatisfied with the presence of the French soldiers,
and all the vehemence of the Spanish character was suddenly roused into action.  Discharges of grape-shot swept
the streets.  The Spanish troops in garrison were attacked
by the French and drew out their own cannon ; but before
they could be fired these were captured by the French by
a brilliant charge, and the artillery men were bayoneted at
their guns.  The insurrection lasted until two in the afternoon.  The French had lost three hundred of their soldiers,
the Spanish troops not so many as their foe.

But the affair was not over, though the streets of Madrid
were assuming at evening their usual appearance.  Men and
women were walking abroad and all danger seemed at an
end, when Murat commenced a massacre.  Spaniards who
had had nothing to do with the riot were seized because
they chanced to be in the streets.  They were dragged before
a French military commission, and sentenced at once to be
shot.  News of these executions spread like wildfire through
the city.  Every family all whose male members were not
under its roof suffered agonies of apprehension.  By distant
sounds of firing all knew that the work of death was going
on.  Two by two the victims were marched out, and massacred by repeated volleys of musketry.  All were denied in
their last moments the consolations of religion.  The work
next morning recommenced, and nearly a hundred victims
had perished before Murat, at the earnest intercession of the
Spanish ministers, put a stop to the carnage.

Such is an account taken from the book of General Foy,
a man of candor and honesty.

"At the distance of twenty years," writes a Spaniard who was in Madrid at the time, "our hair still stands on end at the recollection of that mournful night, the calm of which was interrupted only by the cries of the unhappy victims, or the sound of the cannon and musketry discharged at intervals for their destruction. The inhabitants of Madrid all retired into their houses, there deploring the fate that that moment might be befalling a parent, a husband, or a child. We in our family were bewailing the loss of a young man, one of its members, whose release we had been unable to obtain, when, pale and trembling, he entered the house. He had been saved by the generosity of a French officer, who, touched by his appeal after his hands were tied and he was drawn up for execution, loosed his bonds and set him at liberty. He was hardly out of the limits of the Retiro (the gardens of that Palace were one of the spots where the executions were taking place) when he heard the discharges which terminated the agony of his late companions. Among the victims were many priests, old men, and persons of the most respectable character."

The news of these atrocious acts spread rapidly through all the provinces of Spain, and, together with apprehensions for the fate of their royal family, made men desperate. Then began that hatred of French soldiers which became so frantic and ferocious that the very allies of Spain and the enemies of France threw their personal sympathy into the French scale. The movement was spontaneous. It animated alike Spaniards of all classes, all ages, all professions. Within a week after tidings of the untoward massacre reached Bayonne, the Emperor Napoleon was engaged in the most fierce, cruel, and determined war into which he had ever led or despatched his legions, — war to the death with an undisciplined and high-spirited people, where each man fought for his own hand. Hitherto his battalions had fought regular troops, and these they had always conquered; they were wholly unprepared for the guerilla warfare they were now to face among the mountains and ravines of the Basque Country or Catalonia.

What Napoleon's calculations were in commencing this war with the Spanish people, he revealed in an interview with Escoïquiz, to whom he said: —

" It is of no use to speak to me of the difficulties of the enterprise. I have nothing to fear from the only power who could disquiet me in it. The Emperor of Russia, to whom I communicated my designs at Tilsit, which were formed at that period, approved of them, and gave me his word of honor he would offer no resistance. The other powers of Europe will remain quiet, and the resistance of the Spaniards themselves cannot be formidable. The rich will endeavor to appease the people instead of exciting them, for fear of losing their possessions. I will render the monks responsible for any disorder, and that will lead them to employ their influence, which you know is considerable, in suppressing any popular movement. Believe me, Canon, I have much experience in these matters. The countries where the monks are numerous are easily subjugated, and that will take place in Spain, especially when the Spaniards shall see that I am providing for the national independence, and benefit of the country, giving them a liberal constitution, and at the same time maintaining their religion and usages. Even if the people were to rise *en masse* I could succeed in conquering them by the sacrifice of two hundred thousand men. I am not blind to the risk of a separation from the colonies, but I have long kept up secret communications with Spanish America, and I have lately sent frigates there to obtain certain advices as to what I may expect. I have every reason to believe that the intelligence will prove of the most favorable character."

The news of the tumult and street fighting in Madrid on the morning of May 2 reached Bayonne on May 5, though not probably the news of Murat's massacre. Napoleon at once sent for the old King and Queen, and for their son, — we might say that he *summoned* them to his presence, — and communicated the news he had received of the excitement in their capital. He told both parties that an end must be put to delays and futile negotiations. He had already assured himself of the willingness of the old people to resign their crown into his hands, — indeed they desired nothing but tranquillity and the undisturbed companionship of Godoy, — but he had met with resistance from Ferdinand, who said that while a prisoner he could make no renunciation of his rights, but would do so in Madrid after he was restored to his country. The scene between the parents and the son was painful in the extreme. The Queen was so violent in her rage against Ferdinand that an eye-witness of what took place said he could not bring himself to report her words. Napoleon sternly insisted that to quell the disorders in Spain his brother must be seated on the Spanish throne without delay; thus dissipating the hopes of those who had taken up arms for Ferdinand. Charles IV. bitterly reproached his son for having drawn down disasters on his country and his family, by his precipitate and undutiful behavior. He told him that he alone was responsible for the blood that had been shed, and which might be about to flow, and he concluded by commanding him in an imperious manner to place in his hands forthwith a pure and simple abdication of the crown, under penalty of being treated as a conspirator in case of his refusal.

Ferdinand was confused, and greatly agitated. He would make no reply; but with a few vague words withdrew from the presence of his parents. On reaching his residence he however wrote out his abdication, and sent it unsigned to the Emperor, asking his approval of the document, and entreating his protection for himself, his brother Don Carlos, and the persons who had accompanied them in their journey to Bayonne. This document he proposed to transmit to his Uncle Don Antonio, whom he supposed to be still at the head of the government at Madrid. He wrote also letters which he despatched by couriers, who were intercepted, and their despatches put into the ordinary post. These were opened by the police, and found to contain bitter and disparaging observations concerning "the accursed French," which naturally increased the animosity felt for their writer by the French Emperor. It is a curious circumstance that the correspondence at this time held between Ferdinand and King Charles was mainly the composition of Napoleon; for both sides referred the letters they were to answer to the Emperor, and to the letters of both he returned answers suited to his own views.

After Ferdinand had signed his abdication and put it into the hands of his father, who resumed his rights as King of

4

Spain, a treaty was drawn up between Charles IV. and the Emperor by which the old King ceded, as he said, "for the happiness and prosperity of his dear subjects," all his rights over the dominions of Spain to his august friend and ally the Emperor of the French.

A few days later a treaty was concluded with Ferdinand, in which he renounced all rights to the crowns of Spain and the Indies, but was to retain the titles of Highness and Prince. The parks, palaces, and forests of Navarre were ceded to him, and until the palace in that province could be made ready he, with his brother, uncle, and such friends as composed his little court, were to reside in the interior of France at the country seat of Talleyrand, called Valençay. A pension was assigned to each member of the royal family, in which was included the Prince of the Peace.

The old King and Queen retired to the beautiful Château de Chambord on the Loire, subsequently purchased by public subscription as a present to the posthumous son of the Duc de Berry, known in our own day as the Comte de Chambord, or Henry V. It was made the residence of Abdul Kader during his captivity, by the second French Republic.

The King was much broken in health; the Queen, it was said, seemed to have grown young again. She dressed with elegance, behaved with liveliness and affability, and bestowed every possible mark of attention and regard upon the Prince of the Peace, "as if she were anxious to recompense him for the disasters he had encountered at Aranjuez, and for the odium in which he was held by the whole Spanish people."

After a short residence at Chambord Charles IV. and his Queen removed to Rome. There for the first time the old King was informed by a courtier, who had insinuated himself into his good graces, that the true origin of Godoy's extraordinary good fortune was the guilty passion entertained for him by the Queen. The conviction that this was true broke the old man's heart. He quitted Maria Louisa for the first time during their married life, and went on a visit to the King of Naples. Nothing could heal his wounded spirit, not even a friendly correspondence with his son, and he died a victim to the discovery of what had been known for many years to the world in general.

Maria Louisa preserved to the last the two ruling passions of her life, her devotion to Godoy, and her hatred for her son. Her last illness was brought on by her assiduous attendance on her friend and favorite, who was suffering from sickness.

Ferdinand embittered her last hours by insisting that his ambassador at Rome should demand her diamonds, which were known to be magnificent. The Queen refused to give them up, and in the presence of witnesses declared that so long as she had life they should not go out of her possession, and that she would rather throw them into the Tiber than give them to her son. The moment that she breathed her last the ambassador, in the name of his master, secured her jewels, removing even from the finger of her corpse a gold ring that she had desired should be buried with her.

The old people left pensions to persons who had been in their service during their exile. These Ferdinand refused to pay. He would sanction no liberalities to any of those who had shown attachment to Godoy.

As for that personage, who had experienced so many changes of fortune, he sank into poverty. The Infanta, his wife, had long before retired to a convent, and on her death he married Doña Tudo and legitimized her children. For thus "following the dictates of his heart," he claims great credit in the Memoirs he published for his justification. After the Revolution which placed Louis Philippe on the throne of France he came to Paris, and was put in possession of a small pension. One day (I think it was in 1847) I was walking on the Boulevards with my father, when he touched my arm, and said, "Look at that man!" I did so. He was a small old man, somewhat bent, dressed in black small-clothes and a large black mantle. His face was withered, but his eyes were bright and keen. "Who is he?" I asked eagerly when he was out of hearing. "That is Godoy, Prince of the Peace," said my father. He died, not quite, let us hope, " in a garret," as says the " Biographie Universelle," but in an obscure apartment in Paris, in 1851, being eighty-four years of age.

As for the three princes, Ferdinand, Don Carlos, and their uncle Don Antonio, they were sent by Napoleon under a guard of police to Valençay. Talleyrand, who is very anxious to clear himself of any charge of complicity in the transactions at Bayonne, says he had solicited the presence of these princes as his guests, that he might see that they received proper kindness and attention. Other writers say that Napoleon forced him to give up his ancestral mansion for their prison.

The only account we have of their residence at Valençay is from the pen of Talleyrand, and it may be well to transcribe it here. He says : —

" On the 19th of May the princes made their entrance into Valençay. I had been there several days when they arrived. This moment has left on my mind an impression which will never be effaced. The princes were young, but over them, around them, in their clothing, in the liveries of their servants, could be seen the image of bygone centuries. The coach from which I saw them alight might have been taken for a carriage of Philip V. This air of antiquity, recalling their grandeur, added to the interest of their position. They were the first Bourbons that I saw again after so many years of storms, revolutions, and disasters. It was not they who felt embarrassed, it was I. And I am pleased to say it.

" Napoleon had them accompanied by Colonel Henri, a superior officer of the *gendarmerie d'élite*, one of those police-agents who believe that military glory is acquired by fulfilling with severity a mission of this kind. I adopted with him at once the tone of a master, in order to make him understand that Napoleon did not reign either in the park or apartments of Valençay. This reassured the princes, and was my first recompense. I surrounded them with respect, attention, and care. I allowed no one to present himself before them until after having obtained their permission. No one approached them except in full dress ; I never failed myself in what I had prescribed in this respect. All the hours of the day were distributed according to the habits of the princes : mass, hours of rest, promenades, prayers, etc. Will it be credited that at Valençay I made the princes acquainted with a kind of liberty they had never known when near their father's throne? Never at Madrid had the two elder princes walked out together without a written permission from the king. To be alone, to go out ten times a day in the garden, in the park, were pleasures new to them. They had never before been so unconstrained towards each other."

Hunting, riding on horseback, and dancing had been forbidden them in Spain. Talleyrand gave them an instructor in firearms, who had been gamekeeper to the Prince of Condé. Under him they learned to fire their first shots. For riding-master he gave them a man once attached to the service of Madame Élisabeth. Dances were got up on the terrace of the Château, in which the princes could join, or remain only spectators. Perhaps Talleyrand remembered the explicit instructions of Napoleon to endeavor to put pretty women in their way, Delilahs to whom they might make love, and then reveal to them important secrets.

" I had endeavored," continues Talleyrand, " to have them spend some hours in the library; in this I did not meet with great success, though the librarian and I tried all the means we could imagine to interest them there. We called their attention to the beauty of the editions, and to the books that contained engravings. I am ashamed to say how useless all our efforts proved. Don Antonio, their uncle, who disapproved of the greater part of the books that compose a good library, used all his influence to draw them away. . . . Each day closed with public prayers, at which I required all visitors to the Château, and even the guards, to be present."

But these attentions on the part of Talleyrand — prompted possibly by an hereditary instinct of reverence to the Bourbons — did not last long. Napoleon took umbrage at his civilities to the princes, and at his rudeness to Henri the captain of police, and summoned him to Nantes ; where, in his first conversation with the astute adviser who had disapproved his policy with regard to Spain, he glorified himself

as to the success of his scheme of invasion. "Well!" he
said, rubbing his hands, "where are all your predictions as
to the difficulties I should encounter in regulating the affairs
of Spain? What have they amounted to? I have overcome the people here. They have all been caught in the
nets I spread for them; and I am master of the situation
in Spain as well as in the rest of Europe!" Talleyrand
did not agree with him, and, according to his own account,
spoke his mind plainly. From that day there was increasing
irritation between master and minister, especially as at the
interviews at Erfurth, whither some weeks afterwards Talleyrand accompanied his Emperor, he again crossed the views
of Napoleon; on that occasion their difference was with
respect to the Austrian Empire.

The princes expressed great pleasure in Talleyrand's return
to them at Valençay, after his journey to Nantes to meet
Napoleon. The only event of importance that had occurred
during his absence was the arrival of a letter from the Emperor that Talleyrand found awaiting him. It said : —

"Prince Ferdinand is writing to me, addressing me as his
cousin. Try to have the Duke of San Carlos understand that
this is ridiculous, and that he must simply call me Sire."

When Talleyrand left Valençay for Erfurth the princes
took leave of him with great apparent gratitude and regret.
Each of them offered him the old prayer-book he had used
at church, as a souvenir.

Thus ended I think, the personal intercourse between
Talleyrand and the princes, but he still continued to take
thought for them. He says : —

"The frequent conversations I had with Napoleon at Erfurth
led me to apprehend that he designed causing the princes of
Spain to fall into a snare that his minister the general of police
had laid for them by his order. The results might be fatal to
them ; I believed there was not a moment to lose to forewarn
them of it. I had my secretary leave immediately for Paris,
and call with the utmost speed on the Duke of San Carlos who
was then in that city. His zeal and interest for the princes
were such that it took him only four days to reach the capital."

The affair to which Talleyrand here alludes was that of Kolli, an Irishman by birth, who had lived on the Continent and served as a soldier of fortune. He offered his services to the English government to go to Valençay, enter into the service of the princes, and contrive their escape. The English ministers gave him letters of credit, letters of recommendation, and a quantity of diamonds; an English war-ship on the coast was to await his orders. Ardent in his scheme, Kolli went to Paris, where his servant Richard betrayed him to the police. Kolli was arrested, his papers, money, and diamonds were seized, and Richard was ordered to represent him. Forewarned of this plot by the Duke of San Carlos, who had been forewarned by Talleyrand, Ferdinand would have nothing to say to the project for his deliverance, but at once informed the police. The false Kolli was arrested, but received no punishment. The real Kolli remained in a dungeon at Vincennes until the restoration, when he vainly petitioned for the return of the money and the jewels that had been taken from him.

The princes remained five years at Valençay, till released by what is called the treaty of Valençay, early in 1814, when the empire of Napoleon was tottering to its fall. They had jailers much more stern than Talleyrand, and their most faithful friends, Escoïquiz and the Dukes of Infantado and San Carlos, were consigned to French prisons. They came out from their captivity assuredly no better than they entered it. They had become accomplished hypocrites, who flattered their enemy even so far as to congratulate him when he had won a battle fought in their own cause by subjects faithful to their throne. Truly they had learned the meaning of the words that, it is said, first met their eyes as they crossed the frontier of Spain into France, — an inscription on a triumphal arch across the high-road: "He who can make kings and unmake kings is greater than a king."

At St. Helena Napoleon passed his own judgment on the events I have here related.

"It was that unhappy war in Spain that ruined me. The results have irrevocably proved that I was in the wrong. But there were serious faults in the execution of my plans. One of the greatest was that of having attached so much importance to the dethronement of the Bourbons. Charles IV. was worn out. I might have given a liberal constitution to the Spanish nation, and charged Ferdinand with its execution. If he had put it in force in good faith, Spain would have prospered, and put itself in harmony with our new institutions. If he failed in the performance of his engagements, he would have met with his dismissal from the Spaniards themselves. 'You are about to undertake,' said Escoïquiz to me, 'the labors of Hercules, where, if you please, nothing but child's play need be encountered.' The unfortunate war in Spain proved a real wound, — the first cause of the misfortunes of France. If I could have foreseen that that affair would cause me so much vexation and chagrin, I would never have engaged in it. But after the first steps taken in the affair it was impossible for me to recede. When I saw those *imbeciles* quarrelling and trying to dethrone each other, I thought I might as well take advantage of it to dispossess an inimical family, but I was not the contriver of their disputes. Had I known at the first that the transaction would have given me so much trouble, I would never have engaged in it."

Some one had said of Napoleon's interference in Spain: "If he succeed Spain will be ruined; if he fail he will ruin himself." Both prophecies seem to have been accomplished.

# CHAPTER III.

## KING JOSEPH.

VERY early I conceived a child's enthusiasm for the Emperor Napoleon. My father was reading Scott's Life of him when I was a little girl, and was so much impressed with the greatness and the genius of the man against whose power he had fought for nineteen years that from the passages he read aloud, and the remarks he made in appreciation of the energy and genius of the late Emperor, I conceived the notion that that personage was little less than a demigod. Subsequently I was startled by a furtive perusal of an old pamphlet, found in a lumber room, published as I now believe about the year 1810, which conclusively proved, as it seemed to me, that Napoleon was the Great Beast of the Revelation, that the name of Napoleon, which might be made to sound like Apollyon, clearly made certain his diabolical origin, and was a wonderful example of minute and verbal prophecy. When older I discovered that the facts of history had not borne out the conclusions drawn from Scripture by the author of the tract, and I returned to my old allegiance to Napoleon, with a strong distaste thenceforward for crude guesses drawn from misconceptions of prophecy.

I saw Napoleon's funeral at Paris in December, 1840, and no French girl could have wept tears of more genuine emotion; but the Napoleon of my idolatry has been shattered by his biographers, by whose care his acts, his aims, his private vices, and his public policy now stand in bare deformity. They no longer glitter in the light of his genius, power, and success, which during his lifetime and for many years afterwards made it almost impossible to see them clearly.

I am now inclined to agree with the French writer who speaks of him thus : —

"After Austerlitz Napoleon dreamed of universal dominion. He said openly: 'Before long my dynasty will be the oldest dynasty in Europe.' And at the rate at which he was proceeding to make and unmake kings, this prophecy seemed likely to be accomplished. But he had no fixed plans for accomplishing his purpose. His resolves were shaped by circumstances, though circumstances were expected to bend themselves to his will. He became, as it were, intoxicated with himself. He forgot family ties. He forbade his brothers to address him in the language of fraternal intimacy. He placed them upon thrones, — but it was only that they might become his instruments. He never consulted their welfare or their wishes. He repressed on their part any expressions of affection. He spoke to them, and of them, with irony and rudeness. He forbade them to do any act that was not for the furtherance of his power, glory, and greatness. He interfered with their administration even in trifles; and when, for fear of displeasing him, they did nothing, he hurled at them the reproach that they were *des rois fainéants.* He frequently excited them to action by such words as 'Time presses, — events are hurrying fast; now or never our destiny must be accomplished. *It must!* All means are good that lead on to this end!'"

We have seen that Napoleon was not scrupulous about those means in the case of Charles and Ferdinand ; we will see now how he dealt with Joseph, his elder brother.

Of all the family of Bonaparte Joseph was the most pliable ; yet, next to Napoleon, he was the best educated and the most intellectually endowed. The idea of duty was strong in him. Some writers have accused him of ambition, but it would appear rather that they failed to understand the force of a just feeling for obligations which, having once accepted, Joseph did not consider himself at liberty to lay lightly aside.

His whole life seems in one way or another to have been one of self-sacrifice. He struggled constantly between a desire to please his brother and a wish to do his duty to the people confided to him. Had he been born a king he would have secured the love and gratitude of his subjects ;

KING JOSEPH BONAPARTE.

had he remained a private gentleman he would have won all men's esteem. Placed as he was he could not fail to find detractors, chief among whom was Talleyrand, who never mentions his name without appending to it some remark which proves in what slight consideration he held him.

Joseph was born at Corte in the Island of Corsica, in January, 1768. He was the son of Charles-Marie Bonaparte and Lætizia Ramolino. The personal appearance of his mother gave rise to the idea that in far-off ages she might have had some ancestor of the grand old Saracen race, many of whose tombs are on the Island of Corsica.

Charles Bonaparte was the friend of Paoli and of liberty, which in Corsica meant in those days deliverance from the dominion of Genoa, and annexation to France. When that event took place he went as deputy from Corsica to the Parliament of Paris, — a body with no power to legislate, permitted only to register the King's laws. He became a thorough Frenchman, and refused to be appointed a member of the Supreme Council of Corsica. In 1780 he paid a visit to Italy, taking with him his sons Joseph and Napoleon. In Florence the Grand Duke Leopold of Tuscany was anxious that he should move with his family to Italy, and settle near him. On his declining to do this the Grand Duke gave him letters of recommendation to his sister Marie Antoinette, the Queen of France. On his way to Paris he left Joseph and Napoleon at Autun, where their schoolmasters spoke of them as boys of great promise : of Napoleon, as active and imperious ; of Joseph, as indolent, but full of feeling. The brothers at that time were deeply attached to each other, though we may be sure that the younger always ruled and led. They did not, however, remain long together at Autun. The Grand Duke's letters to the Queen of France procured Eliza di Buonaparte (then called Marianne) admission to St. Cyr, the school founded by Madame de Maintenon, and her patronage probably assisted the appointment of Napoleon to the Military School at Brienne. It had been resolved by the family that Joseph should be a priest, and that Napoleon should enter the navy ; but now that Napoleon was to be a soldier, Joseph wanted to adopt the same career. An amusing letter exists in which Napoleon, in the most pragmatical, head-of-the-family style, begs his uncle to insist on Joseph's adhering to the ecclesiastical profession. He deems him, he says, " unfit for military life ; he is too indolent, too self-indulgent, too luxurious."

Joseph's career, however, was determined by the death of his father, at Montpellier in 1785, when he was called home to take his place as head of the family, protector of his mother and his younger brothers and sisters. He did this nobly. He gave up his own wishes ; he studied law, and conscientiously took up the duties assigned him. In the following year Napoleon came home on a visit, and the two brothers were together again, but already a diversity of tastes and disposition marred their brotherly affection for each other. In 1787 Joseph went for a time to Italy, and was kindly received by the Grand Duke, but he resisted all temptations to remain at the court of Tuscany, and returned to his family after he had finished his law course at the University of Pisa. He was early in sympathy with the French Revolution, and in 1792 was sent as a deputy from Corsica to the National Convention. There he ranged himself among the followers of Robespierre. He became intimate with the younger brother of that mysterious statesman, and is said to have shown some symptoms of becoming attached to their sister. After Napoleon had distinguished himself at the siege of Toulon, he got an appointment as commissary of the first class for Joseph, and places for other members of his family in the same branch of the service. It seems that according to law a commissary of the first class should have been previously in the army, and have risen to the rank of lieutenant-colonel ; so Joseph's papers were sent in declaring him to have been an artillery pupil in 1782, a staff-officer in 1792, and colonel of the fourth regiment of the line ; in short, ascribing to him the military appointments, wounds, and services of his brother Napoleon.

This document has caused great perplexity and annoyance to Napoleon's biographers. It was drawn up, most probably, by Napoleon himself, or by some other member of his family. It was not like the honest Joseph to fabricate such a statement.

In 1794 Joseph married at Marseilles, where his family was then residing, Mademoiselle Julie Clary, the daughter of a man some accounts describe as " a wealthy merchant," while others say he was a soap-boiler. On the day fixed for their gay wedding, news reached Marseilles of the events in Paris on the 9th Thermidor ; and as Joseph was known to have been a friend of the Robespierres, and had accepted a post in Marseilles on a revolutionary committee, he was afraid to draw public attention on himself by a too festive marriage. The young pair left the city unaccompanied by any friends or relations, and were quietly united by the mayor of a neighboring village ; the witnesses being the mayor's son, a municipal officer called in for the purpose, and a hairdresser.

The sister of Madame Joseph was Eugénie Bernardine Désirée Clary. Some love passages had taken place between her and Napoleon, but she subsequently married Bernadotte, and became the Queen of Sweden. Napoleon never cordially forgave her or her husband for this marriage ; and it laid the foundation for an estrangement between him and Bernadotte which led to disastrous results after the campaign of Moscow.

As First Consul, and as Emperor, Napoleon employed his brother in matters of diplomacy. He sent him to Rome as his ambassador, where an insurrectionary movement broke out suddenly in 1797, when Duphot, a French general, was murdered in the court-yard of the embassy ; and Joseph had some difficulty in making his escape, together with his wife and sister-in-law. He had a large share in drawing up the Treaty of Lunéville (1801) and the Peace of Amiens (1802). He invited General de La Fayette to be one of the witnesses to the signatures of this treaty, though the general was by no means in favor with Napoleon.

After Napoleon became Emperor, Joseph was made a prince, and the succession to the imperial throne of France was settled on him and his descendants, in case the Emperor should leave no heirs.   It was about this time that Bernardin de Saint Pierre, the author of " Paul and Virginia," recorded his opinion of Joseph Bonaparte.   " He is," he said, " a philosopher worthy of a throne, if any throne could be found worthy of him."

In 1804 Joseph received his first military appointment, being made a colonel of cavalry, and attached to the great army waiting at Boulogne to cross over to England.   A year later, Napoleon having made himself master of northern Italy, Joseph was offered the crown of Lombardy, but it was declined.   Napoleon then made the same offer to Louis. It was again declined.   Napoleon was made extremely angry by these refusals, and declared that his two brothers had treated him shamefully in the affair.   He then crowned himself with the Iron Crown of Lombardy and made Eugène de Beauharnais his Viceroy.

In 1806 Joseph was sent to take command of the French army in Naples.   The King and his court fled to Sicily on the approach of the French, who thus, almost without bloodshed, took possession of the capital.   Joseph, as commander of the French army of invasion, did not meet with great success in the war he carried on with bandits and guerillas in the mountains of Calabria, nor did he obtain the wound Napoleon repeatedly desired he might receive ; believing that it would increase his qualifications to become possibly, some day, the military ruler of France.   He was engaged in pursuing robbers through the mountains, when he was coolly informed that the Emperor had made him King of Naples.   No time was allowed him to cross his brother's will by rejecting the post assigned him.   Napoleon plainly gave him to understand that, if a second time he refused a throne, he would not only forfeit fraternal affection and imperial favor, but be deprived of his chances of succession to the French throne.

The benefits that Joseph conferred on his Neapolitan kingdom during his brief reign in Naples would take up too much space if recorded here.   They have been thus summed up by a French general : —

"Feudality destroyed; depredations and robberies suppressed; the system of taxation changed; order established in the finances; the internal administration of the kingdom organized; roads constructed; Naples embellished; the lazzaroni taught to work; the army and navy organized; the kingdom evacuated by the English; excavations in Pompeii and Magna Græcia begun."

It should be added, however, that these reforms were commenced, but not completed. Joseph said repeatedly that it was his aim to confer upon his people all the benefits purchased for the French by their revolution, without the price they paid for it in terror, tears, and blood. General Foy has said of Joseph : —

"He was far from coveting a throne. He was almost forty years old. His figure was graceful, and his manners elegant. He was fond of the society of women, of the fine arts, and of literature. His conversation was methodical and abounding with observation. It indicated a habit of speaking, and displayed a knowledge of mankind only to be gained by associating with other men on equal terms. . . . A republican by conviction, Joseph knew the rights of the people too well not to be also aware of the duty of kings."

He was beginning to acquire the confidence and affection of all classes in his new dominions, when the will of Napoleon removed him to another sphere. The Neapolitans did not look upon him as a foreigner. They were accustomed to changes of dynasty; they had no feelings of affection or respect for their Spanish Bourbon kings. Joseph spoke excellent Italian; in a provincial form, it was his mother tongue. He had begun all the improvements enumerated above, though he was hampered by a heavy national debt. He was improving the finances, though the presence of a French army, the cost of its maintenance, and other imperial exactions caused discontent in Naples, as elsewhere, and Napoleon wholly disapproved of his philanthropic ideas of government. Here is a letter written to him when he had reigned about a year in Naples, and was embarrassed by an insurrection in Calabria : —

" In a conquered country, clemency is inhumanity. Nothing need be respected after a conquest. Have three leading persons, chiefs of the revolt, shot in every village. Have no more regard for priests than for others. You must denounce, bring to trial, and send into exile. Since Calabria has revolted, why not confiscate half the property in that country, and make use of it for the army ? It is only by salutary terror that you will make any impression on an Italian population."

Thus Napoleon perpetually found fault with Joseph's administration. He interfered with it in every way. None of his brother's plans pleased him ; they did not carry out his policy ; they did not play into his hands. His will was in all things to be paramount. He was never satisfied unless in his tributary kingdoms he was supreme ruler in everything. Joseph's first thought, on the contrary, was the good of his people. " Tell my mother," he wrote to his wife, " that I am laboring for the kingdom of Naples with the same earnestness that on the death of my father, I worked for his young family. I live only for justice, and justice commands me to make my people happy."

From this task he was called away to meet his brother at Bayonne, May 21, 1808. Napoleon at that date was, as we have seen, on the frontier of Spain engaged in settling to his own profit the affairs of its royal family. He was not in a happy frame of mind at that period. It is possible that his conscience may have reproached him somewhat in the matter of the Spanish princes, but he had a more acute and more personal anxiety. His divorce from Josephine had been already projected. The first steps had been taken. Josephine's appeal to her husband was pathetic, and for a time the matter was postponed.

On December, 1807, four months before trouble broke out at Aranjuez, Napoleon and Joseph had had an interview at Venice, in which the Emperor endeavored to fire his brother's ambition by the exposure of his gigantic plans. In the course of the interview he offered him the throne of Spain, although he had not then seized that country. He had already written : —

"I can no longer have my relations living in obscurity. Those who do not rise with me shall no longer belong to my family. I am creating a family of kings, or rather viceroys; for the King of Lombardy, the King of Naples, and others that I do not name, will all be comprised in a federative system."

Joseph, when summoned to meet his brother at Bayonne, had no wish to leave Naples. He was growing interested in his work, and all classes of the people, except the guerillas and the bandits, were becoming attached to him. He had set on foot many good enterprises, and he wished to see them accomplished. He, however, obeyed his brother's summons, but refused to appoint a Regency in Naples, saying he should soon return.

Napoleon, doubtful if Joseph would consent to exchange Naples for Spain, met him a day's journey from Bayonne, and pleaded with him not to refuse the task of pacifying Spain. He said that the Spanish princes were as far from an agreement at Bayonne as they had been in their own capital; that Charles IV. preferred retirement, and as to Ferdinand he found his character so inferior, so uncertain, and so vague, that it would be indiscreet to commit France to his cause; that no regeneration of Spain was possible under her Bourbon princes; that an assemblage at Bayonne of over one hundred Spaniards, leading men of the kingdom, in rank, information, and character, were convinced of this truth, and had assured him that his brother would be acceptable to them and to the nation. He urged upon Joseph that it was important not to hesitate; that he could not believe that regret at leaving an enchanting country, where no difficulties or dangers remained to be combated, would influence a man like Joseph to refuse a throne, where many obstacles, it was true, would have to be surmounted, but where also much good was to be done.

This was attacking Joseph where he was most vulnerable; Napoleon knew that he was ever ready for self-sacrifice. But Joseph gave no answer.

On reaching the Château de Marrac, now a ruin, but then the residence of Napoleon and his court, Joseph found all the members of the Spanish *Junta* (or Assembly) waiting to receive him, with addresses of welcome. The next day came the Duke of Infantado, and Cervallos, Ferdinand's most influential supporters and friends. They offered their services to Joseph; they assured him that if he showed himself in Spain such a king as he had been in Naples, no doubt could exist that the entire nation would rally round him. The assurance of these Spaniards in Bayonne that he alone could restore tranquillity and prosperity to Spain at last prevailed on Joseph, but he would not give up the throne of Naples without receiving a pledge from his brother that the institutions and reforms that he had set on foot should be preserved and persevered in. A constitution, modelled on that of Naples, was drawn up for Spain, and Joseph and the members of what was called the *Junta* at Bayonne swore solemnly to observe it. The accession of Joseph to the throne of Spain was then announced to the Powers of Europe and (with the exception of England) was acquiesced in by them. He had been already proclaimed King of Spain and of the Indies the day before he reached Bayonne.

On July 8, 1808, Joseph abdicated the throne of Naples, and Murat, who had been severely ill at Madrid ever since the massacre, set out to take possession of the vacant throne.

The new King of Spain was accompanied to the Bidassoa, which divided France from his new dominions, by a splendid *cortége* of one hundred carriages. He crossed the river amid acclamations, and the roar of artillery. It was the last burst of enthusiasm his presence was to awaken on Spanish soil.

Meantime England was thoroughly aroused; the whole country was filled with indignation against the French Emperor, and burned with a desire to hurry to the relief of Spain and Portugal.

I do not propose to give any detailed account of what is called in England the Peninsular War. It has so completely absorbed the attention of English historians when treating of events in Spain from 1808 to 1814 that they tell us hardly anything of Joseph and his administration, of his troubles, of his flight, of his despair, and his humiliation. Napoleon had been entirely deceived in his calculations concerning the English army. He dreaded England's navy, but he held her land forces to be far inferior to the soldiers of France. He forgot that he himself had roused the martial spirit of the nation by his threat of invading England. He was as much deceived concerning the efficiency of the English army as he was concerning the spirit of the Spanish peasantry, and their national modes of warfare.

What is called the Peninsular War is hardly a part of Spanish history. It was a contest between the armies of France and England (either party assisted occasionally by Spanish troops), and the cause supported by England was all the time aided by bands of guerillas, — patriotic, brave, ferocious, and undisciplined. Were I to abridge the military movements of Moore, Wellington, Junot, Bessières, Soult, and Masséna, it would take not 'a chapter but a volume, and I should do no more than bewilder the " general reader." A picture of the warfare may be best gained from such books as " Charles O'Malley," by Lever, from the account of the storming of Badajoz, in Blackmore's " Alice Lorraine," and other books of that kind, whose authors have taken their historical descriptions from the lips of actors and eye-witnesses. I prefer to follow out the history of the government, or rather of the governments, of Spain, during the time that elapsed from July, 1808, to the return of King Ferdinand in March, 1814.

Reassured by the flattering hopes held out to him by all the Spaniards assembled at Bayonne, who seem to have been under the strange charm of personal influence exercised by the Emperor, and with his mind still further set at rest by a letter of congratulation from Ferdinand himself, Joseph set forth on his journey to his new capital; but two days after he entered Spain he wrote to Napoleon, " The spirit of the people is very bad. Madrid gives the tone. I must enter Madrid, and be proclaimed there. I find the soldiers ready to offer their services to whoever will pay them."

The next day he writes from Madrid : " I arrived here, and was proclaimed yesterday, very much against the feeling

of the inhabitants. Persons who hold office dread the populace, which is inflamed by the accounts received from
Saragossa." Then he adds with the frankness of an honest
man : " No one as yet has told the truth to your Majesty.
The fact is there is not a Spaniard who has declared for me,
except a few who are in some way associated with the
Junta, and those who made the journey with me. Others,
who reached Madrid or their own villages before I came,
have had to conceal themselves in dread of the indignation
of their countrymen."

Napoleon, however, persisted in his plans, contemptuously
ignoring the feelings of the Spanish people. At the outset
of the campaign his generals had considerable success in
the northern provinces, but Moncey was repulsed before
Valencia, and on July 22, imperial eagles for the first time
were surrendered to an enemy.

The story of this first defeat inflicted on French legions
by Spanish troops may here be briefly told.

One of the first army corps that entered Spain in April,
1808, in consequence of the convention appended to the
Treaty of Fontainebleau, was under the command of
Dupont, a general who had greatly distinguished himself by
his services in Holland, Italy, Austria, and Germany. Indeed, on two occasions it may be said that he saved the
whole French army by his generalship and personal bravery.
Napoleon said, when he left France for the campaign in
Spain, that he expected him to find his marshal's-baton in
Cadiz. His troops were of inferior quality. There were
few among them of the old veterans accustomed to victory
and glory. They were chiefly young conscripts, who had
been too short a time in the service to have grown accustomed to discipline, or attached to their colors. Dupont's
division marched southward, remained for a short time
within striking distance of Madrid, and was then ordered to
Granada and Andalusia, its objective point being the capture of Cadiz. On its way it took Cordova, which made a
vigorous resistance. The city on its capture was given over
for some hours to sack and pillage, in retaliation, it was said,

for cruelties inflicted elsewhere on French prisoners, which indeed were horrible. The silver vases and other plate belonging to the Cathedral disappeared, and I believe have never been accounted for.

The military situation having somewhat changed, Dupont was recalled from Andalusia, and left Cordova with an immense train of wagons, popularly supposed to be laden with the spoils of Cordova, but said by Dupont to hold stores for the support of his men in their march through a rugged, barren, hostile country. They also transported such of his sick and wounded as were able to travel. Great numbers of his young soldiers were ill with dysentery, a disorder that made frightful ravages among the French in southern Spain. Dupont himself was one of its victims.

The army, twenty thousand strong, reached Baylen, a small town surrounded by olive groves, commanding the entrance to the passes of the Sierra Morena. There they encountered a Spanish army, with a considerable contingent of Swiss and of Walloons, under Reding, a Swiss general, while the general-in-chief was Castaños, of whom I may say *en passant* that, after many vicissitudes of fortune during a life spent in public affairs, he died, aged 96 or 97, in the year 1852.

The weather was fearfully hot, the thermometer ranged over 100° Fahrenheit, the French troops were destitute of food [1] and water. Their general was without information, none could be extracted from the hostile peasantry; the scouting parties he sent out never returned. He was expecting reinforcements, and believed that two French corps were in his neighborhood, one commanded by Dafour, the other by Vedel. They on their part knew not his whereabouts, but were chasing guerilla bands through by-paths in the mountains. On July 19, Reding and Castaños attacked the French, who fought for ten hours; then, exhausted and without hope, Dupont asked for an armistice. Shortly after this, Vedel, attracted to the spot by the noise of artillery, made his appearance. He at once prepared to charge the

[1] Why they were not fed from the stores said to be in the *fourgons*, history does not say.

Spaniards, but orders sent to him by Dupont, who lay on the field sick and wounded, forbade him to do so.

Next day French envoys were sent to the camp of Castaños to negotiate the terms for a capitulation. It had been agreed that the division which had fought under Dupont should lay down its arms. Vedel's corps and Dafour's corps, which had not fought, were to evacuate Andalusia and to retire on Madrid. Especial stipulations were unfortunately made by the French with regard to the preservation of their immense train of baggage.

These terms had not been committed to paper when a messenger reached Castaños from his outposts, bringing a letter captured from a French officer, who had been sent with it to Dupont from Murat at Madrid. This letter commanded Dupont with Vedel and Dafour to return to him at once, as trouble was brewing in the capital.

Having read this news it was impossible for Castaños to allow the troops of Vedel and Dafour to march back with their arms to the very place to which their commander called them. The negotiations were broken off. Dupont sent word to Vedel that he had still time to extricate himself, but Castaños, seeing that his troops were about to move, at once threatened to turn his guns upon Dupont's men, who were completely surrounded. Dupont then thought of breaking through the enemy with the energy born of despair, but his officers assured him that further fighting on the part of his inexperienced troops, young, sick, weary, hungry, and parched with thirst, would be impossible. He gave way, and sent orders to Vedel, who had started on his march, to return. He obeyed, and twenty thousand Frenchmen and seven generals became prisoners of war. By the terms of the capitulation they were to be marched to Cadiz, and thence sent by sea to France. Their baggage was all searched, but the spoils of Cordova were not found there.

My father, then a lieutenant in the Royal Navy serving on one of the English ships lying off Cadiz harbor, saw these men as they were marched into that city, where, as the " patriotic " government of Spain refused to ratify the capitulation, they were put on board of hulks, and kept in hor-rible captivity. He used to describe their march as one of the saddest sights he ever saw, the mob hooting and insult-ing them, pelting them with stones, and rushing at them with knives, the women spitting in their faces, the children casting mud.

From Cadiz, after about six months, six thousand men of the division of Vedel were embarked in ships, and sent — they hoped to France, but knew not whither. At Palma, in the island of Majorca, after a suspense of forty days, they learned that their destination was the desert island of Cabrera.

At Cabrera the most tried courage sank under the horrors of the situation. Upon a pile of barren mountain ridges and sharp rocks, six thousand men were landed, almost with-out clothes, and before long many were absolutely naked. Scarcely a third of their number, after a residence of three years on the island, left its shores.

No habitation was to be found there save the ruins of a castle built by the Moors, nor had the French soldiers any means of building more than a few wretched huts of branches, brought with great labor from a few stunted trees that grew in a remote corner of the island. They had but a bare sufficiency of water to sustain life, and even that was a precarious supply. Provisions were sent to them every four days from Majorca, but were sometimes delayed either by indifference to their sufferings, or by the weather. Then hundreds, already weak, died of famine. Their allowance at the best was only six ounces of bread and a handful of dried beans.

The news of the sufferings of these men reached Sir Charles Cotton, the English admiral at Minorca. It was, according to international law, no affair of his. These French were prisoners of the Spaniards, but in those days British seamen were not strict observers of international etiquette in cases where humanity was concerned. Sir Charles sent my father, then in command of the "Minorca" sloop of war, to make a report to him on the subject.

The " Minorca " found the prisoners in the state I have
described. Almost all of them were naked. Two French
officers, a major and a captain, swam off to the ship as she
approached the landing-place; they were taken on board,
fed, clothed, made comfortable, and my father gave them
passage to Minorca, where Sir Charles soon after arranged
for their exchange. The sailors of the " Minorca," struck with
pity and horror, subscribed three days' rations for the sufferers.
Sir Charles Cotton, on hearing the report, at once had the
" Minorca's" deck loaded with black cattle, and sent her back
to land them at Cabrera. She reached the island at one of
those periods when the bread boat had been delayed, and
as the English ship approached, every tack she made which
seemed to take her out of her course, was watched with the
utmost agitation. The sick and dying had been brought
down to the seashore by their debilitated comrades, and
were encouraged to fix their eyes on her approach that they
might live till food arrived. She let go her anchor within
two hundred yards of the little beach, and in a moment the
sea was alive with men swimming out to her. Not only were
the cattle landed with a supply of food for immediate use,
but slops were served out to many a wretch wholly destitute
of clothing. Sir Charles Cotton sent an energetic report to
the English Admiralty, and the British government followed
this up with representations of the case to the government of
Spain. Matters improved in Cabrera during the few months
the prisoners continued to remain upon the island, and after
the treaty of Valençay at the close of 1813, they were released.

Thiers, describing the cruelties practised on French soldiers
by the Spanish peasantry, says they were sometimes put between two planks and sawn asunder; they were mutilated
and tortured in every way; sometimes they were hanged up
by the arms while fire was lighted beneath their feet; and
other similar atrocities were committed.

English officers to whom these deeds were told were filled
with horror and pity. One day off the coast of Catalonia a
Spanish fishing-smack came alongside the vessel of which

my father was in command. The fishermen wanted to exchange fish for tobacco. "What have you there?" asked my father, observing a bundle covered over with nets, lying at the bottom of the boat. It was a French officer, gagged and tightly bound. His captor, on being questioned as to what he meant to do with him, dragged his forefinger across his throat with a devilish expression of hate and rage. By threats and bribes he was induced to suffer his prisoner to be lifted out of the boat, when my father took possession of him, kept him in his cabin for some weeks, and then landed him under British protection at Gibraltar.

To return to the surrender of Dupont's army. Napoleon was furious. It was the first check his arms had ever received. The French generals were sent to France, where Dupont was at once brought before a very irregular court, nominated by Napoleon. It was remarked at the time that of the thirteen members who composed it the most bitter were civilians, while the most lenient were soldiers. Dupont was condemned to lose his rank, both military and civil, to have the Grand Cross of the Legion, which Napoleon himself had fastened on his breast after distinguished bravery in battle, torn from his uniform, that uniform he was forbidden ever to wear again, and he was condemned to imprisonment in a fortress during the Emperor's pleasure. Dupont remained in prison until the restoration, when Louis XVIII. made him his minister of war, to the great disgust of the French army; for he weeded out old subalterns and non-commissioned officers, and put into the places of Napoleon's old captains returned *émigrés*, court favorites, young men of family, men who had served in the army of Condé. He was also accused of taking revenge on the Order of the Legion of Honor, whose decoration had been torn from him, by distributing crosses indiscriminately to unworthy persons. During the Hundred Days Napoleon took no notice of him, except to forbid his coming to Paris. At St. Helena, however, he seems to have repented his harshness, and spoke of Dupont as a man more unfortunate than culpable.

When Joseph reached Madrid, July 12, 1808, he found

the people bitterly exasperated. A flame had been kindled by the massacres of May 2 which had spread like a flash over all Spain. There had been plenty of inflammable material in the country, and now, the people being convinced of the treachery of Napoleon, fierce passions were aroused, as well as a noble patriotism.

King Joseph, the day after his arrival in the capital, held a reception which men of all ranks and of all parties were invited to attend. There were grandees of Spain, chiefs of the religious orders, members of the tribunals, priests, officers, and generals, the principal capitalists in Madrid, and the syndics of various handicrafts, all astonished to find themselves thus assembled together. King Joseph mingled with the crowd, and conversed freely with those around him about the condition of affairs in Spain, and the motives that had brought him to that country. He said — and continued to say on every occasion — that he should as soon as possible call together a Cortes, whose business it should be to decide on the great question, " Should he, or should he not, be King of Spain? " He said also that he would never consent to any dismemberment of the Spanish kingdom, and that the French troops should evacuate the country the moment peace was declared.

His personality and his promises had made a favorable impression, when six days later, news of the capitulation at Baylen arrived. Then, to borrow a homely phrase, the inhabitants of Madrid were neither " to have nor to hold." They gave the word of resistance to the central and southern provinces, the northern were already up in arms, fighting — they knew not exactly on what side, but their war-cry was " Death to the invader ! "

News of the magnificent defence of Saragossa, then in progress, the inhabitants resisting the French troops of Marshal Lefebvre, had roused patriotism and emulation to the highest pitch.

Saragossa is situated on the Ebro. On June 16, 1808, when first attacked, it contained about fifty-five thousand inhabitants, few soldiers, and no generals. It was defended only by a low brick wall and a fort built on a high hill that overlooked the city. But its houses were substantially built, and its many convents were massive piles almost as strong as fortresses. It had been said of it a century before : " Saragossa is without defences, but the valor of its inhabitants supplies the lack of them."

The siege was begun June 16. The leaders of the townspeople were not military men, but peasants. Calvo di Rozas, the commander, was indeed a man of birth, but his assistants Tio Martin and Tio Jorge were of plebeian origin. Don Joseph Palafox, whose name has been inseparably associated with the defence of Saragossa, was not in the city from June 16 to July 2. He had gone into the neighboring country to collect reinforcements.

For two months twelve thousand French, with a train of heavy artillery, besieged the devoted city. In vain they tried repeatedly to take it by assaults, to subdue it by bombardment, or to reduce it by famine. On August 4, their regular approaches having been completed, they attacked and took possession of one half of the town. The fight of that day seems to have been terrible. In the midst of the confusion the doors of the lunatic asylum were burst open, and madmen, yelling and raging, mingled with the combatants. In the thickest of the fight two powder magazines blew up, scattering death in all directions.

Night closed upon the fearful scene, and in the dark hours Palafox again left the town to procure ammunition, for the way into the country was still open through one gate of the city. In four days he collected three thousand men from neighboring villages, and a large quantity of ammunition and provisions.

Sir Archibald Alison paints a stirring picture of what then took place.

" It may easily be imagined with what transports these reinforcements were received, for in the interim the citizens had had a desperate conflict to maintain, from which they never enjoyed one moment's respite ; from street to street, from house to house, from room to room, the fight was kept up with incredible obstinacy on both sides; every post became the theatre of bloody strife, to which column after column, regiment after regiment were successively brought up, while the fire of musketry, the roar of artillery, the flight of bombs, the glare of conflagration, and the cries of the combatants continued without intermission night and day. But all the efforts of the besiegers were in vain; animated almost to frenzy by the long duration and heart-stirring interest of the conflict, all classes vied with each other in heroic constancy; the priests were to be seen at the posts of danger, encouraging the soldiers, and administering consolation to the wounded and the dying; the women and children carried water incessantly to the quarters on fire, attended the wounded, interred the dead; many even took the places of their slain husbands or brothers at the side of the cannon; the citizens relieved each other night and day in the unceasing struggle. Such was the vigor of the resistance that from the 4th to the 14th of August the besiegers made themselves masters of only four houses. . . . After the arrival of the reinforcements under Palafox the contest was no longer equal; symptoms of discouragement were manifest in the enemy; sinister rumors circulated on both sides of some great disaster to the French at the South. The besiegers were gradually losing ground even in those quarters of which they had obtained possession in the first burst of the assault. Still the fire of the artillery continued, and was particularly violent on the night of the 14th of August; but at daybreak on the following morning it suddenly ceased, and the besieged, when the sun rose, beheld with astonishment the enemy at some distance in full retreat, traversing the plain towards Pampeluna. The victory was complete. . . ."

Nor were the French much more successful in other quarters, and King Joseph by advice of a Council of War, presided over by Savary, quitted Madrid a week after he had entered it. The French troops in central and southern Spain concentrated at Burgos, where he at once put himself and his government under their protection. Wellington was beginning at Lisbon his task of driving Junot out of Portugal, and organizing a Portuguese contingent to his English army.

The Emperor found his presence necessary in Spain, and

early in November, 1808, he joined his army in Galicia. King Joseph met his brother in the North, and after victories over the English, they proceeded together to Burgos on their march to Madrid. "At Burgos they found," says Count Miro di Melito, "all the houses deserted and pillaged, while heaps of broken furniture were lying in the mud. The quarter of the town beyond the river was on fire, and the maddened soldiery were smashing in doors and windows, and destroying everything. The churches had been despoiled, the streets were cumbered with the dead and dying, all the horrors of an assault were there, and yet the French troops had entered the town without resistance. Joseph made remonstrances to his brother, but his complaints were ill received, and his suffering at the sight of this treatment of one of the first towns of the kingdom over which he had been called to reign greatly affected him. I strongly advised him," continues Count Miro di Melito, "to renounce a crown which he could only secure after wading through seas of blood, and which would never recompense him for all the humiliations and disappointments heaped upon him." But Joseph felt his responsibilities, and would not yet resign the hope of saving Spain, though he discovered that Napoleon made light of his promise that Spain should not be despoiled of her northern provinces. Joseph was heartbroken, and protested. He declared that his position was no better than that of a *concierge* at the gates of a hospital at Madrid. His letters to his wife, Queen Julie, who, owing to the uncertain state of affairs in Spain, had not joined him, were full of despair.

The French army with its Emperor marched on Madrid, which yielded to Napoleon with very little resistance, December 3, 1808. Shortly after his arrival registers were opened in different parts of the city on which all those who desired the return of King Joseph were invited to inscribe their names. About thirty thousand persons did so, chiefly men of the more opulent classes, and addresses were forwarded to King Joseph entreating him to return. He came back early in January, 1809. About the same date was fought the battle of Corunna at which Sir John Moore [1] fell. Napoleon, when he heard news of the battle of Corunna, and the complete expulsion of the English army from Galicia, the northwestern province of Spain, said : —

" Everything proceeds well. The English will never make a second effort; in three months the war will be at an end. Spain may be a La Vendée, but I have tranquillized La Vendée. The Romans conquered the inhabitants of Spain, the Moors conquered them, and they are not nearly so fine a people now as they were then. I will settle the government firmly, conciliate the nobles, and cut down the people with grapeshot. They say the country is against me, but there is no longer a population there; Spain is in most places a solitude, without five men to a square league. I will let them see what a first-rate power can effect."

Joseph in Madrid endeavored to organize the administration of his kingdom, and even to set on foot local improvements, but he soon found he had no money, and he was exasperated by an order from Napoleon that French generals should supersede all civil functionaries in any part of Spain where French armies might be found. These generals fully carried out Napoleon's principle that a war must pay for itself; and while the King's treasury was empty, and his sol-

[1] Lady Hester Stanhope, niece of Mr. Pitt, was strongly attached to Sir John Moore. In the spring of 1808 my father was returning to Spanish waters, having been sent home invalided six months before. On board the ship-of-war which carried him as a passenger was Sir John Moore, on his way to meet his death a few months later at Corunna. In 1811 my father was dining at the table of the Governor of Malta, where he met Lady Hester, who had become very eccentric. She was then on her way to the East, where she lived many years. Hearing that my father had come out from England with Sir John Moore on his last voyage, she questioned him minutely, saying in piteous accents repeatedly : " You saw him later than I! You saw him later than I!" At the same dinner were Lord Byron and his friend Hobhouse, returning from their visit to Greece. When my father told this story his hearers would question him eagerly : "And what did you think of Lord Byron ?" He would answer, "I took hardly any notice of him. He was a little, lame lord, who, I was told, had written verses. My attention was wholly absorbed by Lady Hester."

diers and his functionaries were unpaid, they levied enormous contributions from every province in which they bore arms. In Andalusia alone during an occupation of two years and a half, the contributions they exacted amounted to six hundred million *reals* ($60,000,000).

Napoleon had divorced Josephine in 1809, and had married Maria Louisa in 1810. On March 29, 1811, news reached Madrid of the birth of the King of Rome. Joseph, whose position as King of Spain was growing more and more insupportable, with no money in his treasury, and no disposition on the French marshals' part to obey his orders, determined to seek an interview with his brother, and insist on resigning his crown. He was detained at St. Cloud to be present at the baptism of the King of Rome, at which ceremony the Emperor desired to be surrounded by a family of kings, but he could obtain only small concessions with regard to the finances or the government of his kingdom.

Napoleon had commanded him to make war in person, to prove himself a general, and if possible to receive a wound; but in all his enterprises and combinations he had failed. He planned to attack Cadiz, but a Spanish army in alliance with the English anticipated his intention, and frustrated it. At Cordova he had, however, the satisfaction of receiving from the canons of the Cathedral the French eagles that had been taken from Dupont's army. He marched northward to interpose between the capital and the allied army of British and Spanish troops under Wellington. And on June 21, 1813, he fought the battle of Vittoria. King Joseph's Spanish troops were routed, — the French gave way. Joseph fled from the field, and being a poor horseman came very near being captured by a pursuing party, as his horse stumbled in his flight and refused to jump over the ditches. Perhaps had he been taken he would have been glad, for he had written to his wife that he envied the fate of Lucien, captured by the English on his way to the United States, and held in England as a prisoner.

Absolutely penniless, Joseph crossed the French frontier, and reached St. Jean de Luz. Thence he wrote to his wife, who, alarmed by the despairing tone of his letters, was, in spite of her poor health, preparing to join him. He asked her for means to reach her and his home at Mortefontaine, where she was living with her two daughters, her sister Désirée, the wife of Bernadotte (soon to be Queen of Sweden), Catherine of Wurtemburg, wife of King Jérôme, and the Spanish Grand Inquisitor.

Napoleon was in Dresden preparing combinations for his last campaign. On his return to Paris he refused at first to see Joseph, but finally admitted him to an interview, for which the ex-King was forced to ascend the back-stairs.

Napoleon needed troops for his campaign against all Europe. Spain for the present was lost. He would triumph over the English at a more convenient season. He announced to his brother that he had now a plan for restoring Ferdinand VII. to his throne, and uniting him to his own imperial family by marriage. He suggested as the lady of his choice, Zenaïde, King Joseph's eldest daughter. To this Joseph would give no reply, and the matter was not definitely settled when Napoleon started with his legions on the campaign which was to end at Fontainebleau.

When the allies approached Paris Napoleon wrote to Joseph, whom he had named in his absence Lieutenant-General of the Empire, to remove the Empress and the King of Rome from the capital. He did so, and they were escorted by Austrian officers to Vienna after Napoleon had abdicated and had been sent to Elba. By the terms of the abdication liberal pensions were settled by the allies on King Joseph and his brothers.

Joseph and Louis (who was also an ex-king) went to Switzerland, and were forbidden to re-enter France. When Napoleon returned to France in 1815, Joseph joined him during the Hundred Days, but he was not at Waterloo. When all was lost he hurried to Rochefort, where two French frigates were waiting the arrival of Napoleon, who, believing it would be impossible to escape the English cruisers, preferred to throw himself, as he said, " on English generosity." He was too dangerous, however, to be treated with on those terms. He was not allowed to land in England, but was transferred to the Northumberland and transported to St. Helena.

Joseph purchased an American vessel which was taking in a cargo of brandy. His wife dared not risk a sea voyage, but remained in France with her daughters, and subsequently went to Italy.

Joseph took the title of Count de Survilliers, for which one of his biographers amusingly blames him, saying it would have been probably more congenial to the sentiments of Americans had he entered their republican country without a title!

He bought land near Bordentown, New Jersey, — a special act of the legislature enabling him, although an alien, to do so. He built and furnished a beautiful home, which he adorned with many valuable pictures. This mansion in 1820 was burned down. Joseph always considered this fire the work of an incendiary who wished to destroy his papers. He was offered an asylum both by the King of Sweden and the Emperor of Russia. But he pined for a warm climate. His daughters Zenaïde and Charlotte in turn crossed the ocean to visit him.

Joseph resided sixteen years in the United States, and was much beloved and respected by his neighbors in New Jersey. In person he resembled his brother Napoleon, being, however, taller and less stout. In his habits he was regular, temperate, and fond of early hours.

When the revolution of 1830 broke out in Paris, Joseph was eager to return to France, and to advocate the claims of Napoleon II. He wrote to Maria Louisa, imploring her to to authorize him to act for her son, and he spent one half his private fortune in endeavoring to raise friends for his nephew's cause.

In the days when Napoleon had thoughts of adopting Josephine's grandson (the little Charles Napoleon) as his heir, he had started a plan of marrying him to Zenaïde. The child died young, to the bitter grief of his mother, grandmother, and Napoleon. Zenaïde married in later life a son of her uncle Lucien.

Another chance for the imperial throne of France was placed almost within reach of Charlotte, Joseph's younger daughter. She married her cousin, Napoleon Louis, second son of Louis and Hortense. He died mysteriously in 1831 when engaged in an insurrection of the Carbonari, and his "rights" such as they were, descended to his younger brother, Louis Napoleon.

Joseph, after 1832, was at last enabled to take up his residence in Italy, where other members of his family had found a home. He died at Florence in 1844, in the arms of his wife, at the age of seventy-four.

In a piteous letter that he wrote to his brother Louis a few years before the close of his troubled life he said : —

"I have a good wife, but I have not lived with her for the last thirty years. Without ambition I have been constantly engaged in fighting against the enemies of my country. Yet of what that country exacted I could not approve. The most loving man in the world has passed his life always away from his family."

# CHAPTER IV.

## THEIR MAJESTIES OF THE CORTES.

EVERY half-century appears to have its own particular panacea for the evils of society. The experiment is debated, then tried, is found not to accomplish all that its friends expected of it, and gives place to another. The present one is the diffusion of education, — scientific education more or less, too often limited to undigested, undigestible bites of the fruit of the tree of knowledge. It was preceded by enthusiasm for an extension of parliamentary representation ; a parliament or a congress chosen straight from the people would represent, it was predicted, the highest wisdom of the nation, explain its wishes, and promote its best good. Preceding this (and indeed the parliamentary idea was the outcome of it) was the mania for creating constitutions. France during the past hundred years has tried a number of them. That one framed by the Constituent (or Constitution-making) Assembly in 1791 has been the model for almost all its democratic successors. It never could be made "to march," says Carlyle, and indeed it was in force barely two months.

Spain during this century has had seven constitutions, two at a time occasionally. No people, one would think, could be well governed under a constitution until they had had time to grow attached to it, until it was so dear to them that no man might dare to lay a hand upon the Ark of their liberties. This is the case with the English Constitution, and with the Constitution of the United States. Even in our Civil War the crime alleged by the South against the North was that it sought to violate the Constitution.

Spaniards in the different divisions of Spain, — call them as we please, kingdoms, states, or provinces, — learned from very early days how to live under constitutions.   Both Castile and Aragon had free constitutions earlier than the days of Magna Charta.   Under the Gothic kings of Spain, national assemblies were of two kinds : one political, summoned only on extraordinary occasions by the sovereign ; the other legislative, called the Council of the Kingdom, which was intrusted with the ordinary business of the nation.   These bodies bore analogy to the States-General and the Parliaments of France. Under subsequent kings of the various kingdoms that make up modern Spain, this system was continued.   Those who took part in these assemblies were the sovereign, the higher clergy, and the grandees.   Popular representation did not take place until in the Middle Ages ; then great towns throughout Europe began to acquire charters which secured them municipal independence, — independence even of the sovereign.   The earliest appearance of the burgher class in the Cortes of the kingdom of Castile, was in 1169, nearly a century before Leicester's Parliament in England, and forty-six years before Magna Charta.   At about the same date the crown of Castile was declared hereditary.   Leon was joined to Castile, and Toledo was captured from the Moors.

Historians are not able to state what were the qualifications for the franchise, but it is certain that more than one hundred cities and towns sent representatives to a Cortes held in 1345.   The knights formed a separate body in the Cortes of Aragon, and it does not appear that they ever joined the burgesses.   Henry III. died while holding a Cortes, and after his time, that is, in the fifteenth century, the power of the burgesses seems to have declined, — only eighteen towns and cities being thenceforth entitled to send their representatives.

Up to the time of Charles V., great pains were taken to secure purity of election ; bribery, false returns, and undue influence were strictly prohibited, but the ministers of Charles V. interfered openly in elections, and at length in some cities the office of representing the people was publicly sold in the street.

When Charles V. held his Cortes in Galicia, the representatives from Toledo were instructed to pray his Majesty for four things : (1) to take up his residence in Spain ; (2) to hold the Cortes in his kingdom of Castile ; (3) to apply some remedy to prevent the buying of offices ; (4) to put such checks on the Inquisition as would save the innocent from oppression.

The debates of the Cortes were all secret ; their results alone were submitted to the Council and had the force of law, binding even on the King. The Constitution of Aragon provided for four deliberative bodies, and besides had what was called a Justizia, a sort of court of appeal which checked and controlled the sovereign.

So jealous were the Spaniards of the powers they had exercised for long ages over their kings that when, at the beginning of the twelfth century, the Pope sent his Legate to restore King Henry IV., who had been deposed by his subjects, that personage having begun his discourse by the words "I have power to dispose of everything in these kingdoms by the authority of the Holy See," he was promptly checked by the Master of the Order of St. Ignatius, who broke in upon his speech by the declaration that those who had told His Holiness that he had power over the temporal concerns of the kingdoms of Castile and Leon had deceived him ; that he and the nobility of those kingdoms could depose any king for just causes, and set up such an one as they thought suited to the public good.

This patriotic spirit was crushed under the rule of Charles V., and still further under that of his son Philip II.

The sovereigns of Spain ceased to be Spaniards. Their revenues came, not from their European subjects, but from other countries ; the wealth of the Indies flowed into their coffers. They could brave the Spanish Cortes. They were no longer dependent on its vote for their supplies. As money was not wanted, the Cortes ceased to be assembled. The sovereign became El Rey Absoluto. After 1713 no Cortes was called together till 1789. The next was summoned in 1810, when war was raging in every part of Spain, and when a brother of Napoleon professed to rule the country, then a Cortes extraordinary was summoned by a provisional regency in the absence of the natural sovereign, and being unable to assemble at Madrid, which was in the hands of the French, they met at Cadiz, under the protection of an English fleet blockading the harbor.

This extraordinary Cortes was composed of those we now style *doctrinaires,* — men of theory, the most dangerous class who can be called to rule in times of danger. The nobility and the office-holders in Spain had gone over to the French, and served King Joseph; among these was the Marquis de Montejo, father of the future Empress Eugénie. The clergy were scantily represented in the Cortes, and those who came were from the northern provinces. The rest of the representatives, the deputies being chosen by a most complicated electoral system, were nearly all literary men, or of the legal profession. These did not indeed evolve a constitution out of their inner consciousness; they founded it for the most part on the Constitution of 1791, framed for the French in the Constituent Assembly.

By the time the Revolution of 1808, already spoken of, occurred, Spain had sunk to low estate, partly because of the character of her Bourbon princes, partly because the iron hand of the Inquisition had squeezed mind and heart out of her leisure classes, partly because of the corruption of morals induced by court example, and partly because the nobility almost universally absented themselves from their vast landed estates. Nevertheless, the peasantry, though sunk in ignorance and superstition, were exempt from poverty. They were the true Spaniards, brave, bloodthirsty, and independent; loyal to existing institutions, and to their king. Their flocks and their small holdings supported them. They asked and needed no luxuries; many things that seem to us the necessaries of life were quite unknown to them. They had their pleasures, — bloody pleasures for the most part; and if sickness or misfortune overtook them, they claimed help from the nearest convent. There lived their best friends, whose aid was never refused them. The whole kingdom was a Castle of Indolence. The roads were no better than those of the Middle Ages. Many branches of trade were monopolized by the government. The power which took away the means of improvement extinguished the desire to improve. A spell of enchantment seemed to have settled down upon the land. The contentment born of apathy benumbed all classes. The government seemed no concern of theirs. Some one said of them at this period, "The Castilians pride themselves on their loyalty, they even think it a merit to bear every oppression, and suffer every wrong from their lawful prince. They enter into slavery with a sort of chivalrous enthusiasm, and look upon a royal edict as entitled to the admiration of the world."

But all this changed when their princes were led into captivity, when the regency left behind by Ferdinand under the presidency of Don Antonio was displaced by Murat, when French troops occupied their fortresses, cleared their streets with grape-shot, ate up their harvests, and spread themselves over their country; then they had recourse to the only form of government left them, — provincial Juntas which were formed in every province. Spain was again resolved into its former states and kingdoms, nor were the old animosities forgotten. Castilians still jeered at Catalans; still despised the mixed races of Andalusia and Granada; still thought the men of the Basque Provinces a savage horde.

The first written constitution provided for Spain was made at Bayonne in 1808, under the eye, and probably by the dictation of Napoleon. Joseph was to be a constitutional sovereign under the severe and arbitrary will of an imperious and imperial dictator.

Joseph had given a constitution to Naples, and the one he proposed for Spain was framed after that model, but he repeatedly gave his subjects an assurance that as soon as possible a Cortes framed after the model of such assemblies in old times should be summoned to meet him at Granada. His constitution, however, never "marched," it never even stood upon its feet. It had, of course, no attraction for the Spanish people. When Ferdinand's Council of Regency was dissolved, power *ad interim* was exercised by a provisional Central Junta which had been forced to leave Madrid and set up its headquarters at Seville ; thence it was expelled by the advance of the French in January, 1810, but before it broke up it appointed a regency of six persons to administer public affairs. This decree was published in Cadiz on January 31, 1810, and laid down the principles on which an extraordinary Cortes was to be elected. Instead of this new Cortes assembling as of old in three chambers, the Nobles, the Clergy, and the Commons, each body having been elected by separate votes, the whole Cortes was to be elected by a vote of householders, and there was to be only one Chamber, as in the French National Convention or Legislative Assembly.

Since at the beginning of January, 1810, three-fourths of the country was in the hands of the French, election of members of the Cortes which was to settle the form of government and keep up the war in the provinces was conducted mainly within the walls of Cadiz. Into that stronghold patriots had flocked from all parts of the country, animated, for the most part, with French revolutionary fervor. These persons were considered sufficient, under the circumstances, to elect deputies to the Cortes from their respective provinces. The elections for the Spanish-American colonies were made on the same plan. There was to be one deputy for every fifty thousand inhabitants, chosen by the few individuals from each district who found themselves in Cadiz. Galicia, the Asturias, and part of Catalonia chose their own deputies, and from these provinces came the very few nobles and clergy who sat in this extraordinary and most important assembly which was to regulate Spanish affairs.

The Junta which at Seville had governed the country for eighteen months, if not well or wisely, at least with constancy and courage, passed two resolutions before it resigned its functions. It decreed complete liberty of the press, and passed a " self-denying ordinance," which deprived the future Cortes of the benefit of such experience as in eighteen months of administration its members had themselves acquired.

GENERAL JOACHIM MURAT.

A Regency of six persons was appointed, who were supposed to represent the royal authority, but they fell almost immediately under the control of the Municipal Junta of Cadiz, which in turn was completely influenced by the press, which was openly anarchic and revolutionary. One journal thought no shame to call itself the Spanish Robespierre; and indeed Robespierre seems to have been adopted by a faction in Cadiz as its hero, while Marat and Hébert never made bloodier speeches in the French Chamber than their admirers did subsequently in the Cortes which framed the Spanish Constitution of 1812. One member hoped to see the rise of a Christian Robespierre; another declared that a little bit of Robespierre was wanted; a third called for heads to be struck off, and more Spanish than French blood to be shed. A renegade priest clamored for the axe of the executioner, and professed himself ready to wield it. This was, however, in the autumn months of 1810; in the previous February the members of the Junta of Seville who had administered such national government as remained in Spain after Ferdinand went into captivity, were dishonored, persecuted, and imprisoned. One was Calvo, who had borne a splendid part in the defence of Saragossa; one was Count Tilly, who died in prison, but who, if we believe the stories told of him by Blanco White, need not draw largely on our commiseration; his cruelties, however, far from being the cause of his condemnation, should, in the eyes of those who incarcerated him, have redounded to his honor. A different man, the good and stately Jovellanos, was imprisoned, then exiled, and died of a broken heart.

The Regency having got possession of the government, was in no haste to summon the already elected Cortes, which it foresaw might supersede its authority. Public clamor, however, forced it to yield, and at the close of September, 1810, the Cortes commenced its sittings.

One of its first measures was to proclaim its own sovereignty, and, in order to emphasize this claim, it enacted that while the King should be called "Your Highness," its members should collectively be addressed as " Your

Majesty." With all its factious divisions, its subserviency to the French Constitution of 1791, its gross ignorance, and its want of statesmanship, it showed firmness and courage. Although French armies and King Joseph were at the very gates of Cadiz, it issued a proclamation in which its deputies declared that Spaniards would never lay down their arms till they had regained their sovereign and recovered their national independence. They repudiated all treaties or agreements made with their King at Bayonne, or while in captivity, and they swore never to bend their knees to the usurper.

Another point on which they spoke the sentiments of the Spanish people was their determination to maintain the Roman Catholic religion as the sole religion authorized in Spain.

On March 19, 1812, the Constitution devised by the Cortes of Cadiz was promulgated, and met with anything but a cordial reception throughout the country. The Basque Provinces and Navarre were furious at the abrogation of their *fueros*, the especial privileges they had enjoyed under the crown of Spain for hundreds of years, but the commercial cities were enthusiastically in favor of the Constitution; it had been framed to suit commercial ideas, though it stimulated the colonies to revolt, and struck the first blow that severed from Spain her American provinces. In brief, the provisions of the Constitution might be classed as follows. Their Majesties of the Cortes were sovereigns; the King was the executive under their control. He had no right to an absolute veto, and after a recess his conduct during the time the Cortes was not sitting was to be severely scrutinized. The Cortes had the power of making war or peace; of organizing the army; of appointing high officers and judges. Ministers of the King, or officers of his household, could not sit in the Cortes. Trial by jury was not accorded by the Constitution, though it was suggested that if found desirable it might afterwards be granted. A species of local government was provided for the provinces, and the national religion was to be enforced and preserved.

"The reception which this constitution met with in Spain was," says Alison, "such as might have been expected from so great an innovation in a country in which the urban constituencies were so zealous for change, and the rural inhabitants so firmly attached to the institutions of their fathers."

The Duke of Wellington in many of his letters recorded his opinion of it. He said it made no provision whatever for the rights of land-owners. "The Cortes," he writes to his brother, "are unpopular everywhere; and in my opinion deservedly so. Nothing can be more cruel, absurd, and impolitic than their decrees respecting the persons who have served the enemy. It is extraordinary that the revolution in Spain has not produced one man with any knowledge of the real situation of the country. It appears as if they were all drunk."

Six weeks later he went to Cadiz to press the adoption of a measure urged by the English government, namely, that he should be made generalissimo of the Spanish forces, and commander-in-chief of the allied armies in Spain.

Spanish pride would not listen to this for a moment. "Had they agreed," he said afterwards, "I could have saved their country." With respect to what he saw at Cadiz during his visit in December, 1813, he writes:—

"It is impossible to describe the state of confusion with regard to public affairs. The Cortes have formed a constitution only good to be looked at; and I have not met one of its members or any person of any description who considers it the embodiment of a system by which Spain is, or can be, governed. The Cortes have *in form* divested themselves of executive power, and appointed a regency for that purpose, but the regency are in fact the slaves of the Cortes, and neither regency nor Cortes have any constitutional communication with each other, nor have they any authority beyond the walls of Cadiz. . . . In truth there is no authority in the state beyond the libellous newspapers, and they certainly ride over both Cortes and regency without mercy."

It was not long, however, before a change came. Napoleon was already negotiating with Ferdinand, trusting that a weak King of Spain who was entirely under his influence might serve his purposes. Joseph had thrown off his crown in disgust. The imperial prestige was broken. The French troops in Spain were needed elsewhere. Wellington had driven Soult beyond the Pyrenees; and Napoleon made terms with his captives at the close of 1813. He signed his abdication at Fontainebleau, April 11, 1814. Ferdinand had already been released from Valençay, and had reached the shores of his kingdom March 24, 1814, a week before the Allies entered Paris, and nearly three weeks before Napoleon signed his abdication. He came back to Spain to add to the confusions of his divided and distracted people. "Supple, accommodating, and irresolute," says Alison, "he had learned hypocrisy in the school of suffering. His inclination no doubt was strongly in favor of despotic power, but he had great powers of dissimulation, and succeeded in deceiving Talleyrand himself, as well as the liberal ministers imposed on him by the Cortes, as to his real intentions."

Before we close this chapter of Spanish history and take up the reign of Ferdinand, it may not be unwise or irrelevant to give a sketch of the state of feeling among the inhabitants of southern Spain, a few months before the assembling of the Cortes, as we find it in one of the letters of Blanco White which appeared in London in 1821 in the "New Monthly Magazine." These letters were written under the *nom de plume* of Doblado. At the time of their appearance Blanco White was an exile in England, where he became the friend and associate of leading men of letters, and was himself a poet of no small ability in the English language.

He writes (or professes to be writing) from Seville in July, 1808.

"I have arrived," he says, "just in time to witness the unbounded joy which the defeat of Dupont's army at Baylen has diffused over this town. The air resounds with acclamations, and the astounding clamor of the cathedral bells announces the arrival of the victorious general Castaños, who, more surprised at the triumph of his arms than any one of his countrymen, is

just arrived to give thanks to St. Ferdinand for his unlooked-for
success at Baylen, and to repose a few days under his laurels. . . .

"I will, however, relate the particulars of the escape I and my
friend effected from Madrid, six weeks after Murat's intimidat-
ing massacre. Alarm and indignation had spread like wildfire over the country; every gate of Madrid was kept by a
strong force of French infantry. The people indeed could
venture out of their houses, but the public walks were deserted,
and the theatres left almost entirely to the invaders.

"Yet it was visible that the French had a party, which,
though feeble in numbers, contained some of the ablest, and not
a few of the most respectable men of Madrid. . . . Under the
most profligate and despicable court in Europe, a sense of
political degradation had been excited among such Spaniards
as were not blinded by a nationality of mere instinct. The
true source of the enthusiasm which appeared on the accession
of Ferdinand was joy at the removal of his father. As for
the state of dependence on France which would follow the
acknowledgment of Joseph Bonaparte, it could not be more
abject or helpless than under Ferdinand, had his wishes of a
family alliance been granted by Napoleon. It cannot be
denied that indignation at the treatment we had experienced
strongly urged the nation to revenge, but passion is a blind
guide, which thinking men will seldom trust on political measures. Many argued that, though to declare war against an
army of veterans already in the heart of Spain might be an act
of sublime patriotism, it was more likely to bring ruin and permanent slavery on our country than the admission of a new
king, who, though a foreigner, had not been educated a despot,
and who for the want of any constitutional claims would be
anxious to deduce his rights from the acknowledgments of the
nation.

"These are not my own views, but I cannot endure that
blind, headlong, unhesitating patriotism which I find uni-
formly displayed in this town of Seville, and in this province,
— a loud popular cry which every individual is afraid not to
swell with his whole might, and which, though it may express
the *feeling* of a great majority, does not deserve the name of
public *opinion* any more than the unanimous acclamations at an
*auto da fé*. . . .

"We escaped from Madrid on June 15, and walked under a
burning sun to a small inn about three miles from the city,

where we were to take two wagons returning to Andalusia. The heat was dreadful. At a village in Estremadura a crowd of country people collected round us, and began to inquire in fierce, rude tones who we were, and where we came from. Happily the Alcalde soon made his appearance, and testifying that our language was pure Castilian, he at last convinced the villagers that we were not Frenchmen, but he told us we must be prepared to meet with people inquisitive and suspicious, who might do us great harm if they found any flaw in our account of ourselves. . . . The unfortunate propensity to shed blood which spoils many a noble quality in the Spaniards of the South, had been indulged in in most towns of any note, under the cloak of patriotism. Frenchmen of course, though long settled in Spain, were the objects of popular fury, but many Spaniards were called traitors, and owed their fate to private pique or revenge. We found the alcaldes to whom we applied for protection perfectly intimidated, and fearing the consequences of any attempt to check the blind fury of the people under them.

" At Almaraz, where a celebrated bridge spans the Tagus, the Alcalde told us that the people of his district, upon hearing the news from Madrid, and of insurrection in the chief towns of their province, flocked before his house armed with sickles, pickaxes, and other implements of husbandry. The Alcalde, who was a man beloved and popular, came confidently out to them, and asked them what they wanted. Their answer seems to me unparalleled in the history of mobs. ' We wish, sir, to kill somebody,' said the spokesman of the insurgents. ' Some one has been killed in Truxillo, one or two others at Badajoz, another at Merida, and we will not be behind our neighbors. So we will kill a traitor.' As this commodity could not be procured in the village, it was lucky for us that we had not happened to reach it on that day.

" At Merida, however, we had partly undressed and were taking our *siesta*, when we were roused by the noise of a mob rushing down the street and gathering in front of the inn. As far as the eye could reach nothing was to be seen but a compact crowd of peasants, most of them with clasp-knives in their hands. At the sight of us at the window most of them began to brandish their weapons, shouting that they would make mince-meat of every Frenchman in the inn. We hurried on our clothes, and rushed down into the hall to learn what all this meant. There we found twelve Spanish dragoons standing in two lines on the inside of the gate, holding their carbines ready to fire, as the officer in command warned the mob they would do, on the first man who ventured into the house. The inn-keeper walked up and down, bewailing the fate of his inn, which he assured us would soon be set on fire by the mob. A young Frenchman bearing despatches to Junot had been captured on his journey, and was being sent under guard to the Captain General of the Province of Badajoz. The crowd in the street consisted of about two thousand peasants who had been drilling as volunteers in another part of the city. The poor prisoner had been imprudently brought into the town when the recruits were in the principal square, indulging in the idleness of a Sunday. On hearing that he was a Frenchman, they drew their knives, and would have cut him to pieces, but for the haste which the soldiers made with him towards the inn.

" The fury of the crowd was not appeased till the military commander of the place, attended by some of the magistrates, had promised them to throw the young Frenchman into a dungeon. He had done the same thing a few days before on behalf of his own adjutant, against whom these same recruits had risen on parade in so murderous a spirit, that though the man was protected by a few regulars, they had wounded him severely, and would have taken his life but for the interference of the Vicar, who, bearing the consecrated Host in his hands, placed the officer under its protection.

" The Frenchman was accordingly conducted to prison, but neither the soldiers nor the magistrates who surrounded him could fully protect him from the savage fierceness of the peasants, who crowding upon him, as, half dead with terror, he was slowly dragged to the town jail, stuck the points of their knives into several parts of his body. Whether he finally was sacrificed to the popular fury or by some happy chance escaped with life, I have not been able to learn.

" A revolution, however laudable its object, is seldom without some features which nothing but distance of time or place can soften. We were too well acquainted with the inefficiency of most of those men who had been suddenly called into power not to feel a strong reluctance to place ourselves under their government at Seville. The only man of talent in the Junta of that place was Saavedra, the ex-minister. Dull ignorance, mixed with a small portion of inactive honesty, was the general character of that body.

" The effect of revolutionary success on a people at large resembles the effect of slight intoxication on the individual ; it brings forth every good, and every bad quality in a state of exaggeration. To an acute but indifferent observer, Seville, as we found it, would have been a most interesting study. He could not but have admired the patriotic energy of the inhabitants, their unbounded devotion to the cause of their country, and the wonderful effort by which, in spite of their passive habits of submission, they had ventured to dare both the authority of their rulers and the approaching bayonets of the French."

This is a long extract, but it is from the pen of an eye-witness, and an impartial one. It seemed to me fitted to prepare the reader's mind for much that is to follow, and throws light on much that he may have read in the preceding pages. The character of the Spanish people, of the nobles, of the clergy, of the office holders, and of the *bourgeoisie,* but above all of the peasantry, seems to me to be the key-note to the strange vicissitudes that for a century have followed hard upon each other in Spanish affairs. And that character may, I think, be best brought out by such a narrative as I have quoted.

# CHAPTER V.

## THE RESTORATION OF FERDINAND.

THE return of the Bourbons to France, after the downfall of Napoleon and his retirement to Elba, had been
preceded by the restoration of the Spanish Bourbons. There
was no thought of recalling Charles IV. to his throne, the
affections of the people were fixed upon Ferdinand, — their
captive king, in whose name they had fought the French, —
the prince who they fondly hoped would restore Spain
to the place she had held among the nations. They knew
nothing personally of Ferdinand. To them, he was only the
unhappy prince, kept in subjection by his cruel and vicious
parents; the object of persecution by their presumptuous
favorite; the victim of the treachery of Napoleon, and the
king who, in 1808, during his brief reign of ten weeks, had
put forth proclamations full of liberal sentiments, and reassur-
ing promises. Of his unparalleled powers of dissimulation,
nothing was known.

Talleyrand, in his " Memoirs," wrote of Ferdinand : —

" At Valençay he humbled himself to the dust beneath the
hand of his oppressor; he even wrote to congratulate him when
he had gained a victory over Spaniards. He had no sooner
remounted his throne than he made no distinction between
men who had been his faithful subjects and those who, having
brought a revolutionary spirit into the Cortes, had done their
best to annihilate his power, and for the royal authority substitute their own. He condemned all alike to exile, chains, and
even death; among them the very men who had roused their
countrymen in his defence, and delivered him from his captivity, — the men to whom he owed his power to reign. The spirit
of submission that he had exhibited in misfortune suddenly
changed into a mad desire for absolute sway."

Though Ferdinand did not re-enter the kingdom of his fathers until March 24, 1814, the treaty by which he was liberated had been made by Napoleon when disasters thickened round him. One of its stipulations was that the King of Spain should insist on the evacuation of his territory by the English armies. The Cortes refused to ratify this agreement, — called in history the "Treaty of Valençay," — and Ferdinand remained a prisoner until the approach of the allied armies made it necessary to release him unconditionally. He went by water to Catalonia; visited the ruined city of Saragossa, and proceeded thence by easy stages to Valencia, — received everywhere with the noisy acclamations which rise so easily to the lips of a Southern population. He received the honors of war, both from the French and Spanish armies, while the English, by command of Wellington, made haste to evacuate his dominions. He remained at Valencia during the month of April, collecting round him grandees, prelates, and other advisers in whose sympathy he had confidence, and by whose opinions (when he had assured himself that they coincided with his own) he intended to be guided.

The government of the country, meantime, lay with the Cortes, now sitting at Madrid. The deputies had testified great joy at the deliverance of their king, but they did not come forth in a body to meet him, and they were not disposed to resign their sovereignty into his hands, without receiving guarantees that he was prepared to support their new Constitution. They therefore issued a decree by which they enjoined their liberated prince to swear adherence to that document before they would acknowledge him as their sovereign.

As I have already said, the Constitution of 1812 was avowedly a very imperfect one. Based on the French Constitution framed more than twenty years before by the Constituent Assembly, it was a little more restrictive as to the prerogatives of the king, and in some other respects it was more revolutionary.

A Spaniard, writing on the subject to a friend in America, speaks thus of this document: —

*KING FERDINAND VII.*

"You have felt surprise, I doubt not, in common with so many others, that the Constitution, which limited the royal power, which gave to Spain a legislative body, which aimed at reforming abuses and renovating the health of the monarchy, —you have wondered, I say, why so noble and hopeful a scheme as this did not receive the unshaken support of the people; and you have been disposed, maybe, to join in the vulgar cry against the Spanish clergy, and to reproach them as the cause of the strange downfall of the Cortes. But I assure you it was not solely the influence of the clergy which ruined the fabric of the Constitution; it was because that fabric was not founded on the affections of the people; it violated the cherished nationality of several of the provinces; it disregarded the pre-existing institutions upon which and out of which it should have been framed, and the people preferred an absolute king at the head of those institutions, rather than a limited king, obtained at the expense of sacrificing them in obedience to mere political theory."

Then, too, although the Constitution had declared that the Roman Catholic religion must be the sole religion tolerated in Spain, the measures taken against the revenues of the Church, and for the suppression of the convents, made it very distasteful to the peasantry. They had been fighting six years against the French, whose ideas they considered dangerous, irreligious, and revolutionary; they were not disposed, in the name of liberty,— a blessing of which they felt neither the value nor the want, — to make enemies of their parish priests, or of their friends the monks; nor did they desire to tie up the hands of their hereditary sovereign. The Cortes and their Constitution were not popular. Ferdinand was received everywhere with cries of " Long live our Absolute King!" — words probably little understood by those who uttered them. Petitions (most acceptable to royalty) were poured in on the restored sovereign, beseeching him not to ratify the Constitution. Leading generals, and sixty-nine members of the Cortes joined in the cry, and besought him to reign as his fathers had done before him.

Roughly speaking, we may say that at this time rural

Spain was almost to a man enthusiastic for the privileges of the Church and the prerogatives of the King. The army, its generals, and its officers sided with the peasantry. The liberal party had its strength in the cities, in Madrid itself, and above all in the seaport towns.

Thus encouraged to follow out his predetermined resolutions, Ferdinand on May 4, 1814, put forth from Valencia a decree annulling all the acts passed by the Cortes during his captivity, and restoring absolute monarchy over the whole of Spain. He described the Constitution as "a republican form of government, to be presided over by a chief magistrate (the King) deprived alike of consideration and of power." And he concluded : —

"I promise — I swear to you, true and loyal Spaniards, that your hopes of prosperity and peace under your sovereign shall not be deceived. He places his chief glory in being the head of an heroic nation, which by its immortal exploits has won the admiration of the whole world, and at the same time preserved its own liberty and honor. I *detest* — I *abhor* despotism. It can never be reconciled either with civilization or with the lights of the other nations of Europe. Kings never have been despots in Spain; neither the sovereign nor the constitutions of the country have ever authorized despotism, though unhappily it has been sometimes practised, as it has been in all ages by fallible men. Abuses have existed in Spain, not because it had no constitution, but from the fault of persons or circumstances. To guard against such abuses in the future, so far as human prudence can go, while preserving the honor and the rights of royalty (for royalty has its own rights as well as the people have theirs), I will treat with the deputies of Spain and of the Indies in a Cortes legally assembled, composed of deputies from one and the other, as soon as I can convoke them after having re-established the wise customs of the kings our ancient predecessors. . . . No time shall be lost in taking proper measures for the assembling of the Cortes."

This document wound up by annulling the Constitution, and declaring all persons guilty of high treason, and punishable with death, who should attempt to resist this the King's decree. After its promulgation Ferdinand commenced his journey to Madrid, crowds hailing his coming with enthusiasm.

The Cortes lost no time in issuing a counter-proclamation, and sent out troops to oppose the king's progress. But these soldiers joined the multitude with cheers and cries of "Viva el Rey Absoluto!"

The Cortes broke up on May 10, making no effort to withstand the will of the King, and the will of the people. Its members, deserted by all, even by their own ushers, fled in utter dismay toward Cadiz; a few deputies only remained in Madrid, and Ferdinand at once arrested and imprisoned them.

Thus fell the Provisional Government of Spain and the Constitution of 1812 in that country. The people believed in the promises of their King, and looked forward with hope and confidence to his plans for reformation.

The first thing he did was to re-establish the Inquisition, and to recall the Pope's Nuncio; some slight modifications as regarded the use of torture in the proceedings of the Holy Office were, however, made. The monarch forgot all the pledges he had so solemnly given, that he would convoke a Cortes assembled according to the ancient laws and customs of the realm. "He fell immediately," says Alison, "under the direction of a *camarilla* composed of priests and nobles;" and the historian might have added "and of vulgar flatterers and favorites;" for Ferdinand was fond of gossip and low company. When petitions were presented to him begging him to follow up the gracious intentions set forth in his decree, they were received only with displeasure.

The army and its officers, when the decree annulling the Constitution was published, and when they realized that King Ferdinand's promises, being wholly without guarantees, were not likely to be fulfilled, began to show symptoms of dissatisfaction and revolt. Besides this, their pay was in arrears, their clothes worn almost to rags, and when the royal Governor of Andalusia published a decree that any one speaking or acting against King Ferdinand should be arrested, tried by court-martial, and shot within three days of the offence, terror spread among all classes. Ninety persons in one night were arrested in Madrid, and the ordinary prisons were insufficient to contain the many who succeeded them.

Men called the Afrancesados, — that is, those who had assisted or tacitly approved the rule of King Joseph, — were especially persecuted. Ten thousand of them, it is said, fled over the Pyrenees. Here is the apology of those men — many of them the highest in birth, education, and intelligence in Spain — from the pen of one compelled against his will, to be an exile and an Afrancesado : —

"Many persons respectable for intelligence, rank, fortune, and even love of country, attached themselves to the fortunes of King Joseph from deep conviction of the necessity of a change of dynasty, in order to effect the reforms of internal administration which Spain then needed. They saw that Joseph was an intruded king — *rey intruso*, as he was continually called, and that he was imposed upon the country by the arts or the arms of the French, but so also had been Philip V., the first of the Bourbons. They looked to the genius and power of the Bonapartes to give new impulse to the energies of the Spanish nation ; they regarded Joseph's elevation to their throne as a harsh remedy, but one called for by the inveteracy and virulence of the disease. In a word, they submitted to a fraudulent transfer of the crown from one Frenchman to another Frenchman, in the hope of bettering the condition of their country ; and adhered to their new oaths of allegiance from patriotic motives of honest principle, despite the general enthusiasm of the people in behalf of the deposed Ferdinand."

While hundreds of Afrancesados, through fear of death, hurried across the frontier with their families, guerilla bands, well used during the occupation of the French to irregular warfare, made their appearance all over the northern provinces, Aragon, and Catalonia, uniting brigandage with political aims. In Navarre, General Mina, a distinguished partisan leader in the late war, headed an insurrection, but finding less support than he expected from his own soldiers, he sought refuge in France, among the enemies he had so

long fought on behalf of the King who had betrayed the
hopes he formed of him.

On the part of the court in Madrid, and in the southern
provinces, counter revolutions, courts-martial, imprisonments,
and executions rapidly succeeded each other. The Minister
of Grace and Justice under the late government was condemned to serve in the galleys, and the editors of the principal liberal journals in Madrid were sent to prison.

The inhabitants of the great cities were alarmed. Ferdinand ceased to be popular. Secret societies were formed,
the members of which took the name of *communeros;*
General Porlier, who had greatly distinguished himself in the
Peninsular war, and had imbibed from the English with whom
he was associated a reverence for free institutions, took the
lead in a revolt in Galicia, which demanded the assembling
of a Cortes and the dismissal of the King's advisers and
ministers.

But though officers of the army, men of the intelligent
class, and the inhabitants of the cities were full of indignation
against their sovereign and his policy, the peasantry, led by
their priests, were firm in their loyalty to what they considered the cause of Church and King. It mattered little to
them what was the form of the central government, it did
not hinder or promote their own prosperity; only when an
anti-religious Cortes broke up their convents, dispersed their
priests, and confiscated the churches' property, they felt that
all that was most dear to them had been assailed.

The brave General Porlier, notwithstanding the services he
had rendered to his king and country, was taken, brought to
a mock trial, and summarily hanged. His last words were,
" I am not a traitor, but have been the most faithful servant
of the King." He met his fate with dignity and resolution.
Then began those days of tragedy in Spain which ere long
led to the most frightful reprisals on both sides, and for many
long years deluged the Peninsula in blood.

The issue of Porlier's conspiracy in Galicia produced
different effects on the parties who divided the nation. The
oppressed became more and more united, their exasperation

more intense, their numbers increased, and their plans were confirmed. The men who had fought with Porlier in the war of independence, not content with lamenting his fate, were eager to avenge it. The other party found in the insurrection in Galicia a fresh pretext for persecutions. They worked upon the personal fears of Ferdinand. They persuaded him that the liberal party sought his life. They insisted that no quarter should be given in any encounter with the rebels ; that all innovating ideas should be persecuted until not a shadow of them should linger in the country, and all men be reduced to abject submission.

The Canon Escoïquiz, who had given so many proofs of his attachment to Ferdinand, who had followed him faithfully during his misfortunes, and had shared his captivity at Valençay till separated from him by order of Napoleon, was banished from court, and sent into Andalusia, for having told Ferdinand, in reference to the affair in Galicia, that punishments would do less to suppress the spirit of revolt than judicious reforms. Ferdinand grew very angry, and answered that, being King by the grace of God, he was responsible only to the Almighty and his confessor.

The minister of war was Ballesteros, to whom Ferdinand was apparently so partial that when he retired to a village near Madrid for the benefit of his health, his Majesty drove out every day to see him, and passed several hours in his company. During one of these visits Ferdinand told him that he had a great deal of military business on hand, and as he could not get through it without his assistance, he requested him to be in Madrid on such a day. Ballesteros went on the day appointed, but, instead of the business he had expected, he found a decree depriving him of his office, and banishing him from the capital. His offence was that he had presented the King with a project for some reforms in the army which the *camarilla* looked upon as favoring revolutionary ideas.

Instances might be multiplied of individuals of all ranks, high and low, being raised to sudden favor by the caprices of the King, and as suddenly cast down, always with dissimulation. One of these men, Lozano, who had begun life by selling chocolate in Cadiz, retained his master's favor longer than the rest, having persuaded him that the most extraordinary congeniality of temperament existed between them, so that any sickness or misfortune that affected the one would react upon the other.

On the return of Napoleon from Elba and the flight of Louis XVIII. and his court to Ghent, King Ferdinand proposed to march his Spanish armies into France to strengthen the hands of his brother Bourbon, in case he should desire to pursue the Spanish counter-revolutionary policy in France.

Greatly alarmed at the effect this movement might produce, the Duc d'Angoulême hurried to the headquarters of the Spanish generals, and prevailed on them to retire.

Meantime in Madrid political prisoners were being rapidly condemned. Among them was Señor Arguelles, the most brilliant orator in the late Cortes, and a man of moderate political opinions. He was sentenced to ten years' service as a common soldier in a regiment stationed at Ceuta, on the coast of Africa, while another of the late ministers was condemned also to be a common soldier for eight years, and to wear a chain. From time to time there were brief spasmodic indications, on the part of the government, of a disposition to try a more liberal policy. These were probably the result of apprehension concerning the disorganization of the finances, and the depletion of the treasury.

Since the Spanish-American colonies were in a state of anarchy and revolution, the revenues of the mother country from their commerce and their gold and silver mines had been cut off, and her seaport towns were ruined. In Cadiz, where the carrying of bags of gold had led to the formation of a special band of porters for the purpose, these men had no longer any employ. Spanish merchant-ships had become the prey of pirates in the western waters of the Atlantic; the Spanish navy, once so powerful, was ruined, and her men-of-war were unsound.

King Ferdinand had lost his first wife, a princess of

Naples, in 1806. She had urged her husband to resist the influence of Godoy, and had drawn upon herself the bitter hatred of her mother-in-law. She died very suddenly somewhat mysteriously, and of course the court scandal-mongers circulated suspicions of foul play. He now, in 1816, proposed to marry his niece, the Princess Maria Isabel Francisca, daughter of the King of Portugal, while proposals of marriage were made at the same time to her sister by the Infante Don Carlos.

These princesses were both in Brazil, to which country their family had fled in 1808, when Junot was advancing on Lisbon ; but they were brought over safely to Spain, and on September 28, 1816, they were married at Madrid with great pomp to their respective bridegrooms.

Early the next year, 1817, a formidable insurrection broke out in Catalonia, headed by Don Luïs Lacy, a descendant of Hildebert de Lacy, who came over to England with William the Conqueror and was created Earl of Lincoln. A branch of the family in Henry II.'s time settled in Ireland and became Earls of Ulster. Like so many Irish adherents of James II., four brothers of this family escaped to Spain, and were received, like other Irish outcasts, with open arms. To the military skill and gallantry of Don Luïs Lacy, Catalonia was indebted for its liberation from the French, but he had excited the jealousy of the Serviles, that is, the extreme partisans of the absolute policy of Ferdinand, was dismissed from his employment as second in command under Castaños, and was even doomed to a species of restraint in the very province which had witnessed his most brilliant deeds of arms. A considerable force was assembled, and Lacy was joined by another distinguished general, Don Rafael Milans. But their plans were frustrated by the treachery of two officers who had received especial kindness from Lacy in time past, when he was Captain-General of Catalonia. The insurgent soldiers, on learning that their designs were known to the commander of the royal forces, abandoned their generals, who were left to secure their own safety in the best manner they could.

Milans escaped, reached Buenos Ayres, and took part in the affairs of South America, but Lacy and a few companions were betrayed by a farmer in whose house they had taken refuge. In spite of a universal cry for mercy which reached the ears of Ferdinand from the army, and from civilians in all parts of the country, Lacy was condemned to death, but the authorities did not dare to execute him in Catalonia. He was sent to Majorca, under pretence of commuting his sentence to imprisonment. Four days after his arrival the Judge-advocate who had officiated at his trial appeared before him and read his death warrant. " I was not prepared to hear this sentence," said Lacy, " but since it must be so I am ready."

In a ditch of the castle, at five in the morning of the next day, Lacy was shot by a file of soldiers. He had spent his last moments in writing to his wife, and giving directions for the education of their only child, whom he commended, he said, " to the protection of that country which his father had ever faithfully served."

Another revolt soon broke out in Valencia, which was put down with great vigor and severity by General Elio ; and soon after appeared a royal decree prohibiting the importation of "dangerous books," into Spain, among them the works of Voltaire, Gibbon, Robertson, and Benjamin Constant, " such being," in the language of the decree, " false in politics, inimical to the hierarchical order, subversive to the power of the Church, tending to schism and religious toleration, and pernicious to the State."

It would be tedious to enumerate the conspiracies that continued to break out in Spain, all calling on the King to fulfil his promises, to convoke a Cortes, or to restore the Constitution. Meantime the condition of the treasury grew worse and worse, and Ferdinand in his extremity procured a bull from the Pope, authorizing him to exact during six years the sum of sixty million reals (six million dollars) from the revenues of the Church. But large as this sum was, it filled up but a small part of the deficit. A further sum of two million dollars was paid into the royal treasury by the British

Government, being the price agreed on for a decree to be issued by the Spanish government forbidding Spanish participation in the slave trade. So little was this compact observed after the two million dollars had been accepted and paid, that in a short time the annual importation of slaves rose from fifty thousand to seventy thousand in Cuba alone.

The first use made by the royal government of these extraordinary supplies was to obtain a navy. Spain needed ships to transport an army to America. It was felt that with more money a large part of the misfortunes that had fallen on the country since the Restoration might have been averted, and it was from the South American provinces alone that such help could be obtained. Ferdinand therefore bargained with the Czar for a squadron of old, worn-out line-of-battle ships, to which Alexander out of generosity, added three frigates. Such, however, was their state of decay that it took them three months to make the voyage from Cronstadt to Cadiz, where two thousand men were embarked on them for Lima.

In a little more than a year after her marriage, the young Queen Maria Isabel died in child-bed, and her husband was at liberty to form a third matrimonial alliance, which he did very speedily. In about eight months he was contracted to Maria Josefa Amelia, a princess of Saxony. It is said that Ferdinand was really attached to his Queen Maria Isabel, and yet when her funeral procession left the palace, he was playing a game of bowls. The new Queen soon shared the fate of her predecessors. She died a few years after her marriage, leaving Ferdinand free to marry a fourth wife, Maria Christina, daughter of the King of Naples, who became much more conspicuous in Spanish history than the three women who had previously shared his throne.

But while the marriage bells in Madrid were ringing, and artillery saluting the arrival of the young Saxon princess, events of the utmost importance were taking place at Cadiz.

" The disorder of the treasury had pressed more heavily on military men than upon any other class of officers in the State, so much so that arrears of pay to a frightful amount were due them, and even to the private soldiers. The contractors, unpaid, often suspended their supplies. In consequence, the colonels of regiments and the governors of garrisons were frequently obliged to implore the assistance of the rich inhabitants of the towns, to save the troops from actual starvation. In some garrison towns, especially at Ceuta, the soldiers were reduced to such a state of nakedness that, for decency, they were prohibited from going into the streets; and several of them would have died from the inclemency of the season, if the idea had not been adopted of keeping them warm in the ovens in which bread was baked."

The finances demanded some immediate step to save the country from insolvency. The money received from the Church, the two million dollars paid by England, and five millions received from the United States for the cession of Florida, had had little effect on the great mass of national indebtedness. The millions received from the Church had purchased a fleet from Russia, the millions received for Florida should fit out an expedition to recover the revolted provinces in the New World.

In proportion as the evils under which the army suffered increased, and the hope of seeing them corrected grew less and less, hatred to the King and to his government spread rapidly through the army. Those officers who had distinguished themselves in the War of Independence, and had received high military rank, began to be considered leaders by their discontented comrades.

Twenty thousand men had been assembled at La Isla — or the Ile de Leon — a body of land formed into an island by a broad stream flowing from the Bay of Cadiz to the sea, and comprising the peninsula on which Cadiz is situated. These men had been concentrated at La Isla, ready to be embarked for South America.

General Morillo had been appointed their commander. His troops were exceedingly dissatisfied. He managed to embark a few of them on three ships, but some of these he deceived in order to march them to the place of embarkation ; others could not be got on board without being first disarmed ; and their hatred of this colonial war, added to their fear of a long voyage and of an unwholesome climate, took such possession of their minds that they would all of them have been ready to engage in any enterprise, provided they might escape this expedition.

The army was not reassured when news reached them of the two ships that had sailed for Lima. The soldiers and crew of one had mutinied, thrown their officers overboard, and made sail for Buenos Ayres. The other had been captured off the coast of Peru, and the arms she carried had fallen into the hands of the insurgents.

Early in January, 1820, the King issued a proclamation, forbidding his soldiers in South America to give quarter to any foreigners who should assist the colonial revolutionists. This caused additional alarm and dissatisfaction.

The merchants of Cadiz became eager to frustrate the expedition. "Flourishing young republics in South and Central America " — as it was the fashion of the day to call the revolted provinces — were thought likely to promote commerce more than ruined, disaffected colonies. The soldiers at La Isla and the inhabitants of Cadiz professed the utmost respect for monarchy, but they lost no opportunity of disseminating their views of the condition of the country. They urged the displacement of the King's advisers and the assembling of a Cortes. Meanwhile the troops were to set sail as soon as the season should be favorable.

Morillo having sailed with his contingent, a man of Irish descent, named O'Donnell, was made chief commander. His younger brother held a high command in the Spanish army. His Spanish title was El Conde d'Abisbal. He had served with distinction in the War of Independence, had a bold and enterprising disposition, and was a past-master in the arts of dissimulation. He favored a conspiracy formed among his officers, who dreaded the South American expedition ; and having learned all their secrets, he, on the eve of embarkation, when the revolt among the troops at La Isla was to have broken out, assembled the garrison of the city of Cadiz, bound the men by oath to stand by him wherever he should lead them, and marched them to the encampment at La Isla; he then called out the seven thousand men ordered to embark the next morning for South America. He surrounded them with the troops from Cadiz, pointed at them some pieces of artillery, and commanded them to deliver up their officers, whose names he read from a list that he held in his hand. Resistance was impossible. One hundred and twenty-three officers implicated in the conspiracy were put under arrest. Three thousand of the men were compelled to embark at once for the West Indies; the rest were dispersed through Andalusia. The ships that carried the three thousand soldiers reached Havana after a six weeks' voyage. What became of these soldiers subsequently does not appear. Abisbal, having broken up the camp at La Isla, dispersed the assembled troops, and so frustrated the expedition to America, went up to Madrid with his second in command, another Irishman by descent, named O'Daly, and received marks of much royal favor; not possibly as much as he had hoped, and the ministry soon found reason to mistrust him. He was removed from his military command at La Isla, and appointed to the governorship of Andalusia. The ferment in the provinces continued in spite of precautions and arrests, and some places even proclaimed the Constitution.

Little more than a month after the affair at La Isla which has just been related, the yellow fever broke out at Cadiz, and spread rapidly among the troops still remaining on the island. Though the punishment of the galleys was the penalty for any physician who called the fever by its true name, its real character became speedily known. Ten thousand persons in Cadiz and on La Isla were seized with the disorder; the deaths were two hundred a day.

Three months after Ferdinand's marriage to his third wife, the Saxon princess, that is, on January 1, 1820, another revolt broke out, which had its headquarters in Cadiz, but seems to have extended to the whole army. Its leader was Rafael del Riego y Nunez, who has left his name in song and history as a patriot, a soldier, and a martyr. He erred indeed as a statesman, in common with other enthusiasts of his day, but, before age and experience could temper his patriotism into wisdom, he met a fate that his countrymen will mourn for all time. Riego was the son of a small nobleman in the Asturias, and was placed at an early age as a private in the king's body-guard, a post which, after the rise of Godoy, was held to be the first rung on the ladder to fortune. He was still in that corps when the invasion by the French took place in 1808, and, when his regiment was disbanded and dispersed, he joined a band of guerillas. He was next made an officer in a volunteer regiment, but soon after was taken prisoner; he spent several years in France, where he imbibed liberal ideas, and there completed his education. When liberated by the peace, he returned to Madrid, and was made a lieutenant-colonel. His regiment formed part of the force at La Isla destined to embark for South America, and he was thus brought under the influence of the spirit of revolt rampant in the encampment.

On January 1, 1820, at the head of his battalion at Las Cabezas, a town on the mainland opposite to Cadiz, Riego proclaimed the Constitution. He then captured the veteran general, Calderon, who had succeeded Abisbal, together with his whole staff at his headquarters. The exertions of Riego, though he was in a state of great debility from recent illness, are said at this crisis to have been almost incredible. He scarcely took time for sleep, or for refreshment, and communicated a portion of his unconquerable spirit to others. He found an admirable assistant in Galiano, a civilian, one of the most eloquent men in Spain. Galiano was subsequently an exile in England, where he wrote anonymously much that was valuable on the subject of his country; and in 1836 he was a cabinet minister. After his capture of General Calderon, Riego was hailed commander-in-chief of the insurgents, an honor he refused to accept, as it belonged in his opinion to Quiroga, his superior officer. Everywhere he proclaimed the Constitution, and he set up a pillar — *lapida* — in every village. Having united his men with those under Quiroga, who after much delay, owing to bad roads, false guides, and

GENERAL RAFAEL DEL RIEGO.

imperfect information, had at last joined him, both generals pushed on to Cadiz. Both Riego and Quiroga had expected that the town would open its gates to them, but they were disappointed. The city, commanded by its fortress, was not to be taken without a siege, and they had no adequate artillery. Soon they found themselves hemmed in, and their supplies of food were deficient. Then Riego, with his part of the force, broke through the enemy's line, and made a raid through Andalusia. He met but little opposition, but he also met little encouragement. Everywhere he proclaimed the Constitution. The villagers listened and cheered, but few joined him. To his honor be it said that he was guilty of no cruelties.

Barefooted, closely pursued, weary with marching over heavy roads, and discouraged because no permanent success seemed to attend their movement, the little band, reduced to three hundred, passed through Cordova singing Riego's Hymn.[1] No man molested them, but no man joined

[1] Riego's Hymn consists of seven stanzas, and is too long for quotation. Mr. Blanquiere, in his "Spanish Revolutions," gives a translation of it by Sir John Browning. Here are the chorus and two stanzas:—

"The country we cherish
   Hath summoned us now.
To conquer or perish:
   Remember our vow!

"In joy and in triumph
  Serene but delighted,
  Our voices united
   Sing victory's lay.
The Cid was our father,
And proud gratulations
Proclaim from all nations
' His children are they!'

.   .   .   .

"The trumpet is sounding!
  Shrink slavery and folly,
  Our conduct is holy,
   Our conscience is pure.
Ye vassals of tyrants,
Ye tremble — ye tremble,
Our heroes assemble,
   Our triumph is sure!"

8

them. They had been closely pursued on their march by a light column commanded by the younger O'Donnell, and less than three months after the Constitution had been joyfully proclaimed at Las Cabezas by Riego, he found himself among the passes of the Sierra Morena with only three hundred men. Quiroga had fared no better ; Abisbal had frustrated the conspiracy at La Isla, and in southern Spain the attempted revolution seemed at an end. But, as a conflagration subdued in one place breaks out in several others, and grows fiercer for the check given momentarily to the flames, so the revolt, suppressed in Andalusia, gathered strength in the northwestern provinces. The insurgents captured the Governor-General of Galicia ; the cities of Corunna, Vigo, and Ferrol declared for the Constitution, and until the Cortes should be convoked, appointed a provisional government. General Mina again made his appearance in Navarre, and, as Alison says, "lent to the cause of insurrection a name that still spoke to the hearts of all in Spain."

The government, greatly alarmed, called General Elio from Valencia to take military command at Madrid, and despatched O'Donnell, the Conde d' Abisbal, to put down the revolt in Galicia. But the ministers little knew the man in whom they placed their trust. When a few leagues from Madrid he was joined at Ocaña by his younger brother, who commanded the King's troops in Old and New Castile. Together they harangued their men, proclaimed the Constitution, and formed a provisional government in Castile, similar to that in Galicia.

This news at once excited an insurrection in Madrid. In Spain what was called the Pillar (Lapida) of the Constitution took the place held by Trees of Liberty in Revolutionary France. Attempts were made to set them up in all parts of the capital. The soldiers came out of their barracks and fraternized with the insurgents. The Puerto del Sol, the great square from which the principal streets in Madrid radiate in all directions, swarmed with a seething crowd of vociferating people. Ballesteros waited on the King to describe to him the real state of affairs, and ended the audience by informing His Majesty that the government could not calculate on the obedience of a single regiment.  This being fully confirmed by accounts arriving hourly from the provinces, Ferdinand yielded to necessity, and consented to sign a decree in which he promised to accept the Constitution of 1812, and to convoke a Cortes.  The mob, however, mistrusting this news, as "too good to be true," assembled round the Palace shouting for the King.  Urged by his Queen, his brother Don Francisco, and other members of his court, Ferdinand came out upon a balcony with a copy of the Constitution in his hand, and holding it up signified his readiness to conform to the assurances he had already given.  Steps were at once taken to form a Junta to administer the government, to liberate state prisoners, and to abolish the Inquisition ; while in return the people of Madrid shouted with enthusiasm, "Long live King Ferdinand! Long live our Constitutional King!"

The next day, as the ferment in the capital had not subsided, Ferdinand followed up his declaration by a decree, in which he said that to avoid the delays that might arise in the execution of his decree for the immediate assembling of the Cortes, and the will of the people having been pronounced, he had resolved to swear at once to observe the Constitution made and promulgated in 1812.

Not very long before, it had been pronounced high treason to speak a word in favor of this Constitution, — and death the penalty.

It costs little to make promises and to swear oaths never intended to be binding.  Bourbon kings in southern Europe made no difficulty about availing themselves of perjury and blasphemy to escape out of a difficulty.  A supreme Junta was at once formed in Madrid to take charge of the government in a provisional way, and before this body King Ferdinand, on March 9, 1820, took a solemn oath to observe the Constitution.  By his order the grandees in Madrid, and the magistrates, followed his example in the great Square of the Prado.  Bells rang, cannon fired salutes, and the city at nightfall blazed with a spontaneous illumination. All political prisoners were released and marched through the city in procession, amid the shouts of the joyful populace.

All over Spain the ferment spread. In some places vengeance was wreaked on the buildings of the Inquisition. In Valencia the wrath of the populace directed itself against General Elio, whose life was saved only by his being hurried into the fortress and thrown into a dungeon.

Riego, who had been wandering in the Sierra Morena, descended from the mountains, and joining his forces to those of Alexander O'Donnell, the late pursued and their pursuers made a triumphal entry together into Seville.

At Cadiz, however, the fervor of the populace received a check. The military governor of the place, General Freyre, appointed a day and an hour, when in the Square of San Antonio he would meet the people of the city and swear to observe the Constitution.

" On the morning of the day appointed Cadiz exhibited a scene of extraordinary animation; a rich display of tapestries and banners from all its balconies indicated the sentiments of the owners, while groups of both sexes filled the streets and the churches, congratulating each other on the arrival of that day. When it was ascertained that a deputation from La Isla had set out, the town gates were set open, and thousands rushed forth to greet them. Some threw their cloaks on the ground to serve as carpets, others rushed forward to embrace the soldiers, garlands were showered from the windows, and nothing was heard but ' Long live the Constitution! Long live the National Army! Long live its Chiefs!' "

General Freyre kept his promise to the citizens of Cadiz. He met them indeed, but he was then accompanied by the soldiers of his garrison, who fired point-blank into the serried multitude, and having driven them into hiding-places, proceeded to plunder their houses, as if Cadiz had been given up to sack and pillage.

A new ministry was formed at Madrid. It was composed for the most part of men noted for ability, high character, and moderate opinions; many of whom not many days before had been released from prison. Among these was Señor Arguelles, whose condemnation to ten years of service in Africa as a private soldier has been already mentioned.

These men in spite of all they had been made to suffer, endeavored to moderate the revolutionary fervor which had raised them to power, but they cannot be said to have met with success.

The Cortes was convoked for the 9th of July. The elections took place with a due observance of order, but the body was of course highly revolutionary. No grandees were there, and the Church was barely represented. A few members attached to old institutions came from the northern provinces, and were called *Serviles.* One sixth of the Assembly might have been termed Jacobins.

Very soon it began to appear that no man could say where the power of the government resided. Not in the crown, for the King was controlled by his ministry; not in the ministers, for they were controlled by the Cortes; not in the Cortes, which succumbed to the power of the Clubs, which in turn were terrorized by the secret societies; while the Municipal Junta of Madrid seems to have had some mysterious power of imposing its views on legislation.

On the night before the Cortes assembled, an attack was made on the King's palace by a mob, and one of the officers of his body-guard, who opposed the entrance of the populace, was murdered. His death would have been but the natural outcome of a revolutionary riot, had it not been made important by the refusal of the authorities to investigate the affair, or to inflict any punishment.

Many very good measures were introduced in the Cortes, but under the influence of outside pressure others of a different character were passed by a majority.

False rumors of an intention to break up the encampment at La Isla, and to separate the troops again assembled there, began to circulate in Cadiz, and General Riego was sent up to Madrid by his officers, to do all in his power to bring revolutionary pressure on the Cortes, and to influence other branches of the government, who seemed too much inclined to adopt moderate views.

Riego was received in the capital with enthusiasm. He was the hero of the revolution, — the idol of the populace. A week after his arrival he appeared at the theatre, when a large part of the audience rose to their feet, and demanded the singing of a patriotic popular hymn, *Tragala, perro,*[1] which a patriot poet, with more zeal than discretion, had composed as an insult to the clergy and nobility. Riego and his staff stood up and joined in the chorus. Then a riot began. The police interfered, mobs assembled in the streets, shouting for " Riego ! " These mobs the authorities put down by a show of large bodies of troops, and by cannon loaded with grapeshot. The ministers, desirous of discountenancing street riots in the capital, considered Riego the cause of these disturbances, deprived him of his military command, and sent him into retirement at Oviedo. The camp at La Isla was broken up, but gratuities and pensions were voted to the troops, notwithstanding the desperate state of the finances.

King Ferdinand vetoed a decree of the Cortes despoiling the Religious Houses for the advantage of the State. More riots upon this ensued in the capital, and the King as usual gave way. He affixed his name to the decree, and retired to the Escurial.

Then began riots in the provinces ; in some, especially in Valencia, the mob rose against the ecclesiastical authorities ; in northern Spain the riots were in their favor, for the convents had been always the shelter and support of the poor. The idea that their inmates should be turned homeless on the world by a decree of the Cortes, and their revenues absorbed into the treasury of the State, was ab-

---

[1] " Tragala, perro ! " (Swallow it down, dog !) was the burthen of a song in favor of the Constitution sung by its admirers by way of annoyance under the windows of those who were known to be opposed to it, frequently with menacing gestures, scurrilous epithets, and rough music. " Tragala, perro ! " was repeated at the end of every verse, frequently in chorus. — WALTON, *Revolutions in Spain.*

horrent to the peasantry. They rose in many places and prevented the execution of the decree.

Meantime King Ferdinand, shut up in the Escurial, was forming plans for his own deliverance, and with that view he appointed General Carvajal, who was devoted to him personally, to be Captain-General of New Castile. The power of making such appointments was constitutionally with the Cortes, and the King was forced publicly to declare before that body that he had had no idea he was doing an unconstitutional thing in making that appointment.

The next thing that happened was an assault on the King and Queen in their carriage as they were returning to Madrid from the Escurial. The King was much affected by this incident. He felt that it strongly resembled the return of Louis XVI., in October, 1789, to his capital, and he shut himself up in his own apartments.

The revolutionists, backed by the Clubs, had things now all their own way. Riego was made Captain-General of Aragon ; Mina, Captain-General of Navarre ; and other revolutionary officers received similar promotion. Besides this, all the members of the King's first constitutional ministry were accused of moderate opinions, and sent into exile.

The Clubs, like those of Paris in 1792, assumed the direction of affairs. The secret societies professed socialism, thus joining to the views of Robespierre, who favored a democratic despotism, the anarchic theories of Marat.

# CHAPTER VI.

## FERDINAND VII. AS A CONSTITUTIONAL KING.

THE revolutionary fervor in Spain could not but react on France, especially as one duty, self-imposed on Spanish patriots, was to send documents and emissaries over the Pyrenees to stir up disaffection in the French army, and to stimulate revolutionary feeling in the secret societies, to which men of high character, even such men as General La Fayette, belonged.

Several conspiracies, hatched under the auspices of these secret societies, broke out in France, at Rochelle, Colmar, Thouars, Béfort, and other places, and executions of young men, brave but misguided, took place in consequence. Some lives were saved by the supplications of the Duchesse d'Angoulême. There had been a royalist reaction in France, and Louis XVIII. and his ministers were well disposed to follow it up by intervention on behalf of Ferdinand, the Spanish Bourbon, who meantime "was sinking," says Alison, "into that state of impotence and degradation which in troubled times is the invariable precursor of final ruin."

The Cortes of 1820 was no longer in session, and Ferdinand made an effort to recover his authority and prestige by appearing suddenly before the Council of State and making personal charges against his ministers. The effort failed, however, and Ferdinand found himself more prostrate than ever at the feet of his revolution-maddened subjects, whom he had so often and so basely deceived.

The secret societies took heart, and openly encouraged the administration of lynch law to those whose political opinions marked them out to be its victims. One popular orator (ten times more moderate than *L'ami du peuple* in 1792) demanded the execution of thirty thousand individuals in Madrid. In the east of Spain, bands of armed men arrested, on their own authority, in one night, six hundred persons, most of them of high rank, and shipped them, ignorant of their fate, to the Balearic Isles. Animated by the same spirit, a mob broke into one of the prisons in Madrid, determined to take vengeance on a fanatical monk, Vinuesa by name, who had published a pamphlet advocating a counter-revolution. The guard made a show of resistance, but the mob broke open the doors of the prison. The priest presented himself with the crucifix in his hand, and implored mercy in the name of the Redeemer. As he knelt before his murderers on the floor of his cell, one of them advanced and dashed out his brains with a hammer.

This deed might possibly have pleaded in extenuation Spanish bloodthirstiness and the blind fury of lynch law, but no such extenuation was attempted. The press extolled the deed unanimously. The violent revolutionists exulted in the murder, and a popular order of chivalry was instituted, having for its badge a tiny hammer.

In Navarre and the provinces of the North, such deeds of violence provoked opposite feelings. A priest called Merino, who had been distinguished as a patriot in the war with Napoleon, raised a band of peasants to fight the Constitutionalists in what he considered the cause of Church and King. After being successful for a few weeks, he was defeated, four hundred of his men were taken prisoners (a large proportion of them are said to have been priests) ; they were sent to Pampeluna, and were there all shot.

Relieved from the immediate control of the Cortes, King Ferdinand appointed General Morillo, a man of energy, to put down disorder in the capital. Morillo not only showed that he could overawe street mobs, but he took measures against the secret societies in the provinces. He even ordered the authorities at Saragossa to arrest Riego, accusing him and a Frenchman, one of his associates, of sending letters across the Pyrenees to stir up disaffection in the French army and to promote the establishment of a republic.

The arrest of Riego caused great excitement among the Liberals. In Madrid a procession, bearing his portrait as a banner, paraded the streets. Those in the procession had committed no violence, and two regiments of regular soldiers refused to act against them; but Morillo, at the head of the Guards, a body of picked men, mostly royalists, tore down the picture of Riego, and charged the procession with the bayonet. The Jacobin party was for a time subdued, and Madrid relapsed into quiet.

At this date, September, 1821, yellow fever again made its appearance, this time in Barcelona, where it swept off its victims at the rate of three hundred a day. A military cordon was drawn round the city at a distance of two leagues. French physicians and Sisters of Charity hurried over the Pyrenees to aid the sufferers; but it was not until cool weather came that the scourge abated, having cut off twenty thousand persons out of eighty thousand, the estimated population of Barcelona.

The French government made this pestilence a pretext for assembling a large French force on the frontier, to put a stop, as it alleged, to all communication between the two countries.

In southern Spain the ferment caused by the arrest of Riego, the popular hero, went on increasing. The desire " to kill somebody " in retaliation seemed in every breast. In Valencia General Elio, who had already been arrested, was condemned to death for having, in 1814, " acted against the Constitution," — which at that date had been abrogated!

The distracted state of the country, under a central government powerless in the provinces, rendered an Extraordinary Convocation of the Cortes necessary, and it assembled accordingly December 9, 1821. Its first act was to declare that the authorities in Seville and Cadiz, who had refused to receive the governors sent down to them, and indeed had ordered their arrest, should be brought to trial. This excited the advanced Liberals almost to frenzy. With cries of " Viva Riego! Down with the Ministers! Down with the Serviles!" they demanded a reconsideration of the vote, and obtained it, throwing the responsibility of any further action on the King.

This might have been Ferdinand's opportunity, but, as Alison says, " he was as vacillating in his acts as the Cortes were in their votes."

He selected a ministry that pleased no party, and the year 1821 closed with Spain torn in all quarters. It was hard to say whether it suffered most by the furious factions in the cities of the South, or by the hardy peasantry in the valleys of the North, in arms, as they proclaimed themselves, for their Church and their Absolute King.

In vain the better class of Spanish statesmen, Toreño, Martinez de la Rosa, and Calatrava, endeavored to introduce measures into the Cortes which should tend to restore law and order. They were pursued in the streets by howling mobs; their houses were broken open; some of their servants were wounded; and their own safety was secured only by the arrival of troops under Morillo. On the whole, however, the extraordinary Cortes of 1821 may be said to have done less harm than it might have done, which, according to some, is the best that can be expected from any Congress, even in our own days.

The new Cortes that assembled early in 1822 was mainly composed of excited men made violent by the ferment in the provinces and the capital. Before its sentiments were fully known, the King chose a ministry composed of men of moderate opinions, of whom Martinez de la Rosa was the chief. These men held to the Spanish Revolution somewhat the same position that the Girondists had held to that of France. They approved it in its early stages, but desired to put on it the curb of law and order.

Riego, who had been released, was made President of the Assembly, which had but one Chamber according to the Constitution of 1812. Soon fierce outbreaks took place in the provinces, the " Exaltados," as those of the extreme party now called themselves, favoring popular excitement. Riego was powerless to calm the Assembly. When he attempted to bring it to order, he was taunted with inconsistency, being the acknowledged chief of the Exaltados. The deputies might not choose to submit to his authority, but the popular cry was everywhere, "Viva Riego!"

The King, intimidated, quitted his capital. No hand in Spain seemed strong enough to hold the reins of government. Civil war was universal. Among the guerilla chiefs prominent in the royalist faction was a priest, Antonio Miranon by name, but best known as "the Trappist." He had distinguished himself as a partisan leader in the war with the soldiers of Napoleon, and he now took up arms in what he considered the good cause, that of his Church and of his King. His personality is thus described by Alison : —

"Originally a soldier, but thrown into a convent by misfortunes, in part brought on by his impetuous and unruly disposition, the Trappist had not with the cowl put on the habits, or become endued with the feelings of the Church. He was, in 1822, about forty-five years old, — a period of life when the bodily frame is, in strong constitutions, yet in its vigor, and the feelings are steadily directed rather than enfeebled by age. He constantly wore the dress of his order, but beneath it burned the passions of the world. Arrayed in his monkish costume, with a crucifix in one hand and a huge whip in the other, he had a sabre by his side and pistols in his girdle. Mounted on a tall and powerful horse, which he managed with address and skill, he galloped through the crowds, which always awaited his approach and fell on their knees as he passed, dispensing blessings to the right and left with the air of a sovereign prince acknowledging the homage of his subjects. He never commenced an attack without falling on his knees to implore the protection of the Most High. Then, rising up, he led his men into fire, shouting 'Viva Dio! Viva el Rey!'"

It would be tedious to tell in detail the ups and downs of fortune in the guerilla warfare that raged all over Spain at this period, but especially in Navarre and Catalonia. Cruelty provoked cruelty, and whoso studies its history grows sick with horrors. As Sir William Napier writes in his History of the Peninsular War, —

FRANCISCO MARTINEZ DE LA ROSA.

" The guerilla system in Spain was the offspring of disorder.
. . . It is in such a warfare that habits of unbridled license, of
unprincipled violence, and disrespect for the rights of property
are quickly contracted, and render men unfit for the duties of
citizens."

The entire number of guerillas in Spain, even during the
Napoleonic war, never much exceeded thirty thousand ; and
strange as it may seem, no inconsiderable number of these
men were (from 1808 to 1812) deserters from the French and
English armies. Wellington, by desire of his government,
sent presents to the principal guerilla chiefs, acknowledging
their services in the Peninsular War ; but when he afterwards
advanced into Spain and saw them closely, he was forced
to acknowledge that their bands, though active and willing,
were so little disciplined that they could do nothing against
French troops, unless the latter were very inferior in numbers.

The chiefs of the guerilla bands were men from every
class of society, including monks and doctors, peasants, artisans, cooks and collegians. Each had his sobriquet, generally founded on some personal peculiarity or deformity.
There was Juan Martin Diaz, the Empecinado, or *the
spoiled one*, probably in allusion to his having smeared his
face with pitch, and so spoiled his complexion ; and in
Biscay there was a female leader named Martina, whose exploits were so much like those of banditti that Mina was
compelled to hunt her down. He shot her and her gang
when he had surprised them.

Mina himself was by far the most feared and the best
known of the guerilla leaders. Early in the War of Independence he succeeded his nephew Xavier Mina, in command of a considerable band. He was unwilling to accept
the post, saying that he was a farmer, not a general ; but having been persuaded to assume authority, he quelled mutiny
in his band with great severity, and had soon established
discipline of the most rigorous kind. The great feature of
his tactics was perpetual movement. His enemies never
knew where to find him. He kept his officers and men
wholly in the dark as to his plans. He allowed no baggage.

Each man was permitted to possess only a pair of sandals, one pair of stockings, a jacket, and his breeches. Their great success was in capturing convoys bound to and from France through the passes of the Pyrenees. Innumerable were Mina's adventures, and hair-breadth his escapes from the soldiers of Napoleon. On one occasion, when he was surrounded by twenty thousand French, who had received orders to destroy him and his corps at all hazards, he called his officers around him as night fell. " Gentlemen," he said, " our situation is not comfortable. Let every captain look to his own company. The rendezvous will be at such a place [naming one] ; the rallying word is Mina. Now let every man disperse and make the best of his way." The order was obeyed instantly, and without noise. The French deployed their columns early in the morning, sure of capturing their prey. They found nothing but piles of leaves, on which the band had slept ; and five days later Mina was again upon the war-path, executing his usual audacious exploits, not having lost one of his band.

After the general peace of 1814 and the restoration of Ferdinand, Mina soon discovered how treacherous and worthless was the King for whom he and his followers had shed their blood. He attempted a rising in Navarre, his native province, of which the French had been accustomed to call him the King ; but its peasantry could not be roused into enthusiasm for the Constitution, and Mina passed over into France, where Louis XVIII. not only protected him, but gave him a pension. After 1820, when Ferdinand had professed himself a Constitutional King, Mina returned to his country. He went to Madrid, and both he and the Empecinado had interviews with Ferdinand, who flattered them by receiving in good part their advice, especially as it related to the putting down of guerillas. Mina was then appointed Captain-General of the forces in Navarre, Catalonia, and Aragon, but he fell from the King's favor as swiftly as he had risen. He had been invested with power to act against guerilla bands, and all opposed to the Constitution. These instructions he fulfilled by savage proclamations, the massacre of prisoners, and the sack, burning, and total destruction of towns that had held out against him, when they fell into his hands. His military successes and the conviction that dire vengeance would follow resistance struck terror through northern Spain; one by one the guerilla bands were defeated, dispersed, and fled over into France. Thither went the Trappist, when he found that all was lost, and thither went the Baron d'Erolles and Quesada, the most important Absolutist leaders. Thus, although guerillas turned bandits and still in small bands infested the mountains, by the close of 1823 everything like regular warfare in the northern provinces was at an end. Then Mina, feeling that his position was precarious since Ferdinand had begun to disregard his professions of adherence to the Constitution, thought it prudent to leave Spain and to retire to England.

In Madrid news of the successes of the insurgents in the South roused their friends in the Cortes to fury. They demanded the dismissal of the King's moderate ministers, and obtaining a majority in the Assembly, issued decrees that imposed the most ferocious penalties on all persons who might fall under suspicion of giving aid or sympathy to the absolutist cause.

Disputes became fierce and frequent between the troops called the King's Body-guard, and men of the regular garrison in Madrid. In one of these disturbances Captain Landabura, an officer of the National Guard, was shot through the breast while endeavoring to calm the tumult. As usual in such cases, the sympathies of the mob were more fiercely roused on behalf of an individual than a political principle; the name of Landabara became a war-cry.

On July 7, 1822, a regular fight between the body-guard and the garrison took place, the latter being supported by many thousands of the populace. The Guards were forced to surrender, and were ordered to march unarmed out of the capital; but two battalions, dreading lest that disarmament should be a prelude to their massacre, determined to sell their lives dearly while their weapons were still in their hands. They fired on the National Guards sent to disarm them and to escort them from the city, and then charged with their bayonets, forcing their way out of the gates, closely pursued by their enemies.

" The affair ended in the dispersion and destruction of that brilliant corps which a few days earlier had seemed to hold the destinies of Spain in their hands. About the same time the party of El Rey Absoluto, in the south of Spain, met with reverses; and thus, in spite of Mina's successes against the guerillas in the north, the King's authority in the capital was utterly prostrated, and he was deprived of even the shadow of respect which had remained to him. For some days he shut himself up in his apartments and would appoint no ministry. Thoroughly alarmed for his own safety, he was ready to yield anything that was asked of him, provided he might be permitted to retire from Madrid."

As Alison says, " The 7th of July, 1822, was as fatal to the crown of Spain as the 10th of August, 1792, had been to that of Louis XVI."

The Exaltados had things now all their own way, and happy would it have been had they contented themselves with sweeping reforms in the King's household, and with banishing from his person the grandees and priests who were believed to be his ill advisers. But Spaniards are bloody-minded, even in their hours of amusement, to a degree that can hardly be appreciated by a people who after their own Civil War decreed scarcely any executions, and who are now, for the most part, ashamed of the very few that took place.

The first thought of Spaniards on achieving any success seems to have been always whose blood should be shed to celebrate the victory. An officer of the body-guard, named Geoiffeux, who had had no connection whatever with the death of Landabura, was chosen as the first sacrifice to his memory. Next, General Elio, in Valencia, already condemned to death, and at one time rescued from lynch law, was seized in his prison and dragged forth to the scaffold. His last words were a prayer for the pardon of his murderers.

A regency, in the name of the King, had been set up in Navarre and Catalonia, declaring null and void all measures that his Majesty had been compelled to accept "during his captivity." The inhabitants of these provinces repudiated the Constitution, called on the troops to abandon the standard of treason, and engaged to establish a constitutional monarchy, based on the ancient laws and customs of the state. "Thus," concluded the proclamation, "the Spanish name shall recover its ancient glory, and we shall live, not the vile slaves of factions, but subject to the laws which we ourselves have established. The King, the father of his people, will swear, as formerly, to maintain our liberties and privileges, and we shall thus have him legally bound by his oath."

This allusion to the King's oath was unfortunate, for, from his youth up, no oath had been more binding upon Ferdinand than the green withes of the Philistines upon the limbs of Samson.

9

# CHAPTER VII.

## THE DUC D'ANGOULÊME INVADES SPAIN.

IT was becoming daily more and more evident that France would again intervene in the affairs of Spain. The safety of her government, under the restoration, seemed to demand action; her obligations to the Holy Alliance, though not prominently put forward, seemed to exact it. For two centuries the foreign policy of France had been to insist — by force of arms, if necessary — that the rulers of Spain should be in alliance with French sovereigns. This had been the policy of Louis XIV., and of Mazarin; it continued to be that of Napoleon. In after days it has been that of Louis XVIII., of Louis Philippe, and of Louis Napoleon.

The French Cabinet, in which M. de Chateaubriand was foreign minister in 1823, was very desirous to secure the good-will (it dared not hope for the co-operation) of Mr. Canning, who in August, 1822, on the death of Lord Londonderry (formerly Lord Castlereagh) had become leader of the House of Commons, holding at the same time the portfolio for Foreign Affairs.

Crowds of starving peasants, who had been fighting in the northern provinces of Spain, in the cause of El Rey Absoluto, flocked over into France with piteous tales of suffering. Compassion, religion, the duty of self-preservation and pressure from without, prompted King Louis to act. A large army was already assembled on the frontier, and war with Spain, if successful, was likely to be extremely popular; for had not French soldiers suffered defeats on Spanish soil? Might not the same men who had been driven back over the Pyrenees in 1814 repass them nine years later as conquerors? The old legions of Napoleon burned to take up arms again to fight for France, no matter in what cause. It was their country, right or wrong, which called on them to do her service. Sympathy with revolutionary theories had died out in the French army; visions of glory, promotion, and plunder dazzled their eyes. They were weary of inaction. All were ready for the word "March!"

While this was the feeling in France and among French soldiers, diplomacy was considering the subject at the Congress of Verona. Public opinion in England was all in favor of a constitutional government in Spain.[1]

The immense amount of capital that previous to 1822 had been invested by foreigners in Spanish loans and in the revolted Spanish colonies, caused the moneyed men of England to feel the sympathy of the pocket, as well as of the heart, for Spanish constitutional government, and for the cause of independence in the Spanish-American colonies which had set up for themselves. They were spoken of in England as "healthy young republics," arising in the fertile regions of tropical South America, giving promise that they would equal England's lost colonies in rapidity of growth, wise government, and prosperity. It was also predicted that they would speedily become good markets for English manufactures.

"No one doubted that these young republics would spread the cause of liberty and independence over the whole of the

---

[1] I was born in those days. Next door to my grandfather's house in London lived Major Cartwright, a man who had been identified with liberalism for fifty years. In his house met all the Spanish patriots who were refugees in England. With them my father became acquainted, and deeply he sympathized with their disappointments and their wrongs. Almost from my babyhood, I was educated to take an interest in Spanish patriots, — an interest that deepened when in my girlhood I became sincerely attached to our friend, the dear old Canon Riego, brother of the leader of the Exaltados. I own that since I have been old enough to understand the subject, my enthusiasm has cooled for the so-called Spanish patriots, more zealous for the success of their faction than for the good of their native land.

New World, and it was assumed that, having been rescued from the colonial oppression of Spain mainly by the sympathizing arms of England, and the valor of the disbanded veterans of Wellington, they would speedily become powerful states in close alliance with Great Britain."

Perhaps the best way in which we can take a brief view of the motives and opinions of the Powers on the question of an invasion of Spain by France, will be to quote the instructions given to the envoys sent to the Congress of Verona by their respective governments. Those of England to the Duke of Wellington were as follows : —

" If there be a determined purpose to interfere either by force or by menace in the present struggle in Spain, so convinced are his Majesty's ministers of the uselessness and danger of any such interference, so objectionable does it appear to them in principle, as well as impracticable in execution, that when a necessity arises, — or rather, an opportunity occurs, — your Grace will at once frankly and decidedly declare that to any such interference England will not be a party."

The French representative, M. de Montmorency, was, on the contrary, instructed by his government that the situation of France would make no formal declaration of war with Spain necessary ; but if France took up arms in the cause of Ferdinand, she must be the sole power that should act with troops, and be the sole judge whether and how to do so. Russia, Prussia, and Austria, afraid of contagion from revolutionary Spain, were earnestly in favor of French intervention. They were so determined to sustain King Ferdinand and to put down the Constitutionalists, that France dreaded that if she did not act, they might march their own armies through her territory.

The representatives of these Four Powers at last signed a document called a *procès-verbal*, declaring that the state of affairs in Spain menaced the tranquillity of Europe ; and they stated frankly to Ferdinand that if he could not reduce his subjects to obedience, their ambassadors must be withdrawn from his court, and an armed force sent to restore his royal authority.

The Duke of Wellington, on the part of England, wholly dissented from these views, and in an interview he had with Louis XVIII. on his way home from Verona, he found that sovereign of the same mind. The desire of Louis XVIII. was that his brother Bourbon should follow his example, and no longer aim to be El Rey Absoluto, but give his subjects a suitable constitution, and a parliament composed of an Upper and a Lower House, to act as checks upon each other.

But France was impelled into war by two different forces, — the Powers, who desired her to put down revolutionary aspirations in Spain, and the spirit of *chauvinism*, not only in her army, but among her masses. They were eager to seize this opportunity to replace France in the front rank of military powers. The soldiers of France had quitted Spain as fugitives; now they aspired to overrun her plains as conquerors.

Both Talleyrand and Canning believed that the war, if commenced, would be long and bloody. The former was superstitious about French interference in Spain, and though his prognostications were not justified by the event, seven years later found the French Bourbons in exile, much of the spirit against them having been roused by their interference in Spanish affairs.

King Louis declared war, not precisely against Spain, but against the Spanish Revolution. He made a speech to the French Chamber, January 28, 1823, saying, —

"France owes to Europe a prosperity no nation can ever attain but by a return to religion, legitimacy, order, and true liberty. France is now giving that salutary example, but divine justice permits that after having long made other nations feel the effects of our own discord, we should ourselves be exposed to similar calamities by a neighboring kingdom. . . . The infatuation with which my efforts to preserve peace have been rejected at Madrid leave little hope of a peaceful accommodation. I have ordered the recall of my minister; a hundred thousand men, commanded by a prince of my own family, the Duc d'Angoulême, are ready to march, invoking the God of Saint Louis to preserve the throne of Spain to a descendant of

Henri IV., to save the kingdom from ruin, and reconcile it to France. . . . Let King Ferdinand be free to *give* his people the institutions they can never hold but from him, and which, in securing the repose of his kingdom, will dissipate the just anxieties of France."

The Cortes and the Constitutional Ministry at Madrid were not to be intimidated. They put into the mouth of King Ferdinand words that must have sounded strangely from the lips of a man notorious for his broken promises. In his speech from the throne in answer to that of Louis XVIII., he said : "The nation that enters into negotiations with an enemy whose bad faith is well known is half subdued. The removal of my person, and the Cortes, to some place less exposed to military operations than Madrid, will defeat the projects of our enemies."

In the House of Commons, Mr. Brougham made an impassioned harangue on the situation of affairs on the Continent, and prophesied that, should the designs of the despotic Powers be unchecked, Russia would gain possession of Constantinople, and Prussia would absorb Hanover into her kingdom.

A magnificent speech on February 15, 1823, was made by M. de Chateaubriand in the French Chamber. It closed with these words : "Our king with generous confidence has intrusted the guard of the White Flag to captains who have triumphed under other colors. They will teach him the path to victory ; he has never forgotten that of honor."

He was answered by Talleyrand, who, giving the Spanish people credit for far more military skill than they possessed, and for a spirit of national union, gave warning to the Chamber in these words : —

"It is sixteen years to-day since I was called by him who then governed the world to give him my advice on the struggle in which he was about to engage with Spain. I had the misfortune to displease him because I revealed the future, — because I unfolded the misfortunes which might arise from an aggression as unjust as it was imprudent. Disgrace was the reward of my sincerity. Strange destiny! — which now, after

LOUIS ANTOINE, DUC D'ANGOULEME.

so long an interval leads me to give the same counsel to a legitimate sovereign!"

Nevertheless the Chamber with enthusiasm voted twenty million dollars for the expenses of the war, though sixty deputies, among them La Fayette, Manuel, General Foy, and Casimir-Périer, signed a protest. Large bodies of troops were hurried forward to Bayonne and Perpignan, and the warlike spirit of the nation was " roused to the highest pitch by the prospect of vindicating the tarnished honor of the arms of France on the fields of Castile." The Duc d'Angoulême set out from Paris to take the command of his army on March 15, 1823.

Meantime those interested in the success of the Spanish Revolution, so sadly compromised by Jacobin excesses and by civil strife, endeavored to induce the old soldiers of Napoleon to abandon the White Flag and take the side of their revolutionary brethren. A curious anecdote in this connection is told in Nolte's "Fifty years in Two Hemispheres," and is as follows : [1] —

"One morning at New Orleans in 1826, Lafayette spoke to me of the Bourbons, on whose political and moral unimportance he looked with pity, and from whom he wished that France were freed as soon as possible. The well-known remark of Talleyrand that they had forgotten nothing, and learned nothing, he thought described them better than all that other men had said about them. 'France,' said Lafayette, 'cannot be happy under the Bourbons, and we must send them adrift. It would have been done now but for Lafitte.' 'Indeed!' I said, 'how so?' 'It is not too long ago,' said the General, 'for you to remember that two regiments of Guards, ordered to Spain under the Duc d'Angoulême, stopped at Toulouse, and began to show symptoms of revolt. The matter was quieted, however, and kept as still as possible. But all was ready, as I know by my private correspondence with some of the officers, — all that was wanted to make a revolution succeed was money. I went to Lafitte, but he was full of doubts, and dilly-dallied

[1] I gave this anecdote in "France in the Nineteenth Century," and some apology is due for telling it again. — E. W. L.

with the matter. Then I offered to do it without his help. Said I, " In the first interview that you and I have, without witnesses, put a million of francs in bank-notes on the mantel-piece, which I will pocket, unseen by you. Then leave the rest to me." Lafitte still fought shy of it, deliberated, hesitated, and at last concluded he would have nothing at all to do with it.' I could not," adds Nolte, "conceal my surprise, and said, ' Had I heard this story from any one but you, General, I could not have believed it.' Lafayette merely answered, '*C'était pourtant ainsi.*'"

The troops were not corruptible by fine words, unsupported as they were by money. They were not eager to give up the prospect of continuing their trade of war, and wiping out the remembrance of their old defeats on the battle-fields of the Peninsula.

On arriving at Bayonne the Duke found himself confronted with an unlooked for difficulty, not unlike that experienced, forty-seven years later, by the French armies at the outset of the Franco-Prussian War. One hundred millions of francs ($20,000,000) had been voted for army supplies ; but nothing had been done to provide forage for the horses or transport for the wants of the army, not even had provision been made to move forward the artillery. It seemed impossible for the troops to advance. The greatest alarm prevailed in Paris when this account reached the capital. Marshal Victor, then Minister of War, was sent in haste to the front, and every nerve was strained to procure transport and forward supplies. There must have been dangerous delay, however, had not Ouvrard, the financier, stepped forward. The length of his purse enabled him to overcome every obstacle ; in a few days plenty reigned in camp, and the means of transport were amply provided.

The army at Bayonne numbered ninety-one thousand men. Its divisions were commanded, it was said proudly, by old soldiers of Napoleon ; but, with the exception of Marshal Oudinot, their names appear only in a dim light in the Napoleonic annals. The Spanish forces were more than equal in numbers to the French, but were very inferior in appointments and discipline. Eleven-twelfths of the Spanish people were, thinks Alison, hostile to the cause for which they were to fight, and there was no *esprit de corps* or unanimity of feeling among the soldiers.

On April 9, 1823, the French army was massed on the banks of the Bidassoa. The Spaniards had made preparations to receive them; but their main dependence was on the effect that they expected would be produced by a band of French refugees in the worn uniforms of the Old Guard, with the tricolor and the eagles for their standard. As the French column crossed the bridge, their first ranks were confronted by this body of Frenchmen, small indeed, — only two hundred, — whereas the Spanish leaders had promised themselves an imposing array of eight hundred veterans. The little band chanted the soul-stirring "Marseillaise," and waved their colors. The advanced guard of the French paused. The moment was critical. Suddenly an officer galloped to the head of the column, and ordered a gun to be discharged over the heads of the enemy. The men in the uniform of the Old Guard shouted, "Vive l'Artillerie!" but their cry was premature; a second and a third gun fired at close range into their ranks made havoc, and dispersed them. The invading army then passed the Bidassoa, and the main body, forty thousand strong, pushed on rapidly by the high-roads to Madrid. At Vittoria, where, within the memory of all of them, a French army had suffered defeat, they were received with arches and acclamations. So it was all along their route. Nowhere did they meet with opposition. As they advanced, the Pillars of the Constitution were thrown down, and those who acted under constitutional authority were dispossessed of their employments.

The French army, well provided with money, paid for everything upon its route, and thus strengthened the good opinion of the small shopkeepers and the peasantry.

On May 17, little more than a month after the army crossed the Bidassoa, their commander received a flag of truce from O'Donnell (the Conde d'Abisbal) whom the Cortes had left in command at Madrid, asking on what terms he was expected to surrender the capital. The Cortes had retired to Seville on the approach of the French, taking with them the King, against his will, and all the royal family.

Madrid received the French with triumphal arches. The Duc d'Angoulême, so far from imposing terms of capitulation, was ready to yield anything it pleased the Spaniards to request of him. Already in the northern provinces and in upper Catalonia the French had been received as friends; only the fortresses of Barcelona and Lerida held out for the Constitution.

The entrance of the French army into Madrid had been fixed for May 24; but before that time an insurrection broke out among the populace, and D'Abisbal only saved his life by flying for protection to Marshal Oudinot.

The Duc d'Angoulême issued a proclamation calculated to calm the apprehensions of the moderate Constitutionalists. It declared " to the generous Spanish nation" that the French were not at war with Spain, that they came only to raise up its altars, to deliver its sovereign, and to restore justice, peace, and order. The Duke promised respect for property, and safety for all persons. He appealed to the conduct of his army since it had entered Spain. He alluded to the enthusiasm with which it had been welcomed in the provinces, and added that so soon as King Ferdinand should be set free to govern his own subjects, the French army would retire, and its mission would cease. Meantime the ancient Supreme Council of Spain, and the Council of the Indies, requested him, in the King's absence, to nominate a Regency.

All that flowers and garlands, tapestries, music, and shouts, could do to welcome the French army into the capital, was done by the Spaniards, apparently with rapture and enthusiasm. The main body, commanded by the Duc d'Angoulême (not an imposing figure), entered by one gate; Marshal Oudinot with his division by another.

No time was lost in sending a force toward Seville to pursue the Cortes, who were in full retreat, and to deliver the King. But the Cortes, with their escort of six thousand men, marched so rapidly that the French never came up with them until they had established themselves safely in Seville.

The complete success of the French, almost without any effusion of blood, had been entirely unlooked for by statesmen and diplomatists. It had been expected that the fierce spirit of the Spaniards would lead them to rise at once *en masse* against a foreign invader. The reception given to the French damped foreign enthusiasm for the cause of the Constitution.

The Cortes, soon after they reached Seville, declared the King incapable, and deposed him. They made no longer any secret that they held him in captivity. Seville not being thought safe, they removed themselves and the royal family to Cadiz. In vain Ferdinand protested, and the moment that the Cortes and the King were out of Seville, riots began and continued, until the French took possession of the beautiful city.

In Cadiz, the Cortes shut themselves up with their captives, under charge of a garrison of twenty thousand men. Although they had deposed Ferdinand, it was found convenient still to act in his name, and to make use of his authority.

Riego, who now commanded in La Isla (the Île de Leon), made his way into the mountains, and vainly endeavored by his personal influence to rouse the inhabitants of the Sierra Morena to make head against the foreigners.

The Duc d'Angoulême, leaving only a garrison in Madrid, marched at the head of his army to Cadiz. From Andujar, while on his march, he issued a proclamation which not a little impaired his popularity among the Spanish people. He was alarmed by the savage cruelty of the exultant royalists in places where no French were on the spot to put a check upon their passions. In Saragossa, fifteen hundred persons had been arrested, and their houses pillaged ; and this example was being followed in other cities, often with much effusion of blood. The Duke ordered the release of all such prisoners, and declared that no persons should be arrested by the Spanish authorities for other than a criminal offence, without the authorization of some French officer. This was considered usurpation, and the assumption of the authority of a conqueror by the French commander.

On this subject Alison remarks that " with the Spaniards loyalty to their sovereign seemed identical with thirst for the blood of his enemies ; " and the decree of the Duc d'Angoulême was publicly denounced as worse than any act of the Emperor Napoleon.

Cadiz is situated on the extreme point of a tongue of land, which stretches upward abruptly from the coast, forming one side of a large bay. The city at the narrow entrance to this bay defends it ; La Isla, a small province of Andalusia formed into an island by a river, is on the south of the peninsula and the bay of Cadiz. Porte Sainte Marie, or Puerto di Santa Maria, is on the main line of the Andalusian coast, northeast of Cadiz and its harbor. Of the forts that defended the approach to Cadiz the most formidable was the Trocadero (a name now associated with shows and festivities in the French capital). It had been strengthened with great care, but was assaulted by the French during the last week of August, 1823. The assault, which took place at early dawn, was the first real military exploit of the war. The Spaniards repulsed the attack with bravery, but by nine o'clock the French had gained possession of the place, and they then had a point from which they could throw bombs into the city. The Duc d'Angoulême, although never trained to war, exposed himself freely ; but the hero of the day was Charles Albert, Prince of Savoy-Carignan, who had been condemned by his kinsmen to do penance for his liberal opinions in Piedmont, by serving in the French army against those who upheld the Spanish constitution. The warlike instincts of the Princes of the House of Savoy were animated by the excitement of a real conflict, and the father of Victor Emmanuel, the first king of Italy, bore himself to the admiration of all who fought beside him. Perhaps, despairing and unhappy, he was seeking death as he did in 1849 at the close of the lost battle of Novara.

Riego, whose attempt to organize a peasant army in the

central part of Spain had met with no success, was at the head of a small force closely pursued by General Ballesteros, whose troops, enlisted under the Constitution, had gone over to the royal cause ; but when they saw their old companions-in-arms, and heard their cries of " Viva Riego ! Viva la Constitucion ! " they deserted back again. They forced their general to do as they did, and to clasp Riego, his old comrade, in his arms.

But Riego failed to effect a junction, as he had hoped, with Mina ; his followers dropped off from him in the mountains ; wounded and exhausted, he sought shelter in a farmhouse, and was betrayed to the French, who captured him. He was conducted under a strong guard to Madrid, his escort with difficulty preventing his being torn to pieces. At Andujar he said to a French officer who in a riot covered him with his body at the hazard of his life : " The people who are now so excited against me, — the people who but for the succor of the French would have murdered me, — that *same* people last year, on this very spot, bore me in their arms in triumph. The city forced on me against my will a sword of honor; the night which I passed here, the houses were illuminated, the people danced till morning under my windows, and prevented me by their acclamations from getting a moment's sleep."

The Cortes now got Ferdinand to sign a letter to the Duc d'Angoulême, asking for peace. The Duke refused to offer any terms till the King was out of the hands of his rebellious subjects. The defence of Cadiz was then continued, until, thoroughly alarmed and disheartened, the Cortes dissolved itself September 28, 1823, and three days afterwards King Ferdinand, having published another proclamation assuring his people of a general amnesty and everything desired by reasonable Constitutionalists, embarked on board a small ship and sailed to Porte Sainte Marie.

The Duc d'Angoulême was waiting to receive him, at the head of a brilliant staff, and bent his knee as Ferdinand stepped on shore.

An anecdote told of his disembarkation gives a black but a

true picture of Ferdinand's character. Two Constitutionalist generals, Valdez and Alava, had been deputed to see him safely into the French lines. Ferdinand conversed with them down to the last moment of the gratitude he was convinced he owed them, and of the need he felt of experienced and popular ministers to guide him in his new reign. He invited them to put full trust in him, — to land with him, and quit forever a city where their kindness to him might be imputed to them as a crime. They, however, distrusted his sincerity. They had had too many proofs of his treachery and dissimulation. So soon as the royal family had landed, they pushed off from the shore. "Miserable wretches!" muttered the King; "they do well to withdraw from their fate!"

The first act of Ferdinand on regaining his liberty was to issue a decree that all laws passed from March 17, 1820, to October, 1823, were null and void, "seeing that he had during that time been under the orders of a revolutionary government."

In vain the Duc d'Angoulême, in accordance with his promise, pleaded for amnesty, moderation, and humanity. "But unhappily in the Spanish character the desire for vengeance and the thirst for blood are as inherent as the heroism of adventure and the spirit of resistance." Ferdinand had never learned that forgiveness of injuries is the highest of Christian virtues.

Riego was his first victim. He was brought to trial, but no lawyer was found bold enough to undertake the once popular hero's defence. The people clamored for his death with cries of "Muera Riego! Death to the traitor! Long live our Absolute King!" Amidst the clamors of those present in the court-room, the sentence of death was passed, and a few days afterwards he was executed, November 7, 1823. Stripped of his uniform, shrouded in a white cloth, with a green liberty cap placed in derision on his head, his hands tied behind him, on a hurdle drawn by an ass, he passed to the place of execution. At the foot of a scaffold forty feet high, he received absolution, and then was lifted up, still

*MARIA TERESA DEL RIEGO.*

bound and helpless, pale and attenuated, already half dead, to the top of the scaffold. When the rope was passed round his neck, a monster struck him a blow in the face, and he was launched into eternity.

Such is in substance the account of this execution, as given by Sir Archibald Alison, and by Lamartine, who derived their information from contemporary narratives.

His brother, the Canon Riego, who subsequently wrote his life, escaped to England, having under his protection his widowed sister-in-law; all that affectionate brotherly devotion could do to soothe her sorrows and prolong her life was unavailing. She died at Chelsea June 19, 1824, seven months after the execution of her husband.[1]

---

[1] From 1836 to his death in 1844, we constantly saw the Canon Riego, who, my father often told us (I know not on what authority), would, had his brother succeeded in his plans, have been Archbishop of Toledo. His devotion to his sister-in-law was very touching. Almost all the little money they had saved was spent during the sad months of her illness in making her comfortable. When she died the Canon was reduced to almost absolute poverty; but he had permitted himself to spend money before her death for a beautiful miniature, which he would show to his friends with much emotion. A Spanish servant insisted on remaining with him, and together they went into obscure lodgings. He wrote a memoir of his brother published in London in 1824, and he printed a volume of Mediæval Spanish poems, published under the patronage of H. R. H. the Duke of Sussex in 1842. He was very desirous that the life of his brother should be written by Mr. Prescott, then engaged on the "Conquest of Mexico," and were this a suitable occasion, I could tell an amusing story in that connection. Sometimes he wrote verses in English. One poem he addressed to my little sister; each line was correct as to its number of syllables, but absurdly wrong as to its accents. He had many books, some of which he gave to friends, and some he sold when other resources failed him. He also occasionally sold Spanish wines. My father purchased a quarter-cask from him of what he held to be the purest Xeres. But our palates, accustomed to port and sherry as doctored for the English market, could not brook it; and my father was persuaded to invent some pretext to give it back to the Canon as a present, without hurting his feelings. Not long after he was summoned by a policeman to attend an inquest. The Canon had been found dead in his bed with a vial containing some of the wine clasped in his

The King and Queen entered Madrid in triumph a week after this tragedy. They were seated on an antique chariot twenty-five feet high, drawn by one hundred young men in splendid fancy dresses, and surrounded by dancers in operatic costumes, both men and women. But the promised amnesty proved far different from what was hoped. It was so full of exceptions that it was rather a declaration of war against the adverse party than an offer of peace. Arrests multiplied, and the prisons overflowed. The Duc d'Angoulême was deeply hurt by the little account taken of promises he had made in the King's name, and of his own known wishes. Even Russia, through her Corsican minister, Pozzo di Borgo, ventured to remonstrate; and as Ferdinand held Russia's good opinion in high esteem, her intervention resulted in the change of his fanatical, severe, and unpopular confessor.

Thus the revolution ended, and Ferdinand held absolute power thenceforward to his death. Spain was not in the least pacified, only the factions were held down. The finances of the kingdom were in a state of bankruptcy. Prosperity was at an end. The only activity in the whole kingdom was that of arrests; the only energy displayed was when one enemy sought the destruction of another. Nothing kept the peace but the presence of the French; and when the main body of their army was withdrawn, thirty-five thousand men were permitted to remain in possession of the principal fortresses.

Portugal in 1823 was under a Constitutional government, but the presence of the French in Spain provoked an insurrection in favor of absolutism. This was put down for a time; but events in Spain infused new spirit into Don Miguel, the head of the Absolutist party. He made his

hand. The coroner's jury found that he died from natural causes. Probably feeling faint and ill, he had got out of bed, and possessed himself of some of the pure Xeres wine as a cordial. Loving and generous, no one ever heard him allude to his poverty; on the contrary, he was always making little presents, and doing little kindnesses for half-grateful friends. I remember his sending his servant to make us chocolate, after the Spanish fashion, and a *puchero*, an unsavory hash, composed chiefly of mutton, garlic, and beans. — E. W. L.

escape from Lisbon, and put himself at the head of some revolted regiments. The mob assembled round the palace; the King came out, and was forced to tear the white Constitutional cockade from his breast; the ministry was changed; the Cortes dissolved, and an Absolutist revolution was effected without bloodshed; and without punishment to the leaders of the party which had suffered defeat.

It was at this time that Mr. Canning developed his foreign policy. Alarmed at the disturbance of the balance of power, he protested that if France was to have supreme influence in Spain, she should not domineer over "the Spain of the past," — Spain with the Indies. He would favor the recognition of the young republics torn from her in South America; and he concluded his speech in the House of Commons on this subject with these memorable words, "I have called a New World into existence, to redress the balance of the Old."

10

# CHAPTER VIII.

WHEN Ferdinand was restored to his capital and resumed the cares of government, he found everything unhinged and in disorder. Misfortunes in new shapes followed fast upon one another. The more the state of the country was inquired into, the more ruin and disaster came to light. The treasury was empty ; foreign credit was destroyed. Ferdinand himself not unaptly described the situation when he spoke of being the cork in a bottle of beer. Little as we may feel disposed to extend any sympathy to Ferdinand, he is entitled to justice. Spain was the battleground of factions. No statesman was wise enough to say which was the strongest one. The Constitutionalists demanded reforms ; the northern provinces were fanatical for their ancient institutions. Republicans agitated for revolution. The men *plus royalists que le roi* wanted to bring back the monarchy of Philip II. and the rule of the Inquisition ; and Ferdinand, weak, vacillating, and without principle, was called to reign over a congeries of fierce, untamed, selfish, and ignorant populations, eager for revolt, whether for the Constitution or the Inquisition. If we look under the surface of things, after the second restoration of Ferdinand we may cast less blame on him than we should do on a superficial view. He was governed by fear, and fear makes kings tyrants, as it has made a Robespierre.

The General Amnesty, published May 20, 1824, was, as I have said, the cause of anguish, disappointment, apprehension, and terror. It contained twelve classes of exceptions, so that it was in reality a sentence without trial against several thousand persons, under the false name of an amnesty. The exceptions were : (1) the authors of military rebellion; (2) all concerned in the Madrid conspiracy of March, 1820; (3) all military chiefs concerned in the Ocaña mutiny, particularly the Conde d'Abisbal; (4) the authors of the Provisional Junta; (5) those who signed the document depriving the King of his royal functions and appointing a Regency; (6) all members of secret societies; (7) writers or editors who had written or published anything against the state religion; (8) persons concerned in the Madrid conspiracy of 1823; (9) all concerned in the murder of General Elio; (10) all concerned in the murder of Archbishop Vich, or the priest Vinuesa, or the *noyade* of prisoners from the Castle of Antonio;[1] (11) members of the Cortes, who voted for the King's deposition, July 11, 1823; (12) those who composed, or promoted the formation of, a Regency. No wonder that the publication of such an amnesty stirred up strife instead of appeasing it. Many

[1] This deed was so abominable that it certainly deserved little mercy. I have several accounts of the atrocity, but copy that from a very good "Short History of Spain," by Professor Harrison, of Washington and Lee University:—

"The guns in the French warships, before Saint Sebastian commanded the bay, in consequence of which a number of royalists, confined in a pontoon, rose upon their guards, cut the cables, and drifted out to sea. Fearful that the other prisoners in the Castle of San Antonio might equally escape, the military governor ordered fifty-two of them to be brought into the town, and in the afternoon they were lodged in the prison; but the civil authorities objecting to this step, in consequence of the crowded state of the prison, the unhappy men were put into a small vessel and conveyed down the bay. After doubling the point on which the castle stands, and in front of the lighthouse called the Tower of Hercules, they were brought up in pairs from under the hatches, bound together back to back, and then thrown into the sea. One of the victims, seeing the fate which awaited him, jumped into the water before his hands were tied, and endeavored to escape by swimming, but some of his executioners pursued him in a boat, and beat out his brains with their oars. The tide cast the bodies of these unfortunate creatures on shore, where they were the next morning found by the French sergeant on guard. The French general sent in a flag of truce complaining of this atrocity, but the officer in command, who had given the order for its perpetration, had in the mean time, together with several other patriots, made off in an English vessel."

of the persons excepted fled to England, and were there supported either by a government allowance, or by private benevolence.

From time to time rash expeditions were planned by restless men ; one under Valdez, one of the two officers from Cadiz, who, having escorted the royal family to the Duc d'Angoulême, was so insolently spoken of by Ferdinand. He seized for a few days the town and castle of Tarifa, but his rash raid had no results.

Many persons not excepted in the amnesty, but who had served under the irregular and revolutionary government, gave in their formal adhesion to that of the King. These men were spoken of as *the Purified,* — a term equivalent to *Reconstructed* in our vocabulary after the Civil War. But while statesmen of all parties in England, France, and even Russia were blaming King Ferdinand for his harsh and unforgiving spirit, riots broke out in Catalonia, — the royalists in that kingdom having taken offence because too many persons who had fought for the Constitution between 1820 and 1823 had been *purified.*

The war minister appointed by Ferdinand was General Eguia, an earnest royalist, who in conjunction with two others had headed the Army of the Faith in Navarre and Catalonia in 1822. The Commander-in-Chief was the Count de Espana, who, being ordered to restore tranquillity in Catalonia, put down the disaffected royalists with horrible cruelty. It was supposed that under this revolt of the Catalans lay a plan for raising Don Carlos to the throne. But the Infante was indignant at having his name mixed up in the affair. He was already his brother's heir presumptive, and could afford to wait for his dissolution. King Ferdinand, however, had become jealous of the brother to whom he had been so closely united at Valençay in the days of their captivity. Don Carlos was a favorite of the people. He was considered more loyal to ancient institutions than King Ferdinand. But his habits were retired. He took no part in politics, though he sometimes tendered his brother advice, which was not often accepted.

One of the most active agitators who engaged in raids and risings was General Torrijos. The Marquis de Custine, who travelled in Spain in 1831, tells how he met with an Irishman named Blake, a member of some International Revolutionary society, who was then working as its agent in Andalusia. Torrijos had been drawing on himself the attention of the police, and was in hiding. Blake managed to get him to Gibraltar, where his presence was a great embarrassment to the Governor, for the Spanish ministry demanded that he should be given up to punishment. Blake persuaded the captain of an English frigate in Gibraltar roads, who was about to sail for Alexandria, to allow him to smuggle Torrijos on board. This was done, and the Governor with satisfaction reported to his own government and to that of Spain that Torrijos was no longer in his power. But Blake, who favored the presence of the revolutionary leader in Spain, had succeeded in deceiving everybody by substituting another Spaniard for Torrijos, who remained safe at Gibraltar planning another insurrection and preparing a manifesto in which he assured his countrymen that he did not seek to re-establish the Constitution of 1812, but that his aim was to destroy the faction that surrounded the King, to call a Cortes, and to leave ulterior questions to its decision. In December, 1831, lured by treacherous promises from the Governor of Malaga, Torrijos and a party of his friends landed in the province of Malaga, were taken prisoners, led to the city, and shot upon the strand. An obelisk in the Plaza di Riego now commemorates their names as martyrs to the cause of liberty.

Spain was greatly excited by the Revolution in France in 1830. Custine says that they regarded France as an infected country, and every French traveller as carrying contagion about his person. A cordon of soldiers was placed round the French Embassy in Madrid, for fear its inhabitants should be injured in some popular outbreak.

General discontent prevailed throughout the country; men complained that no Cortes had been summoned, no improvements introduced into the general government; but yet the people in general, weary of war, were patient and not disposed, even in the northern provinces, to join fresh attempts at revolution. The revolutionary leaders found their chief support in London and Paris, where public sympathy encouraged them and cheered them on. They had not learned, what subsequent history might have proved to them, that spasmodic revolutionary raids and risings involve only the loss of brave men's lives, and stimulate increased vigilance on the part of the governing powers. Neither did they appreciate the folly as well as wickedness of sending infernal machines through the post-office, an atrocity which then first came into fashion. Such machines were sent to the King, to his ministers, and to members of his family. Only one person, General Eguia, was injured by them; but alarm became so great in the public offices that another machine was invented for opening heavy and suspicious packages safely. The author of these infernal machines was never discovered.

Mina in 1830 again crossed the Pyrenees, and succeeded in penetrating a few miles into Spanish territory. The British public had been assured that the population of Navarre would flock to his standard, and that the road to Madrid lay open to him; but nobody joined him, his personal followers fell off from him, and after wandering almost alone among the woods and precipices of the mountains, he was glad to escape into France again.

From 1823 to 1830 the best-managed department of the Spanish Government was that of the finances. The King's government succeeded in reducing them to something like order, under the management of Gary, a man of low birth, who showed zeal and ability.

Brigandage, however, was rife in Andalusia and Granada, to say nothing of Aragon and Catalonia; and Custine tells amusing and almost incredible stories of the influence of its chiefs, Apollinario and José Maria. The former once robbed a Franciscan monk, who produced such an impression on him by his eloquent appeals, while he was stripping him, that he became a penitent, and publicly renounced his profession.

He returned to it, however, after a time, and was as formidable as ever. José Maria never repented, and his power
was greater than that of the King in the districts he fre-
quented. The Governor of Granada, being about to set out
on a journey of twenty miles without an escort, was reproved
for foolhardiness by a friend, when he drew from his pocket
a *laissez passer* signed by José Maria, for which he had paid
a handsome sum.

At the close of 1830, there was hope that a new era had
commenced in Spain. Liberal and Absolutist insurrections
had been put down, and the kingdom was apparently in a
state of quiet and peace.

Ferdinand was again a widower. His third wife died on
the night of May 16, 1829, and immediately negotiations
were begun under the auspices of the Infanta Doña Luisa
Carlota of Naples, wife of Don Francesco di Paula, for a
marriage with her sister Christina. In less than four months
the marriage contract was signed.

Ferdinand's first wife was a princess of Naples, an active,
intriguing woman, bitterly opposed to the influence of
Godoy. His second, Maria Isabel, a Portuguese princess,
and his own near relative, was amiable and beloved. The
third, Maria Josephine Amelia, was a lady of like character,
but the Princess Christina was a different woman. She was
sister of the Duchesse de Berry, and niece to Queen Marie
Amélie, wife of Louis Philippe, a woman holy and pure,
whose life as wife, mother, queen, and Christian is too
sacred for mere praise.

Ferdinand, after his fourth marriage, was observed by his
court and household to be much altered. He was "everything by turns, and nothing long." Sometimes he tried
a little liberalism. At this, Absolutists took the alarm.
They complained that he did not care enough for priests,
that his favor was all given to monks ; and they turned their
eyes upon Don Carlos, in comparison with whom Ferdinand
was held to be a recreant to Absolutist principles, and a protector of men who held revolutionary views. Popular
opinion believed that Don Carlos, when he came to the

throne, would re-establish the Inquisition with all its horrors. The King's old confessor, Father Cyril, General of the Franciscans, who had been dismissed by Ferdinand and exiled to Cadiz, through the influence of Russia in 1823, was looked upon as head of the Carlist party. Father Cyril was a bigot and an Absolutist, but he was also a statesman, and a very remarkable man. He was a Grandee of Spain of the First class, Head of the Council of Castile, and had the cordons of many European orders.

But to return to King Ferdinand : During the last years of his life he took an aversion to public business, in which he had before seemed to take an interest. He disliked to appear in public. He became a prey to melancholia. Up to that time he had been popular in Spain, — popular, that is to say, with the great body of the populace. His people made allowances for the great difficulties of his position, and they never forgot his persecution by Godoy. He was the first Spanish king who held daily public audiences, and he patiently received with his own hand innumerable petitions. The lower orders looked upon him as their friend, and had formed an idea that he was the champion of their ancient institutions, as well as of the religion of the state. "*Per contra*," as Mr. Walton remarks, "no monarch was ever beset by so many conspiracies ; no one had more enemies abroad, or at home was exposed to so many contending influences."

His attachment to his brother — already weakened by jealousy — from the time of his fourth marriage decreased, and there began disputes among other members of the royal family, who had hitherto lived in outward harmony with one another.

Ferdinand, like all weak men, was jealous of any interference with his authority, and his former queens had not dared to offend him by meddling in public affairs ; but Christina was of a different stamp. She became the life and soul of the administration. Through her influence and at her nod, the secret springs in every department of the State were moved. Scarcely had the King a will of his own.

*QUEEN MARIA CHRISTINA.*

The Queen's first wish was to secure the throne to her own offspring. To this end, as soon as she knew herself to be *enceinte*, she desired to make sure of a liberal party in favor of herself, in opposition to the ultra-royalists, who hoped to see Don Carlos on the throne. To this end, she made concessions to liberalism, after the example of France. It was believed in Madrid that she was encouraged to do this by letters from her aunt, Marie Amélie, who had urged her to use her influence with her husband to induce him to grant institutions in accordance with the wants and wishes of Spain.

The announcement that the Queen was likely to give birth to a child (it was hoped that that child might prove a son) caused great excitement in Madrid, and disconcerted the friends and followers of Don Carlos, whose claims to the throne, if the babe should prove a girl, were protected by the Law of Succession, passed when Philip V. ascended the throne.

The Queen and her friends therefore made haste to provide against such a contingency by manœuvring for the abrogation of the Salic law.

We have already seen that fickleness was characteristic of Ferdinand in the choice of his friends and advisers. He threw them aside with as little reason and as much suddenness as he had exalted them into favor. To the favorite of the moment was intrusted the task of obtaining Ferdinand's consent to the abrogation of Philip V.'s law of succession. It was not easy to bring Ferdinand over to the scheme that his wife had so greatly at heart. At the first hint he resisted and grew angry, but in all things he was changed. Nothing now could interest him or amuse him. Formerly he was jocose, stirring, and inquisitive; now languor and indifference pervaded all his actions. He ceased to ask questions; his hands trembled with nervousness; and in this condition he was in no state to combat those who were bent on bringing him over to their plans.

The Law of Succession was precise. It was part of the agreement sanctioned by all Europe, when Philip V.

mounted the Spanish throne. So long as there was a male descendant, however remote, of Philip V., no female could wear the crown. For one hundred and twenty years this law had been held to be the only rule of succession. It was feared that to abrogate it would introduce tremendous changes, and give rise, in all probability, to disastrous civil war.

Ferdinand held firm as long as he could, but Christina brought her strong will and all her fascinations to bear upon him. As a means to her end, she set herself to rouse his slumbering jealousy of his brother's popularity, especially in the northern provinces. The earliest step taken in the matter was a private message, sent by the King to the Minister of Grace and Justice, directing him to send up all records of the proceedings of the Cortes of 1789, regarding the succession, for his Majesty's perusal.

It seems that Charles III., not long before his death, had grown uneasy about the working of this law. His son (Charles IV). had been born in Naples, and the law said distinctly that the prince who succeeded must have been born on Spanish soil. Don Luis, his next son, had deeply offended him by refusing to be a priest, and marrying a lady not of royal blood. No steps, however, had been taken in the matter when Charles III. died in 1788, and Charles IV. succeeded him without opposition. But the new King's mind was not at rest on the subject of the succession. Ferdinand was frail and sickly ; he was an object of positive dislike to both his parents. The King's desire was to be empowered by the Cortes, to set aside the law of 1713, and to leave his crown, in case of his early death, to Maria Carlotta, his daughter, who was some years older than Ferdinand. With this view, he sent out writs for the assembling of the Cortes in 1789, to do homage and swear allegiance to his son, the Crown Prince, "and also to treat of other matters, should they be proposed."

"The deputies, to the number of seventy-six, met on September 14, 1789. After their first meeting, a second was ordered to be held in secrecy. The deputies were then told that their concurrence was wished to alter the Law of Succession as it then stood, by revising Law 2, Title 5, of the Partidas, whereby females might succeed to the crown on a par with males. By this most extraordinary stratagem the proposed measure was carried, and the Cortes petitioned Charles IV. to have a law passed to the effect desired. To the petition Charles appended the following answer, bearing date Madrid, September 30, 1789. 'I have adopted the resolution pursuant to the accompanying petition, enjoining the greatest secrecy to be kept for the present; this being expedient for my service.' This reply being communicated to the Cortes, a fresh petition was submitted to the King, praying him to adopt the usual formalities,[1] in order that the old law might be observed in preference to the new one. To this the following reply was returned: 'I answer you that I will ordain those of my Council to issue the Pragmatic Sanction usual in such cases, bearing in mind your petition, and the opinions thereon taken.' Here the matter ended. The deputies dispersed, and, being bound to secrecy, the whole affair was buried in oblivion. No new law was enacted, and that of Philip V. continued in force. . . . Of this power unconstitutionally granted, and rendered obsolete, Ferdinand VII., forty-four years after, desired to avail himself to bar the rights of his brother, and secure the throne to his daughter, the Princess Isabel." [2]

No further notice of the matter was taken, and the papers relating to the Law of Succession lay forgotten among the archives until Ferdinand expressed his wish to examine them. He kept them twelve days, and then returned them with a marginal note in his handwriting, " Let them be published." The minister ventured to remonstrate, but was overborne when the King sternly said to him, " Such is my will ! "

On April 6, 1830, all Madrid was astounded by the appearance in the " Gazette " of the incomplete decree projected by Charles IV. in 1789, with the words : " Ordered to be published by his reigning Majesty for the *perpetual* observ-

[1] It would appear that though the Cortes had ostensibly been summoned to swear fealty to Ferdinand, that oath had not been taken.

[2] From Walton's Revolutions of Spain, 1837.

ance of a law for the succession to the Crown of Spain."
And at midday the law was publicly proclaimed, in torrents
of rain, by magistrates and heralds, to the astonishment of
the people. It was like a bomb thrown into the camp of
the Carlist party. Not only did Don Carlos protest on
behalf of himself and his three sons, but every male descendant of Philip V. in Europe objected likewise. Foremost among them was the King of Naples, father of Queen
Christina and great-grandson of Philip V. The King of
Sardinia joined the protest, the Bourbons of France, and
even Louis Philippe, then Duke of Orleans. But there was
hope that Ferdinand's interference with the Law of Succession might have no results, since in a few months a
prince, heir of his body, might be born.

The Queen's next care was, to keep such strict guard
over the King that he might neither have a moment for
reflection, nor see any one likely to alarm his conscience
and make him change his design. New rules were established in the palace. All friends of Don Carlos were kept
at a distance.

Early in October, 1830, the confinement of the Queen
was expected, and took place. At that time the northern
provinces were in dread of an invasion, the Spanish refugees
having assembled in some numbers near the frontier of the
Pyrenees, while in Malaga Torrijos attempted the revolt
which led to his seeking refuge at Gibraltar.

The peasantry in the Asturias (after which province the
Crown Prince is always named) sent up a deputation to
petition that if the child born should be a son, they might
be the first to do him homage. If the babe should prove a
prince the royal standard was to be hoisted on the palace ;
if a princess, a white flag.

On October 10, 1830, at two o'clock in the afternoon,
all the official persons required by court etiquette being
present, the child began the troubled life which at this date
(1897) still continues. "What is it?" cried the King, im-
patiently. "A robust daughter," replied the physician.
The King turned pale, and an expression of disappointment

escaped him; but according to custom, he had to receive the infant on a silver salver, and turning to the assembled officials and grandees, declare it to be his daughter. The babe was christened Isabel, treated as a royal heiress, and military honors from her birth were paid her.

The Queen's next care was to strengthen her influence in the army. All officers supposed to be in the interest of Don Carlos were removed. When her health was re-established, she presented banners to some regiments, embroidered by her own hand, and in a speech to the officers expressed a hope that under these banners they would defend the rights of King Ferdinand and of his issue.

Meantime the King's health grew more and more feeble. He had severe attacks of gout, and seemed daily to decline. In January, 1832, about fourteen months after the birth of her first child, the Queen became the mother of a second daughter, christened Luisa.

Eight months later, the King, on his way to his palace of La Granja, at San Ildefonso, was attacked with gout in the stomach, and lay almost lifeless for some hours. Couriers sent off to Madrid carried news that he was dead, and it spread thence over Europe by special messengers to all the Spanish embassies. In Madrid several influential grandees then in the capital urged Don Carlos to lose not a moment in asserting his rights to the crown. But Don Carlos replied that, not being assured of the King's death, he would take no step unbecoming in a subject or a brother. He was then urged to assume the Regency, but he assured his advisers that he had full confidence that the law would protect his rights.

The King for some time before his last illness had been wavering. He felt that the country was on the eve of a great crisis. At times, something of his old love for his brother revived.

"He felt too that he had outlived his popularity with the masses, and saw himself deserted by the royalists, the party to whom he had hitherto looked for support. His bed of sickness was surrounded by strangers; even the attendant who had shaved him for twenty years and had accompanied him to Valençay, had been removed; and though Don Carlos was daily at La Granja to inquire for his brother's health, he was never allowed to enter his chamber. When the King recovered sufficiently to notice what was passing round him, he was grieved and astonished to find his old barber superseded by a stranger; he also expressed regret at being deprived of his brother's visits, as well as those of other old friends. But the Queen made every exertion to soothe him and to keep him calm and tranquil."

It was affirmed and believed in Madrid that as the King lay insensible, cold, and motionless, the physicians at his bedside had believed him dead. It was only when his attendants were preparing to lay out the corpse that a slight convulsive breath startled them. The doctors were called · in, and through their skill and promptitude the King's life was saved. It was said that a more remarkable case of suspended animation never existed.

As the King grew better, the Queen herself could not contemplate with equanimity what might happen in case of his sudden death. She endeavored to win Don Carlos over to her party, and to make him consent to the accession of Isabella, by offering him the appointment of co-regent, — the other regent, herself, having been already appointed; she also proposed a marriage between his eldest son and her daughter. This offer Don Carlos firmly declined, declaring that he would never bar his own right or that of his three sons to the succession, in case his brother should die without a male heir; and he added that the nation was with him.

The night after this proposal had been made and refused was spent by Christina and her supporters in anxious deliberation. The next morning the King, very weak and exhausted, commanded the Count of Alcudia, who had the day before been employed to negotiate with Don Carlos, to summon the Minister of Grace and Justice. Señor Calomarde therefore appeared before the King, when Ferdinand, with a voice of deep emotion, asked if his ministers were aware of the dangerous aspect that affairs were assuming. Señor Calomarde answered that they knew well, and that it was evident the crisis would end in blood. Here the Queen cried out, " Not blood! No, anything but that! not blood! " " But what can be done? " asked the King. " My wish is only for the welfare of my people. Prepare a decree of *derogation* abrogating the late Law of Succession; but I enjoin you not to let any one know of it till my eyes are closed. Take care that until then it is not published or allowed to go out of the department of Grace and Justice." " But," said the minister, " it is proper that the other ministers should know of it; and they must also witness your Majesty's signature." The King agreed. The hour for signing was fixed for six o'clock in the afternoon.

The decree was drawn up. This was the form of it:

" Desirous of giving my people a fresh proof of the affection I bear them, I have deemed it proper to derogate from the second law, Title 5, *partida* the second, respecting the succession to the crown, and from all clauses in my will which might be contrary to this last determination. I ordain that this decree be deposited with the Ministry of Grace and Justice until after my death. You will so understand it, and see to its execution.

" I, THE KING."

At the hour appointed, the ministers assembled round the King's bed. Señor Calomarde read aloud the paper. The King said, " It is well." The Queen took a pen, and handing it to the King, placed a blotter under the paper to which he was to affix his signature. The King executed his sign-manual, and turning to the Minister of Grace and Justice, asked him if he wished that his name should be signed in full. The minister replied that it would be advisable. The King therefore signed Fernando after his sign-manual, after which his ministers (with the exception of the Minister of War, who was absent) signed their names; and the document so signed and witnessed was delivered to Señor Calomarde.

From this moment the King seemed more composed,

and said on the following day to Señor Calomarde, affectionately pressing his hand at the same time, " Of what an
enormous weight my heart is now relieved! I shall now
die in peace."

A week later Te Deums were chanted in the churches,
in gratitude for the improvement in the King's health.
But he was not fit to attend to business, and Queen
Christina was appointed Regent till he should be able to
do so.

Don Francisco di Paula had leaned towards the liberals,
through dislike to other members of his family, who had
never been cordial to him. His wife (a Neapolitan princess, sister of the Duchesse de Berry, and of Queen Christina)
was not friendly to her sisters-in-law. The court indeed
was divided into two factions, the Neapolitan and the
Portuguese. To the latter belonged Doña Francesca, wife
of Don Carlos, — sister of King Ferdinand's second wife
Doña Maria Isabel, — and the Princess of Beira, widow of
the Infante Don Pedro, another sister of the same Queen.

While the King was believed to be at the point of death,
some attempt was made to reconcile these factions, and
Queen Christina made overtures of amity and forgiveness
to the wife of Don Carlos, but so soon as the King was
convalescent, war began again.

Don Francisco di Paula and his wife had been at Seville
while events of importance were taking place at San Ildefonso. No sooner did the Princess Luisa Carlota learn
what had happened, than she hastened to La Granja, travelling four hundred miles in forty hours, over rough roads and
mountain passes. She was furious with her sister for having
allowed the King to sign the decree of " derogation," and
reproached her for having sacrificed the welfare of Spain
and the future of her children. She demanded that the
important paper should be given up to her. This Señor
Calomarde refused to do ; but being threatened with assassination by some of the Queen's friends, he believed it was
no longer safe in his hands and gave it into those of the
President of the Council of Castile, from whom, before long,

Doña Luisa Carlota contrived to obtain it. Copies had, however, been sent into the various provinces, not to be opened till the King's death, and these remained.

Ferdinand had now become so weak in mind and body as to be almost imbecile. The Queen Regent exercised all the functions of royalty. She dismissed the old ministers, and appointed new ones, moderate liberals, and good men; but she showed little moderation in many of her other actions. She punished Señor Calomarde by ordering a carriage to his door, compelling him to enter it and to leave the capital. She endeavored to disband the body-guard, composed of royalists, all likely to favor Don Carlos rather than Isabella. She promoted secret societies in the army, pledged to favor her views, and she published a decree of amnesty, not with motives of clemency, but to bring back into Spain about twelve hundred energetic members of the liberal party, who might support her own claims. All the generals and all governors of the provinces were changed.

The decree of amnesty excited fierce opposition in Madrid. The exiles themselves published in a Paris paper a protest against being pardoned. They said it was not themselves, but King Ferdinand, faithless and forsworn, who needed pardon. This paper was surreptitiously shown to King Ferdinand by an attendant, in a moment when his mind was more clear than usual, and it greatly excited him. He was very angry with the Queen, and reproached her for promoting the return of persons who had voted for his deposition at Seville, and had carried him off to Cadiz against his will.

Señor Zea Bermudez was the prime minister. He was absent from Spain when first appointed, and did not return to Madrid for some weeks, when he found the Cabinet divided, two of the ministers being inclined to royalist opinions, the other two to advanced liberalism. Zea did not approve of the decree of amnesty, which would bring back to Spain men likely to increase the general agitation. He put forth a document assuring foreign powers and the Spaniards that false reports had gone abroad; that the Queen

Regent had no designs of making any religious or political innovations in the government. But this circular only shook the confidence of the liberals in the Queen, as head of the advanced movement, while the confidence of the royalists in the King had been shaken already.

On December 31, 1832, the Queen Regent summoned the Archbishop of Toledo, the ministers, court officials, nobles, and dignitaries in Madrid, to the King's chamber; and in their presence the King made a protest, in which he alleged that in signing the decree of " derogation " on September 18, he had been taken by surprise in the moments of an agony to which he had been reduced by a serious illness ; that disloyal and deluded men had then surrounded his bed, and led him to believe that the kingdom was opposed to the repeal of the Salic law, and that torrents of blood would flow if he changed the Law of Succession. They had therefore obtained from him the decree of derogation by surprise and misrepresentation, and that it was consequently to be considered null and void.

The first idea of the Queen and her party had been to deny the existence of such a document as the act of derogation, since it had been probably destroyed when it came into Doña Luisa Carlota's hands ; but there were too many copies in existence to make that falsehood available. There was no remedy but to make the enfeebled and declining King go back on his own words.[1]

[1] A brief restatement of the foregoing facts may make them clearer.

In early times, the Crown of Castile could descend to females, as we see in the case of Queen Isabella and her daughter Juana. In 1713, when the first Bourbon prince, Philip V., mounted the Spanish throne, the Law of Succession was altered by the King, with the approval of the Cortes; and by the treaty of Utrecht, it was guaranteed by the European powers.

Charles III., before his death, became uneasy as to who might be his successor. He had a misgiving that his son Charles (afterwards Charles IV.) might be considered ineligible because he was not born on Spanish soil. He did not like his son, and he particularly disliked his wife, Maria Louisa. Don Luis, his second son, had forfeited his favor, and he wished to have the privilege of altering

The next care of the Queen was to rid herself of the presence of her rival. A Carlist revolt broke out in Toledo, to which Don Carlos gave no countenance; but the King was persuaded that his life, and those of his Queen and of his children, were not safe from conspiracy so long as the Portuguese faction at court remained undisturbed. An order was issued that the Princess of Beira, under pretence of visiting her family in Portugal, should leave the kingdom. Struck with dismay at the blow which for his sake had fallen on his sister-in-law, Don Carlos hastened to the King, and begged to be allowed to accompany the Princess into exile. The King, who retained some fraternal feelings, insisted that his brother must not leave him, but was subsequently persuaded by Señor Zea that the task of government could be made much easier if Don Carlos and his wife were out of the kingdom; so Ferdinand gave his consent to all that was required of him, but "he could not part without emotion from a brother who had given him so many proofs of attachment, had shared his captivity in France and all his dangers in Spain, and who, but for his rectitude of character and his fidelity as a subject, might have found numberless opportunities of taking possession of the crown."

by will, if he so pleased, the Law of Succession. He took, however, no action in the matter; but shortly after his death, his son Charles IV., who also desired to have power to alter the Law of Succession, assembled a Cortes under false pretences, and then submitted to them in a secret session, and under an injunction of secrecy, a request that they would petition him to make such changes in that law as would give him power to appoint his successor, and permit the accession of females. The Cortes sent in the required petition evidently with reluctance. The papers remained for forty-four years neglected and forgotten. They had never been completed, and had no legal force or form until in 1830, Ferdinand desired they should be brought to him, and wrote on them the words, *Let this be published.* "Published," in such matters, has not the meaning we commonly attach to it. It means that a decree shall be publicly proclaimed as the will of the King, with all due ceremonies, and so become law. On September 18, 1832, Ferdinand abrogated this law, and restored that of 1713, by what was called "an act of derogation." On December 31, 1832, he reversed this abrogation. None of these changes in the law of the land received the approval of a Cortes.

The exiles — eight members of the royal family — left Madrid, March 16, 1833. Orders had been given that no honors should be paid to them upon their journey ; volunteers were forbidden, under pain of imprisonment, to appear on their route in uniform, and the clergy were required not to allow church bells to be rung. Yet proofs of respect and attachment were tendered them along their way, by sorrowing spectators, and several officers who had the boldness to come forward and kiss the hand of Don Carlos were put under arrest and deprived of their pay.

June 20, 1833, was the day fixed for what was called the *jura.* All persons of rank and dignity who could be assembled in Madrid moved in procession to the royal monastery of St. Jerome, through streets decorated with hangings of silk and velvet, and protected by an immense body of guards. In the church of the monastery, these exalted persons, together with seventy-six deputies from the provinces, took oaths to consider the Infanta Isabel her father's heir. Don Carlos published his protest against this, and the envoy of the King of Naples read a similar paper, expressing the sentiments of his master. The Archbishop of Toledo, head of the Church in Spain, refused to be present. There was little or no enthusiasm among the spectators, and even at a magnificent bull-fight, with which the court entertained the populace, there were few *vivas* when the unhappy King, emaciated and weak, appeared on a balcony and bowed to the forty thousand spectators.

Three months later, September 29, 1833, the day of St. Michael, the King, who was supposed by his attendants to be asleep, was found to be dead. He had died without an opportunity having been given to administer to him the last sacraments. Mr. Walton, in his " Revolutions of Spain " (up to 1837), thus closes an account of this King's career :

" As far as the royal patient himself was concerned, his death was a happy release. For more than twelve months he had been a martyr to disease, both of mind and body ; yet in that deplorable condition he had been constantly dragged forth from the seclusion of his sick chamber, and exposed to the public

gaze, to satisfy the populace that he was still living.   The prolon-
gation of his existence, under the repeated paroxysms by which he
had been assailed, seemed so extraordinary that no reliance whatever was placed upon the bulletins Inserted in the 'Gazette.'
The people required the more substantial evidence of ocular
demonstration; and the unhappy sufferer was more than once
inhumanly paraded through the streets, strapped, for the sake
of support, to the back part of his carriage."

# CHAPTER IX.

## THE SPANISH-AMERICAN COLONIES.

I APPROACH in this chapter a part of my task which looked to me hopelessly difficult. It is no doubt desirable to say something concerning the Spanish-American colonies which revolted when they received news of the disorders of Aranjuez and the designs of the French in 1808; but after having gathered round me the books needed for reference, I was appalled by their number, their intricacy, and their confusion.

From 1808 to 1821, every one of the Spanish provinces of South America had not only been in revolt, but nearly all of them, it may be roughly said, had had its semi-annual revolution. All were at war with Spain, and all were apparently at the same time at war with one another. Each had its prominent patriot, its revolutionary leaders, its successes, its reverses, its paper constitutions, its *pronunciamentos*, and its alliances. How was it possible, within the limits of this chapter, to work such material into a connected or interesting narration?

I was tempted altogether to omit the subject, when I remembered a monograph of my own on "General Rosas, Buenos Ayres, and Montevideo." It had been written many years ago, published in an English magazine in 1846, and had been rewritten, enlarged, and used as a parlor lecture. I read it over, and decided that it might answer my purpose. At any rate, it will try my readers' patience less than if I attempted to construct for ten republics, during ten years of revolution, a continuous and connected narrative. It gives glimpses of the distracted state of the Spanish South American colonies during the period when they were all in a state of revolution. This appears to be all that could be done within my limits without crowding the reader's memory with unfamiliar names and a confused chronology.

To this I have added some long quotations from Mr. Carlyle's picturesque Essay on Dr. Francia. That essay is perfectly accessible, but probably the greater part of my readers may not have the book at hand.

I have also indulged myself with a piece of naval biography. The interest of the story must be my excuse for introducing it, for it hangs upon the subject before us by a very slender thread.

There were two Spanish viceroyalties in South America: Lima, which comprised the countries now known as Peru, Ecuador, Venezuela, Costa Rica, and the Guianas; and Buenos Ayres, which included, besides the present Argentine Republic, the Banda Oriental (or Uruguay), Chili, Paraguay, Upper Peru (or Bolivia), and an anticipatory interest in the uncivilized wastes of Patagonia.

Now the history of these ten states is (with the exception of that of Paraguay) the same thing ten times over. Each was inhabited by four classes: the Indians, the *mestizos*, or half-breeds (partly white and partly Indian), the Creoles, — that is, white men born on the soil of South America, — and Spaniards who were born in Spain. These last held all the offices under government; the Creoles were treated as an inferior race. Occasionally they were conciliated with decorations and with titles of nobility, but they had no share in the government of their native country, and no future lay before them. The Indians were trampled under foot, and the half-breeds fared little better.

The events of 1808 in Spain, and the pretensions of the brother of Napoleon to the Spanish throne, followed by an infusion of French liberal ideas into the Peninsula, stirred up the people in Spanish America to political aspirations.

Every one of the colonies was shaken as by the tremors of an earthquake. There was some attempt made to repress revolution on the return of Ferdinand, and we know the history of the expeditionary force at La Isla ; but state after state in South America had already declared itself independent, and in 1824 Mr. Canning proclaimed England's intention that they should not be interfered with by any European power.

Alas ! those petty republics, provided with brand-new constitutions of the latest pattern, — constitutions which rarely fitted them, — clothes which they found it difficult and inconvenient to wear, have not fulfilled the expectations of their patrons and admirers ; and instead of attempting to disentangle the perplexing history of these various states, I will tell, as specimens of what took place, stories about Buenos Ayres and its tyrant Rosas ; about Paraguay and its dictator, Dr. Francia ; about Bolivar, the Peruvian patriot ; about Chili, and its English champion, Lord Cochrane ; and leave my readers to infer the history of the rest, whose main features are the same, with only slight variations.

In the days when Spain and Portugal, by virtue of a papal bull and private enterprise, divided between them the whole of South America, the possessions of Portugal consisted of all those countries (in an area larger than Europe) that are watered by the Amazon and its tributary streams. These formed what was called subsequently the Empire of Brazil, while the colonies of Spain, — larger in extent, but less compact, — with an extensive seaboard on both the Atlantic and Pacific oceans, were divided, as I have said, into two viceroyalties.

The residence of the Viceroy of Buenos Ayres was in the city of the same name ; and the only other town of much importance in his dominion was Montevideo, on the left bank of the Rio de La Plata. Buenos Ayres, on first approach, is less imposing than its rival, and has a miserably inferior harbor. It lies on the right bank of the La Plata, about a hundred miles farther from the sea than Montevideo.

There is properly no such thing as the *Rio* de La Plata, that name being given to a magnificent estuary formed by the united waters of the Parana and the Uruguay, which meet at some distance above Buenos Ayres and spread out into a fresh-water sea, thirty miles wide before the city, and growing broader thence for nearly two hundred miles until it joins the South Atlantic Ocean. The *pamperos*, or mountain hurricane, has, however, been known to sweep over it with such violence as to cause half of its waters to disappear. In 1811, the inhabitants of Buenos Ayres were one morning amazed to find themselves six miles away from their river (or bay). A long smooth beach of that width lay stretched before them, while a Spanish ship that was blockading their harbor (for in 1811 the city was in revolt) lay high and dry upon the sand, and could easily have been captured by a troop of cavalry.

In 1806, England, then at war with Spain, attacked her American dependencies. Buenos Ayres was taken, but was recovered by the Spaniards. When this news reached England, a large force was fitted out under the command of General Whitelocke. It was reinforced by a body of British troops, eleven thousand strong, that had just captured Montevideo.

Buenos Ayres was at that time distracted by disputes between the Creoles and the native Spaniards. It is strange that a Spaniard, a royalist, a public officer, and a man who hated Creoles, should have headed the first movement of revolt in the Spanish colonies of the Western World. Don Martin de Alzaga, Mayor of Buenos Ayres, who was all these, called a public meeting and proposed to depose the Spanish Viceroy. This resolution was adopted, and carried into effect. General Liniers, a French officer, was made military commander, while the mayor and municipality kept the civil administration themselves. General Whitelocke, meantime, was approaching Buenos Ayres (June, 1807), vowing to take it, and to raze it to the ground; but he landed his men twenty miles below the city in a swamp, his force having marched from Montevideo, on the left bank, and forded the river. Draggled, disheartened, weary with their march, and dispirited by the loss of much baggage and some artillery, the English troops reached Buenos Ayres. The inhabitants had had time to prepare for their reception. They fought from the flat roofs of long lines of white houses, and before General Whitelocke was half repulsed he offered to make terms. " Put in that the British must evacuate Montevideo," said the energetic mayor to Liniers, who was drawing up the articles of capitulation. " Impossible ! " replied the soldier, " the English are but half beaten ; we must not provoke them to essay their strength." " Put it in," returned Alzaga ; " it can but be withdrawn." General Whitelocke did not object to the stipulation. He only proposed that in return all prisoners should be given up, and in a short time the English had abandoned both banks of the Rio de La Plata.

For his services on this occasion Liniers was appointed viceroy, but the little notice Spain took of the gallantry of the Creoles was the cause of fresh murmurs and disputes. Liniers, as has been said, was by birth a Frenchman, and although a Spanish viceroy, his sympathies were with his own people ; so dazzled was he by the fame of Napoleon that when the news arrived of his interference in 1808 in the affairs of the Peninsula, and of the appointment of his brother Joseph to be King of Spain, he was disposed to acknowledge the authority of the new sovereign in Buenos Ayres. Alzaga and the native Spaniards adhered to the cause of the Spanish Bourbons, and concerted plans with Elio, governor of the Banda Oriental, who lived at Montevideo. A municipal deputation waited on Liniers, and forced him to sign an abdication, but that night Alzaga and his colleagues found themselves seized and conducted to the seashore. The whole naval force of Buenos Ayres, consisting of one ketch, the " Hydra," mounting four guns, was waiting to receive the prisoners. It was a dark and stormy night, and before they had well got over their sea-sickness, they found themselves landed on the coast of Patagonia without having been permitted to communicate with their families. There they remained until the Governor of Montevideo sent a party to release them. Alzaga

after a time returned to Buenos Ayres, entered into new
intrigues in the cause of Ferdinand, and at last was publicly
executed, after one of those revolutions which before long
became frightfully common in the revolted provinces.

The Supreme Junta at Seville, which, in connection with
the Council for the Indies, attempted in 1809 to administer
the government of the Spanish colonies in the name of the
captive sovereign, angrily displaced Liniers for his energy
on this occasion, and an old Spaniard who had commanded
a line-of-battle-ship at Trafalgar, Cisneros by name, was sent
out as the new Viceroy. He had all the roughness and
none of the *bonhomie* popularly attributed to his profession.
He came out to carry matters with a very high hand, and
to enforce the ancient laws of the Council of the Indies. One
of these, which was always a great grievance in the eyes of
colonial Spaniards, prohibited all commercial intercourse
between Spanish South Americans and foreigners. But during the administration of Liniers, a profitable trade had been
opened with other countries, and Cisneros was implored,
in an eloquent address by Marius Moreno, the wise man of
the province, not to destroy the opening prospects of what
should be eminently a commercial land. Cisneros yielded,
but by yielding lost the support of his own party, and the
Spanish-born faction plotted his downfall.

The first act of a revolution which speedily spread through
every state in Spanish South America took place on New
Year's Day, 1810, when news arrived that the French had
driven the existing Spanish government out of Seville. It
was then politely intimated to Cisneros that, since all the
military in his viceroyalty were against him, there was no
course left him but to resign. He accepted the situation,
and took a humble seat at his own council table ; until
at last, having been detected in a political intrigue, he was,
together with the whole bench of judges, shipped off to the
Canary Isles.

Buenos Ayres then constituted herself a republic with
General Saavedra as her president. Having done so, her
first thought was propagandism. She sent forth an army

to march into all the Spanish provinces that had made part of the former viceroyalty of La Plata, and peremptorily invited them to follow her example. As the invitation included submission to the supremacy of Buenos Ayres, all who were powerful enough to have a public opinion refused to submit to the dictation of a sister province, and two or three of them took up arms against the once vice-regal city.

One of these revolted provinces was then called Upper Peru. It is now called Bolivia, being so named after Bolivar, the Revolutionary President and General in Colombia, to whom it applied for a code of laws, in 1825, when it was formed into a republic.

The general in command of the army of Buenos Ayres marched into Paraguay, preceded by a proclamation in which he compared himself to Hercules, Theseus, and Socrates. This modern combination of Greek heroes did little by force of arms, though Paraguay was persuaded to effect her revolution, which she did, and soon after placed herself under the dictatorship of Dr. Francia.

Among all the wars and revolutions that from 1810 to 1820 succeeded one another in the Spanish South American colonies, we cannot but sigh over the hard fate of Liniers. Pursued by seventy-five men, and a general of the new republic (for a republic Buenos Ayres was, though Ferdinand VII. was its acknowledged head), he was taken prisoner in the mountains, and with six of his officers was summarily shot.

Chili too was up and busy with its revolution, though it took seven or eight years to accomplish it.

The rural population of what had been the viceroyalty of Buenos Ayres was largely composed of cattlemen, called Guachos, who were scattered at wide intervals over the enormous *estancias*, or cattle-farms. The male Guacho had his good points, but was wild and untamable, like the horse that he bestrode. He realized the fable of the Centaurs, save that in the Grecian fable the half-man had pity on the half-horse, while any attachment between man and horse upon the Pampas was seldom or never heard of. Every

Guacho had an intense hatred of the Indians, and an inborn, jealous, inflammable dislike to all the inhabitants of the other South American republics, to which he had not the honor to belong.

The Guacho women (for the Guachos, unlike the cowboys, were by no means bachelors) led more indolent and monotonous lives than Turkish women in a harem. They found no employment even in cookery or needlework, for beef — endless beef — was the sole diet of the country; the children ran naked; the men covered themselves with *ponchos ;* and the Guacho wife (in a country where even a male beggar asked alms on horseback) seldom rode, except to her own wedding. On this occasion the bridegroom, mounting her *en croupe,* set off some few hundred miles to seek the nearest *curé,* and having been joined to her in the bonds of holy matrimony, brought her back in the like fashion to his rude and desolate mud-built home.

In the provincial towns women of a richer class spent their lives in a round of *siestas,* pumpkin-chewing, *cigarrillos,* and *maté,* the substitute for Chinese tea in South America. The men roused themselves to an interest in politics only on the eve of an election, when passions awakened by political excitement were exhibited in all their fierceness and in all their folly.

The political changes that took place in Buenos Ayres from 1810 to 1817 were not more frequent than those in the other provinces. From 1810 to 1817 Buenos Ayres enjoyed peace for four months only. She underwent fourteen revolutions ; the city was twice blockaded, and once bombarded by the Montevideans ; she put down a civic conspiracy and a military insurrection ; four general Congresses were elected, but only two assembled ; she was at war with Chili and Peru ; she was endangered by two Spanish expeditions, and she won a great naval victory over the Montevideans, with the loss of two men killed and one wounded. It is melancholy to add that having annihilated the maritime power of her rival, she had no further use for her own ships, and put her whole navy up at auction, — the " Hydra " ketch, four corvettes, a brig, a cat-boat, and a polacca. By and by a ten years' war broke out between Buenos Ayres and Brazil, which did not cease until England stepped in to settle it in 1828.

Were I to record the names of the various governors and rulers of Buenos Ayres that succeeded one another rapidly, each being deposed, and another elected by some sort of political convulsion, my readers would certainly not care for the information. At one time there was a proposition to form a stable government by electing a king, and Louis Philippe, the ex-Duke of Lucca, and Don Francisco di Paula were the candidates under consideration. The affairs of Buenos Ayres fell in 1829 into the hands of two military chiefs, General Dorego and General Rosas, who trampled all paper constitutions under foot, and by turns made themselves military dictators. When Dorego was murdered (as of course happened at last), Rosas became head of what had been called the Federal party. The original name " Federal " lost its significance. It meant thenceforward the party of Rosas.

It was not, however, till 1835 that Rosas formally accepted supreme power, although he had exercised it for seven years. The main source of his strength lay in his celebrated Masorcha Club. We have all read of the Vehmgericht, that secret tribunal that selected its victims and had them killed mysteriously; "but worse than the doings of any other known secret society," says an English officer, " were those of the Masorcha Club. The Vehmgericht murdered in secret, the Jacobins openly guillotined, the Masorcha tortured and killed."

" It took its name [I am quoting from contemporary documents] from the inward stalk of the maize when deprived of its grain." That is, in plain American, *masorcha* means a " corn-cob." These " cobs " were used as instruments of torture in a way that can hardly be put into words.

When I first wrote an account of Rosas and Buenos Ayres, I had in my hands a collection of documents made by an English naval officer sent by Lord Palmerston to La Plata to report on its affairs. One of these thus computes the loss of life for political reasons in six years, from 1838 to 1843, under the administration of Rosas : "Died by poison, 4 ; by cutting the throat, 3,766 ; by shooting, 1,393 ; by the poniard, 722 ; in battle, 14,920 ; by various persecutions, including executions for attempting to desert, 1,600."

For twenty years Rosas successfully defied any naval or military force that could be brought against him, but in 1852 he and his Guachos were defeated by a body of Schleswig-Holsteiners, brought over to South America by the Republic of Uruguay. Rosas escaped to Europe on an English war vessel, accompanied by his daughter, the charming Manuelita.

All this having taken place after the recognition of the independence of the South American republics by the great European powers, and their separation from their mother country Spain, has, properly speaking, nothing to do with the present narrative. I would say, however, that Rosas, having established his authority over the city and state of Buenos Ayres, endeavored to bring under his dictatorship the other provinces that had formed part of the Buenos Ayrean viceroyalty in the times of the Spanish dominion. He carried on perpetual warfare with what was called the Banda Oriental, now the Republic of Uruguay, whose capital is Montevideo. The French took part in this war. They had been insulted by Rosas, and seem to have been unwilling to allow the English to bring about a peace until they had punished him. In fact, they looked on the Republic of Uruguay as a sort of French colony, and French immigrants began to flock in there. During the years of this contest our own government at Washington was perpetually grumbling at the interference of European powers in transatlantic affairs. In the end Buenos Ayres has succeeded in forming a federation of provinces on her own side of the La Plata, and these Confederated States are now known as the Argentine Republic, — or as Argentina.

I hardly think that after this brief narrative of events in Buenos Ayres a similar account of every one of the other South American States would interest my readers. Each had precisely the same history, — revolt from Spain, civil war, war with neighbors, intervention of foreigners, insurrections, barbarities, assassinations, exilings, new constitutions, dictatorships, and general confusion. Paraguay alone, for thirty years, pursued a different course under the rule of its dictator, Dr. Francia. Of course on this subject I shall be largely indebted to Mr. Carlyle's delightful essay.[1]

Carlyle begins his article with a brief summary of what he calls "the confused South American Revolutions, — a set of subsequent revolutions, which, like the South American Continent itself, is doubtless a great confused phenomenon." And as I ought to make such a summary myself, I am sure my readers will have no reason to object if I prefer following in the picturesque path traced out by Mr. Carlyle : —

"Iturbide," he says, "the Napoleon of Mexico, who was he? He made the thrice celebrated Constitution of Mexico, — the Plan of Iguala, a constitution of no continuance. He became Emperor of Mexico, and reigned seven months, — most serene Augustin I.; was then deposed, banished to Leghorn, to London; decided on returning; landed on the shore at Tampico; was there met and shot. This, in a vague way, is what the world knows of the Napoleon of Mexico, most serene Augustin I., most unfortunate Augustin the last. Oblivion and the deserts of Panama have swallowed this brave Don Augustin.

"And Bolivar, the 'Washington of Colombia'? — Liberator Bolivar, he too is gone without his fame. Melancholy lithographs represent to us a long-faced, square-browed man, — a man, if stern, consciously considerate, a man of hard fighting, hard riding, and manifold achievements; of whom, except that melancholy lithograph, the cultivated European public knows as good as nothing. Yet did he not fly hither and thither, often in the most desperate manner, with wild cavalry clad in blankets, with the cry of War of Liberation to the death?

"With such cavalry, and artillery to match, Bolivar has ridden, fighting all the way, more miles than Ulysses ever sailed. He has marched over the Andes more than once, a feat analogous to Hannibal's. Often beaten, banished from the firm land, he always returned again, truculently fought again. He was Dictator, Liberator, almost Emperor. Three times over did he in solemn Colombian parliament lay down his dicta-

---

[1] It came out in the "Foreign Quarterly Review" in 1842.

torship with Washingtonian eloquence, and as often, on pressing request, take it up again. Thrice — or at least twice — did he painfully construct a Constitution, the reasonablest Democratic Constitution you could well construct, and twice did the people, on trial, find it disagreeable. He was of old well known in Paris; has shone in many a gay Parisian *salon* this Simon Bolivar, — truly a Ulysses whose history were worth its ink, had the Homer who could do it made his appearance.[1]

" Then, too, of General San Martin there is something to be said. Did the reader ever hear of San Martin's march over the Andes into Chili? It is a feat worth looking at, comparable most likely to Hannibal's march over the Alps, when there was yet no Simplon or Mt. Cénis highway, and transacted itself in 1817, when the people of Buenos Ayres, having driven out their own Spaniards and established the reign of freedom, — though in a precarious manner, — thought it were now good to drive the Spaniards out of Chili and establish the reign of freedom there."

An account of this march was written by General Miller,[2] an Englishman who was with the army; and in the Essay on Dr. Francia, his narrative has been graphically abridged by Carlyle : —

" The army of San Martin, descending from the hills, struck the doubly astonished Spaniards with dire misgivings, and com-

---

[1] Bolivar lost the favor of his countrymen. In 1826, indignant at the charges brought against him of treason and ambition, he retired into private life. On September 10, 1827, he was called back to power. He died in 1830, having consolidated the two provinces of Venezuela and New Granada into the Republic of Colombia, and given a Constitution to the other republic called by his name. Bolivar was a native of Caracas, the capital of Venezuela. — E. W. L.

[2] I was a child, who, to my knowledge, had never seen a hero, when I was told that my father had invited such a person to dine. To my horror, however, the hero shook hands with me with his right hand covered with a black kid glove, of which two fingers were empty. On being afterwards justly reproved for having shown my aversion to the mutilated hand, I was told he was a great warrior, whose exploits had been the most remarkable of any man's in the fights that had taken place in Bolivia, Peru, Ecuador, Chili, and the State of Colombia. Tall, stiff, lean, dark, how well I remember him, looking embarrassed and uncomfortable in unaccustomed evening clothes. — E. W. L.

pleted the deliverance of Chili, as it was thought, forever and a day. Alas! the deliverance of Chili was but commenced, — very far from completed. Chili, after many more deliverances up to this hour, is always being delivered from one set of evil-doers to another set."

San Martin next manœuvred to liberate Peru, to unite Peru and Chili, " to become some sort of Washington-Napoleon, but this did not prosper so well. The suspicion of mankind began to arouse itself. Liberator Bolivar had to be called in, and some revolution or two to take place in the interim. Then San Martin saw himself peremptorily, though with courtesy, complimented over the Andes again." And finally, more happy than most dictators, presidents, liberators, and generals in those countries, he settled down in his own whitewashed house in Mendoza, with his own portrait hung up between those of Napoleon and the Duke of Wellington.

" Governing," concludes Mr. Carlyle, "'is a rude business everywhere, but in South America it is of quite primitive rudeness. They have no parliamentary way of changing ministers, as yet nothing but the rude, primitive way of hanging the old ministry on gallows, that the new may be installed. . . . But undoubtedly the notablest of all these South American phenomena is Dr. Francia and his dictatorship in Paraguay. For nearly thirty years Dr. Francia, practitioner of law and doctor of divinity, practically sealed up his little inland state. If any man entered Paraguay, and the doctor did not like his papers, his talk, his conduct, or even the cut of his face, it might be worse for such a person! Also, no one could leave Paraguay on any pretext whatever."

Once he seized on a French naturalist, M. Aimé Bonpland ; and not all diplomacy, backed by Humboldt and the world of science, could for a long period get him back again.

Dr. José Gaspar Rodriguez Francia was the son of a cattle-raiser not far from Asuncion, *the* city (for I think there was but one) of Paraguay. His father is thought to have been an immigrant from France, who, relinquishing his real name, called himself Francia. There were other young Francias in the family, of whom one went mad, and the great doctor himself was subject to fits of melancholia. His friends designed him for the church, and he studied divinity; but the moment he became his own master he exchanged divinity for law. He soon worked his way into practice, and was esteemed a just and true young man.

Francia's private studies at this period were in the books of democrats and those of the encyclopædic philosophers, — Raynal, Volney, Voltaire, Rousseau & Co. In his law practice he was conspicuous for rectitude; in his domestic relations he was unhappy, for he quarrelled with his family, after which he and his father never spoke to each other again. Meantime the French Revolution had run its course, and the provinces of Spanish America had begun to bestir themselves; "the subterranean element," says Carlyle, "shock on shock, shaking and exploding in the new hemisphere, as in the old, from sea to sea."

"The people of Paraguay, lying far inland, with little speculation in their heads, were in no haste to adopt the new Republican gospel. Buenos Ayres, Tucuman, and most of the other La Plata provinces, had made their revolutions, brought in the reign of liberty, and unluckily driven out the reign of law and regularity, before the Paraguenos could resolve on such an enterprise."

But at last an expedition from Buenos Ayres came up the Parana on a mission to propagandize them. The people of Paraguay defeated and dispersed these revolutionists, and it was more than a year before ideas of revolution got well worked into the popular head. Then Francia assumed his place as a leader among his people. "The fruit being drop ripe," continues Carlyle, "at the first shake fell."

A National Congress, a President, two Vice-Presidents, and Dr. Francia as Secretary, formed the powers of government. But it was not long before every public matter was in such wild confusion that the one man who might have set things right grew disgusted and withdrew. Here is a picture of him as he lived in retirement during this interval.

It is from the pen of Mr. Robertson, a Scotch trader. The time is the year 1812. Robertson was out shooting one fine day: —

"Suddenly I came upon a neat and unpretending little cottage. Up rose a partridge. I fired, and the bird came to the ground. A voice behind me called, *Buen tiro* — a good shot. I turned round and beheld a gentleman about sixty years of age, dressed in a suit of black, with a large scarlet *capote*, or cloak, thrown over his shoulders. He had a cup of *maté* in one hand, a cigar in the other; and a little urchin of a negro, with his arms crossed, was in attendance by the gentleman's side. The gentleman's countenance was dark, and his black eyes very penetrating, while his jet-black hair, combed back from a bold forehead, and hanging in natural ringlets over his shoulders, gave him a dignified and striking air. He wore in his shoes large golden buckles, and at the knees of his breeches the same."

This gentleman was Dr. Francia, who, with primitive hospitality, invited the stranger to his house, where his *sanctum* was found strewn with his papers, his gloves, his mathematical instruments, French and Latin books, Euclid, and treatises on algebra.

The year 1812 was productive of all kinds of disorders in the home department of the new Paraguayan government, while without it was threatened by ambitious Buenos Ayreans. Something had to be done. The old Congress was dissolved, and a new one was elected, which named two Consuls, — one of them Dr. Francia. In 1814 a third Congress made Dr. Francia Dictator.

Francia's experience of Congresses had not prejudiced him in their favor; he never called another to help him to govern Paraguay.

"With Francia's entry on the government, a great improvement in all quarters began to show itself. The finances were regulated; every official person in Paraguay had to bethink himself and begin doing his work, instead of merely seeming to do it. The soldiers were paid and drilled, and effectual military protection was afforded against the Indians."

The land had peace. Elsewhere South America was in a blaze. Francia broke off all intercommunication with other revolutionary governments. By degrees what he called "a sanitary line" — a rigorous line of demarcation — was drawn round Paraguay. No intercourse, no importing, no exporting, except by the doctor's especial permission, was allowed. "Paraguay stood isolated; a rabid dog-kennel raging round it, wide as all South America, but kept out, as by lock and key."

But in 1819, the second year of the dictatorship of Francia, came rumors of plots, — even dangerous plots. A paper fell into Francia's hands revealing a plan which had been hatching two years, for massacring himself and his chief adherents, and changing the policy of the country. Francia allowed the insurrection to break out, then pounced on it with fury, and tore it and the makers of it to shreds. It was the only plot hatched in his dictatorship.

The period of the suppression of this plot is called Dr. Francia's Reign of Terror. However, only forty persons were executed for it; how few in comparison with all the murders, executions, and massacres I have told of elsewhere!

In the midst of this political Reign of Terror came an agricultural Reign of Terror, a visitation of locusts in 1820, which ate up every green herb. Francia came to the rescue, and obliged the farmers, under penalty of punishment, to sow late crops. The farmers obeyed, though without hope; but they reaped an average crop before winter set in. The doctor's idea was that agriculture, and not foreign trade, was the road to prosperity in Paraguay, where the land is fertile, and, in his time, the inhabitants only two to the square mile; but besides the attention he gave to agriculture he took care to encourage other things. He introduced schools, and justice, sure and swift, into his dominions. He put down highway robbery. He improved the streets of Asuncion, straightening them by his own work with the theodolite; "above all, he expected every man to do his duty, and he himself spent laborious days to see that it was done."

Dr. Francia never married. Probably he had in early life

taken ecclesiastical vows. He prescribed no religion for Paraguay; all forms of Christianity were tolerated; but he said he would have no atheists among his people. He led a regular and lonely life, taking constant precautions against assassination. His five servants were mulattoes, and were strongly attached to him. His sister at one time tried to live with him, but he seems not to have been satisfied with her society.

He was delighted when he could get an opportunity to converse with cultivated Europeans; and at one time he tried to open a trade with England. Napoleon he greatly admired, and a touching anecdote is told by a German traveller, who showed him a small engraving of Napoleon, with which he was greatly delighted. Thinking to please him, the German would have left it with him as a remembrance; but, as he refused to take pay for it, Dr. Francia had it returned to him beyond the frontier. For thirty years he was himself the sole government of Paraguay. He died Sept. 20, 1840, the people crowding round the Government House in tears.

He was succeeded in his dictatorship by three dictators at once; the most notable of whom was a man named Lopez, who governed the country for six or seven years, and left his power to Francisco Solano Lopez, his son. This young man, who had been educated in Paris, seems to have been smitten with a desire to imitate the Third Napoleon. He made his own *coup d'état*, and became sole dictator. Then he provoked a war with his neighbors, Brazil and Buenos Ayres.

"Never," says a writer in Macmillan's Magazine, — "never was a ruler, a chief, better served by his subjects than Francisco Solano Lopez, and never did any one less deserve, personally, such devotion and fidelity. . . . For him Paraguay lavished without a murmur three-fourths of her life-blood, saw her towns destroyed, her villages wasted, her wealth plundered to absolute bareness, nor even then submitted, only ceased to strive. Lopez was chased into the mountains of Brazil. There, hemmed in and at bay, he turned on his pursuers, and fighting to the last, died, with his eldest son, Panchito, at his side, more nobly than he had lived. Hardly any of his followers were made prisoners ; nearly all died with their chief. A few, however, escaped to neighboring wild tribes of Indians."

Paraguay was for a short time united to Brazil, but that connection has ceased, and she is now a republic enjoying peace. "She is," says a recent writer, " one of the most flourishing states of South America, and has reduced her army to five hundred men." She has also a railway one hundred and fifty-five miles long, in the hands of an English Company.

As soon as the Republic of Colombia secured her independence, she issued letters of marque to privateers, ostensibly to prey on Spanish commerce in the Caribbean Sea. The "privateers" were in most instances pirates, who made no distinction in their captures, and gave the United States navy great trouble for many years. After passing through several revolutions, changes, and civil wars, Colombia is now at peace under a constitution of eleven years' standing. Venezuela broke off from her in the year 1833, and has since been another independent republic.

Before entering on an account of the war of independence in Chili, which in its main features is a duplicate of all the rest, let me relate one of the saddest stories in modern history, — that of the champion of Chili, Thomas, Lord Cochrane, afterwards Earl of Dundonald.[1]

He was the eldest son of a very scientific, eccentric, impecunious old nobleman, descended from that Cochrane, the favorite of James III., who, because he loved house-decoration, castle-building, and the refinements of life, was so vehemently hated by the Scottish barons that he was hanged by them with a silken cord.

---

[1] My father held him in esteem as the Bayard of modern England. We had at one time his portrait, tall, manly, and in full naval uniform, on which my father loved to gaze. They were sympathetic in politics, and in some points sympathetic in temperament. Lord Cochrane was the older officer by some years, having done brilliant deeds in the Mediterranean as captain of the " Impérieuse " before my father was old enough to be made a commander. — E. W. L.

Thomas, Lord Cochrane, went into the navy when he was eighteen, an unusually late age in those days, when midshipmen began their sea life at twelve or thirteen. Wherever he was employed, he distinguished himself by almost reckless bravery. He took an immense Spanish vessel when in command of a little sloop, the "Speedy;" and Lord Gambier's great success in the Basque Roads, where he cut out the French fleet, was due mainly to Lord Cochrane's skilful handling of some fire-ships which he had invented. But brilliant and successful as he was, he was a thorn in the side of the English Admiralty.

He was too vehement and irrepressible to find favor with his superiors, and was as eager to attack his enemies in his profession or in politics as if they had been Spaniards or Frenchmen. Finding his claims not recognized as fully as he hoped after his distinguished services, he obtained a seat in Parliament, where he worried the ministers by his cries for Reform. An enthusiastic young nobleman who could command the sympathies of all naval and military men, who had wrongs of his own to press on Parliament, and wrongs of the people, could not but be terrible in the eyes of Lord Castlereagh and his government. Notwithstanding his brilliant services, the Admiralty kept him unemployed from 1809 to 1813, in which year his uncle, Sir Alexander Cochrane, having been appointed to the command of the British squadron on the North American station, offered him the post of his flag captain. This offer Lord Cochrane accepted joyfully, and was busy with preparations for the cruise, when on Feb. 21, 1814, came the fatal day in his history. At that date Napoleon was making his last struggle against the allied armies. His cause was tottering; any great success on his part, or on that of the allies, would bear or bull the stock market.

About one o'clock in the morning a man came to the door of the Ship Inn at Dover, shouting loudly for admittance. Men landed in those days upon the coast from France, from open boats, and in some such way this man had presumably reached Dover. He was rather foreign to look at, but he

*THOMAS COCHRANE, EARL OF DUNDONALD.*

wore the English scarlet uniform, and was brimming over with good news, which of course it was his business to communicate first to the War Office. He said, however, this much, that he was an *aide-de-camp* of Lord Cathcart. He let out, too, that his news concerned the discomfiture of Bonaparte, and that the war was as good as ended. In those days if a government messenger, or an *aide-de-camp*, brought good news, he hung his post-chaise with wreaths and flags, and waved his hat as he passed people on the road, and cheered lustily.

By the middle of the next day three persons, one of them this traveller, whose name was Du Bourg, crossed London Bridge in a post-chaise, waving and cheering. Stocks rose with a bound; the city was in wild commotion, — but no further news came. By night it had been ascertained at the Horse Guards that there was no Colonel du Bourg in the British army, that the news was a fraud, — a hoax set on foot by speculators to make the stocks rise.

I must here mention that Lord Cochrane had another uncle who was a partner in a London banking house, and who, when he engaged in business, had changed his name to Johnstone. He was a very canny Scot, not scrupulous in a bargain, and to his nephew he had recommended a Mr. Berrenger to go with him to North America as his private secretary. This man, he said, would help him in some rocket experiments he was desirous of making, and would superintend the rifle drill of the ship's company. Now, Du Bourg and Berrenger were the same.

About noon, on February 22, Lord Cochrane, who was at a lamp factory (he had invented a new street lamp, and was trying to apply the principle of it to lanterns at sea), received a note so badly written that he said afterwards he could not make out the signature. The servant, however, told him that the gentleman who gave it him was in uniform, and had asked for an immediate interview that he might communicate to his lordship "some affecting news." Dreading that this might be the death of his brother, who was serving in the Peninsula, Lord Cochrane hastened home, and was relieved when he found that his visitor was Berrenger.

Berrenger said that he had come to ask if his lordship could receive him secretly on board his ship, as the Admiralty had refused him the place of private secretary, on the ground of his being a foreigner. Lord Cochrane said he could not do this, but advised him to see some persons of influence on the subject. " I cannot go in these clothes," said Berrenger. He was wearing a sort of fancy uniform, — green with a gray overcoat. He asked Lord Cochrane to lend him a hat. This Lord Cochrane did, and then, noticing that his green coat showed under his overcoat, he picked up an old black coat lying on a chair, and offered it to him. Berrenger, or Du Bourg, as we will now again call him, put it on, wrapped his green coat in a towel, and went away, carrying a small portmanteau, " in which," said Lord Cochrane afterwards, " he doubtless concealed the red uniform he had displayed at Dover."

Unhappily, that very morning, owing to the supposed good news from the seat of war, Lord Cochrane's broker had sold out for him £4000 in stocks, which some weeks before he had been ordered to sell as soon as there was a rise.

Du Bourg, on reaching the environs of London, had stepped out of his post-chaise into a hackney-coach and driven straight to Lord Cochrane's door. The coachman was found, and, being a bad man who expected a large reward for the conviction of so distinguished a criminal, swore that when Du Bourg entered Lord Cochrane's house he wore a red, not a green uniform. This man had been in prison before for cruelty to his horses, and was afterwards transported for robbery. His evidence about the red coat was the only thing that connected his lordship directly with the transaction.

As soon as Lord Cochrane joined his ship, and there learned that the mysterious Du Bourg was Berrenger, and that he had been traced to his house, he hastened back to London, and at once published a full and frank account of their interview.

But government was determined this time to be avenged

on him. It was believed, and no doubt truly, that Du Bourg
had been employed by Cochrane Johnstone.

Cochrane Johnstone and Lord Cochrane were tried together for fraud and conspiracy. They were not allowed to
separate their cases. Cochrane Johnstone's guilt was clear,
but the only evidence against Lord Cochrane was disproved
by showing that Du Bourg had with him a green coat, which
he must have put on in the hackney-coach or the post-
chaise, and hidden the red one.

Lord Cochrane was found guilty. His uncle escaped by
flight. Lord Cochrane was sentenced to pay a fine of
£1000 ($5000), to be imprisoned for twelve months, and
to stand in the pillory one hour. But his constituents at
Westminster were loud in their expressions of perfect confidence in his honor. Sir Francis Burdett, his colleague, said
that if Lord Cochrane were placed in the pillory, he would
stand beside him, and government remitted that part of the
punishment, fearing to provoke a riot in Westminster. But
he was expelled from the House of Commons, his name was
struck from the Navy List, and from the roll of Knights
Commander of the Bath, his banner was taken down from
its place in Henry VII.'s Chapel, and officially, and *literally*,
*kicked* out of Westminster Abbey.

When his twelve months' imprisonment expired, Lord
Cochrane refused to pay his fine. He paid it at last, however, in a £1000 note, now preserved in the Bank of England, on which he wrote : " My health having suffered from
long and close confinement, and my oppressors being resolved to deprive me of property or life, I submit to robbery
to protect myself from murder, in the hope that I shall live
to bring the delinquents to justice."

It was after this that, suffering as only such a high-minded
and brave man could do under unmerited disgrace, Lord
Cochrane took service in the Chilian navy. It was 1818 ;
Chili had begun her revolt from Spain in 1810. San Martin
had made his famous march over the Andes to her assistance, and had afterwards been sent back again. The hero
of Chili was a native Chilian of Irish descent, Don Bernado

O'Higgins. Probably the greatest blessing O'Higgins conferred on Chili was his marvellous improvement of her mountain roads.

I need not trace the course of the Chilian revolution; it resembled all the rest, except in this, — the Spaniards who still bore rule in Peru, and possessed the splendid ports of Callao and Valdivia, had a formidable naval force, which brought supplies to their troops wherever needed. With this they blockaded the coast of Chili and bombarded Chilian towns.

In this emergency an agent was sent to London to secure if possible the services of Lord Cochrane as Chief Admiral of the Chilian Republic. The agent was also to procure a war steamer. Lord Cochrane accepted the proposal. It opened professional employment to him, and gave him hopes of again distinguishing himself in the world's eyes; it also gave him once more a professional income, for the loss of his pay and the expenses of his lawsuit had almost ruined him.

He embarked for Santiago in 1818, taking with him Lady Cochrane and his children.[1] When he reached Chili he found the Spaniards preparing to invest Santiago, having swept the seas with their fleet, and they were at the same time organizing an attack on Valparaiso. The patriotism of the Chilian admiral who had just captured a Spanish fifty-gun frigate, and who, in all the flush of his success, declared that he could know no greater honor than to serve under such a commander as Lord Cochrane, prevented any difficulties as to the command of the fleet.

Lord Cochrane's squadron consisted of seven ships, three carrying fifty guns, while the other four were very small vessels. The Spanish fleet was just double that number.

---

[1] The most celebrated of Gretna Green marriages was Lord Cochrane's. The engraving we see sometimes in shop windows of two carriages and four, the one pursuing the other, the gentleman in the foremost carriage standing up and shooting one of the leaders in the carriage that has almost come up with him, is Lord Cochrane. He was proud of that exploit till the day he died.

Though Peru was the last stronghold of Spanish power in South America, and up to 1821 had not achieved its independence, it contained plenty of sympathizers with the patriotic movement in Chili; and Chili's best policy seemed to be to carry the war into Peru, and make it safe for her people to join the liberators. Three expeditions were made by Lord Cochrane against the Spaniards. In the first he failed to take Callao; in the second he stormed Valdivia; in the third Lima was taken, and the Spanish fleet was so broken that it never again appeared upon those shores.

General Miller was Lord Cochrane's military chief aid in these expeditions; but the last one was accompanied by a land force under General San Martin, who had no sooner taken possession of Lima than he turned traitor to Chili, and proclaimed himself Protector (that is, Dictator) of Peru. He also refused the pay and the gratuities that had been promised to the men and officers of the Chilian fleet. After spirited and repeated remonstrances Lord Cochrane helped himself to a large amount of treasure which San Martin had captured from the Peruvian stores. With it he paid his men and officers, but took not a farthing for himself. All that remained over when the fleet was paid, he put into naval repairs. "Years of reflection," he wrote forty years afterwards, "have convinced me that if I were in the same circumstances I should pursue the same course over again."

During the three years he served Chili he destroyed the Spanish fleet, made independence possible along the western coast of South America, and it now remained for the people to show if they had virtue and patriotism enough to rise as the United States had done after their revolution.

Lord Cochrane for a while went into retirement; but the miseries of his poor comrades in the fleet, left unpaid, unclothed, and unprovisioned, drew him back into controversy with the Chilian Government.

San Martin, having run his course of petty tyranny in Peru, was obliged to resign his protectorate, and seek refuge in Chili. Chili chose to treat him as her hero. Lord Cochrane considered him a traitor. San Martin was pitted against

O'Higgins. Cochrane hated the one, and admired the other. Finding that the fickle public sided with San Martin, he sent in his resignation. "As to the sums owing to me," he said, " I forbear to press for their payment until government shall be freed from its difficulties."

Before that time he had received invitations to enter into the service of Brazil, Mexico, Spain, and Greece. Mexico and Spain he declined, but Brazil he accepted. Peru, sadly abused by San Martin, and almost won back to Spain, was rescued by the valor and wisdom of Bolivar; while Chili, destined to much future trouble, was temporarily rescued by a new revolution in favor of General Friere, a better man than San Martin.

In March, 1823, Lord Cochrane reached Rio, and was made Admiral-in-Chief of the Brazilian Navy. The Emperor he found loyal and true, but those under him little better than the officials he had left in Chili; and he subsequently bitterly repented having taken command of the Brazilian fleet. Success, however, attended him in all his undertakings, and the Emperor was not slow to recognize the value of his services. But it did not take long to set him at loggerheads with the officials of the government. It was the old story of pay withheld from the navy, and Lord Cochrane championed the rights of his men and officers. He partially succeeded this [time in having justice done them, and then threw up the service of Brazil, and returned to England. All Europe rang with his achievements. In the House of Commons Sir James Mackintosh asked, "if a greater display of judgment, calmness, and British valor was ever shown?" and ended by heartily wishing "such advice might be given to his Majesty's councillors as would induce them to restore Lord Cochrane to the country which he so warmly loves, and to that noble service to the glory of which I am convinced he would willingly sacrifice any earthly consideration."

But, no doubt, across Lord Cochrane's name in the Black Book, said to be kept at the Admiralty, had been written, " Impracticable, Troublesome."

In 1825 he went to Greece, but the war was nearly over,

and though he threw himself into the cause with his usual gallantry, Kanaris, Miaulis, Frank Hastings, and Sir Edward Codrington share with him the naval glories of that war.

Lord Cochrane lived to 1860. He became Earl of Dundonald on his father's death, and at the age of eighty wrote his charming " Autobiography of a Seaman." In it of course he blazed down on his political and professional enemies with the fire-ships of his " wrathful indignation."

" Meantime, slowly but surely has justice to Lord Dundonald been accomplished. In the first place, the £1,000 he paid as a fine before he was released from prison, and part of his legal expenses, was restored to him by a penny subscription raised throughout Great Britain, and two million six hundred and forty thousand people gave this practical proof of belief in his innocence. When William IV. came to the throne, one of the early acts of his reign was to reinstate Lord Dundonald in the navy. No sentence can be reversed. Theoretically justice cannot err, so he was given a 'free pardon,' and the naval rank he would have attained had he remained in the navy; namely, that of rear-admiral.

" Three lord chancellors and a chief baron have pronounced their opinion on his case, all of whom had been present at his trial. Lord Erskine, in 1835, spoke of the injustice and oppression he had suffered; Lord Brougham deplored ' that cruel and unjustifiable sentence,' which had brought him so much suffering. Lord Campbell, in his Lives of the Chancellors, thinks that the case of Lord Cochrane weighed heavily on the conscience of Lord Ellenborough (the judge who tried him), and that it hastened his end. The chief baron regretted ' that his country could not blot out from her history that dark page.' "

In 1847 the Queen restored Lord Cochrane his knighthood in the Order of the Bath in the most gracious manner. At the time of his disgrace he had been K.C.B. (Knight Commander of the Bath). Her Majesty gave him the Grand Cross of the Order. He was appointed commander-in-chief on the North American station, to which, in 1814, he was to have sailed as flag captain; and his banner, that had been kicked with contumely from Westminster Abbey, was replaced with ceremonious honor.

A few words remain to be said of the battle of Ayacucho

and the formal recognition by England of the independence of the principal states of South America.

In 1822 a large force had been sent out to Peru from Spain, under General Morillo; and on December 9, 1824, was fought at Ayacucho a battle which was considered by Spaniards the most disastrous defeat experienced by modern Spain. The Revolutionary or Colombian forces were under the command of General Sucre, with General Miller and other generals under him. The Spaniards were commanded by La Serna, who had been appointed Viceroy of Lima. The battle resulted in the total defeat of the Spaniards. La Serna was taken prisoner, with the loss of eighteen hundred men in killed and wounded. The rest of his army surrendered. The news of this splendid victory filled all South America with rejoicings, as it effectually accomplished the deliverance of Peru from Spanish rule. In Spain it was considered a disgrace as well as a disaster.

In January, 1825, Mr. Canning made a formal communication to the foreign ambassadors in London that his government had come to the determination to appoint *chargés d'affaires* to the Republics of Colombia, Mexico, and Buenos Ayres; and in the King's speech on February 3, it was declared "that in conformity with the declarations that have been repeatedly made, measures have been taken to confirm by treaties the commercial relations already existing between Great Britain and those countries of South America which appear to have established their separation from Spain."

This announcement was received with loud cheers from both sides of the House of Commons; and coming, as this official announcement did, at a time when the minds of men were strongly excited on the subject, and the spirit of speculation was more than usually awake, operated with magical effect on the classes which had money.

"There was no end to the projects set on foot to work out the inexhaustible riches of South America, and for a time there seemed equally no limit to the profits realized by the fortunate shareholders. The gain made in the shares of some of the South American companies, in a few months at this period, exceeded fifteen hundred per cent. These extravagant profits spread a sort of madness through England. It seized upon the most sober and retired members of society, pervaded all ranks, swept away all intellects, and in the end ruined not a few fortunes. Joint stock companies were set up in every direction and for all imaginable undertakings. There was nothing so absurd as not to be set on foot; scarce anything so unfortunate as not for a few days or weeks to realize large profits to the original shareholders. When *they* had got their shares off their hands, and landed them in those of the ignorant, — the widow and the orphan, — they were indifferent how soon their schemes went to the ground. The country bankers, trusting to the unbounded supplies of specie expected from South America under English management, poured forth their issues without end, and their notes were universally received amidst the general prosperity and sanguine spirit of the times. In the beginning of 1825 there were two hundred and seventy-six joint stock companies in existence in Great Britain, the subscribed capital of which was no less than £174,000,000 sterling. . . . But South America, which it had been expected was to prove an inexhaustible source of mineral wealth, turned out quite the reverse. It became the greatest drain on the metallic resources of England that had ever been experienced. An immense export of gold took place to South America; little or no gold came back in return. During the political convulsions which had deluged that country with blood for fourteen years, the whole capital of the Spanish colonies had been destroyed ; the mines, unworked, had in a great part come to be filled with water ; and the supply of specie which for ten years back had been obtained for the use of the world, had been almost all picked up from the refuse thrown out of the mines in former days, or the gold and silver plate and ornaments, which the necessities of the former proprietors and capitalists who worked them had compelled them to melt down and bring into the market. The new mines set on foot by the English companies during the mania of 1825 could be worked only with English capital. Hence the drain on the Bank of England, the monetary crisis, the general distress which soon overtook Great Britain, and through her brought disaster and distress upon the rest of the world."

Thus spoke Sir Archibald Alison. Since the Spanish South American colonies achieved their independence, they have ceased to be an important gold-producing portion of the world.

# CHAPTER X.

## CARLISTS AND CHRISTINOS.

ON King Ferdinand's death the revolutionary fires which since 1820 had smouldered throughout Spain, especially in the northern provinces and Catalonia, burst into a flame. The Spaniards had always evinced a scrupulous respect for ancient forms, and made strong opposition to any change in their existing institutions. They rebelled when they were told by the party who modelled their Constitution on that of the French Constituent Assembly that they must have nothing that did not bear a modern stamp. The alterations in their government that the liberals of France and England proposed to force Spaniards to accept were premature. They were no more adapted to the feelings and the wants of the state of society required to receive them than the fancy cottage of Nurse Eleanor, in Miss Edgeworth's "Ennui," to the wants and habits of an Irish peasant woman. Besides, the people of Spain resented foreign influence, and had never been free from it since the dawn of the nineteenth century. France and England by the Quadruple Treaty signed April 22, 1834, bound themselves in concert with the existing rulers of Spain and Portugal to settle the affairs of the Portuguese and Spanish peoples according to their own ideas of what would best promote their prosperity.

We must remember, too, as Mr. Walton tells us, "that for centuries Spain had been a family of confederated kingdoms, several of which had a language of their own, each one was opposed to the others by political prejudices, most of them were independent within their own separate spheres, and yet revolving round a central authority held by the sovereign."

By the close of 1833, the date of Ferdinand's death, this Spain of the past had been shattered to pieces.

The Queen had taken care during her regency that not a single "royalist" at the time of her husband's death should hold any office in the country, either civil or military. All "royalists" who had held such offices were displaced, degraded, closely watched, and stripped, as far as possible, of influence and power. Don Carlos, an exile in Portugal, had received his brother's commands to embark with his family on board a Spanish ship-of-war, and seek an asylum in the Pontifical states. This order, to the consternation and regret of his partisans, he was preparing to obey, when prevented by the capture of Lisbon by Dom Pedro's forces. This was one of the phases in the civil war raging at that time in Portugal.

Queen Christina, as soon as her husband was dead, summoned round her all the ministers, generals, and other high dignitaries whom she herself had appointed. They sat in council till a late hour of the night, apprehending a royalist rising in the capital, but there was no "royalist" leader at hand to direct the movement.

After four days, when the crisis seemed passed, Christina relaxed her watchfulness, but ordered troops to surround Madrid, and issued a manifesto, in which she promised to leave untouched the fundamental laws of the State, and to oppose all dangerous innovations. "She made, indeed, a bid for popularity by affecting to surpass Don Carlos himself in royalist sentiments. This manifesto, which did not allay the fears of the royalists, exasperated the liberals, and made the prime minister, Señor Zea Bermudez, distrusted and unpopular." He was a statesman who had passed many years out of Spain, knew very little of Spanish feeling, and was endeavoring (to use the language of American politics) to sit upon the fence, and balance himself between conservatism and liberalism.

When Don Carlos had received in April an order from

the King that he should join in recognizing the Infanta Isabella, as Princess of the Asturias, and heiress to the Spanish throne, he wrote the following letter : —

DEAREST BROTHER, — This morning at ten o'clock my secretary came to inform me that Cordova, your envoy, desired to know at what hour it would suit me to receive the communication of a royal order. I sent to say that twelve would be a convenient hour. He came a few minutes before one, and I immediately received him. He gave me the official document, which I read; after which I told him that my dignity and character allowed me only to answer in a direct manner, that you were my king and lord, and moreover my brother, — a brother well beloved whom I had attended in adversity. You desire to know whether I intend to take the oath of fidelity to your daughter as Princess of the Asturias. I need not tell you how much I should wish to take that oath; you know me, and can judge that I speak from my heart. Nothing would be more agreeable to me than to be the first to recognize your daughter, and to save you all the trouble and embarrassment my refusal must occasion, but my conscience and my honor forbid it. The rights I possess are so sacred that I cannot put them aside, — rights which I derived from God, when He caused me to be born in my present station, and of which He only can dispossess me by giving you a son, an event which I desire perhaps more than yourself. Besides, it is my duty to defend the rights of those who may come after me, and therefore I think myself bound to transmit the accompanying Declaration, which I address to you in the most solemn manner, — to you, and to all the sovereigns to whom I hope you will communicate it. Adieu, my dear brother, doubt not that I shall be ever devoted to you, and that your happiness shall ever be the object of your brother

CARLOS.

DECLARATION.

I, Carlos Maria Isidore de Borbon-y-Borbon, Infant of Spain, fully convinced of my legitimate rights to the crown of Spain, if I survive your Majesty, you having no male issue, do declare that my conscience and my honor forbid my acknowledging any rights but my own. To our King, from his affectionate brother and faithful vassal

(Signed) The Infant DON CARLOS DE BORBON-Y-BORBON.

PALACE OF RAMALHAO, April 29, 1833.

DON CARLOS, COUNT DE MOLINA.

It was in the same spirit, and almost in the same words, that Don Carlos again received Cordova, when on October 4 of the same year he brought him the official news of King Ferdinand's death, together with an order from the Queen Regent, addressed as to a subject, to leave Portugal at once for Rome.

The partisans of Don Carlos (now calling himself Charles V.[1]) had been wholly unprepared for the news of King Ferdinand's death. Their prince had steadily refused to sanction any preparations for the event which partook of the nature of conspiracy. So long as the King his brother lived, he was too royalist to be disloyal.

The northern provinces of Spain, as soon as they heard of the King's death, rose *en masse* against the Queen's troops, and proclaimed King Charles. Guipuscoa and the soldiers stationed there at once did likewise; Navarre the same. All over Spain, in short, in Granada, La Mancha, Andalusia, and Valencia, as well as in the north and east, there were risings, but the local leaders had no one to direct them; their men were without discipline, unarmed crowds, who brought to the cause for which they would cheerfully have made any sacrifice only their bare hands and their enthusiasm. Local leaders, mounting their steeds, placed themselves at the head of small knots of their followers, who in many places melted away for want of arms. In others they swelled into imposing bands, " which, after all, were but armed mobs, a body without a soul, every one commanding, no one obeying, till they were dispersed by the government troops almost without an effort."

Since Don Carlos was in Portugal near the Spanish frontier when he received the news of his brother's death on October 4, 1833, it seems inconceivable why he did not, by some stratagem, or in some disguise, get back to Spain, and put himself at the head of the bands of insurgents who had proclaimed him in the northern provinces. He possibly

---

[1] To avoid confusion, it may be well to say that the Emperor Charles V. (King of Spain from 1516 to 1555) was Charles I. of Spain, and fifth Emperor of that name in Germany.

believed that the strength of his cause lay in clinging to that
of his nephew, Dom Miguel, then in arms as the legitimate
and Absolutist candidate for the throne of Portugal, in opposition to the claims of Doña Maria da Gloria, supported
by her father, Dom Pedro. At all events, Don Carlos did
little but write letters and protests to foreign courts, and
despatch assurances to his supporters that he would soon
be in the midst of them.

As we read the memoir of his faithful and energetic
adherent, the Baron de Los Valles, a Frenchman in his service, and see how *he* contrived to cross and recross from
Portugal to Spain, from Spain to England, and thence back
to the northern provinces of the Peninsula, though he was
condemned to death by the Christinos and a price set upon
his head, we are surprised that no such enterprise was
attempted by Don Carlos, who, hunted, "like a partridge on
the mountains," from place to place along the Spanish
frontier, by the troops of the Spanish general, Rodil, an old
Republican who had given in his adherence to what he
believed to be the Constitutional party, seems to have made
little effort to put himself at the head of his friends.

The accounts published of the many hair-breadth escapes
of Don Carlos and his family in Portugal from October, 1833,
to June, 1834, read like incidents in one of Stanley Weyman's
thrilling novels. With great difficulty the Baron de Los Valles
obtained permission (when the affairs of Dom Miguel grew
desperate) to open negotiations with the English Admiral
Parker, then blockading the coast, with the object of pro-
curing vessels from his fleet, to carry the fugitives to England. Protection and transport were at once offered to
Don Carlos and his family. The baggage of the royal party
had been captured by Rodil, the servants in charge of it,
twenty-three in number, had been murdered, and their masters were reduced to extreme poverty. The Infanta Maria
Francesca, Don Carlos' queen, and her sister, the Princess
of Beira, sold their jewels to help their adherents, but could
obtain only one hundred thousand francs for what was
twenty times more valuable. "I have literally nothing left

but the clothes I have on," said Maria Francesca to Los Valles; and it is said that one night during their wanderings, when the children in the royal party cried for their supper, they were suffered to go out and ask the guards who were their escort, for some fragments of bread from their rations. But, alas! the soldiers, hungry as themselves, had eaten all before the request reached them.

The cause of Dom Miguel was lost when he capitulated at Evora, stipulating that he would renounce his claim to the throne of Portugal, and never return to that country. He embarked on board the "Stag," an English ship-of-war, for Genoa, where, be it said, he repudiated the engagement he had made at Evora, but he subsequently lived quietly in extreme poverty in Rome and Baden.

The separation of the two royal families of Spain and Portugal, and of Don Carlos from Dom Miguel, took place on May 30, 1834, in the gray of the morning. It was heart-rending in the extreme. The party of Don Carlos was followed by a crowd of Spanish officers, some on foot and some on horseback, for they would not abandon their king while in the power of his enemies. He was also attended by Colonel Wylde, an Englishman charged to protect him by the English ambassador. But for Colonel Wylde the troops of Dom Pedro would have massacred the Spanish officers.

The next morning, June 1, Don Carlos and his family, with many tears, took leave of those faithful friends whom they were forced to abandon, and embarking on board H. M. S. "Donegal," with royal salutes from the French and English squadrons, they commenced a rough voyage of twelve days, when the ship dropped anchor off Spithead; but they did not land till June 18, Lord Palmerston not having made arrangements for their disembarkation. An under secretary of state was sent, however, with a letter from the English minister, proposing that Don Carlos should renounce his right to the Spanish crown, in consideration of which a large sum of money should be paid him by the Spanish Government, which, with handsome pensions to his family, should be guaranteed by England. It is needless to say that Don Carlos rejected these terms.

On leaving the "Donegal" the Infante addressed the captain and officers in these words : —

"Gentlemen: I cannot take leave of you without expressing how sincerely I congratulate myself on being favored with an opportunity of appreciating the merit of English naval officers; they are deserving of the reputation they enjoy throughout Europe. Never can I forget the attention and solicitude you have evinced toward me and my family. Have the goodness to accept my thanks, and to believe that my only cause of regret is the shortness of my stay among you."

The Prince had resolved to preserve a strict incognito during his stay in England, and called himself the Duke of Elizondo, in recognition of the town of that name in which his kingdom of Navarre had assembled a Provisional Junta.

Soon after, a vessel arrived at Hamburg, bringing one hundred and fifty officers of the suite of Don Carlos from Spain. Eighteen of these had been severely wounded by Pedronite soldiers, who broke in upon them when they were asleep, and stabbed and hacked at them. Admiral Parker was indignant at this outrage. He was requested by the ministers of Dom Pedro not to report the circumstance to his government, but he replied that silence with regard to such a crime would make him an accomplice.

Leaving the Duke of Elizondo and his party in safety, we will return to the northern provinces of Spain, and in order to understand the nature of the conflict, a brief description of the country may be valuable. I extract my information from a book by Captain C. F. Henningsen, published in 1836, in London, and entitled " A History of Twelve Months' Campaign with Zumalacarregui."

"Navarre is situated between the Pyrenees on the north, Aragon on the east, the Basque Provinces on the west, and the Ebro and Castile on the south. Its population is computed at two hundred and eighty thousand. From the northernmost extremity, where the famous pass of Roncesvalles leads into France, to the large and fertile plains in the vicinity of the Ebro, called the Riviera, it is but one succession of mountains, where the stranger is lost and confused in the labyrinth of long and narrow valleys, deep glens, and wild and gigantic rocks. In the northern part, adjoining the Pyrenees, the hills are higher and bolder than in the southern districts, but there is no part where cavalry can march a whole day without dismounting. In some parts the mountains are girt at their base by forests of chestnut trees, or the Spanish oak called *encina*, whose acorn, roasted, is as palatable as the chestnut; higher up they are clothed with brushwood, or mere heath or furze, and their summits exhibit in all its nakedness the gray or black stone of which, lower down, huge and fantastic masses show themselves. . . . A singular feature of every peasant's house, however mean, is the arms rudely sculptured over the doorway. The furniture is rude and simple; but in some houses a few chests inlaid with ebony and ivory, and of antique workmanship, show that the forefathers were either richer or more luxurious than the present generation. . . . Whether rich or poor, there is little variation in the Navarrese peasant's costume. If old or middle-aged, he wears a cap, breeches, and jacket of the coarse brown cloth used by the Franciscan friars, having round the waist a red or blue sash. If young he sports a *beret*, or blue round cap woven all in one piece, and black velveteen trousers. In the mountains sandals, manufactured of hemp, are worn instead of shoes, and the peasants wrap in winter a piece of cloth round the leg, which is tied by a horsehair cord. . . . From one cluster of villages to another the distance is usually from four to twelve miles, but generally there are formidable defiles and deep precipices to encounter before reaching them. Paths which cut straight over the mountains are too difficult for anything but a goat or a Navarrese to tread,—rugged and steep, and at times so narrow that you may almost span the way with your extended fingers, with, perhaps, a ravine of some hundred feet gaping, or a torrent roaring below. In winter the way, which has been worn in the ascents of the solid rock, and into which the rain has beaten the soil, form a succession of reservoirs of mud a foot or two in depth, and considerably impede the traveller's progress; and in summer it presents a ragged and irregular flight of steps, where every instant the iron of the mules' or horses' shoes is slipping on the naked stone. Men who have to traverse such ground, particularly if they have to carry the baggage of regular troops, are exhausted by the shortest marches, while the people of the country go through wood and ravine, straight as the fox or the wolf, and can always overtake without the possibility of being overtaken. In some places the ground is so much covered that an invading force has no idea of the proximity of the enemy. That enemy has his spies and guerillas, but the invader dares not detach men on expeditions of discovery, because when a few hundred yards from the main body they are always liable to be cut off."

Navarre has been a kingdom from very early times. When, in the fifteenth century, part of it was united to Spain under Ferdinand the Catholic, it was allowed to retain all its ancient laws, customs, and usages, since it had then been for about six centuries an independent kingdom. Never till the Cortes promulgated its Constitution in 1812 had those privileges been interfered with. It claimed to be governed by a viceroy, to be exempt from all duties as well as from all levies of men and money, except in extraordinary circumstances, when danger threatened the King. In everything the ancient mode of government was retained. Similar *fueros*, or privileges, were also enjoyed by the provinces of Guipuscoa, Biscay, and Alava, which recognized no monarch, the King of Spain being only "the lord" of those provinces which were seigniories to the crown. "So tenacious are they in this particular that, when the King (Don Carlos) reviewed the Carlist army, after the battalions of Navarre and Castile had been deafening the air with their shouts of 'Viva Carlos Quinto!' 'Viva nuestro Rey!' those of the Basque provinces, though much more clamorous, changed the cry as he passed to 'Viva nuestro Señor!' or, 'Viva el Rey nuestro Señor!' Long live the King, our Lord."

A great mistake of Don Carlos and his advisers at the very outset was that overtures were made to Rodil to join the Legitimist cause with the troops under his command in Portugal upon the Spanish frontier, and not to Sarsfield. Sarsfield was descended from an Irish Rapparee renowned in the war between William III. and James II. His father was from Limerick. The general had a high reputation for bravery and military skill, and he had always been known as a Legitimist. When the death of King Ferdinand took place, he remained for five days without sending in his adhesion

to the Queen's government, waiting, it was thought, for overtures from him whom he considered his legitimate sovereign;
but when he found that communications had been made to
Rodil, an officer of inferior rank to himself, he despatched
his adhesion instantly to Queen Christina. He was a man
of hasty temper, and at times liable to be excited by drink.
On one occasion, during the War of Independence, he
made a bet that he would strike a nail into the gate of Barcelona, then in possession of a French garrison, and calling
to his staff that all who did not follow him were cowards, he
commenced a mad gallop, with a hammer and nail in his
hand, and was not stopped until half the officers round him
had been swept down by grapeshot, discharged from the
walls.

Though he had given in his adhesion to Queen Christina,
had been made her Viceroy of Navarre, and placed in command of one of her most important armies, his predilection
was evidently for the cause of legitimacy. For some weeks
he did all in his power to favor the insurgents, so far as he
could, without compromising himself, and it has been generally believed that it was his intention to pass over with all
his division to Don Carlos and to proclaim him king had
that prince made his appearance among his adherents, or
had he seen a reasonable prospect of success.

At last, fearing to compromise himself by further inaction,
he advanced on Bilbao. The place was taken without any
resistance, and the inhabitants were treated with so much
lenity that Sarsfield was removed from his command. He
was furious at this disgrace, and especially at the reason
given; namely, "that his health was delicate." He refused
a command when it was subsequently offered him, and the
most competent military commander in Spain fades out of
the page of history.

The leader on whom the hopes of the Navarrese were set
was General Don Santos Ladron. He had already distinguished himself in previous wars. From 1820 to 1823 he
had commanded the royalist volunteers, and in recognition
of his services was made governor of Pampeluna. When

Christina made her changes in 1832, he was exiled to Valladolid, and placed under surveillance. On the death of Ferdinand he contrived to escape. Returning to Navarre, he proclaimed Charles V., and in a few days a thousand men had put themselves under his command. The Queen's authorities placed a price upon his head; and General Lorenzo, with a considerable force, marched against him. Ladron was considered by his countrymen a man of military ability and of undoubted courage. On this occasion he displayed neither. He went into action with Lorenzo's troops so dazed, benumbed, and incapable of action that his men always believed he had been treacherously drugged. Perhaps it was a case of illness like that of General Barratieri before the battle of Adowa, in Abyssinia. Another account says that Ladron was treacherously wounded when retiring from an interview with Lorenzo, who had been his personal friend. However this may be, he was captured, and his men dispersed. Lorenzo sent him to Pampeluna, hoping that from his great popularity in that city the government would not dare to take his life. The Viceroy and his judges did indeed hesitate, but were overruled by an officer of carbineers, who threatened that if they delayed the execution, he would be the first to accuse them to the government. It is said that on a former occasion Don Santos Ladron had saved the life of this man.

The death of Ladron, which took place the next morning, October 15, 1833, in the moat of Pampeluna, excited more indignation and fury throughout the northern provinces than any other execution in the course of the war. Three hundred [1] young men who were under surveillance and suspicion, left Pampeluna the next day to join the Carlists. But all accounts say that at this time, though all over Spain

---

[1] That my readers may judge how difficult it has been to procure exact details of these obscure events, I will mention that the first account I read spoke of seven hundred young men on this occasion; the second placed their number at five hundred, the third at three hundred. Possibly had I had the means at hand of searching further, the number might have been diminished still more. All my authorities were Carlist sympathizers.

partial risings had been effected, the cause of Don Carlos
was at a low ebb. The insurgents, although brave and
full of hope, were everywhere without plan or arrangement,
nor was there any man among them with *The Gift*, — "the
supreme gift that inspires other men to hail him as their
leader." Their bands were quickly crushed by the generals in command of the regular troops, who overran the
provinces, proclaiming martial law and executing it with
the utmost severity. "Generally," says Captain Henningsen, "the Carlists were punished so effectually and so
promptly that the very names of those who first raised the
standard of Legitimacy remained unknown to their fellow-
partisans in other provinces." At this period of depression
there appeared in the mountains, among the discomfited followers of Ladron, a man clothed like a peasant in goatskin
jacket, hempen sandals, and a Basque cap. That man was
Don Tomas Zumalacarregui.

This hero was born at a small town in Guipuscoa, near
the frontier of France. He was the son of a man much
esteemed among his neighbors, a Basque in the highest
sense of the term. His family consisted of three sons : one
was bred to the Church, and became the pastor in his birth-
place ; one became a lawyer and sat in the Cortes of 1810 ;
while the youngest one, Tomas, has left his name indelibly
inscribed on the annals of his country. That name, Zumalacarregui, was of old Gothic origin. It was too long and too
hard for general use among his soldiers ; they called him El
Tio Tomas, — Uncle Thomas, — or more often they abbre-
viated it into El Tio. In the war of independence, when
scarcely more than a boy, he joined the band of Mina, and
"was considered one of that chief's best officers for the surprise of a convoy, or a night march that required secrecy
and celerity." When the war ended he entered the regular
army, and was made a lieutenant-colonel. Eguia, King
Ferdinand's unpopular war minister, was his patron and
often consulted him. When the expedition under Abisbal
was being formed for South America, Zumalacarregui was
offered high rank in it, but declined. In 1832, Morillo,

acting in the interests of Christina, removed him from the command of his regiment at Ferrol. He then went with his wife and three daughters to Pampeluna, where he became an object of jealous suspicion to the Madrid government. His political opinions were well known; his military talents were unquestionable. He had been intimate with Santos Ladron, and was struck to the heart by his cruel fate. He determined to join his fellow-royalists. His wife encouraged him. At parting she distressed him by no useless lamentations, but begged him not to be anxious upon her account.

"On the last night of October, at the hour when country people in the town of Pampeluna were warned by beat of drum that the gates were about to be shut, Zumalacarregui, in the dress of a peasant, mingled with the crowd, and passed out, unobserved by the sentinels. Alone, and not venturing to trust any one, he struck into by-roads, and after travelling nine dreary leagues during the night, joined the royalists at sunrise, at Los Arcos."

He was chosen at once commander-in-chief of the insurgents in Navarre, and made Ituralde, whom he superseded, his second in command. His peculiar tact in disciplining recruits, and the ascendency he could gain over his officers and men, soon became visible.

I will here give his portrait in the language of an officer who served under him : —

"He was a man, when he joined the band, in the prime of life, being forty-five years of age, and of middle stature, but on account of the great width of his shoulders, his bull neck, and habitual stoop, the effect of which was much increased by the *zamarra*, or fur jacket, which he always wore, he appeared rather short than otherwise. His profile had something of the antique, — the lower part of the face being formed like that of Napoleon, and the whole cast of the features bearing some resemblance to the ancient basso-relievos which have given us the likeness of Hannibal. His hair was dark, without being black; his mustachios joined his whiskers; and his dark-gray eyes, overshadowed by strong eyebrows, had a singular rapidity and intensity in their gaze, — generally they had a stern and thoughtful expression, but when he looked about him his eye seemed to travel over the whole line of a battalion, making, in that short interval, the minutest remarks. He was always abrupt and brief in his conversation, and habitually stern in his manners. . . . His temper changed much during the last two years of his life. Latterly he was subject to sudden gusts of passion. Those who have undergone the painful experience of a civil war like that which in those years desolated the north of Spain, will agree with me in thinking that the scenes of strife and massacre, the death of friends and partisans, and the imperious necessity of reprisals on fellow-countrymen, often upon friends, exposure to innumerable hardships and privations, the sufferings and perils in which his followers were placed, and his serious responsibility, were enough to change, even in a brief space of time, Zumala-carregui's nature. . . . To him fear seemed a thing unknown, so that often he outstripped the bounds of prudence, and committed such acts of rashness that when he received his mortal wound, everybody said that it was only by a miracle he had escaped so long. His white charger had become such a mark for the enemy that all those of a similar color, mounted by officers of his staff, were shot in the course of three months, though his own always escaped. His costume was invariably the same, — the round national cap of the provinces, stretched out by a switch of willow inside; the *zamarra*, or fur jacket, of the black skin of the merino lamb, lined with white fur, and an edging of red velvet with gilded clasps; gray, and latterly red trousers, and the flat heavy Spanish spur. The only ornament he ever wore was the silver tassel on his cap. As he rode or walked, according to his wont, at the head of his columns, his staff, about forty or fifty officers, following behind, and his battalions threading the mountain roads as far as the eye could reach with their bright muskets and grotesque accoutrements, the whole presented a scene novel and picturesque. . . . To me Zumalacarregui, in character and feeling, as well as in costume and manner, seemed always like the hero of a by-gone century. He was of a period remote from our own, where the virtues and vices of society were marked in a stronger mould, partaking of all the stern enthusiasm of the middle ages."

The two great wants of Zumalacarregui and his followers were the want of ammunition and the want of their king, who continued in Portugal, and with whom it was almost impossible to hold communication. But one immense advantage that they enjoyed was the ease with which, through their sympathizers, they could send intelligence, or receive it with celerity. Anywhere north of the Ebro, a Carlist officer had only to give a paper into the hands of an *alcalde*, or even a verbal message, to be forwarded in any direction; the alcalde would immediately pitch on a house-holder, who, if thus selected, was bound to go himself, or to provide a messenger. On reaching the next village, this man would hand it over to another. If the paper was marked for especial despatch, he might, if tired, give it into the hands of the first man he met. The herdsman was bound to leave his flock, the laborer his plough, to carry it; and any man refusing, or betraying such a trust, would have been looked on with scorn by his family and his neighbors.

The strict blockade of the coast by the English, and the vigilance of the French police in the Pyrenees, made it difficult for the Carlists to obtain arms or ammunition. The time came when but for the scarcity of the latter they might have marched on Madrid.

Meantime Zumalacarregui used every effort to open com-munication with his king. On May 19, 1834, he wrote to his sovereign, and it was the first letter containing anything like details that Don Carlos had received from his northern provinces. It must have reached him shortly before the capitulation of Dom Miguel at Evora. It said: —

SIRE, — Listen to the voice of your faithful subjects, for the sword of justice is now unsheathed in your favor through the whole of your faithful Kingdom of Navarre, whose natives most anxiously expect you, in order to surround the throne, which you, Sire, will raise among them, and on which they will defend you. Never were hearts more filled with enthusiasm; and of it avail yourself, lest the dread of not seeing you should dishearten them. . . . Our consciences and our honor, Sire, oblige us to beseech you to come among us, — your presence alone will suffice. If you once tread the soil of Navarre, or the coast of Guipuscoa, rely on it, Sire, you are safe. We will all fly to receive you. Ten thousand bayonets, wielded by as many vet-eran soldiers, will you have at your side the moment that you reach the Spanish territory; and a few days afterward many thousands more. May the happy moment of your arrival come!

Listening rather to the advice of the Baron de Los Valles than to those who habitually counselled him, Don Carlos, on his arrival in England, June 18, 1834, determined to lose no time in responding to such appeals, by traversing France in disguise, attended only by the Baron. With some difficulty passports were procured for two Spanish gentlemen from Trinidad : one Alphonse Saoz (Don Carlos) being a merchant, while Los Valles took the name and passport of Thomas Sarebot, a real native of Trinidad, then in London. Fortunately the description of Sarebot on his passport singularly corresponded with the person of the Baron. The gentlemen around Don Carlos considered the risk of a long land journey too great; but it would have cost much money to fit out a suitable vessel, and the royal exiles were very short of funds. Los Valles had taken all precautions, — he had had experience in such journeys, in false passports, and in disguises, — and he was anxious that their departure should not be delayed. The family had moved to London, where they occupied Gloucester Lodge, the late residence of Mr. Canning.

On July 1, at evening, the Prince was to walk out with a friend, take a hackney-coach at the first stand they came to and drive to Welbeck Street, where the Baron would meet him, and where his mustachios could be cut off, and his hair dyed. At Gloucester Lodge it was to be given out that Don Carlos was ill. So well was this all arranged that the gentleman of the bedchamber himself, who kept watch in an adjoining room to that of the Prince, did not for two days know of his departure.

The Baron de Los Valles must have been born for a conspirator, his precautions were at once so minute and so complete.

All went well, though Don Carlos was deficient in the "politeness of princes," and his friends in Welbeck Street waited two hours for his arrival. The travellers crossed the channel from Brighton to Dieppe in twelve hours, with no inconvenience but sea-sickness. The Baron had obtained a promise from his companion that he would express neither

14

surprise nor objection, whatever happened, and after some trouble, having received their passports at the *bureau de police,* and their luggage from the custom-house, they continued their journey.

"Why," said the Prince to his companion, "did you insist so much on obtaining our passports at the bureau before every one else? I thought your earnestness might rouse suspicion." "Quite the contrary, Sire," the Baron replied. "It was the best way to avert it. The man who holds up his head and makes a fuss is never suspected. Suspicion falls on the timid man who endeavors to elude observation."

The most remarkable incident on their journey was, that when, towards evening, they entered Paris in their travelling carriage, and passed through the Place de la Concorde, glittering with lights and thronged with carriages, Los Valles was just pointing to the spot where he conceived the place of Louis XVI.'s execution to be indicated by a painted model of the Obelisk of Luxor,[1] when a gay, open carriage passed them, for which their coachman drew out of the way. It was Louis Philippe and his family driving out to Neuilly.

"I quickly," said the Baron, "pointed him out to my King, saying, 'Look, Sire! Behold your august cousin, the King of the French, who comes to wish you good luck on your journey.' Charles V. hastened to look at his worthy relative, who erroneously fancied that some one was bowing to him, and raised his hand to his royal gray hat, graciously lowering it to his Spanish Majesty. Queen Amélie and the princesses vied in courtesy with their husband and father. Charles V. laughed heartily at Louis Philippe's salutation, and whispered to me: 'My worthy cousin of Orleans does not suspect that I am traversing his dominions without his leave, and am preparing to tear up with the point of my sword his Quadruple Treaty.'"

They crossed the frontier in disguise, having travelled some miles to the last French village on their route in com-

---

[1] The guillotine stood really where the fountain nearest to the river now plays.

pany with the commander of the *gendarmerie,* who little suspected that " the Englishman" with whom he conversed so pleasantly was the *soi-disant* King of Spain, whom he ought to have arrested.

It was not safe for the King to declare himself till he reached Elizondo, on the 10th of July. Then the news of his arrival spread through his kingdom of Navarre with electric rapidity. The entire population gathered round their prince; they pressed upon his steps, threw themselves on their knees, and kissed his hands. " It called to mind what Henri IV. once said of the Parisians, that ' they thirsted to see a king.' "

Before the close of the year Don Carlos received news of the death of his wife, Doña Maria Francesca, *née* Princess of Portugal. She died on September 4, 1834, at Alverstock near Portsmouth, of bilious fever. Her health had been impaired by her sufferings, privations, and fatigues during the anxious months she spent in Portugal. Her sister, the Princess of Beira (whom Don Carlos afterwards married), attended her death-bed, and took a mother's care of her sons. The eldest was earnestly desirous to join his father; but that father, hunted by Rodil through mountain passes, thought the risk too great for his son. Doña Francesca had been greatly moved by the summary execution in Portugal of the twenty-three servants captured in charge of her baggage, and afterwards by the attack made on the officers they had left behind to follow them into exile. She and her sister sold everything of value belonging to them, and distributed the proceeds among these unhappy men; but such feeble resources were soon exhausted.

This excellent lady, against whom no word of court scandal was ever breathed, died at the age of thirty-four, and was buried at the foot of the altar in the little Roman Catholic Chapel at Gosport. She had desired that if ever her husband recovered his crown, her remains might be removed, not to a royal vault in the Escurial, but to a convent she had founded at Valencia, where daughters of noblemen were to receive their education, or, in times of storm and stress, find a sure refuge. The English admiral at Portsmouth ordered all marks of respect to be paid to the memory of the deceased princess, and the Duke of Sussex sent to the Princess of Beira a letter expressing his sincere sorrow for her loss, and his regret that he was not able in person to assure her of his sympathy.

# CHAPTER XI.

### ZUMALACARREGUI.

" SPAIN," says an English writer in Blackwood in 1845, " is a country which England has been fighting, or diplomatizing about, without intermission, since the beginning of the present century; a country, to which by its intestine broils and frequent political changes, the attention of the English public has been continually invited, while that of the moneyed and commercial classes has been especially directed to it by the frequent fluctuations, and consequent specula-tions, in what are facetiously called Spanish ' *Securities*.' It therefore seems singular that no one should have produced a book fully elucidating Spanish affairs. The probable cause of this is that no country has been so diffi-cult to follow and to comprehend through all its countless changes; an indispensable key to which is a thorough knowledge of the national character. On the other hand, that knowledge is doubly difficult to obtain at a period when, as now, the people and the institutions of Spain are in a state of transition."

On the truth of these remarks I base my own apology.

No sooner had the news of Ferdinand's death reached the court of France than the French ambassador at Madrid had orders to declare that his government was disposed to acknowledge the young Princess as soon as the official notice of the demise of the Crown had arrived.

There can be no question that, viewed from the old stand-point of legitimacy and legality, Don Carlos had an un-doubted right to the Spanish throne; but "legitimacy" had ceased to be a word of power. Legitimacy had been set aside in nearly every country in Europe during the eighteenth and nineteenth centuries. A Constitutional Government and a Constitutional King replaced it as a watchword; and Queen Christina, who was utterly devoid of honor, principle, or integrity, perceived at once that if she was to keep the power she had usurped, she must join the cry, and rally round her the friends of constitutional order.

Don Carlos was represented as an Absolutist, — which he certainly was, — but all through his career he gave no evidence of a disposition to misuse absolute power. He was denounced as a bigot, — a man likely to uphold the Inquisition, to carry Spain back to the days of her last Austrian rulers, — but although in his exile and his wanderings he was surrounded by ecclesiastics and far too much governed by monks and priests, he was a man of his word; and if he entered into engagements he always fulfilled them, — far different in this from his brother Ferdinand and the Bourbon Kings of Naples.

When Ferdinand VII. breathed his last, the care and craft of the Queen Regent and her advisers had left not a single "royalist"[1] in any military command, or in any important civil position. Nevertheless, as I have said, no sooner did the news of the King's death reach the provinces than risings took place all over Spain, and Charles V. was proclaimed in many places.

Before the arrival of Zumalacarregui from Pampeluna, on November 1, 1833, Colonel Benito Eraso, who had raised the valley of Roncesvalles, issued proclamations to the inhabitants and to his soldiers, in which, after begging them not to be discouraged by the misfortune of Santos Ladron, he added: "No vengeance! Oblivion of the past, and a religious observance of the decree of amnesty."

The minister in power at Ferdinand's death was Zea Bermudez. He was a monarchist at heart; that is, although opposed to Don Carlos and to Civil War, he was equally opposed to the policy and plans of the advanced Constitu-

---

[1] In other words, a Legitimist; a supporter of the claim of Don Carlos.

tionalists. In his zeal to replenish the treasury he did what was above all things calculated to inflame with anger the inhabitants of the northern provinces, — especially those Basques of whom some politician once said that rather than govern them, he would tame lions. Zea Bermudez revoked their *fueros*, and imposed taxes on the people of the Kingdom of Navarre and the northern provinces as well as on other Spaniards. At once, those provinces, already agitated, broke eagerly into rebellion.

The contestants in Portugal were Dom Pedro and Dom Miguel. Ferdinand had favored the latter ; but Christina took the part of Dom Pedro, who professed Constitutionalism. English and French diplomacy supported his cause, and that of his daughter Maria da Gloria.

Zea Bermudez was not long considered satisfactory at the helm of state, and was overthrown by the Exaltados.

He was succeeded by Martinez de la Rosa, a gentleman, a poet, a former exile, and a man who in the last years of Ferdinand's life had been employed on diplomatic missions. He was a native of Granada ; had been a member of the Cortes which in 1812 completed and promulgated the Constitution, and on the return of Ferdinand from his captivity he shared the fate of other prominent liberals who were transported to Africa. There he composed a tragedy of much merit, and wrote several poems. In 1820 he was recalled by the events at La Isla, and was sent by his native city as its representative to the Cortes. Later Ferdinand placed him at the head of the Department for Foreign Affairs, but the ministers with whom he was associated were soon overthrown by the *decamisados*,[1] the shirtless populace. He then took refuge in France, where he lived seven years, and became well known as a poet and a man of letters. He even wrote a tragedy in French verse which was acted on the Parisian stage. In 1830 he came back to Spain, and was employed in diplomacy. His first act when appointed premier by Queen Christina was to recall his personal friends from exile, — Arguelles, Galiano, and many others. His

[1] The Spanish equivalent for *sansculottes*.

elevation to power was thought to be the work of the English ambassador at Madrid, and was consequently not looked on favorably by M. de Reynéval, the French minister, that gentleman's diplomatic rival.

Martinez de la Rosa hastened to put forth for the government of Spain a new Constitution, his own work in his own study, called the *Estatuto Real*, which pleased no one, and was virulently attacked by both the monarchical and constitutionalist parties. He also, in April, 1834, signed the Quadruple Alliance, a treaty by which England, France, and the existing governments of Spain and Portugal agreed to combine to restore peace and order in the Peninsula, and to uphold constitutional government. The ministry of Martinez fell in less than six months, and he deemed it prudent to go again into exile. He was a man entirely honest and incorruptible, one who commanded universal respect on account of the moderation and dignity of his character, but he was not fitted to guide the Ship of State in stormy seas. His ministry was succeeded rapidly by others, " so that at length no sooner was the accession of any individual to the management of affairs announced, than his fall was looked for by the public ; and persons at a distance, without being able to unravel the confused and almost chaotic condition of Spanish affairs, scarcely believed it possible that the government could be much longer controlled without the aid of a foreign intervention to sustain it."

The administration of Mendizabal, which shortly succeeded that of Martinez de la Rosa, began by organizing a national guard throughout the country. These men, who were very turbulent and disorderly, were popularly called *urbanos*. He also suppressed the military orders, decreed the sale of church property, and the abolishment of several of the Provincial Juntas. These measures were unpopular with the great body of the people, and the unpopularity of the Queen Regent was aggravated by her conduct with regard to Muñoz, a man now established as her favorite, or if we borrow the language of an old colored woman in Virginia, he occupied the position of her " illegitimate husband."

The acquaintance of Queen Christina with the handsome captain in her body-guard was thus brought about. Three months after her widowhood she set out in the midst of winter to make a mysterious journey to La Granja, her summer palace, twelve leagues from Madrid on the other side of the Guadarama Mountains. The object of this visit was to secure some valuables locked up in safes and secret chambers at La Granja, for the greed of Queen Christina was very great, and it became notorious in after years.

"She left Madrid at an early hour one winter day accompanied by one of her equerries, the adjutant-general, and a party of body-guards commanded by their officer. On reaching the defile of Novacerrada, notwithstanding the precautions taken, the road being covered with ice, the carriage slipped down the hill, and had it not been stopped by coming in contact with a cart laden with timber, must have been precipitated into a ravine. The Queen alighted, and finding it impossible to pursue her journey, reascended the hill on foot, leaning on the arm of the commander of the guard, who happened to be Captain Muñoz. It was thus their intimacy commenced."

Muñoz was the son of a postmaster in a small country town in the province of Toledo. But the fact that he and his brother had been admitted into the royal body-guard is proof of the nobility of their descent. Both were considered "royalists;" and when the Guard was weeded out in 1832, the younger was dismissed for his political opinions, and Muñoz would have been dismissed too, had he not chanced at the moment to be absent. He was handsome, gentlemanly, and at the time he became the favorite of the Queen was thirty-eight years of age. Although so much was in his power, he never seems to have sought wealth or title for himself, nor did he ever forget his early royalist principles, but several times befriended Carlists when in adversity.

For the affair that took place on August 13, 1836, I had rather borrow the account given in the graphic pages of that delightful book, Borrow's "Bible in Spain," than tell the story in my own words. Mendizabal, the minister from whom much had been expected in the way of reform, had been dismissed. He was a Jew by descent, and Jewish in his features; he was also supposed to have the Jewish talent for finance, but a strong opposition had been formed against him by the *moderados;* and finding himself thwarted in all his projects by the Queen Regent and General Cordova, the Commander-in-Chief, whose pecuniary demands he was not willing indiscriminately to supply, he resigned his premiership and left the field open to his adversaries. He was succeeded by Isturitz, Galiano, the Duke de Rivas, and Quesada as War Minister. These were "all honorable men," but they had not held office more than a few weeks when Mr. Borrow had an interview with Isturitz, who had the Department of the Interior.

"Two or three things," he says, "connected with my interview with Isturitz, struck me as being highly remarkable: chiefly the air of loneliness which pervaded his audience-room and his antechamber. There were no eager candidates for an interview with the great man, who, when I entered, sat upon a sofa, with his arms folded and his eyes cast on the ground. When he spoke there was extreme depression in the tones of his voice, his dark features wore an air of melancholy, and he exhibited all the appearance of a person meditating to escape from the difficulties of life by the most desperate of all acts, — suicide. And a few days showed that he had indeed cause for much melancholy reflection. In less than a week occurred the revolution, as it is called, of La Granja. The Granja, or Grange, is a royal country seat, at San Ildefonso, situated among pine forests, on the other side of the Guadarama hills, about twelve leagues distant from Madrid. To this place the Queen Regent had retired in order to be aloof from the discontent of the capital. She was not, however, permitted to remain long in tranquillity; her own guards were disaffected, and more inclined to the principles of the Constitution of Cadiz than to those of absolute sovereignty, which the *moderados* were attempting to revive again in the government of Spain. Early one morning a party of these soldiers, headed by a sergeant named Garcia, entered her apartment, and proposed that she should subscribe her hand to this Constitution and swear solemnly to abide by it. Christina, however, who was a woman of considerable spirit, refused to comply with this proposal, and ordered them to withdraw. A scene of violence and tumult ensued, but the Regent still continuing firm, the soldiers at length led her down to one of the courts of the palace where stood her well-known paramour Muñoz, bound and blind-folded. 'Swear to the Constitution, you she-rogue!' vociferated the sergeant. 'Never!' said the spirited daughter of the Neapolitan Bourbons. 'Then your *cortejo* shall die!' replied the sergeant. 'Ho! ho! my lads, get ready your arms, and send four bullets through the fellow's brain.' Muñoz was forthwith led to the wall, and compelled to kneel down; the soldiers levelled their muskets, and another moment would have consigned the unfortunate man to eternity, when Christina suddenly started forward with a shriek, exclaiming, 'Hold! hold! I sign, I sign!'"

I cannot forbear adding to this account Mr. Borrow's report of what took place in Madrid toward evening of the next day, when the Puerto del Sol was filled with an excited crowd, and where two bodies of troops stood inactive, uncertain as to what it was expected they would do. One was a squadron of cavalry, who, together with their officer, shouted for the Constitution; the other was a body of infantry, sent to preserve order, but who made no attempt to do anything.

"Suddenly we heard the clatter of horses' feet hastening down the street called the Calle de Carretas. As the sound became louder and louder, the cries of the crowd diminished, and a species of panic seemed to have fallen upon all. Once or twice, however, I could distinguish the words, 'Quesada! Quesada!' The foot-soldiers stood calm and motionless, but I observed that the cavalry, with the young officer who commanded them, displayed both fear and confusion, as Quesada, in complete general's uniform, and mounted on a bright bay thorough-bred English horse, with a drawn sword in his hand, dashed at full gallop into the area in much the same manner as I have seen a Manchegan bull rush into the amphitheatre when the gates of his pen are suddenly flung open. He was closely followed by two mounted officers, and at a short distance by as many dragoons. In almost less time than is sufficient to relate it, several individuals in the crowd were knocked down, and lay sprawling on the ground beneath the horses of Quesada and his two friends, for as to the dragoons they halted as soon as they entered the Puerto del Sol. It was a fine sight to see three men by dint of valor and good horsemanship strike terror into at least as many thousands. I saw Quesada repeatedly spur his horse into the mass of the crowd, and then extricate himself in the most masterly manner. The rabble were completely cowed, and gave way. All at once Quesada singled out two Nationals who were attempting to escape, and setting spurs to his horse turned them in a moment and drove them in another direction, striking them in a contemptuous manner with the flat of his sword. He was crying, 'Long live the Absolute Queen!' when suddenly a bullet had nearly sent him to his last account, passing so near to his face as to graze his hat. Quesada seemed to treat the danger from which he had escaped with cool contempt. He glanced about him fiercely for a moment, then leaving the two Nationals, who sneaked away like whipped hounds, he went up to the young officer who commanded the cavalry, and who had been active in raising the cry of the Constitution. To him he addressed a few words with an air of stern menace. The youth evidently quailed before him, and, probably in obedience to his orders, resigned the command of his party, and rode slowly away. Whereupon Quesada dismounted, and walked slowly backward and forward before the Casa de Postas, with a mien that seemed to bid defiance to mankind. This was the glorious day of Quesada's existence, his glorious and his last day. I call it the day of his glory, for he certainly never before appeared under such brilliant circumstances, and he never lived to see another sun set. Tranquillity was restored to Madrid throughout the remainder of the day; the handful of infantry bivouacked in the Puerto del Sol. No more cries of 'Long live the Constitution!' were heard, and the revolution seemed to have been effectually put down. It is probable indeed that had the chiefs of the Moderate party but continued true to themselves for forty-eight hours longer, their cause would have triumphed, and the revolutionary soldiers at La Granja have been glad to restore the Queen Regent to liberty; but they were *not* true to themselves. That very night their hearts failed them, and they fled in various directions, — Isturitz and Galiano to France, and the Duke of Rivas to Gibraltar. The panic of his colleagues even infected Quesada, who, disguised as a civilian, took to flight. He was not, however, so successful as the rest, but was recognized at a village about three leagues from Madrid, and thrown into prison by some friends of the Constitution. When the news reached Madrid a vast mob of the nationals, some on foot, some on horseback, some in cabriolets, instantly

set out. 'The Nationals are coming,' said some one to Quesada. ' Then I am lost!' he said, and prepared himself for
death."

That night in a large and brilliant coffee-house in Madrid
Mr. Borrow saw a large body of rejoicing Nationals enter.
They untied a blue handkerchief, out of which they took a
gory hand, hacked from the dead body of the brilliant general
who had cowed the mob twenty-four hours before. They
called for a bowl of coffee, and horrible to relate, stirred the
contents with the dissevered fingers.

While these transactions took place in Madrid, the Carlist war went on in the northern provinces. The most
dreadful feature of that war was the barbarous system of
reprisals. Zumalacarregui, like Riego before him, was a
man of humanity, anxious to keep war within the limits prescribed by the law of nations. "I shudder at these acts of
retaliation," wrote Zavala, one of his generals; "they are
opposed to the rights of war, and to that noble generosity
with which those ought to be treated who surrender themselves, but I feel compelled to proclaim to my army the
adoption of just reprisals, having learned that Col. A. Que-
veda was shot on the 11th instant, not in an engagement, but
four hours after he was taken prisoner."

Mr. Walton, who served with the army of Don Carlos until
the death of Zumalacarregui (June 23, 1835), speaks thus
on this subject : —

"The war assumed a ferocious character on both sides, but
only one side was to blame for its beginning. The whole guilt
of both parties rests on that which took the lead in these horrors, and obliged the other in self-defence to shed blood for
blood, and to take life for life. The Spanish civil war has been
represented as a mere alternation of mutual massacres, in which
both parties have been equally to blame; and some who could
not deny the notorious excesses of the Christinos have endeavored to excuse them by alleging that the Carlists have also
perpetrated bloody deeds. But in examining the account in
question, it seems to me that, to all not wilfully blind, it must be
evident that the Christinos set the example which the Carlists
were obliged to follow. That the former acted from choice and

predilection; the latter reluctantly yielded to a stern and imperious necessity."

Before Don Carlos arrived in Navarre, Zumalacarregui had defeated the troops under General Quesada, who, much mortified and displeased in consequence, went back to Madrid, and a year later met death as we have already seen. It was thought that, had the Carlists had cavalry, the battle, which was fought on a plain near Pampeluna, might have been a total rout; as it was, much spoil was captured, and the " ragged and shirtless " of Zumalacarregui's force were equipped in new shirts and breeches at the expense of the Queen Regent Christina.

The fate of one of the prisoners taken moved all hearts, even that of the General, who condemned him to death with tears in his eyes. The story may be given as a specimen of many more of the same class, related by Mr. Walton and by several other Englishmen : —

" Among the officers captured was Colonel Leopold O'Donnell, only son of the Count de Abisbal, whose unfortunate end deserves some notice. When taken he was running up a hill, but the ground being rough, his foot slipped, and he fell. At this moment half a dozen Carlist soldiers and a sergeant came up and told him to surrender. O'Donnell did not rise, but in an inclined posture begged his life, observing to his captors, ' We are all — all brothers.' The privates shared among them three dollars and a half found on his person. And the sergeant, wishing to have a *prenda*, or keepsake, took his handkerchief and gloves. That night, when the Carlist general was established in his quarters, the fate of the prisoners was decided on. Zumalacarregui believed himself to have an act of just retaliation for recent outrages to perform, and desired to give it as far as was in his power the grave and deliberate character of a judicial retribution. He sent to the nearest Christino authority a formal notice that he should order O'Donnell and other officers and men to be shot by way of requital for the execution of a certain number of Carlists, whose cases he specified. When this resolution was announced to the unfortunate prisoners, O'Donnell's firmness forsook him. He burst into tears, and with earnest and repeated supplications entreated Zumalacarregui to reverse his sentence. The latter was all but overcome.

He was moved by the youth and the name of the suppliant, and felt a soldier's reluctance to extinguish a title which had been won on the field of battle in an honorable cause. While he was yet wavering he was informed that O'Donnell had offered a large sum of money for his release. This sealed the prisoner's doom. Zumalacarregui was now inflexible. After having been allowed ample time for his last arrangements, young O'Donnell, with six officers and six privates, was led out to be shot. Before they proceeded to the place of execution they acknowledged that the same death would have been the doom of Zumalacarregui had he fallen into Quesada's hands."

Quesada, in spite of his own bull courage, had found his Spaniards of the South unable to cope with the insurgents in their mountain fastnesses. He was superseded by Rodil as Viceroy of Navarre and generalissimo. Proud of his success in Portugal, the new Viceroy, at the head of his army of ten thousand men whom he brought with him, made no doubt of capturing Don Carlos, and of sweeping the country from the Pyrenees to the Ebro. No general ever assumed a command with greater confidence of success ; but it is simply bewildering to read details of the military operations in this campaign. It must suffice to say that the Carlists, under their beloved leader Zumalacarregui, were everywhere successful. A battle in which a small body of Carlists repulsed an overwhelming force by which they were surrounded, convinced Rodil that he had a formidable enemy to contend with, and not mere isolated bands of peasants and guerillas. Don Carlos had been with his troops during this engagement, but afterwards was persuaded by Zumalacarregui to retire to Elizondo, and so avoid the fatigue of forced marches on foot, the mountain paths being often impracticable for horses. Besides this, the General conceived that his own plans of operation had been hampered by solicitude for the safety of his sovereign, to say nothing of the interference of his ignorant advisers. Don Carlos was in truth no soldier. He had not been bred to arms, and though personally brave, he seems to have been as useless in the field as a woman in a storm at sea on ship-board. On arriving at Elizondo he received news that a man was coming to assassinate him for a reward of twenty thousand francs. The man was arrested, refused to give his name or to tell his country, and was shot. The weapon with which he proposed to do the deed was found upon him.

Talleyrand in his letters spoke very severely of Rodil for his dilatoriness in capturing Don Carlos, the task he had been set to accomplish ; and the Marquis de Miraflores, the Spanish ambassador in London, wrote home that the two great Powers who were parties to the Quadruple Alliance were much dissatisfied. Additional articles had been added to that treaty. France bound herself to use every exertion to prevent arms, ammunition, or reinforcements from crossing the Pyrenees to the insurgents ; while England engaged to send supplies of all kinds to the Christinos. In consequence of this the Carlists began to manufacture gunpowder in the mountains, saltpetre being more easily smuggled for their use than gunpowder. They also contrived to cast several cannon and some mortars. In England Lord Palmerston persuaded Parliament to authorize the formation of what was called the Foreign Legion. It was to be placed under the command of Colonel Evans (subsequently Sir De Lacy Evans), an Irishman by birth, and a radical member of Parliament. He had served in the Peninsular War, and was part of the British force which in 1814 captured Washington, but was repulsed at Baltimore. He was made a lieutenant-general in the Spanish service, and his force was supposed to consist of ten thousand men, though it fell short of that number. After two years' service in Spain, the remnant of the army in 1837 returned home. It had consisted principally of the sweepings of the streets, the unemployed or dissolute of London and other large cities. As the Legion effected little or nothing, and was wholly unfitted for mountain warfare, I need say no more of it than that the Spanish Government failed to pay the men, who returned ragged and penniless to their own country.[1]

[1] I have never seen such miserable, tramp-like objects as the poor fellows in tattered green uniforms, who were scattered about London, many of them with birch brooms, soliciting charity for having swept

Zumalacarregui and his officers, having all the inhabitants of the country in their favor, could choose their own ground, refuse to encounter the enemy in open fight, and carry on a war which to mountaineers was mere play, while it exhausted the soldiers of the State by useless marches over rugged paths and dangerous roads.

The more Rodil pushed his way through the northern provinces, the more exasperated he became at the proofs of attachment and devotion to the royal cause that he met with everywhere.

Reaching a ridge of mountains which divides the provinces of Alava and Guipuscoa, he cast his eyes upon a convent of Franciscan friars.

" The slopes and hollows of the mountains were cultivated by the industry of these monks, and wore the appearance of hanging gardens. In return for the voluntary labor of the peasantry, the friars, besides giving spiritual consolation to all around, fed the hungry, attended the sick, and administered medical relief to all who needed it. In the course of time this convent became a rich and romantic sanctuary, and was visited from far and near on account of a miraculous image of the Virgin which was preserved in the church. The traveller always met with a kind reception, and in winter, if needy, received warm clothing when he went away. The friars had sheltered some Carlist fugitives, and it was this offence which Rodil prepared to punish as he went upon his way. The first officer, El Pastor, whom he ordered to destroy the convent, started back in horror, and refused to obey. Another was less scrupulous. At nine in the evening he and his band arrived at the convent gates, and were hospitably received by the friars. The men were comfortably lodged, the officers invited to supper in the refectory; the best wines were brought out, and officers and men professed themselves delighted with their reception. When the convent clock struck eleven the monks prepared to retire. The *padre guardian* lingered to pay his last compliments to the officer in command, when his late guest seized him

the crossings. Many persons doubtless felt as we did. They looked so wan, so starved, so tattered, so discouraged, so miserable, that my father and mother never could refuse, as they passed them, to place pennies in their hands. — E. W. L.

by the throat. He told the venerable old man to fly and save himself. 'For,' he added, 'I am about to set fire to this convent, my peremptory orders being to see it reduced to ashes before two o'clock to-morrow morning.' No supplications availed; the order was executed. The troops sent on the expedition were not regular soldiers, but what were called *peseteros*, a corps raised by the Queen Regent from the turbulent population of Madrid. Their promised pay was a *peseta* a day, and they were notorious for their unscrupulous cruelty and robbery. The little the monks saved was stripped from them by these *peseteros*, and the next morning the friars, carrying nothing with them but the coarse garments of their order on their backs, and their breviaries in their hands, were marched to distant provinces. The sacred image of the Virgin, which, when the flames were ready to reach it, the Superior had obtained permission to rescue, was hastily placed on a hand-barrow. About thirty of the monks succeeded afterwards in joining the Carlists, as did their dispersed servants and lay brothers. Some splendid paintings, a valuable library, a well-stored dispensary, and a *hospice* with fifty beds, were all consumed with the edifice. No act of the war so outraged the feelings of the peasantry as this destruction of the Convent of Aranzazu."

Rodil, irritated by the letters he received from his own government urging him to press forward, set out to pursue Don Carlos through the mountains. He was by no means disheartened. He said he had divided his army into three strong columns, "each capable of beating the rebels, even in case they united in advantageous positions." And he added that he himself "intended to take care of the Pretender, whilst his generals must look after Zumalacarregui." He was so confident of success that he had written to the French commander at Bayonne to provide quarters in his citadel for his royal prisoner.

Never but once had Rodil any chance of making his intended capture. It was in the Pass of Roncesvalles, where Don Carlos had stayed two days in a convent overlooking the Plain of Roland. The convent was burned by Rodil, and the monks dispersed.

Scarcely did a day pass without the perpetration of some new atrocity. The mother of a Carlist general, ninety years of age, was stripped, led out into a street at early dawn, and exposed to every imaginable indignity.

Why recapitulate these things? Yet before leaving the subject I will add a page from the book of Mr. Borrow, because it seems to bring forcibly before the reader the state of family life and family feeling, so distracting and so terrible in that pitiless war. All Rodil's marches and counter-marches served only to make his name a byword for cruelty in the northern provinces, so widespread were the devastations and incendiarisms which his soldiers committed. At a mountain inn in Biscay Mr. Borrow was travelling with his French servant Antonio, who, perceiving a young man he knew in a crowd round the inn door, suddenly quitted his master. He returned some time after, showing signs of great emotion. On being questioned, he said : —

"You know, *mon maître*, I told you of the noble family I once lived with: father, mother, and two sons, from whom I parted by reason of a quarrel with my mistress about a pet quail? A short time before the troubles, — I mean before the death of Ferdinand, — Monsieur the father was appointed Captain-General of Corunna. Now, monsieur, though a good master, was rather a proud man, and fond of discipline, and all that kind of thing, and of obedience. He was, moreover, no friend to the populace, — to the *canaille*, — and he had a particular aversion to the Nationals. So when Ferdinand died it was whispered about at Corunna that the General was no Liberal, and that he was a better friend to Don Carlos than to Christina. *Eh, bien*, it chanced that there was a grand fête or festival at Corunna on the water, and the Nationals were there and the soldiers. And, I know not how it befell, but there was an *émeute*, and the Nationals laid hands on M. le Général, and tying a rope round his neck flung him overboard from the barge on which he was, and then dragged him astern about the harbor till he was drowned. They then went to his house and pillaged it, and so ill-treated *madame*, who was in delicate health, that in a few hours she expired. I tell you what, *mon maître*, when I heard of the misfortune of *madame* and the general, you would scarcely believe it, but I actually shed tears, and was sorry I had parted from them in unkindness on account of that pernicious quail. The eldest son, as I told you, was a cavalry officer, and a man of resolution, and when he heard of the death of his father and mother he vowed revenge. Poor fellow! So what does he do but desert with three or four discontented spirits of his troop, and going to the frontier of Galicia he raised a small faction, and proclaimed Don Carlos. For some little time he did considerable damage to the Liberals, burning and destroying their possessions, and putting to death several Nationals who fell into his hands. However, this did not last long. His faction was dispersed, and he himself taken, and hanged, and his head stuck on a pole.

"The young man we have just met, when he saw me, could only weep and sob. His story is soon told. He returned from his travels, and the first news that met him in Spain was that his father was drowned, his mother dead, and his brother hanged, and, moreover, all the possessions of his family were confiscated. This was not all. Wherever he went he found himself considered in the light of a factious and discontented person, and was frequently assailed by the Nationals with blows, and sabres, and cudgels. He applied to his relations, and some of those who were of the Carlist persuasion advised him to betake himself to the army of Don Carlos; and the Pretender himself, who was a friend of his father and remembered the services of his brother, offered to give him a command in his army. But, *mon maître*, as I told you, he was a pacific young gentleman, as mild as a lamb, and hated the idea of shedding blood. He was, moreover, not of the Carlist opinion, for during his studies he had read books, written a long time ago by a countryman of mine, all about republics, and liberties, and the rights of man, so that he was much more inclined to be liberal than to be Carlist. He therefore declined the offer of Don Carlos, whereupon all his relatives deserted him, while the Liberals hunted him from one place to another like a wild beast. At last he took refuge in this desolate place, where we have just met him."

A change of ministry in England at last produced a change in her policy towards Spain; not that the Tory Cabinet, under Sir Robert Peel and the Duke of Wellington, repudiated the Quadruple Treaty, but Lord Eliot and Colonel Gurwood (known as the editor of Wellington's despatches) were sent to both the Carlist and Christino headquarters in Navarre and Biscay, to effect an arrangement for the safety and exchange of prisoners. They were also to see what could be done toward making an amicable settlement of the quarrel. They proposed that Isabella should marry the eldest son of Don Carlos, but this proposal was at once rejected by the young man's father. An arrangement was, however, made for an exchange of prisoners, and the safety and liberation of the sick who might be captured in hospitals. The Christino generals signed the agreement, but did not observe it. Zumalacarregui, on his part, endeavored to do so. This, however, somewhat anticipates events, for the convention was not signed till May, 1835, when it excited great indignation among the population of Madrid, who declared that the insurgents had been recognized as belligerents by foreign powers.

Rodil having failed utterly, Mina, the old guerilla chief, was appointed to succeed him. The campaign of the winter of 1834–1835 was terribly exhausting, even to Carlist soldiers ; the cold in January was extreme, and the snow several feet deep in the mountain passes.

It was supposed that Mina would make use of his knowledge of the country to do what Valdes, Quesada, and Rodil had failed to do ; but his knowledge of the country and of the kind of warfare suited to it only inspired him with a feeling that times were changed, — situations reversed. When he had fought before it was with mountaineers against regulars ; the peasantry were all with him ; now he commanded regular soldiers, and the inhabitants of the country were opposed to his cause. Besides this, Zumalacarregui in the war of independence had served under him. "I am glad they have sent Mina against us," said that general to his staff officers. "I shall know his plans almost as soon as he has formed them."

Rodil, in disgrace, took up his residence at Port St. Mary, near Cadiz, where he embarked in commercial speculations as a wholesale wine merchant. Meantime he had the satisfaction of knowing that Mina, upon whom such hopes were fixed, met with no better success than himself, and early in 1835 was superseded by General Valdes, who was thus raised to the command a second time.

On the 10th, 11th, and 12th of May, 1835, there were

serious riots in Madrid, where the cholera had broken out, and monks were accused of poisoning the water. The mob demanded the head of Martinez de la Rosa, who had dared to sanction a convention made for the exchange of prisoners with insurgents, whom it was the duty of his generals to exterminate. In vain the minister argued that the object of the convention was to mitigate the horrors of civil war. The *urbanos* (that is, the National Guard) were thirsting for blood and revenge ; and in the commotion that ensued the friends of Martinez de la Rosa had great difficulty in saving his life. He then went into voluntary exile, as I have said already, being afraid to trust himself among the rabble of the capital.

It is believed to have been Zumalacarregui's plan to defeat general after general in the northern provinces, to discourage and demoralize their forces, and then, concentrating his own troops, make a rapid march on Madrid. The time was nearly ripe for the execution of this project. It only remained to take Bilbao. Zumalacarregui was not in favor of losing time by laying siege to the place, but the measure was urged by advisers round the King's person, and the General consented. He was in high spirits and full of confidence. Here is a part of a letter that he wrote to the Baron de Los Valles, dated Durango, June 10, 1835 : —

DEAR FRIEND, — We have lately gained much good, for we take the Christinos as in nets, and whatever the French journals may have said respecting our successes during the last ten days, they are still below the truth. While I was besieging Villa Franca, Espartero marched to relieve it; the only advantage he derived from that attempt was that of losing twelve hundred prisoners. On the 9th we took Villa Franca, after playing upon it with our artillery, — we even used the bomb. The enemy have abandoned Tolosa ; and the town of Bergara, containing a garrison of twelve hundred men, surrendered soon afterwards. In fact, they have withdrawn all their garrisons from the Bastan and the three provinces, except those of Salvatierra, Orchandiane, and two other places on the coast. It seems, therefore, that their intention is to abandon this part of the country, and to retire on the Ebro. For my part, I expect to be in Bilbao in three days, and at Vittoria in twelve. Eylar surrendered yesterday.

GENERAL FRANCISCO MINA.

Bilbao is situated near the Bay of Biscay six miles from the mouth of a broad and winding river. Durango, where Zumalacarregui and the King had their headquarters, is about seventeen miles to the southeast. Bilbao is a handsome city, and probably at that day, with the exception of Cadiz and Barcelona, was the most commercial Spanish seaport. On the 12th of June, 1835, two French war-vessels and an English frigate were in the harbor. The officers of these ships had an interview with Zumalacarregui, who treated them very politely, promised protection to English subjects in the city, if they would hoist the union jack over their houses, and furnished the British consul with a pass to communicate with the English naval commander.

The General had determined to take the city by assault. It had a garrison of thirteen thousand men, and plenty of artillery, much heavier than his own two little 18-pounders. A breach had been made in the wall, and the assault was to take place as soon as it was practicable. I will now quote from Captain Henningsen : —

"Lots had been drawn, and it had fallen on the first and second companies of guides to lead the way for the storming party. Zumalacarregui in a few words informed the men that the first hundred who entered the place should each receive an ounce of gold; if they fell their families should be each provided for, and six hours' pillage would be allowed. He was answered by loud shouts to send them on. A delay occurred, however, owing to the non-arrival of ammunition, and the assault was postponed till the next day. There was a tall tower next to a church which afforded a commanding view, and, though it was within easy gunshot from the enemy's works, early the next morning, notwithstanding the representations of his staff, Zumalacarregui, who would see everything himself, went out with a telescope into the balcony, although the woodwork of the window was like a riddle, and all the bars, excepting three, were torn away by grape-shot. Seeing a man so exposed, and, by his telescope and black fur jacket, perceiving him to be a superior officer, all the men lining their batteries and the works commenced firing on him. Some say the bullet that wounded him was fired by an English marine, but this is mere conjecture; a hundred men were firing at once. The bullet, bounding from one of the bars of the balcony, struck him in the inner part of the calf of the right leg, passed without hurting the *tibia*, broke a small bone without having the force to penetrate, and dropped two or three inches lower in the flesh.  The General came slowly out of the balcony, but, finding that he could not conceal his lameness, admitted that he was wounded. . . . I reached Bilbao early the same morning, having been sent for from an outpost to accompany Dr. Burgess, whose medical assistance was required, but who had difficulty in making himself understood. I met the General as he was carried, bed and all, by twelve soldiers, along the road.  He seemed in some pain, but conversed and smoked his *cigaretto* all the way, as if nothing had happened.  Notwithstanding this, the necessity of quitting the army, and being unable to direct the operations of the siege, seemed to prey upon his mind.  All along the road the news of Zumalacarregui's being wounded had flown like wildfire ; the peasants and soldiers thronged around his couch.  He took chocolate twice on the road, saying, 'I suppose I must not take anything else,' which the doctors confirmed.

" It was already late, owing to the slowness of our march, before we reached Durango.  All the ministers were in waiting for the General's reception.  As Zumalacarregui had never been on cordial terms with those about the King, he received them rather bluntly.  On examining the wound it was found as I have described.  He had a little fever, which increased during the night.  His first observation when left by the King's people was : ' The pitcher goes to the well till it breaks at last.  Two months more only, and I would not have cared for any sort of wound.'  He was attended by the surgeon of his own staff, — a man who had deserted from the Christinos a few weeks before, and in whom he seemed to place confidence, — the King's own physician, and Dr. Burgess.  The two Spaniards were of opinion that in a month, so slight was the wound, he would be again on horseback ; the latter gave a still shorter time for his recovery.  Burgess was of opinion that the ball should be at once extracted ; this was opposed by the other two, and even dressing the wound was postponed till the next day. . . . Don Carlos came to see him and they conversed at considerable length.  Tears stood in the King's eyes, and the interview was very affecting.  The General looked very pale and exhausted. He read over and signed several papers.  Then he dismissed Burgess, saying that as they all considered his wound but slight, he had better go back to the front, where his services would be of more use to the wounded.  He also dismissed me to join General Eraso's staff, who *ad interim* was commander-in-chief. He was then carried in a litter thirty miles to Segura, passing through his native village Ormaistegui, which he had thrice seen on the march during the war. He died (June 23, 1835) the eleventh day after he received his wound; he was then delirious, and in his temporary derangement fancied himself leading on his followers in some desperate action. The day before he died the surgeons at last decided on extracting the ball, but the operation had been rendered more difficult by the delay, and was conducted in so barbarous a manner that he suffered intense pain, from the effect of which he fainted. To lull this they gave him opium, in too large a dose it appears, for soon after the bullet was extracted he died in delirium."

His body was placed in a leaden coffin. For the sake of appearances it was interred with all the honors of war in a neighboring church, where the bones of his ancestors repose; but it was afterwards secretly disinterred, and conveyed to a hiding-place known only to Don Carlos and to the curate of Ormaistegui, the General's brother, it being feared that if the Christinos ever recovered the place, their savage resentment would not respect even his grave.

Empty titles of Count and Duke were subsequently conferred on him, but no title could add lustre to his own ancient name. He died lamented not only by his own troops and by the prince whom he looked upon as his sovereign, but by all men of honor, loyalty, and patriotism, whatever might be their feelings regarding legitimacy. All Zumalacarregui's fortune at the time of his death (for he was recklessly generous) consisted of fourteen ounces of gold — $240. This he left to his household; his widow and three daughters he commended to the grateful remembrance of his sovereign.[1]

---

[1] I have written of Zumalacarregui while reading at leisure moments the wonderfully picturesque and heart-stirring account of the siege of Delhi, in Mrs. Steel's remarkable book "On the Face of the Waters." It seems to me that Zumalacarregui and General John Nicholson were "made of the same clay," if I may borrow an expression often used by French writers. It is a clay used sparingly by Him who fashions us.

# CHAPTER XII.

## CLOSE OF THE FIRST CARLIST WAR.

THE last words spoken by Zumalacarregui to his sovereign were addressed to him from his litter at the moment he was leaving Durango, when Don Carlos with tears in his eyes asked him who, in case of his death, ought to command the army. "Your Majesty," was the prompt reply, and he confided to the King a little box containing papers, supposed to be his plans of a campaign for marching on Madrid and terminating the war.

The commander-in-chief *ad interim* was General Eraso, who was wasting away with consumption, and died not many weeks after. He was considered by the Carlists their best chief after Zumalacarregui. It was to Eraso that Zumalacarregui when he joined the army in Navarre after the death of Ladron offered to give up the command on account of his seniority of rank, but Eraso, frankly acknowledging that he believed Zumalacarregui's talents greater than his own, refused to accept it. He was aware that he was dying. "At the fall of the leaf I shall die," he said to a friend some months before, when he was taking leave of him. "And," adds that friend, "he begged me to give him a copy of the head of Zumalacarregui that I had taken and which was considered a good likeness by all who had known him."

Bilbao remained unassaulted and untaken. The reason why Don Carlos and his advisers insisted on its capture before Zumalacarregui carried out his plan of taking Vittoria, and thence marching on the capital, was that the want of money in the army was very great, and they conceived that the capture of a rich commercial city might furnish them with funds. " Can you take Bilbao?" Don Carlos had said to his great general. " I know I can take it," was the answer, " but it will be at an immense sacrifice, not so much of men, but of time, which is now so precious."

So the evil counsels of the courtiers, speculators, and ecclesiastics who surrounded Don Carlos prevailed; but Zumalacarregui insisted that if the city must be taken it should be taken by storm. His wound prevented the assault, and, unhappily, as soon as he had relinquished the command, the plan of storming the place was given up, in spite of the earnest remonstrances of Eraso.

"The King was persuaded that abandoning a city to the horrors that must follow this desperate resource of warfare would be an unwarrantable act, as one-third of the inhabitants of Bilbao were Carlists, and innocent and guilty might all perish alike. . . . This false mercy, or rather weakness, which the Bourbons have so often been guilty of, caused oceans of blood in the end to be spilled. . . . The consequence was that when the troops were informed that they were to storm the forts, — and the forts only, — to run all the risk, and be cheated of the recompense which the soldier in all times and places has been taught to look upon as the reward of desperate efforts, — they naturally refused to mount the walls, or rather (from the observations that were made) it was evident they *would have done so*. . . . But when news of the death of Zumalacarregui reached them they loudly demanded to be led to the storm of the city to avenge his death. 'We will go without pillage ! — we will go without the hundred ounces ! — we will go if hell itself be before us ! ' were their incessant exclamations."

News of the Carlist commander-in-chief's death put fresh spirit into the Christinos. They strengthened their works, made two sorties from Bilbao, and fired with new vigor on the batteries of the besiegers. Their eighteen thousand troops in the surrounding country marched at once to effect a junction with Espartero, that together they might relieve Bilbao.

This approach of the enemy must have convinced the counsellors of Don Carlos, when too late, how ill they had advised him. It was now determined to attack the army advancing to the relief of the city. Carlos himself assumed the command of his forces, Moreno was made chief of his staff, and Eraso, with a small force, was left before Bilbao ; but little by little so many of his soldiers were drawn off that he was obliged to raise the siege.

The main army of the Carlists meantime, finding itself two hours too late to attack the advancing enemy in an advantageous position, did not venture on an engagement.

At Zumalacarregui's death the Carlist army, which a year before had numbered six thousand men, amounted to thirty thousand, but it was very deficient both in artillery and cavalry. Horses were rare in the mountain provinces, and, owing to the strict blockade on the French frontier, they were very difficult to procure.

We must not forget that two armies were fighting in the cause of Don Carlos, the Army of the North, and the Army of Aragon and Valencia. These armies were composed of very different materials. The Army of the North under Zumalacarregui was animated by his spirit ; Cabrera, at the head of the Army of the East, infused *his* spirit of savage cruelty into the soldiers under him.

" The Carlist standard uplifted in Aragon became a rallying point for the scum of the whole Spanish people. Under Cabrera's banner murder was applauded, plunder tolerated, vice of every description freely practised ; and accordingly escaped galley slaves, ruined profligates, the worthless and abandoned, flocked to its shelter. To these may be added the destitute, stimulated by their necessities, the ignorant and fanatical led away by turbulent priests, the unreflecting and unscrupulous, seeking military distinction where infamy alone was to be obtained. From the commencement the war was of a very different nature in Navarre. To Navarre repaired those men of worth and respectability who conscientiously upheld the rights of Don Carlos ; the battalions were composed of peasants and artisans. . . . They were to defend certain local rights and immunities, whose preservation they were taught to believe was bound up in the success of Don Carlos. In eastern Spain the mass of the respectable and laboring classes were of liberal opinions, and the ranks of ' the faction ' were swelled by the dregs and refuse of the population."

This account is corroborated by every contemporary writer. Señor Cabello, who wrote the history of the Carlist war in the eastern provinces, supports his statements with documents, and gives us the same view. It is not pleasant to discover that the favor of Don Carlos and his advisers inclined more to Cabrera than to Zumalacarregui. The personal relations between the latter and his prince were respectful, but never cordial. The chief counsellors of Don Carlos were distasteful to Zumalacarregui. All the passions, bold or mean, all the jealousies, all the intrigues that vegetate rankly in the older courts of Europe, were found flourishing in the little court that assembled round the Pretender.

"There was not a Christino general more disliked by the hangers-on of Don Carlos than Zumalacarregui. They feared him, they respected him, but they hated him. And the General was not long in finding out what experience soon confirmed, viz.: that his royal chief was worse than a nonentity, and that the royal suite were actively in the way. Lord Bacon has said: 'It is the solecism of princes to think to command the end, and yet not to endure the means.' Don Carlos was always commanding the end, while his generals were left to find the means as best they could."

So speaks Lord Howden, K. C. S., one of the Englishmen who were in the court and camp of Don Carlos, and who left the service of that prince when Zumalacarregui was dead.

"In the personal intercourse between the King and his great general Don Carlos felt himself under the restraint that a strong mind imposes on a weak one. They were both uncomfortable. Zumalacarregui never flattered the prince on his chances of success. He laid before him his difficulties, almost insuperable in his own opinion, — for let it be known as a fact that Zumalacarregui always in his heart despaired of the ultimate upshot of the war."

Little more than three months before the death of Zumalacarregui, Ramon Cabrera became general-in-chief of the Carlist forces in Aragon and Valencia. He was a Catalan, son of a sea-captain, born at Tortosa in 1806. His parents destined him for the church, and desired to equip him with a good education, but, uncontrolled at home by his adoring family, he led the life of a scapegrace rather than that of a hopeful scholar. He soon became notorious for precocity in vice, and proved himself in character and propensities better fitted to be a devouring wolf than a meek and humble shepherd. His savage disposition led him to imbibe all the abominable and sanguinary doctrines of the Inquisition. But though spoiled by indulgence and the esteem in which he was held by his family, no sooner was the cry of insurrection raised in Aragon than he hastened to become a soldier, — according to his own view, a soldier for the Faith. In November, 1833, he joined General Carnicer, who had already planted the standard of Charles V. on the walls of Morella.

For the first sixteen months of the war Cabrera acted as a subaltern under Carnicer, and in no way distinguished himself, as we are told, except "by occasional acts of cruelty." Indeed, he had had no military education, and no guerilla experience whatever. At the beginning of 1835, a few months before Zumalacarregui's death, the Carlist chiefs in the eastern provinces of the Peninsula were reduced to wander in the mountains at the head of scanty and disheartened bands. Furious at this state of things, and still more so at the conduct of Carnicer, to whose lenity towards the population and the prisoners he attributed their reverses, dissatisfied too with his own subordinate position, Cabrera, who had powerful supporters among the ecclesiastical advisers who influenced Charles V., resolved on a bold attempt to get rid of his chief, and assume the command in his stead.

On his arrival at the camp of Don Carlos, where he was received as the chief of the apostolical or ultra-absolutist party, he was admitted to a private audience with the prince, and so worked upon his mind, by accusing Carnicer of weakness and mistaken humanity, and urging the necessity of more severe and sanguinary measures, that he was sent back to Aragon bearing orders for Carnicer to make over his command to him, and repair at once to Navarre.

Carnicer obeyed, and on the 9th of March, 1835 (three months before the death of Zumalacarregui), he set out with an escort for the Basque country. On his way he fell into the hands of the Christinos, and was shot.

The death of Carnicer has always been attributed to treachery on the part of Cabrera, and there is much circumstantial evidence to prove that he was betrayed.

"For eighteen months the kingdoms of Aragon and Valencia had groaned beneath the calamities of civil war. Their cattle were driven, their granaries plundered, their sons dragged away to become unwilling defenders of Don Carlos; the unfortunate inhabitants could hardly conceive a worse state than that of continual alarm and insecurity under which they lived. They had yet to learn that what they had endured was light to bear, compared to the atrocious system introduced by the ruthless successor of Carnicer. From the day that Cabrera assumed the command the war became a butchery, nor were its inflictions confined to the armed combatants on either side. Thenceforward the infant in the cradle, the bedridden old man, the pregnant matron, were included among its victims. A mere suspicion of liberal opinions, the possession of a national guardsman's uniform, a glass of water given to a wounded Christino, a distant relationship to a partisan of the Queen, was sentence of death. The rules of civilized warfare were set at nought, and Cabrera, in obedience to his sanguinary instincts, committed his murders, not only when they might possibly advance, but even when they must positively injure, the cause of him whom he styled his sovereign. 'Those days that I do not shed blood,' said he in July, 1837, when waiting in the antechamber of Don Carlos among a group of Carlist generals, 'I have not a good digestion.' During the five years of his command his digestion can rarely have been troubled."

This extract is taken from "Blackwood's Magazine," September, 1846. That magazine during the Carlist struggle might have been termed almost the organ and advocate of the Carlist party in England. It denounced the policy of the English Government in upholding the cause of Queen Christina, and sending to her aid ships, men, and supplies. But the atrocities of Cabrera met with its vehement rebuke, as did the counsels of the ecclesiastical advisers of Don Carlos, who surrounded him at his headquarters. So long as the magazine treated of the Carlists in the northern provinces during the first three years of the war, it gave its support to the cause of legitimacy, but on Cabrera it had no mercy. I will relate only one of his atrocities, enacted before February, 1836. It will be remembered that the Eliot convention for the exchange of prisoners and the protection of sick prisoners in hospitals applied only to the armies of the North, and was not extended to those of Valencia and Aragon.[1]

On September 11, 1835, Cabrera suddenly appeared before the town of Rubielos de Mora. The garrison, taken by surprise, defended themselves for two hours, but part of the town was set on fire, and at last, overcome by fatigue and thirst, scorched, bruised, and exhausted, they accepted the terms offered, and surrendered.

" Their lives were to be spared, and they were to retain their clothes, and whatever property they had about them. Cabrera and his second in command signed the agreement, and sixty-five national guardsmen and soldiers of the regiment of Ciudad Real, marched out, and were escorted by the Carlists in the direction of Nogueruelas.

" On reaching a plain near that town, known as the Dehesa, or Pasture, Cabrera called a halt that his soldiers might eat their rations. The prisoners also were supplied with food. The meal over, the Carlist chief formed his infantry and cavalry in a circle, made the captives slip off every part of their clothing, and bade them run. No sooner did they obey his order than they were charged with lance and bayonet, and slaughtered to a man."

These atrocities everywhere excited horror, and a clamor rose for reprisals. Unhappily, the Christino General Nogueras, early in February, 1836, yielded to the public voice;

1 By what was called the Durango Decree, issued by Don Carlos shortly after the death of Zumalacarregui, the humane provisions of the Eliot convention were stated as not being intended to apply to " mercenaries " in the Christino army, — that is, to men of the British Legion serving under General Sir De Lacy Evans. The Durango Decree led to great indignation in England, and at the expiration of two years' service to the withdrawal of the Foreign Legion.

his troops captured Cabrera's mother, and he ordered her execution, threatening that of Cabrera's two sisters, if the atrocities of the troops under his command did not cease.

" The act itself was cruel and hasty; its consequences were terrible. It is thought that Nogueras repented of his order, and might have revoked it had he not been absent from Tortosa at the time. The deed was at once repudiated by the Spanish Government, and condemned by the nation, but in the eyes of Europe it went far to convert Cabrera from a pitiless butcher into an injured victim."

When he received the news of his mother's death he issued a furious proclamation, and ordered torture and execution for four unhappy ladies who had fallen into his hands. It would serve little purpose to give the details of the massacres he committed by way of reprisal.

As a general in 1836, the energy and skill shown by him were wonderfully great: he succeeded in organizing his irregular forces until they became a regular and disciplined army, and then he descended from his mountains, and marched into La Mancha.

" He was," says Mr. Borrow, "within nine leagues of Madrid with an army nearly ten thousand strong. He had beaten several small detachments of the Queen's troops and had ravaged La Mancha with fire and sword, burning several towns. Bands of affrighted fugitives were arriving every hour in the capital bringing tidings of war and disaster, and I was only surprised that the enemy did not appear, and by taking Madrid, which was almost at his mercy, put an end to the war at once. Many thought that the Carlist generals did not wish the war to cease, for as long as the country was involved in bloodshed and anarchy, they could plunder and exercise that lawless authority so dear to men of fierce and brutal passions."

The fears of the Madrileños led them to magnify the strength of Cabrera's army; he had four thousand infantry and three hundred dragoons. The activities of the enemy opposed to him were unsupported by their government,

16

whose whole attention was directed to the war in Galicia, where Espartero was alternately obtaining important advantages, and suffering discouraging defeats. He, however, by help of the English ships, raised the siege of Bilbao. But at last, roused to a sense of the importance of the contest carried on in the eastern provinces, the government ordered General Narvaez, at the head of a brilliant brigade, to detach himself from the army of Espartero and march into Aragon. He crossed Spain from the Bay of Biscay to the Mediterranean in nine days, and commenced operations with great activity. He was about to attack an important Carlist corps, when an orderly, bearing despatches from Madrid, arrived in haste. The General was ordered to leave Aragon at once and to march in pursuit of Gomez, who was proceeding south, apparently intending to attack the capital. " Yonder rebels," exclaimed the General, pointing to the army he was about to encounter, "may truly say that they continue to exist by royal order."

A rebellion had broken out in Madrid, and General Gomez, now chief among the Carlist generals, was on the march threatening the capital. Being in need of reinforcements he too sent messengers into Aragon, asking for assistance, but he would send no messenger to Cabrera, whom he held in horror, as did all the better class of Carlist generals.

Nevertheless Cabrera, without orders, joined Gomez, bringing with him, however, only his staff officers, and one of his clerical advisers. Gomez treated him with great contempt, and would give him no command in his division. Still, Cabrera stayed to share the fighting, and was foremost on several occasions.

"If Gomez disliked Cabrera, Cabrera on his side heartily despised Gomez; to have captured three thousand national guardsmen at Cordova and not to have shot at least a couple of thousand of them, to have spared the fifteen hundred men composing the garrison at Almaden, were inexcusable weaknesses in the eyes of the Aragonese leader. Moreover, his own name was omitted in the despatches and proclamations announcing the triumphs of the division; and at this he was in-

GENERAL BALDOMERO ESPARTERO.

dignant, viewing it as a stain upon his reputation, and a dishonor to his rank. At last, so troublesome did he become, constantly murmuring at whatever was done, and even conspiring to promote mutiny, that Gomez, in order not to shoot him, which he would otherwise have been compelled to do, insisted on their parting company."

So Cabrera set out with a small escort for the mountains of Toledo. He passed through La Mancha, his force increasing as he went, intending to cross the Ebro and lay his wrongs before Don Carlos, who was then at Onate. Before his party reached the river, however, they were attacked, the escort was cut to pieces, and Cabrera, while endeavoring to find a refuge, was slashed with a knife and stabbed with a bayonet. He succeeded in escaping to a forest, where he was found and removed to the house of a village priest, who concealed him until his wounds were healed.

Gomez, notwithstanding some successes at the beginning of his campaign, was generally routed when his men had to engage regular troops, and was at last driven back into the Basque provinces. There were bitter dissensions among the Carlist generals, all of whom seem to have resented the partiality of Don Carlos for Cabrera. Several spoke out their minds freely. One general, Cabanero, repeatedly assured the prince that he would rather serve as a private in the army of Navarre than as a general under Cabrera. So high did this quarrel run that Quilez (second in command to Gomez when he marched southward) and Cabanero, finding that Don Carlos supported Cabrera in everything, separated themselves from his army, and went to make war elsewhere.

In the summer of 1837 Don Carlos, now with the army of Cabrera, approached Madrid by forced marches. It was defended only by national guards, but Espartero arrived in time to bring relief, and Don Carlos retired. Espartero followed him, and Don Carlos, finding it hopeless to pursue his plans, sent Cabrera back to Aragon, and made his way almost as a fugitive to the Basque provinces. A loan and recognition by the Northern Powers had been promised him could he establish himself in Madrid, but this was now impossible. Beset on every side, Don Carlos became so discouraged that he suffered the war to languish, and his prospects became hopeless, except in Aragon, where Cabrera carried on hostilities with occasional success.

In the summer of 1839, General Maroto was in command of what remained of the Carlist army in the North. There is a story that finding himself confronted by Espartero with greatly superior forces, and having made up his mind that the cause of Don Carlos was lost, he asked an interview with Espartero, probably to arrange terms of capitulation, but began by offering to throw dice with him, as to whether or not he should surrender; the offer was accepted, and Espartero won. Be this as it may, a convention was entered into at Bergara (or Vergara, as it is sometimes written), by which the war was ended in Navarre, Biscay, Galicia, Guipuscoa and Alava, and Don Carlos with some thousands of his followers passed over the frontier into France. There the town of Bourges was assigned to him as his residence, but he was kept under strict surveillance by the police. He was at last permitted to retire to Austria, where he took up his residence at Trieste, assuming the title of Count de Molina. He married Maria Theresa, Princess of Beira, his own niece and his deceased wife's sister. It is probable that nothing short of his steadfast devotion to the cause of the Papacy could have procured him the necessary dispensations.

In 1849, when all Europe was in a state of revolution, he was in London, where Cabrera went to see him, hoping to persuade him to authorize another attempt to gain his crown. But Don Carlos was not to be persuaded. He said that in 1844 he had solemnly renounced his rights in favor of his son. How that son, the Count de Montemolin, and his youngest brother, the Infante Don Fernando, fared, must be read in another chapter.

Besides these sons (his eldest and his youngest), Don Carlos, when he died at Trieste in 1855, left behind him another, his second son, Don Juan; his widow then took up her residence in Venice, and long survived him.

When the convention of Bergara ended the war in the North, Espartero marched into Aragon with forty thousand infantry and three thousand cavalry. But he remained inactive all winter, hoping that Cabrera would open his eyes to the inutility of further resistance. He offered him the same terms that had been accepted by the other generals, which were very liberal, far more so than could have been expected by men who had made war like savages. But these offers were contemptuously rejected.

At last Cabrera, worn out by six years of anxiety, activity, and agitation, fell ill during the winter. Besides, he had led a dissolute life from a very early age, and his continued debaucheries told upon him. His vexation and rage at the Convention of Bergara had also affected his health, and for some weeks his life seemed in peril. He recovered, but his illness had weakened both his bodily strength and his courage.

In the latter part of February, 1840, Espartero attacked two of his strong places. The garrisons defended themselves bravely, but at last, overcome and exhausted, they hung out a white flag.

" They were Spaniards," wrote Espartero in his despatch to Madrid, " blinded and deluded men, who had fought with the utmost valor ; and I could not do less than view them with compassion." So their lives were spared, and the wounded were carried to the hospitals in the arms of their recent opponents.

The last stronghold that remained to be taken was Morella ; it was a place dear to Cabrera ; it was the scene of his early triumphs ; it had given him his title. But, believing that its fate was sure, he marched out of it before the siege began, with his personal followers. Nor did he make any effort to relieve the place, though it held out for eleven days. It was the last stronghold attacked by Espartero, and when it was taken the war was at an end.

Cabrera with a considerable force made his way to France. Crossing the Ebro, he took occasion to drown a number of national guards he had with him as prisoners. Others were shot, while some few were dragged bound over the frontier, and released by the French authorities. On July 6, 1840, Cabrera quitted Spain with two hundred cavalry and twenty battalions. We shall hear of him again; he has not yet passed out of this story.

# CHAPTER XIII.

BEFORE recording what took place at Madrid after the close of the Carlist War, it may be well to recapitulate some of the events which, during the seven years that that war lasted, had distracted the ever turbulent and uneasy capital of Spain.

It is impossible to describe the various parties in Spain by terms employed to denote political parties in the United States, but we may do so by borrowing party terms from English politics, which are probably sufficiently familiar to all my readers.

The term "Royalist" was, as I have said, used only to denote the Carlist faction, — not the adherents of the two Queens. Theirs was the Liberal or Constitutional party, which may be said, roughly, to have had three divisions, the Moderados, the Progresistas, and the Exaltados. The Moderados were the Tories or Conservatives; the Progresistas the Whigs; the Exaltados the Radicals, of various degrees of revolutionary fervor.

Zea Bermudez, the first prime minister of Queen Christina, was a Moderado. He came into office in 1832; he quitted it at the close of 1833, and was succeeded by Martinez de la Rosa, one of the leaders of the Progresista party. Zea was supposed to be supported by French influence; Martinez de la Rosa was accused of unduly leaning to English interests and ideas. As I have said, he came into office with a new constitution in his pocket, evolved during his exile, from his inner consciousness. It was called the Estatuto Real, or Royal Statute. Its author professed to have formulated it on the ancient and long disused liberties and customs of Spain. It created an Upper and a Lower House of Parliament, — the

Proceres and the Procuradores. The Upper House, that of the Proceres, consisted of the clergy, grandees, and high functionaries of every description. The Estatuto went into operation ; the Proceres and the Procuradores met ; their quarrelsome discussions excited agitation in the streets, and obliged Martinez de la Rosa to retire. After him came a brief ministry under Toreno, an advanced Liberal, — one of the few Spanish writers who have furnished us with any account of their own times. He was followed by Mendizabal, who was bred a banker. He was the author of three measures, popular with the Radicals, but highly distasteful to other men in all parts of the country. These three measures were : the closing of the monasteries ; the sale of lands belonging to the regular clergy ; and the formation of a National Guard ; in other words, he put arms into the hands of the turbulent and dangerous classes in the cities. Mendizabal fell after a few months. Isturitz and Galiano succeeded him. I have thus recapitulated what I have said in a former chapter, and have brought our story down to the Revolution at La Granja (August 12, 1836), the death of Quesada, and the resignation and flight of the Cabinet Ministers.

Christina found herself after this in the hands of mutineers ; and after a week of the disorders that in Spain attend upon a revolution or a revolt, a ministry was formed of some of the best men of the advanced Liberal party, who summoned a Constituent Cortes to set aside the Constitution of 1812, and the Estatuto Real, and to create what is called the Constitution of 1837.

Arguelles assisted largely in the construction of this new Constitution. In his youth he had been one of the framers of the Constitution of Cadiz, had been sent to Africa by Ferdinand in 1815 to serve as a common soldier, and in 1820 had been recalled by him to form a ministry. Being a wise and honest man, he had profited by experience, and the Constitution of 1837 was more conservative than the Constitution of Cadiz ; it therefore displeased and disap- pointed the Exaltados and a large part of the Progresistas.

It will be thus seen that from 1832 to 1837, Spain lived under three constitutions, was governed by six ministries, and had twice been thrown into the vortex of a revolution, to say nothing of having throughout these years to carry on a desolating civil war. If the reader finds all this confusing and confused, I will quote to him from an able article in the "North British Review" of March, 1865, which speaks thus on the subject : —

"Spain has slipped of late years so thoroughly out of the notice of Europe that it would be affectation to imagine that one person in a thousand knows even the A B C of her recent history and politics."

Soon after the Constitution of 1837 had been promulgated, the ministry brought into power by the affair of La Granja succumbed to another military revolt, and General Espartero, who had won laurels in his campaigns against the Carlists, was called for a brief period to the head of affairs. But, defeated in the elections for a new Cortes, he was succeeded by a strong Conservative or Moderado ministry, which had the support of the Queen Regent and her *camarilla*. At its head was Ofalia, of whom it was once said that, if there was any truth in metempsychosis, his soul must have once dwelt in the body of a mouse.

During this time of ministerial changes, revolutions, and the making of constitutions, Gomez, with his Carlist army, had with little or no opposition made a sort of military progress from one end of Spain to the other. His advanced posts had been seen from the walls of Madrid, but he was forced to retire beyond the Ebro, and in 1839 the convention signed at Bergara drove Carlos Quinto into exile, and virtually ended the Carlist war.

Espartero had had honors heaped upon him, and was now field marshal and Duke of Vittoria. His attitude with regard to politics had become of the greatest possible interest to all Europe, as well as to all parties in Spain. He was evidently inclining more and more towards the Progresista party, while his relations towards the Moderado ministry, then in power, became colder. He was dissatisfied with some arbitrary measures they had taken to get rid of Progresista deputies in the Cortes, and the party that was making revolutionary plans relied on his assistance.

The Congress of 1840 had no sooner met than a fierce struggle began in which the galleries took part, as they used to do in the French National Assembly; indeed, at one time the scenes of 1793 seemed likely to be repeated; nevertheless the Moderado ministry succeeded in passing several reactionary laws.

After the close of the Carlist war, the Basque provinces offered to acknowledge Isabella, on condition that their *fueros* — their ancient privileges — should be restored to them; and Espartero, now powerful as a successful commander-in-chief, insisted that the Queen Regent should not only accept these terms, but loyally adhere to them.

At this moment, while all the country was in a divided state, the young Queen was advised to take salt sea baths at Barcelona, and to that place she repaired, accompanied by her mother. The Queen Regent had not been long absent from Madrid, and believed herself to be under the protection of O'Donnell and his northern army, when she announced to Espartero that she had given her assent to a new law affecting the municipalities, and had no intention of renewing the local privileges so dear to the inhabitants of the Basque provinces. The new law was also intended to diminish the influence of the Liberals, and to increase considerably the powers of the Crown. Espartero at once resigned his military position. The Queen Regent refused to accept his resignation. He then informed her that he was about to retire from the city, as he could be of no further use to her. Hardly had he done so when Barcelona broke into revolt, and the Moderado ministers who had accompanied the court fled hither and thither. The revolt spread rapidly over Spain. On the first of September Madrid had its *pronunciamiento*. After this the Queen Regent gave way, and Espartero was desired to form a ministry. The General required of Christina two things, namely: that the Cortes now subservient to her influence should be dissolved, and that the law concerning the municipalities should not be carried into execution; also he desired that she should issue a manifesto throwing all blame for recent events on her late Cabinet. This Queen Christina indignantly refused to do. She again endeavored to place herself under the protection of the troops commanded by O'Donnell, but failing in this, and not daring to go back to Madrid, she abdicated the regency, abandoned her royal children, and took ship for France. At Marseilles she delivered herself of a proclamation denouncing her enemies, and expressing her tender attachment to the children she had forsaken and the country she had misgoverned and betrayed.

She repaired at once to Paris, where she took up her residence in the Quartier Beaujon in the Hôtel de Courcelles. She was received with every mark of consideration by Louis Philippe and the Parisians; and for three years she carried on all manner of plots and intrigues against the Spanish Government.

Espartero had his revenge. He published documents to prove that the Queen Regent had been married to Muñoz not long after her widowhood. This placed Christina between the horns of a dilemma. If she was really the wife of Muñoz, she could not, according to law, have been Queen Regent of Spain, and the nation might call upon her to refund the $150,000 per annum that she had received from the country for her services in that capacity. If the wife of Muñoz, she was a swindler; if the widow of Ferdinand, she was something worse. Christina made her choice; avarice, her ruling passion, carried the day. She boldly averred that she had *not* been married to Muñoz, although there had been no secrecy kept up at court or elsewhere that before 1840 she had had three children by that handsome cavalier. In 1844, when it could no longer be possible that any revolution in Spain should restore her to the regency, she acknowledged her marriage, fixing its date, however, in that year. Muñoz was made Duke of Rianzares, and was received at court and elsewhere as husband of the ex-Queen.

He took little part in politics. No charge was ever brought against him, except that he had a taste for stock-jobbing, by indulgence in which he from time to time dissipated large sums from his wife's hoards; for Christina had laid hands on everything that she could carry out of the country. Her savings and plunderings were enormous, and she invested everything in foreign lands. Not only money, but jewels, plate, lace, and other valuables, she carried away with her,[1] and one of Espartero's first duties was to buy diamonds for the little Queen, then ten years of age, that she might appear suitably adorned on public occasions.

Queen Christina having fled, the office of regent was vacant, and it became necessary that it should at once be filled. The Progresista party desired to have three regents; the friends of Espartero desired only one. On May 8, 1841, Joaquin Baldomero Espartero became Regent of Spain. His father had been a coachmaker in a small town in La Mancha. He was born in 1792, the youngest of nine children, and had been educated for the priesthood; but in 1808, when sixteen years of age, he volunteered to fight the French. He entered what was called the Army of the Faith, and served so well that when the war ended he obtained an appointment to the Military School, established in the Île de Leon. In 1815 he went out as an officer to Peru with Morillo. He fought in seventeen battles, received three wounds, and returned to Spain in 1825 a brigadier-general, with a beautiful wife and a large fortune (made partly at the gaming-table). In 1833 he declared for Isabella II. Eight years later he found himself a field marshal, Duke of Vittoria, Count Lucana, and the acknowledged ruler of Spain. But no sooner was he fairly installed into office than the foundations of his power began to shake.

Washington Irving, appointed United States Ambassador to Madrid in the early part of Espartero's regency, spoke thus of him in a private letter: —

---

[1] Isabella's christening robe was, it is said, offered for sale at the American embassy.

" The more I get acquainted with the present state of Spanish politics and the position of the government, the more does the whole assume a powerful dramatic interest, and I shall watch with great attention every shifting of the scene. The future career of this gallant soldier, Espartero, whose merits and services have placed him at the head of the government, and the future fortunes of the isolated little princesses, the Queen and her sister, have an uncertainty hanging about them worthy of the fifth act of a melodrama."

The first care of Espartero was to appoint proper persons in the household of the Queen. Madame Mina, widow of the general of that name, was made governess to Isabella and her sister; Arguelles was made their guardian, and a learned preceptor was secured for them. In 1868, the Queen (whose statements always need corroboration) published a pamphlet in which she bitterly reproached Espartero, as well as her mother, for the complete ignorance in which she was brought up. It is true that when at the age of thirteen she became a reigning queen, she knew less than the most ordinary schoolgirl in America, but those persons placed about her by Espartero found it almost impossible to make her learn. A friend of Cherbuliez describes how he saw her when she was five years old, driven to see some wild beasts at the Retiro : —

" She was a delicate child, but was clothed in royal splendor, with flying feathers, lace, and jewels; and as she drove up in a State coach, drawn by six horses, and surrounded by a squadron of guards, the men of Madrid uncovered, and bowed before her as if she was something infinitely precious, almost divine. When she walked in the garden, they followed her every movement with the tenderest anxiety, and when she stumbled one might have thought from their faces that some dire calamity had befallen the State. The little Queen, far from being discomposed by the attention lavished upon her, seemed to enjoy it, and clapped her hands and laughed with delight. Evidently she was none the worse for the storms that had raged around her cradle."

The child seems even then to have exhibited such of her better qualities as she showed through life, — the easiest good-nature, the friendliest readiness to be pleased with everybody and with everything, which made her for many years very popular among her people.

As a result of plots hatched by Christina in the Rue de Courcelles, and countenanced and favored by Louis Philippe (her uncle by marriage), General O'Donnell, who was in Navarre in command of an army, seized on the citadel of Pampeluna, six months after Espartero's elevation to the regency, and proclaimed Maria Christina Queen Regent once more. A plan was also formed to seize the person of the young Queen, and the Infanta, and carry them off to O'Donnell's army. Two generals in Madrid, Concha and Leon, had been gained over to the plot. They contrived to have only a few guards at the palace on a dark, tempestuous night, when, with a number of their followers, they entered the main portal and rushed up the grand staircase to the Queen's private apartments. But in the corridor they met with eighteen veteran halberdiers, who made a vigorous resistance. The halberdiers ensconced themselves within an anteroom, and fired through holes made in the door the moment they heard footsteps at the head of the staircase. Many of the assailants were slain and wounded.

" In the mean time the situation of the poor little Queen and her sister may be more easily imagined than described. The repeated discharge of firearms which reverberated through the courts and halls of the palace ; the mingled shouts, and curses, and groans, and menaces which accompanied the attack, joined to the darkness of the night and the howling of the storm, — filled their hearts with terror. They had no one with them but their *aya*, or governess, Madame Mina, and some of their female attendants, except their poor singing-master, who was as much frightened as any of the women. Ignorant of the object of this attack, and fearful that their own lives were menaced, the poor children gave themselves up to tears and outcries. The Queen threw herself into the arms of her governess, crying : ' *Aya mia !* who are they? Are they rebels? What do they want of me ? ' The Princess was in convulsions in the arms of an attendant, making the most piteous exclamations. It was with the greatest difficulty that Madame Mina was able to soothe them into some degree of calmness. The noise of firearms continued; attempts were heard to force a door leading through a private passage; two or three musket balls broke the windows of their apartment, but were stopped by the inside shutters. In the midst of these horrors the poor little Queen, trembling and sobbing, called to one of the ladies in attendance: 'Inez, I wish to say something to you; Inez, I want to pray!' The wish of the innocent child was granted. They all knelt down and prayed. 'And I felt relieved,' said Madame Mina, in her narrative of this eventful night, 'by the tears I shed in contemplating the situation of these two innocent beings, who, full of fervor, directed their supplications to Heaven to protect and deliver them from a peril the extent of which no one knew so well as I.' . . . The gallant defence of the halberdiers effectually defeated this atrocious attempt. They kept the assailants at bay till assistance arrived. The alarm spread through Madrid. The regular troops and national guards assembled from all quarters. Espartero hastened to the scene of action, and the palace was completely surrounded. Concha and Leon, seeing that the case was desperate, left their fellows in the lurch, and consulted their own safety in flight. They spurred their horses to the open country, but Concha, being in ordinary dress, returned unobserved to Madrid, concealed himself there, and ultimately escaped out of the kingdom. The heedless Leon, being in full general's uniform, was a marked object; he was discovered and arrested at some distance from Madrid, and, though great interest was made in his favor, he was ultimately shot."

The result of this attempt was to throw more odium on Maria Christina, and on Louis Philippe and his ministry, who were secretly aiding and abetting another revolution.

Before the month of October ended, Espartero was called away from Madrid to put down a military revolt in Barcelona. Discontent in Catalonia had been carefully fostered by Christina and her ally, who infused into the minds of the Catalans an idea that the friendship for England attributed to Espartero would lead him to favor the importation of English cotton goods into Spain, which might injure the cotton factories of Catalonia. This idea disposed the population to side with the troops, who were bent on the restoration of the Moderado party, and the return of Christina. The departure of the Regent Espartero for the scene of the revolt was witnessed by Mr. Irving, and in his letters it was graphically described. He said of Espartero : —

"He is a fine martial figure, and was arrayed in full uniform, with towering feathers, and mounted on a noble gray charger, with a flowing mane and a long silken tail that almost swept the ground. He rode along the heads of the column, saluting the soldiers with his gauntleted hand, and receiving cheers wherever he went.[1] He stopped to speak particularly to some troops of horsemen, then, returning to the centre of the esplanade, he drew his sword, made a signal as if about to speak, and in an instant silence prevailed over that vast body of troops and the thousands of spectators. I do not know when I was ever more struck by anything than by this sudden quiet of an immense multitude. The Regent then moved slowly backward and forward with his horse, about a space of thirty yards, waving his sword and addressing the troops in a voice so loud and clear that every word could be distinctly heard to a great distance. The purport of his speech was to proclaim his determination to protect the present constitution, and the liberties of Spain, against despotism on the one hand, and anarchy on the other ; and that he confided to the loyalty of the national guards during his absence the protection of the capital and the safeguard of the young and innocent Queen. His speech was responded to by enthusiastic acclamations, and he sallied forth in martial style from the great gate of Alcala."

I think my readers will hardly blame me for giving one more extract from the letters of Mr. Irving. He was presented to the little Queen upon her Saint's Day, together with all the rest of the *corps diplomatique*, and it must have been for the poor child a trying ceremony, as, followed by

[1] It is singular how political feeling will color the impression made on the most honest observer, when gazing for the first time on the person of a great man. Calderon de la Barca, who was a Moderado, in the interest of the court, and opposed to Espartero, speaks very differently of his appearance when he met him at a Cabinet dinner, in the autumn of 1853: "In Espartero's outward man there is little to attract the popular fancy. Divested of his uniform and multitudinous crosses, he would appear an ordinary-looking individual, rather in feeble health, devoid of strength, either moral or physical. His manners are grave, his features no way remarkable. Except that he is a man of the people, one looks in vain for the qualities which have made him the hero of the popular cause." He died in 1878, at the age of 86.

her sister, she passed down the diplomatic line, her duty being to receive and reply to a speech from each of the foreign representatives.

"I felt almost as much fluttered as herself," says Mr. Irving. "She is growing fast, and will soon be quite womanly in appearance. I cannot say she is strictly handsome, but her sister, the Infanta, is decidedly pretty enough to answer all reasonable notions of a princess. I had been so interested in contemplating the little sovereign that I had absolutely forgotten to arrange anything to say, and when she stood before me, I was, as is usual with me on public occasions, at a loss. However, something must be said, so I expressed my regret that my want of fluency in the Spanish language prevented my addressing her as I could wish. 'But you speak it very well,' said she, with a smile and a little flirt of her fan. I shook my head negatively. 'Do you like Spain?' said she. 'Very much,' I replied; and I spoke sincerely. She smiled again, gave another little dash of her fan, bowed, and passed on. Her sister followed. She had not the womanly carriage of the Queen, being more of a child. I told her I hoped she had been pleased at the opera, where I had had the honor of seeing her a few nights before. She said, 'Yes; she liked the theatre,' and then glided on after her sister."

Mr. Irving mentions subsequently a speech of Espartero to the diplomatic corps, when some months later he was about to go forth to confront another revolt, set on foot by divers factions, who had formed a coalition to pull him from his place and put an end to the existing Progresista government. He said it was his wish to cultivate cordial relations with all countries, but particularly with those who had representatives at the Spanish court, and who recognized the constitution of Spain, the throne of Isabella, his regency, and his loyal devotion to the constitution and the throne; that his sole and uniform ambition was to place the reins of government in the hands of the Queen on October 10, 1844, when she should have attained her legal majority. Then he trusted to place under her command a peaceful, prosperous, and happy country; meantime he would resist every attempt to throw that country into a state of anarchy.

17

"But, alas!" says Mr. Irving, "I cannot but feel that he sallies forth this time with much more doubtful prospects than in his former expedition against Barcelona. The spirit of rebellion is more widely diffused, and is breaking forth in various places."

A month later Madrid was in confusion and alarm. An insurgent force, under General Espiroz, had been threatening it for several days, while General Narvaez, who had returned from recent exile, was bringing another army to co-operate with him. A government army, under Generals Soane and Zurbano, was hurrying up for the defence of the capital. A sort of siege of the city then took place, and the diplomatic corps, fearing for the safety of the Queen in the absence of the Regent, offered to rally round her; but on the approach of the government forces, the rebel generals drew off to encounter them. "Espartero," says Mr. Irving, "has been the only man for many years calculated to be a kind of keystone to the arch, but his popularity has been undermined, and whether he be displaced or not, I fear he will no longer have power and influence to prevent the whole edifice falling to ruin and confusion."

Treachery helped the work that disunion had begun. In August, 1843, a week or two after Mr. Irving wrote thus, the idol of September 10, 1840, was on his way to England, whither he was shortly after pursued by a decree which stripped him of all his honors, titles, and decorations.

His reception in England was not only cordial but enthusiastic, which probably did not assist his popularity in Spain. Mr. Irving paid a visit to his wife the Duchess of Vittoria on the eve of her departure to join her husband. "She said that it was a matter of pride and consolation to her that they left the regency poorer than when they had accepted it. Nor did she speak with acrimony of any of the political rivals who had effected the downfall of her husband; but with deep feeling mentioned the conduct of some who had always professed devotion to him, who had risen by his friendship, and who had betrayed him. General Narvaez and General Serrano, the new commander-in-chief and the minister of war, had sent her offers of service. 'As to General Narvaez,' she said, 'he has always been the avowed enemy of my husband, but an open and frank one ; he practised nothing but what he professed. I accept his offers with gratitude and thanks. As to Serrano, he professed to be my husband's friend, he rose by his friendship and favors, and he has proved faithless to him. I will accept nothing at his hands.'"

She departed for England by way of France, with an escort furnished by Narvaez to protect her in her journey through Spain.

All was now changed under the provisional government set up by the successful generals. Lopez, who had been in Espartero's Cabinet, was made prime minister, but as all power was in the hands of the Moderado generals, he found his position so untenable that he induced the Cortes to pass a bill accelerating the legal majority of the child queen. Thus instead of coming of age at fourteen on the 10th of October, 1844, she was proclaimed a reigning queen eleven months earlier. This done, Lopez placed his resignation in her hands, and a Moderado ministry came into power.

Madame Mina, Arguelles, and all the official characters placed by the late Regent about the person of the Queen were superseded, the old nobility flocked back to court, where everything was brilliancy and mutual congratulation, while the girl of thirteen who had passed as it were to a throne from the nursery, thoroughly enjoyed the pageantry and the flattery with which she was surrounded.

But though the court was Moderado, policy prescribed for a short while a Progresista prime minister. That office was bestowed on Olozaga, a man of high character and conscientiousness. But hardly was he in possession of power before an intrigue was set on foot to get rid of him. It was desirable that a new Cortes should be chosen which would give the Progresistas a considerable majority. Ever since Queen Christina had been an exile she had kept up in her Hôtel de Courcelles an almost daily correspondence with her daughter, and under her instructions, either to the child herself or to those about her, the extraordinary controversy occurred that amazed Madrid, the Cortes, and the outside world. Already Queen Christina had sent creatures of her own to Madrid to form around her daughter a *camarilla*, — that household body of irresponsible advisers who have always directed affairs in a Spanish court. These ladies and gentlemen were all devoted adherents of Christina, Moderados in their politics, and strongly tinged with absolutist principles, although most hostile to the claims of Don Carlos.

Olozaga retained office only a week. During that week he had presented to her Majesty a decree dissolving the Cortes, and ordering a new election. The Queen refused to sign it, pleading that it was the Cortes that had declared her fit to reign. Olozaga insisted, and she finally signed. It was at once rumored in Madrid that her signature had been procured not only by moral pressure, but by personal violence, and these rumors seemed confirmed by a second decree revoking the order for the dissolution of the Cortes, and dismissing the minister.

The next day a new prime minister took his place in the Cortes, — Gonzales Bravo, editor of a satirical journal in the capital. He took from his portfolio a paper which he proceeded to read. It was a full account, signed by Isabella, of the violence which she averred had been used towards her by Olozaga.

It was impossible to believe the story. It was not in character that Olozaga should have conducted himself like a ruffian to his sovereign. He made an explanation to the Cortes, after which even his enemies held him to be blameless, and for the sake of the reputation of the child-queen the matter was hushed up as speedily as possible. It was a poor beginning of the forlorn child's reign, but from her earliest years those about her had said that she was capable of great dissimulation.

The truth seems to have been that the young girl had been somewhat frightened by the minister's unaccustomed sternness, had complained of it to her attendants, who,

QUEEN ISABELLA II.

delighted to find a pretext for the dismissal of Olozaga, had magnified it into the account which Isabella signed. After Olozaga's self-vindication in the Cortes, no one believed that he had locked the doors, had seized the Queen's hands, and had declared that, *nolens volens*, she must sign the paper. Nevertheless, though all men exonerated Olozaga, he found it necessary, for fear of assassination, of which he had received several hints, to withdraw from Madrid secretly. "Portugal," says an English resident, at that time in the capital, "presented the readiest asylum, and following very nearly the course of the Tagus, the exile, escorted by twenty well-armed *contrabandistas*, crossed the frontier on the back of a mule, disguised as a trader."

"Olozaga," adds another writer, "was used to that sort of thing, having already had to fly for his life in the time of Ferdinand. On that occasion he drove out of Madrid in the disguise of a *calesero*, accompanied by his friend Garcia, who was also obliged to fly from the vengeance of the *camarilla* of the day. They reached Corunna in safety, and embarked for England. The facile versatility with which Olozaga smoked, joked, and drank his way, adapting himself to the humors of all he met, and admirably supporting his assumed character, had in no small degree contributed to save them from detection."[1]

---

[1] In 1869 a letter written by Olozaga when ambassador at Paris appeared in a London paper. A man named Murillo had committed a murder, and was condemned to death. He had implored the ambassador to intercede for him. This was in part his answer : —
"Mr. Murillo, you are a Spaniard, and you have been condemned to death. I who represent Spain in this empire have been nearer to the gibbet than you are to the guillotine. . . ."
Then after telling him that he will do his best, but has little hope of succeeding under the circumstances, the ambassador goes on to say : —
"The less hope you have, the better. When I was in the extremity in which you are now placed, my sole consolation was to say to myself : Be persuaded that the day which now lights thee will be the last thou shalt see ! By this means the hours which exceeded the day were always more agreeable."
This was all the consolation the ambassador could suggest, but he sent a special messenger to provide his correspondent with comforts, and in the end succeeded in saving his life.

At last when the time for the *camarilla* selected by Christina to complete her designs, was ripe, a Moderado Cabinet was formed, the chief places in which were filled by Narvaez, and Sartorius the Count de San Luis. Christina was recalled from exile, and returned with the full intention of exerting all her influence to marry her royal daughters in such a way as would give satisfaction to her uncle and ally, Louis Philippe, who in the event of the success of their plans, had promised (so men said) to stand between her and any attempt that might be made in Spain to force her to disgorge the wealth that the Spaniards accused her of having stolen.

Here is Mr. Irving's account of her return in a letter dated March 16, 1844 : —

"We are preparing for great ceremonies and festivities on the arrival of the Queen Mother, who has lately entered Spain from France, and is slowly making her way to the capital, to be restored to her children. The little Queen and her sister departed from Madrid some time ago, to meet their mother on the road. . . . The meeting is to take place at Aranjuez. A temporary structure has been put up on the road for that purpose. She returns by the very way by which she left the kingdom in 1840, when the whole world seemed to be roused against her and she was followed by clamor and execrations. What is the case now? The cities that were almost in arms against her now receive her with fêtes and rejoicings. . . . The impatience of the little Queen and her sister would not permit them to remain quiet in the tent; they were continually sallying forth among a throng of courtiers to a position that commanded a distant view of the road to Ocaña, as it sloped down the side of a rising ground. Poor things! — they were kept nearly two hours in anxious suspense. . . . At length the royal *cortége* was seen descending the distant slope of the road, escorted by squadrons of lancers, whose yellow uniforms, with the red flag of the lance fluttering aloft, made them look at a distance like a moving mass of fire and flame. As they drew near, the squadrons of horse wheeled off on to the plain, and the royal carriage approached. The impatience of the little Queen could no longer be restrained; without waiting at the entrance of the tent to receive her royal mother, according to etiquette, she hurried forth through the avenue of guards quite to the road, where I lost sight of her amidst the throng. . . . The old nobility, who have long been cast down and dispirited, and surrounded by doubt and danger, look upon the return of the Queen Mother as the triumph of their cause, and the harbinger of more prosperous days."

The next day the Queen and her mother made their entrance into Madrid, the mother sitting on the left side of her daughter. The houses were all decorated with tapestry, and the populace showed much enthusiasm.

While this pageant was taking place the excellent Arguelles breathed his last. He had been in bad health for some months, and recent political agitations hastened his end. His life had been one of great vicissitudes, and he had bravely borne all kinds of change of fortune.

"When he had the guardianship of the young Queen," says Mr. Irving, "he was entitled to a salary of about seventy thousand dollars. He only accepted one tenth. On the triumph of the Moderado party he retired from office poor. . . . He was faithful in his guardianship of the little Queen and her sister, and was strongly attached to them. He was represented by his political opponents as an enemy of the Queen Mother, but, though he may have disapproved of her political course when in power, he did justice to the amiableness of her character, and in a conversation with me, lamented that she was separated from her daughters, as her presence could have been of vast advantage to them, especially to the young Queen. When the Queen Mother was entering Madrid in state in company with the little Queen and her sister, an officious courtier rode up to the carriage, and announced to her with congratulation the news of the death of her enemy Arguelles. 'Hush!' said the Queen Mother, 'do not let the children hear you, for they loved the old man!'"

# CHAPTER XIV

QUEEN CHRISTINA found herself restored to Spain by permission of General Narvaez, Duke of Valencia. He was not at that time prime minister, but he held supreme authority. Lopez, when he resigned his place as head of the provisional government, had said that he was hopeless of doing anything for the country in what he called, " that mephitic court atmosphere, in which thought and soul every moment sank in the wretchedness of personal interests, pretensions, and intrigues."

It was possibly with some view of controlling this " mephitic atmosphere " that Narvaez entered into close relations with the *camarilla*. For more than two hundred years the court of Spain had been governed always by a *camarilla*, a group of irresponsible advisers, men and women, who owed their position solely to the sovereign's favor, and kept it by flatteries and counsels suited to his mind. The most influential member of the *camarilla* placed round poor little Isabella by the care of Queen Christina was the Duchess of Vera Cruz, — a woman whose character was not above reproach, but who had been *aya*, or governess, to the young Queen during her infancy. When Christina ceased to be Queen Regent in 1840, the Duchess was replaced by the widowed Madame Mina, but the former lady resumed her place at court when Espartero fell. To her is supposed to have been due the conduct of the Queen in the affair of Olozaga.

Narvaez, whilst awaiting the time when he should find it convenient to exchange his post of commander-in-chief for the position of prime minister, filled the place by Don Luis Gonzales Bravo, of whom it has been said that he united some of the most singular disqualifications for the post ever

possessed by a prime minister. He had gained notoriety as
the editor and chief contributor to a scurrilous popular
journal, the " Guirigay," or " Slang," — a paper remarkable for
its coarse personalities and its unscrupulousness. He had
begun life as an active member of the Thunder Club, — an
association of riotous young men who amused themselves
after nightfall by imitating the " Mohawks " of London in
the days of the early Georges. They molested peaceable
citizens, they knocked down watchmen, and practised such
like intellectual and dignified diversions. When he became
editor of the " Slang," his attacks were first directed against
Queen Christina ; and when she was expelled from Spain, it
was thought that he had contributed to her downfall by in-
flaming against her the popular mind. Four years made a
great change in his opinions. As he said in his own defence,
" A man makes himself ridiculous when he stands always in
one position." So from an Exaltado he became a Moderado, and in both cases he adopted extreme views. He had
gained influence and popularity while in the opposition ; but
when he became prime minister, his incapacity for government grew so evident that his popularity and influence were
at an end. He did not give up his connection with the
" Slang," and he lost no time in taking care of himself and
of his friends. His father, who had been dismissed from
some government employment because of irregularity in
money affairs, he made under-secretary of the treasury ; and
his brother, a hanger-on of one of the theatres in Madrid,
received a post in the Queen's household.

Narvaez himself had the faults and the virtues of a soldier of
fortune, — " prompt decision, great energy, and determination,
on the one hand ; cruelty, impolicy, and violence on the other."

" His character made him popular with a portion of the army,
and over the officers in particular he exercised great influence.
His severities, however, especially his shooting of eight men in
the autumn of 1844 for demanding what had been solemnly
promised them, — permission to quit the service, — lost him
many adherents, and made him numerous enemies in the ranks.
But his deadly foes were the ex-national guards of Madrid.

That they had been disarmed, disbanded, and then sabred and bayoneted when assembled for peaceful purposes, were matters they were not likely to forget or forgive. . . . But, if we except a portion of the period of Espartero's rule, there were no three months during the ten years from 1835 to 1846 which would not, if transplanted into the annals of any other country, form an era of bloodshed."

It was only by the exercise of despotic cruelties that the cabinets chosen by Narvaez checked insurrection and prevented civil war. He defended his severities by the argument that the sufferers were rebels against the established government of their country, and as such deserved their fate; "but in a country in which revolution flourishes like an evergreen plant how is it to be decided who is the rightful governor, and who is the usurper?"

Such were the excuses for sanguinary executions, but none such could be pleaded for street massacres.

"On many a *fiesta*, or saint's day," says an Englishman long resident in Spain, who published in 1846 the clearest and most impartial account given of Spanish affairs at that period, — "days which Spain regards as of especial holiness, — plots and snares were thickly strewn around the people's footsteps; murder lurked beneath the wreath of festivity, and the day which began with prayer concluded with mourning."

Especially was this the case during the three days of rejoicing on occasion of the Queen's majority. "They invited us to a ball," said the people of Madrid, "and we had to assist at a funeral."

Narvaez, like most men in Spain (for a certain Orientalism lingers in the Spanish character), had notions regarding outward decency, and feminine observance of conventional propriety, far stricter than those that prevailed at the court of Naples, where Queen Christina had her early training; and the question was often asked, "Considering what Queen Christina is, why should the government and the populace have welcomed her return to the court of her innocent child?" But Maria Christina, false, cruel, avaricious, and licentious as she was, even according to her own admission, had at least the instincts of a woman. Narvaez estimated the dangers that might beset the child-queen on her entrance into womanhood, and he knew that Christina understood how to reconcile her vices with appearances. She was wanted in Madrid for the excellent example she would set, if her unhappy daughter's ill-regulated passions should burst all bounds of propriety. Narvaez sanctioned her return to Spain only on condition that she should take no part in politics, but he could not prevent such part from being taken by her ally, Louis Philippe, or by the *camarilla*, composed of men and women appointed to act according to her views. She returned to Spain with Muñoz, now Duke of Rianzares, as her acknowledged husband. She had made a pilgrimage to Rome during her exile, and had purged herself of sins committed in that connection. It is believed that she at that time (1841) went through the ceremony of marriage with her second husband, but for reasons sufficient to herself she would not acknowledge her nuptials.

"When she left Spain in 1840 a committee of the Cortes, appointed to report on the sequestration of her property, had contrived, with spiteful and perhaps not very honorable dexterity, to show that Spain had claims against her for a very large amount of money unlawfully received, as she could not legally have been Queen Regent while the wife of Captain Muñoz. The committee had stated the alternative with malignant clearness. Christina refused to be called a swindler, because in that case she might have been called upon to restore money appropriated under false pretences. Rather than lose her property, she consented to confess herself to be what most women would consider something worse. But on her arrival in Madrid in 1844 she openly avowed her marriage, fixing the date of it in the spring of the same year."

She had had three daughters of whom Muñoz was the father, before her first exile in 1840. While she resided in the Rue de Courcelles, these children were kept out of sight, and were sent to live with a governess near Vevay in Switzerland. On her return to Madrid in 1844 they were brought forward, acknowledged by Queen Isabella to be her sisters, and were treated by the court almost as infantas.

Lady Louisa Tenison, who travelled in Spain about this period, and wrote an interesting book, with admirable illustrations from her own pencil and pen, thus speaks of Queen Christina : —

" Her former beauty has now disappeared, as she has grown very stout; but she possesses still the same fascinating voice, the same bewitching manner, and the same siren smile which make all who speak to her bow before the irresistible charm which she knows so well how to exercise. Queen Christina might have worked an immense amount of good for this unhappy country, had she devoted her talents and energies to the improvement of the nation; had she exerted her powerful influence in a good and noble cause, how much might she not have accomplished! But instead of earning a reputation which would have called forth the admiration of posterity, she preferred sacrificing the interests of the kingdom for the sake of gratifying her own inordinate love of wealth, and has, in fact, proved herself worthy of the Neapolitan family from which she sprung."

Her popularity was once great, her talents undeniable, the power of fascination she could exercise over all those brought into contact with her was universally acknowledged. She was popular as the representative of anti-Carlism and of constitutional monarchy, and she might have made herself greatly beloved. A large majority of the Spanish nation — which has ever been noted for its loyalty and its monarchical predilections — would have asked nothing better than to esteem and to protect her. As it was, they could only look upon her as a necessity, accepted because anything appeared better than the rule of the vacillating Don Carlos and the tyranny of his priest-ridden advisers. But it was soon discovered that, while professing to combat absolutism, Christina was at heart an absolutist and a tyrant ; that all her political tendencies were retrograde ; and that she was utterly selfish, degradingly sensual, and unboundedly covetous.[1]

[1] The above paragraphs are taken from " Blackwood's Magazine," October, 1853, in an article reviewing the work of Lady Louisa Tenison.

During the administration of Narvaez there was a Cortes composed almost entirely of Moderados. The Progresistas had been weeded out ; but although all power was in the hands of one party, that did not imply a harmonious or peaceful rule. Those who called themselves Moderados split up into groups or factions, holding a variety of opinions, and squabbles in the Cortes were as frequent and as excited as if it had contained its due proportion of Exaltados and Progresistas.

The Progresistas, finding themselves not only deprived of power, but objects of persecution, began to turn their eyes toward the northern provinces, and occasionally to dream of a coalition with the Carlist cause. The nation had endured so much, had suffered so terribly from civil wars, rebellions, reactions, and the like, that all it expected, almost all it asked, was to be tyrannized over gently. Spain had not had time to recover from her state of exhaustion and suffering, during the honest and conscientious, but brief rule of Espartero. Never had rulers a grander chance than the Moderados of 1843 when they came into possession of power. "The ball was at their foot; they had but to pick it up ; instead of that, they threw it away. No sooner were they in power than they abandoned themselves to their evil instincts, and thought only of filling their pockets. Christina reverted to her old system of unscrupulous appropriation ; and Narvaez, having filled the higher grades in the army with his own supporters, believed himself to have made the army his own by pampering and flattery, and gave free rein to his instincts as a despotic ruler."

Espartero, in his anxiety to lessen expenses and to replenish the treasury, had at the close of the Carlist war reduced the army to fifty thousand men, which was probably too little for an efficient peace establishment in so turbulent a country ; but Narvaez increased it to a hundred thousand. In this army the officers were much more numerous, proportionately, than the soldiers. It was calculated that there was a general for every four hundred men ; and at one time, about this period, there were said to be two hundred and fifty generals congregated in the capital.

Narvaez projected great reforms and many useful public works, some of which, while he remained in power, were begun. He also entered into negotiations with the Pope, who since the death of Ferdinand had given all his influence to Don Carlos, and refused to acknowledge Isabella, or to give investiture to the bishops she appointed ; in fact, the attitude of Rome had been exceedingly detrimental to the Queen's cause because it sent a vast number of priests (always active and influential partisans) over to the side of the Pretender.

But the question that most agitated men's minds after 1844 was that of the marriage of the Queen and her heiress presumptive, the Infanta.

The question of Isabella's marriage was first mooted a few days after her birth. " She shall be married," said her father, "to a son of my brother, Don Francisco di Paula." When Christina bore a second daughter, the King said, " They shall be married to my brother Francisco's two sons."

If this story be true, there was in 1830 and 1832 no mention of the sons of Don Carlos, which, as he was then on good terms with his brother Ferdinand, would have seemed natural ; but a bitter feud was raging in the palace between the two Neapolitan princesses (Christina and Luisa Carlota) on the one hand, and the two Portuguese princesses (Maria Francesca, wife of Don Carlos, and her sister, the Princess of Beira) on the other. The project of a double marriage was doubtless contrived by Luisa Carlota, the strong-minded sister of Christina ; and the Queen Regent, in her conversations and correspondence with that lady, frequently referred to it, and expressed a strong desire that the marriages should take place, though the children were double cousins, their fathers being brothers, and their mothers sisters, — but such considerations never seem to have been taken into account in the matrimonial alliances of the Spanish Bourbons. When, in 1846, the question of the Queen's marriage was the one thing uppermost in all men's minds, a letter was published in a Madrid newspaper, written (or purporting to have been written) in the year 1834, by Queen Christina to her sister. It spoke of the intention expressed by the late King that his daughters should marry his brother's sons, and then continued: "This idea has always flattered my heart, and I would fain see its realization near at hand, for it was the wish and will of the beloved Ferdinand, which I will ever strive to fulfil in all that depends on me."

The *beloved Ferdinand* was at that time supplanted by the still more beloved Muñoz, but it suited Christina to play the rôle of a tender-hearted widow.

Two years later she was offering her child's hand to a son of Don Carlos, whose army in 1836 was threatening Madrid. But the Carlists having been driven back to their strongholds in the mountains, the matter was shelved. Next came a project for the Queen's marriage with an archduke, a son of the House of Austria, who should share the regency with Christina, and be made commander-in-chief of the Spanish army. Perhaps the choice might have fallen on poor Maximilian, — lucky would it have been for Isabella if it had; but when Zea Bermudez went to Vienna to negotiate the marriage, he stipulated as an indispensable condition of success that Louis Philippe should know nothing about it. No sooner, however, had he set out upon his mission than Christina told all to her uncle, and the project of an Austrian marriage was at once nipped in the bud. Again the idea of marrying Isabella to the son of Don Carlos was brought forward; and the minister Toreno was charged to prepare the public mind for this alliance by announcing in the Cortes that wars like the one then devastating Spain could only be terminated by a compromise, — in other words, a marriage. But the Cortes did not take kindly to this suggestion, and the war was brought to a close in another way.

When in 1840 Queen Christina found herself an exile in Paris, and had the means of daily personal intercourse with her astute uncle at the Tuileries, every resource of money and of intrigue was employed to get poor little Isabella into that uncle's power; even the plot to carry her by night out of her palace, and mounting her *en croupe* behind a dragoon, to bear her off to O'Donnell's army, which had declared for

Christina as regent in the place of Espartero. Enormous bribes were offered to men in place and power to enter into partnership with the principals in the conspiracy. One especially of an immense sum was tendered to the military commandant of the important fortress of Montjuich, commanding the town and harbor of Barcelona; but to the honor of that officer it was declined.

It was the great ambition of Louis Philippe's life to accomplish what Louis XIV. and Napoleon had failed to do. With one of his sons on the Spanish throne, and with Algeria in his possession, the Mediterranean would indeed have become a French lake. We smile and sigh as we read the alarm created in England as the cunning old monarch developed his policy. The denunciations of the English press against his ambition, his treachery toward England, and his truly Bourbon disregard of solemn promises, were directed against his state policy rather than against him as a man. Time speedily proved that England had had little cause to concern herself about the former. Events in the womb of the future at the time of the Spanish marriages were, two years later, to make the success or failure of that policy of no consequence to Spain, England, France, or the rest of the world; but it was the sacrifice of a poor, ill-taught, worse than orphaned child-queen that makes us indignant; that would have caused us to rejoice that the plan was frustrated by almost any means, short of the cost of a woman's honor!

Espartero refused, during the three years of his regency, to have anything to do with the question of his Queen's marriage. He said that as she was not to marry until she came of age, when he should be no longer regent, his government had no occasion to busy itself with the selection of her husband. It might have been better had he been less scrupulous, for Christina and Louis Philippe, who had interests of their own to serve, were by no means inclined to do nothing in the interval.

The French King's first plan was to marry the young Queen to his son, the Duke d'Aumale, a man whose subsequent career proved him to be one of the wisest, most accomplished, and most conscientious men in Europe. In 1843 he was known to be a fine young man, very rich, and highly educated. Queen Christina highly approved the plan. If she had any motherly instincts left with regard to her eldest daughter, she could not but feel that her future would be thus committed into safe and worthy hands. Besides, she was to receive from Louis Philippe, as the price of her concurrence in his scheme, a promise that her own guardianship accounts and private peculations, which the Cortes was so anxious to interfere with, should not be too curiously investigated if her daughter married his son.

In view of this plan to marry Isabella to the Duke d'Aumale, an envoy was sent early in 1843 to London and the principal courts upon the Continent, on the part of King Louis Philippe, who, calling himself the head of the House of Bourbon, said that he felt bound to declare that, according to the spirit of the treaty of Utrecht made in 1713, the Queen of Spain could marry no other than a prince of that family. This assumption of Bourbonism by no means met with a cordial response. England replied that, according to the Constitution of Spain, the Cortes must decide on who should be the Queen's husband, and whatever prince the Cortes should select would be favored by England. Nor were the replies of the other courts more satisfactory.

In June, 1843, Espartero, the only conscientious and constitutional ruler with whom Spain for long years had been blessed, was, by the bribes and intrigues of Queen Christina and her uncle, driven from power. In 1845 Queen Victoria paid a visit to the King of the French at his family château of Eu. Louis Philippe was paternal, the Queen pleased and cordial. Lord Aberdeen and Monsieur Guizot, the respective premiers, had long conversations on the subject of the Spanish marriages. Louis Philippe urged that if the marriage of Isabella to the Duke d'Aumale was not acceptable to England, that country might at least consent to the marriage of his youngest son, the Duke de Montpensier, with the Infanta ; and an express or implied promise was person-

18

ally given by Louis Philippe and his minister to Queen Victoria, Prince Albert, and Lord Aberdeen, that the marriage of the Duke de Montpensier and Luisa should not take place until after Queen Isabella had been married, *and had had a child.* As a concession, the English Minister for Foreign Affairs was induced to declare that it was desirable that the Queen of Spain should wed a descendant of Philip V.

There had been, previous to this time, some talk of two candidates from the House of Coburg. One, the now widowed Ferdinand of Coburg, who had made an admirable husband to the Queen of Portugal, the other a somewhat distant cousin of Prince Albert's, a young prince of the Catholic branch of the same family. But Ferdinand of Portugal did not desire the hand of the Queen of Spain, and the claims of the other Coburg were barred by the assent of England to the proposal that the Queen should marry a prince of the House of Bourbon. Of these there were four marriageable princes to choose from : a son of Don Carlos ; the Prince of Trapani, who was a prince of Naples ; and the two sons of Don Francisco di Paula, — Don Francisco d'Assis and Don Enrique. Of these it was desirable to choose the most ineligible, in order to provide, as far as possible, against the contingency that the Queen (whose health was delicate) might give birth to an heir. To be sure, there was a promise that Montpensier and Luisa should not be married until the Queen had issue, but — by good management a royal promise always could be broken.

The consent of the Cortes was at that time necessary to the Queen's marriage, but the deputies were decidedly opposed to Trapani. They had had enough of the Neapolitan connection. Trapani himself was a miserable creature. The populace of Madrid treated with scorn his very name, which had some analogy to the Spanish word for a dish-clout.

The next step in the intrigue was to call for a reform of the Constitution of 1837, — a measure acceptable to the Moderados. The Constitution was so " amended " that it did away with nearly all the liberal clauses of the Constitution of

*DON FRANCISCO D'ASSIS.*

1837. The Senate, for instance, was to be nominated by the
Crown, not chosen by the people ; but the most important
clause was that which made it no longer necessary for the
deputies to assent to their sovereign's marriage ; that event
was to be merely announced to them, whether before or
after it had taken place. Christina and her sister objected
strenuously to any one of the three sons of Don Carlos ;
there remained therefore only two candidates, Don Francisco
d'Assis and Don Enrique. Of these the elder, Don Francisco d'Assis, was known to be so imperfectly organized that
there was no hope that he would ever be the father of heirs
to the Spanish Crown. He was under-sized, had a little
squeaking voice, and was wholly without ambition, or force
of character. He was gentlemanly in his manners, could
talk agreeably, and indeed converse in several languages.
Don Enrique, who it was thought had found some favor with
his cousin, was a blunt, rough sailor, with small reverence for
religious observances, and extremely rude in his manners ; but
the nation considered him the candidate to be preferred. As
a Spaniard, he was more pleasing to the Spanish people than
a foreigner ; in energy and decision of character he was far
superior to his brother Don Francisco. " He had been
brought up in a ship and not in a palace, had lived apart
from *camarillas* and their evil influences ; and though little
was known of his political predilections, it was hoped that
he might govern the country constitutionally by majorities in
the Cortes, and not by the aid, and according to the wishes,
of interested politicians." But his selection would have
spoiled Christina's schemes. He was banished from Spain
on some slight pretext, and became the object of persecution. This increased his popularity ; and had he been
placed at the head of a party bent on getting up a revolution in his favor, he might have plunged his country into
another civil war. He refused overtures from Louis Philippe, made in hope of inducing him to favor the marriage
of the Duke de Montpensier with his cousin, and was obsti-
nately opposed to any alliance with the French King.

Christina and her ally had made up their minds as to the

Queen's marriage to Don Francisco d'Assis. They availed themselves of a very flimsy pretext to get rid of the promise made to Queen Victoria and Lord Aberdeen at Eu. They said that Lord Palmerston had written in one of his despatches, "whoever the Queen of Spain may marry, whether it be a Coburg or some other prince." . . . And this was distorted into the enunciation of a purpose on the part of the English Government to uphold the pretensions of the Coburg candidate.

It only remained to force the poor young Queen to consent to marry Don Francisco. All one night her mother and M. Bresson, the French ambassador, were with her. Sobs, cries, and entreaties were heard by dwellers in the palace, but when morning dawned consent had been forced from the unhappy girl. A courier was at once sent to summon Montpensier, who was waiting on the frontier, and with hardly any time for bridal preparation, the marriages were celebrated on the same day, October 10, 1846, — but *one after the other*; thus "keeping," said M. Guizot, in reply to the indignant complaints of the English Government, "the promise that the Infanta should not be married until *after* her sister." He omitted to allude to the important stipulation, — " until Queen Isabella had had a child."

Thus Louis Philippe was made confident that his son, or at any rate one of his descendants, would after a few years ascend the Spanish throne, and M. Guizot prided himself in the thought that he had achieved for France the greatest triumph she had won for more than a century in the field of European diplomacy. He so expressed himself in the Chamber of Deputies, and also to his friends in private, to whom he showed Queen Isabella's picture, "sent him," he said (by Queen Christina, of course), "in acknowledgment of his services in promoting her marriage."

It needed a strong body of Spanish troops to escort the Duke de Montpensier to Madrid after he crossed the Bidassoa, so opposed was the nation to the French alliance, so heartily did it hate all Afrancesados. The French Government sent a deputation with the young prince to Madrid, to report the particulars of the marriage. Alexandre Dumas was one of the envoys, and his account of the bull-fights that took place on the occasion is one of his most spirited pieces of description. General Boulanger, then a very young officer, was also present on this occasion in behalf of his government.

Every exertion was made to have the marriage procession of the sisters as splendid and as military as possible. The wedding took place on Isabella's sixteenth birthday, October 10, 1846. The Patriarch of the Indies, the highest ecclesiastical dignitary in Spain, presided at the nuptials. All that the magnificence of Catholic ceremonial could accomplish was done to celebrate what, in the case of one couple, was an unholy union.

The brides wore dresses of white lace embroidered with gold. The Queen and her mother wore crowns. " I give your Royal Highness a helpmate, not a servant ; may you love her, even as Christ loveth the Church," were the words addressed to the young Duke de Montpensier by the Patriarch after the ceremony. What words he addressed to the other bridegroom have not been recorded.

It had been taken for granted that the marriage of the Queen and King (for Don Francisco d'Assis had been raised to that dignity) would be childless, but Queen Isabella set at nought these expectations.

" At the time of her marriage Isabella was at an age when much might yet have been made of her, if her husband had been a man whom she could either love or respect; for, so far at least, though she had given no indication of great ability or strength of character, her conduct had been without reproach except in the matter of Olozaga. But once tied to a man whom she so thoroughly despised that she never even troubled herself to hide her contempt, she threw off all restraint. Narvaez had convinced her that as a Constitutional sovereign her power in the State was rigidly limited, but she resolved that in her own house she would rule supreme. She exiled Don Francisco without ceremony to a country residence. Christina, who had lost all influence by bringing about the marriage, was given to understand that her interference would not be tolerated, and the

Queen, little more than a child in years, threw herself into a course of reckless gayety that made the sovereigns of Europe stand aghast. Well might Prince Metternich exclaim, 'Queen Isabella is revolution incarnate, in its most dangerous form.' She banished all etiquette from her court, and turning night into day, made it the scene of wildest dissipation; while she openly showed her affection for General Serrano, the handsomest man in Spain; and when her Moderado ministers remonstrated she threw herself into the hands of the Progresistas."

As regarded the union of Montpensier and Luisa, it was a very happy one. She became the mother of four beautiful and promising children, admirably brought up and educated. She was also a loving and beloved wife, shielded by the amiability, cultivation, and strict respectability of her husband's family from all the evil influences which beset her unhappy sister.

The political events that followed the Spanish marriages may be deferred till the next chapter; we will here briefly narrate the second Carlist rising in Spain.

Don Carlos (Charles V., Duke of Molina) renounced his claims to the Spanish throne in 1844, in favor of his eldest son, — Carlos, *soi-disant* Charles VI., Count de Montemolin. In 1848 the advisers of this young man conceived that the propitious moment had arrived for another Carlist insurrection. The Spanish peasantry in the Basque provinces and Catalonia were not eager for insurrection; their country had been exhausted by the disquietudes and exactions of a long civil war. Nevertheless, the disturbed state of Europe seemed to offer a favorable opportunity for political outbreaks of any kind. Cabrera sought Don Carlos, and endeavored to persuade him to head another rising; but Don Carlos, always faithful to his word, said he had renounced his rights, and would do nothing to reassert them. Then the eyes of his supporters turned to his son Carlos, the Count de Montemolin, who agreed to strike another blow for the Carlist cause. Sanctioned by him, Cabrera, in 1848, raised a force in Catalonia. For seven years he had been living in the south of France, recruiting his health, and, it is fair to say, unlearning the savagery that in the late war had blighted his reputation. He was now prepared to take the field, not as a marauding chief, but as a civilized general. The cause of Isabella, the Constitutional Queen, had lost in three ways during the interval from 1840 to 1848. She had proved herself to be in heart not a Constitutional, but an Absolutist sovereign; the downfall of Louis Philippe had pushed a most important prop from under the Spanish throne; and by the summary dismissal of Mr. Bulwer, the English ambassador, from Madrid, the administration had deprived itself of English support and sympathy.

Cabrera crossed the Pyrenees, and returned to the scene of his former exploits. The report that he had done so was discredited in Europe. Men said that he who had left Spain eight years before, with ten thousand hardy, well-armed soldiers, because he would not condescend to a guerilla warfare, after having won towns and fortresses and fought pitched battles, was not likely to recross the frontier with a handful of invaders, when the cause he had come to support was destitute of arms, money, and organization, — of everything, in short, necessary for the prosecution of a war. But Cabrera emerged from his retirement, not expecting to find an army, or money, or organization, but prepared to create all three.

In disguise he moved through eastern Spain, acquainting himself with the feeling of the country, visiting his old partisans, reviving their dormant zeal, infusing into them fresh spirit, and raising recruits. He seemed ubiquitous. He traversed Catalonia in all directions, rarely recognized in his own person, often disguised as a priest. His prodigious activity and perseverance wrought miracles. By the close of 1848, the government papers in Madrid estimated his forces at eight thousand men; the Carlists themselves at ten thousand. They had not fought; it can hardly be said that they had been opposed. Their duty had been confined to levying contributions, to organizing themselves into a disciplined army, to awaiting from French and English manufacturers supplies of arms, and from Carlist sympathizers in foreign lands supplies of money. Regularly rationed and supplied with tobacco, they waited cheerfully until the moment for action should be announced to them; in other words, until the military chest should be filled. Their martial pride had been gratified with conspicuous uniforms: one brigade wore green with black facings, one wore dark blue, another was dressed in scarlet coats and dark trousers, like English soldiers; but all wore the national Basque flat cap, or a low-crowned shako. What they needed most was some strong fortress as a centre of operations; and several attempts were made to surprise fortified towns, but without success.

During the winter of 1848–49, Cabrera lay ill, and his army was inactive. No attempt of importance was made by the government to molest them. Cabrera was a short man, muscular, square-built, and rather round-shouldered. His dark eyes, notwithstanding his reformation, never lost their cruel expression. But, warned by the past, in his second war he gave up the cruel system of reprisals. Mercy and humanity seemed to be his device, as they undoubtedly were his best policy. His aim was to win followers by conciliation, instead of compelling them to join him by intimidation and cruelty.

Although during the winter the forces of the Queen made no attack upon those collected by Cabrera, frequent and often successful attempts were made to lure or bribe his soldiers from his standard. No less than three generals, Posas, Pons, and Monserrat, passed over to the enemy; but in almost all these cases their men deserted back again, taking with them the pay they had received for changing sides. In vain great offers were made to Cabrera, — gold, titles, rank, and governorships. Having convinced his enemies that he would not accept such offers, he deemed it prudent to guard himself against assassination; and he is said to have worn a shirt of mail under his sheepskin jacket, and a wonderful metal-lined pair of thick leathern trousers. He might very well conceive that his life was all-important to the success of his cause.

Meantime affairs in France seemed likely to assist the Carlist plans in Spain. Louis Napoleon, the French President, had been on friendly terms with young Montemolin when they were both exiles; and Narvaez, fearing the influence of this old association, sent his wife (a distant connection of the Bonapartes) to intrigue, in concert with the Duke of Sotomayor, the Spanish ambassador at Paris, in the interests of her husband's government.

Letter after letter was despatched by Cabrera and other promoters of the Carlist cause in Spain, urging that at any sacrifice a sum of money should be procured; but this was beyond the power of the incapable plotters and advisers who surrounded the young pretender. Without conduct, energy, or dignity, they had not a single quality calculated to obtain credit or induce confidence. In all their attempts to raise money they miserably failed. Foreigners who had the command of funds were loath to embark them in so hazardous a speculation as the restoration of the Count de Montemolin. Nor was he himself a person who inspired confidence. He was not deficient in natural ability, but he was infirm of purpose, and, like his father before him, was led by a clique of selfish and unworthy advisers, among whom were more than one man who had been the evil genius of Charles V., and some who exercised over the young count in his manhood the influence they had had over him from his cradle. With great difficulty, and with little aid beyond that of contributions levied in Catalonia, Cabrera had subsisted his troops during the winter; in March a rumor was spread that the Count de Montemolin was on his way to join his faithful adherents.

Then came counter rumors. It was said that the Prince had crossed the Pyrenees, and had been arrested on the Spanish frontier; then that he had never left London; while some Carlists, who credited the reality of his journey, declared that their conviction from the first had been that he would be betrayed before he got through France, by men who dared not refuse to accompany him, but who were unwilling to risk themselves for what they felt sure must prove in the end a lost cause.

Cabrera, disgusted with the feeble and pusillanimous Junta of advisers who swayed and bewildered the Count de Montemolin by their intrigues and dissensions, lost all hope, and abandoned a contest in which it was impossible to fight with success, since the party had neither money nor head. Already several of his subordinate chiefs, disgusted that no reply had been received to the frequent and indignant letters and messages forwarded to London, had left him. His little army fell to pieces, and he himself was arrested by French authorities when he crossed the French frontier. After a brief detention, however, he was allowed to go at large. He retired to London, resolved never again to take up arms for the Carlist cause. He married a rich Englishwoman, and spent the latter years of his life tranquilly in England or in Italy.

It seemed as if the last hopes of Carlism had been crushed — or rather Carlism had fallen of itself without crushing. But, says a writer in " Blackwood's Magazine " in 1849, to whose articles I am indebted for much information concerning the campaign of Cabrera : —

" Spain is the country of anomalies ; and nothing in the political conduct of Spanish affairs will ever surprise us until we find them conducted according to the rules of common sense, and the dictates of prudence that govern the every-day life of ordinary humanity."

# CHAPTER XV.

## THE REVOLUTION OF 1854.

A WRITER in one of the great quarterly magazines of England speaks thus of the ten years that followed 1844 : —

"Those who would understand the politics of Spain during the period that immediately preceded or immediately followed the marriage of the young queen, must find the clue to half a dozen plots, in which the interests of courtiers, ministers, and confessor are confusedly interwoven with the hopes of the Carlist, French, Neapolitan, and Portuguese competitors for the doubtful blessing of the royal hand. Most readers might be satisfied to see six ministers rise and fall successively in an incredibly short interval, — all of them more or less Moderados."

The ministry in power in 1848 was that of Narvaez ; and Sartorius, lately a bookseller's clerk, and afterwards the Count de San Luis, was one of his underlings. Narvaez, who had insisted on outward propriety at court, had obliged the Queen to appoint General Serrano Captain-General of Granada, a post that removed him from the capital, and broke up a court scandal. He also insisted on the return of the King, and on October 13, that personage, accompanied by the Papal Nuncio, and by Queen Christina, who never approved the open irregularities of her daughter, resumed his place at court as the Queen's husband. Riots in the provinces of Spain followed the French revolution of 1848, which overthrew all the plans and hopes of Louis Philippe and Christina. These riots were put down firmly by Narvaez ; and it was his unconstitutional severities on this occasion that provoked a remonstrance from the British ambassador.

With the return of Don Francisco to court, there were petty conspiracies against the established order of things. The King was given charge of the palace, and of some other family affairs. The court at once swarmed with his favorites, and he formed an ultramontane *camarilla*, the chief personages in which were Father Fulgencio and Sister Patrocinio, who had the gift of working miracles and was marked with the *stigmata*. The King and these people aimed at re-establishing an absolute monarchy, and they very nearly succeeded. A few days before the assembling of the Cortes which had been summoned by Narvaez, Don Francisco persuaded his wife to demand of the premier his immediate resignation. A new ministry was appointed, but Narvaez in twenty-four hours swept it away. This was "the flash of lightning" ministry. The King was more Catholic than the Pope, more Absolutist than Ferdinand VII. Whenever he had an opportunity of putting his ideas into practice the result was defeat and disaster. On this occasion Narvaez sent Father Fulgencio to a monastery of his order, and Sister Patrocinio was imprisoned at Talavera, in execution of a sentence by which she had formerly been condemned. As for the King, it was intimated to him that he must give up governing the palace and administering family affairs.

But the nun and the priest subsequently returned to court when the repressive hand of Narvaez had been thrust away. He was the only one of Isabella's ministers who understood how to manage his unfortunate queen. He treated her as a spoiled child, to be humored and flattered, but who must at the same time be given to understand that there were bounds that she could not pass, and that there were limits to the license accorded her.

Narvaez had insisted upon outward decency, and obliged the Queen to appear with her husband at her side on all public occasions, but there was one point on which she would listen to no remonstrances. Tricked into a disgraceful marriage, she conceived herself at liberty to conduct as she pleased her amorous affairs. Serrano soon gave place to Colonel Gandara, Gandara to Don Josef Arana, and so

*GENERAL NARVAEZ.*

on, through a list of favorites longer than ever disgraced Catherine of Russia, who at least conducted such alliances with a sort of imperialism.

I will give one quotation relating to this subject which will be enough for my readers; and then, *Non ragionam di lor, ma guarda e passa:* —

"Many things are doubtless exaggerated, many false reports are spread; but it is true, and undeniably true, that a young cavalry officer is all-powerful at court, where he has introduced a number of his own friends, and established a sort of *coterie*, or *camarilla*, that surrounds and influences the Queen. It is true that applicants for court favor know no surer channel by which to obtain their wishes than this young man; that aspirants to power — I mean to the highest offices of state, to the ministry, and the presidency of the council — seek his society, flatter him, admit him to their intimacy, and show themselves in public as his friends. Nor do some men high in office think it beneath their dignity to avail themselves of his influence and intercession to carry in high quarters points which they might otherwise have to abandon."

"It is Madame Dubarry over again," says another contemporary writer, "only that the Spanish Madame Dubarry, instead of powder and patches, wears a sword and spurs."

Of Isabella herself in 1852 Lady Louisa Tenison tells us : —

"She has now grown immensely stout, and with the most good-natured face in the world, has certainly nothing to boast of in elegance of manner or dignity of deportment. She looks what she is, — most thoroughly kind-hearted, liking to enjoy herself, and hating all form and etiquette; extremely charitable, but always acting on the impulse of the moment, obeying her own will in all things, instead of being guided by any fixed principle of action. She dispenses money with a lavish hand, while her finances are not by any means in a flourishing condition. Her hours are not much adapted to business-like habits; she seldom gets up till four or five o'clock in the afternoon, and retires to rest about the same hour in the morning. She has one most inconvenient fault for a queen, being always two or three hours behind time. If she fixes a *Besa-manos* (or reception) at two o'clock, she comes in about five; if she has a dinner-party announced at seven, it is nine or ten before she enters the room; and if she goes in state to the theatre and the performances are announced for eight, her Majesty makes her appearance about ten."

The Queen had been twice *enceinte*. In 1848 her first child, a boy, was born. He lived only three days, but in 1851 she gave birth to a daughter. The child was adored by her mother, who, fearful of accidents and suspicious as to the fate of her first-born, kept her by her side on all occasions. Her first words when wounded by the priest Martin Marino on the steps of the Church of Atocha, whither she went on Candlemas Day, to return public thanks to God for the birth of her little girl, were, " My child! my Isabella!" and her next, " I don't wish the man to be punished!" But the citizens of Madrid, wild with excitement and reawakened loyalty, insisted on Marino's execution, and even burned his dead body themselves, when the executioner refused to do so. " When the Queen drove in state to church to return thanks for her escape, the people embraced her horses in the intensity of their enthusiasm, for, strange to say, while other sovereigns were striving hard, and often in vain, to win the love of their people, Isabella, whose whole course of life was a public scandal, was for years a popular idol. Her good-hearted, happy-go-lucky nature seemed to cast a charm over her subjects. Her total lack of reticence appealed to them; they could follow so easily the workings of her mind, whether she was petulantly reproaching her ministers with betraying her, or confessing with remorse that she had wronged them."

" If her sins were open, so was her repentance. Year by year when Holy Week came round, she kneeled in church by the hour together, and with loud sobs and groans proclaimed her sorrow for the past and her resolution to make atonement in the future. Her subjects, seeing her sorrow, sorrowed too, and when Easter Day arrived were as convinced as she was that a new era in her life was at hand.

" The Maundy Thursday ceremony never failed to win for her hearty adherents; she washed the feet of the beggars with such manifest zeal, spoke to them such kindly, loving words, served them with food as if she thought it a privilege to do so, and at the close of the feast cleared the table with a dexterity that showed her heart was in her work. Her splendid robes — she always wore full court dress on these occasions — seemed to enhance the touching humility of her attitude; and although the free-thinking part of the community scoffed at what they called the popish mummery of the whole affair, that was not the feeling with which the bulk of the population regarded it. One year, while she was serving at table, a diamond fell from her head-dress on to the plate of one of the beggars. A dozen hands were stretched out to restore it, but the Queen motioned to the man to keep it, saying, 'It has fallen to thee by lot.' Her generosity was unbounded. It was not in her nature to say no to a beggar. The one point on which she made a firm stand against her ministers was to insist upon her right to exercise mercy; and the hardest struggle she ever had with them was *à propos* of a pardon granted at the request of Ristori. A queen has many chances of doing little gracious acts, and Isabella never failed to seize each one as it came in her way; not, however, for the sake of popularity, but simply to follow the bent of her own nature." [1]

I have said that Narvaez was in power at the time of the Queen's marriage. He was also in power when in 1848 there was a dangerous crisis, and mutiny and revolt broke out in the provinces. It was on this occasion that Sir Henry (then Mr.) Bulwer excited a furious burst of anger in Madrid by formally remonstrating with the Spanish administration. Moderados, Progresistas, Exaltados, and Republicans, nay, even the insurgents, united in demanding that the audacious Englishman who had dared to give advice to Spain unasked should be turned out of the country. This led to a cessation of diplomatic intercourse for several years between Spain and England.

Narvaez was not Moderado enough or Apostolical enough to satisfy the court party, in which Christina was by degrees regaining her influence. He had commenced many of the reforms and industrial enterprises recommended by Burgos, the Afrancesado whose introduction into the Cabinet had

[1] The Gentleman's Magazine, 1889.

caused the downfall of Espartero in 1840. Railways all over Spain were projected, the administration believing — what the event has proved — that nothing could tend more to improve Spain than the establishment of great main lines of railroad. But the difficulty was how to find the money with which to build them. The unpaid national debt was so enormous, and the credit of the government so low, that relief could be obtained only at a cost of twenty per cent, and even then foreign capitalists were very slow to lend their money.

In Madrid Narvaez was stimulated to emulate Baron Haussman in Paris. He pulled down a number of houses in the Puerto del Sol, and proposed to replace them with handsome buildings, but this movement increased his rising unpopularity. The frequenters of the Puerto del Sol grumbled at the dust and the rubbish which encumbered their evening lounging-place; the shop-keepers complained that their stores were pulled down; and it was even matter of complaint that the great clock which had marked time for Madrid for several generations was no longer in its place. " Have you no watch? " asked an Englishman of a young man of fashion who was commenting angrily upon its removal. " Yes," was the reply; " but who wants the trouble of pulling out his watch every time he has occasion to know what time of day it is? " There was general activity throughout Spain during the administration of Narvaez; and as no efforts were made to pay off the immense loans contracted during the past forty years with foreign capitalists, there would have been sufficient money for public works could the revenues of Spain have been so administered as to flow into the public coffers, and not into the pockets of a few illustrious swindlers and a legion of corrupt underlings. There is a saying in Spain that money is like oil; those who measure it out are sure to find some of it sticking to their fingers.

In 1847, when Pio Nono was in difficulties, Narvaez sent to his aid, and to that of his ally, King Ferdinand of Naples, a Spanish army under General Cordova; and subsequently, when the Pope returned to Rome, he made a Concordat with Spain which settled the relations of Church and State in that country. Besides this, in recognition of Isabella's zeal on that occasion, his Holiness forwarded to her the Golden Rose, — a gift bestowed annually on the pious female who has done most during the year for the service of the Church, generally a female sovereign.

But Narvaez was powerless to alter the preposterous tariff, in which sixty thousand smugglers conceived themselves to have vested interests, since through its anomalies they gained their bread. Catalonia, as we have seen, rose in rebellion against Espartero when it suspected him of an intention to favor commercial relations with England. Yet, after all, her cotton factories employed only thirty-two thousand persons. Spaniards in general have little taste for mechanical operations, and a reform in the tariff would have greatly benefited those who made their living by work in the open air.

The crisis of 1848 put Narvaez for a short time out of power at a moment when peace and the stability of his administration seemed to be assured. But he speedily returned to office, though after three years he once more succumbed to clerical machinations. The clerical party was very strong at court; the Nuncio and the cardinals played a large part there, as well as the nun Patrocinio, who appears to have been what we should now call a "medium." When the second administration of Narvaez fell, the court party — Absolutist and Apostolical — came into power. The Moderados and the Progresistas were alike set aside; little or nothing was practically left of the Constitution, and the court and its party at length attempted to rule the country by decrees. Then, for the first time the Throne and the Church were both openly attacked by a people whose loyalty to both had been exceptional. The scandals of the court had brought into existence a Republican party.

For three years — from 1851 to 1854 — the *camarilla* tried to govern Spain by a succession of ephemeral ministries, each holding office long enough, however, for all its members to retire with life pensions, which are always bestowed in

Spain upon ex-ministers. Those that held office longest were the Bravo Murillo, the Alcoy, and the Lersundi ministries. To the latter succeeded, in the autumn of 1852, a Cabinet of which the premier was Sartorius, Count de San Luis, who had served in a previous administration under Espartero. The Sartorius ministry became speedily more unpopular than any of its predecessors. It, however, contained at least one honest man, as its Minister for Foreign Affairs, Señor Calderon de la Barca, selected, it was said, on account of his knowledge of the United States and Mexico, as in 1853 a bitter quarrel was impending between Spain and the United States, on account of American interference in Cuban affairs. Señor Calderon de la Barca had at one time made part of the Spanish Embassy in Washington. He had been minister to Mexico, and had married a lady so well known in the United States as to be almost considered an American. She was the eldest of three sisters, the Misses McLeod, who came from Scotland to the United States, and engaged in educational work in Boston and Baltimore. While in Mexico Madame Calderon corresponded with Mr. Prescott, affording him great assistance in his work on Cortez by her descriptions of localities and scenery. She afterwards gave her experiences to the public in a very sprightly and interesting volume. In 1855 she wrote another book, called "The Attaché in Madrid," disguising herself as a young German diplomat writing to his family, of whose letters she professed to be only the translator. This book gives a most graphic account of the Revolution of 1854, from the palace side of the question, while letters of the same date, published monthly in a leading magazine in England, tell the same story.

Madame Calderon de la Barca was subsequently placed in charge of Queen Isabella's children. The Queen was an affectionate mother, and was so conscious of her own lack of proper training that she was very desirous of securing what had been wanting to herself for her three daughters and her son. They could not have been committed to better hands than Madame Calderon's, and all have turned out intelligent, amiable, and well conducted. Of course

Madame Calderon's relations with the court imposed upon her certain reserves in the book of the "Attaché."

"Queen Isabella," it is said by a writer, who published a *chronique scandaleuse* of her court in the "New Review," "had no idea of what is meant by ruling over a nation, and made no attempt to do so, well or ill. She carried out the formal functions to which her position condemned her with a sort of resigned *ennui.* But she never really grasped the meaning of the conflicts that went on around her; she never realized the play of forces, the struggle of ideas, the supreme interests which it was in her power to decide. If, however, she was not troubled by the exercise of a power of whose extent she was unconscious, she was only too ready to use that power in a futile manner, and to bring about terrible conflicts for mere personal ends. . . . Indifferent to the great questions of State, incapable of even knowing whether she was taking the side of Liberalism or Absolutism, she was very sensitive to personal influences. A man who acquired power over her could attract her either way. Progresistas, Liberals, Moderados, or Absolutists, — any of the twenty-six parties said to exist in Spain, — all incarnated themselves in her eyes in certain men, and according as these men pleased or displeased her, for purely personal reasons, just so did the Queen become Liberal, Moderado, or Absolutist."

Bravo Murillo, while he held the helm of State, had had a project of effecting a complete revolution, — of introducing, under the name of "reform and the interests of morality," which from that time became a war-cry, — changes which would have restored to the ministry of the day the absolute power wrested from Ferdinand VII.

There were three conflicting influences in the palace during the three years that succeeded the downfall of Narvaez: Maria Christina; the ultra-clerical, or "apostolical" party, which included the King Don Francisco; and the party of the Queen's favorites.

The immediate cause of the overthrow of the Sartorius ministry — or rather of the events that preceded that overthrow — was the question of government concessions to the numerous railways begun or projected in Spain. It was not long before these railway concessions became matters of shameful traffic. To obtain a concession became, for the friends of the palace, an easy way of getting money. It was soon well known that Christina and her husband, when shares went up, pocketed their gains; when shares ran down, their losses were made up to them out of the Treasury.

Sartorius, the Count de San Luis, was a man of considerable energy, but not endowed with much tact. He began his administration with a few liberal promises, but soon went on to inaugurate an ultra anti-Liberal policy. Being defeated in the Cortes on some measure connected with railroad concessions, he at once suspended that body, and removed the generals and high officials who had voted against him.

Spain is a country in which, though the press may be silenced, tongues are free. And all tongues seemed now turned against the inhabitants of the palace, the Queen, and the ex-Regent Queen Christina. Republicanism up to this time had hardly shown itself in Spain, but now there was talk of a change of dynasty, and a new party was added to the twenty-six, — a party which dreamed of a union between Spain and Portugal under the sceptre of Dom Pedro V. of the House of Braganza.

As the public journals were silenced, and foreign journals (even the London "Times") were denied entrance into Spain, hand-bills were secretly prepared and circulated. Here is one which Isabella found one day on her toilet-table: —

"Spaniards! you have suffered enough. The abuse of power has reached its height. The laws are outraged. The Constitution no longer exists. The minister is no longer a minister of the Queen; he is the minister of an imbecile and ridiculous favorite, a man without reputation, glory, talent, or heart; without any other titles to favor than those afforded by his sovereign's caprice. A new Godoy, he would fain plant his heel on the throat of this heroic nation, immortal mother of the victims of Murat's massacre of the 2d of May; of the heroes of Saragossa and Gerona; of those who fought at Arlaban, Mendigorria, and Luchana. Shall we suffer this shame in silence? Are there no swords in the land of the Cid? Are there no more staves?

Are there no more stones? Up, up, Spaniards! To arms, all of you! Death to the favorite! Long live the Constitution! Liberty forever!"

At the beginning of January, 1854, the Queen gave birth to another child. According to etiquette, the babe had to be presented immediately on its birth, upon a silver salver, to the ministers, ambassadors, and high officials, by the King, whose duty it was to proclaim himself its father. But the day was bitterly cold, the room in which the dignitaries were assembled had no fire, the poor little Infanta was, according to etiquette, unclothed, and caught such a cold that she died three days after. Those who would like to hear of all the pomp and ceremonial of her funeral in the vaults of the Escurial, may read them in many sprightly pages in the letters of the "Attaché."

Before the Queen had recovered from her confinement, she received a manifesto signed by a great number of senators, deputies, nobles, high officials, capitalists, proprietors, and writers, demanding the reopening of the Cortes. Alarmed by the state of public feeling, the Count de San Luis inaugurated a Reign of Terror. In Spain a military officer who is not employed can be assigned a residence by the war office; and those in disgrace with the administration are sent to remote and undesirable places. The advocates of the ministry said that its measures, severe as they were, were not severe enough. Don Manuel Concha, Marquis of Duero, was ordered to proceed to the Canary Isles; another general to Majorca, General José Concha to the same place, and General O'Donnell to Teneriffe. General Concha disappeared into France, and O'Donnell sank out of sight, his hiding-place being a mystery. He was, however, living quietly in Madrid, even venturing sometimes by night upon the Prado. He was visited by his friends in his retreat, and was actively engaged in organizing a conspiracy; but the authorities could find no trace of him, although orders for his arrest were sent into all the provinces. It is said that persons going to the house in which he was hid, were secretly warned by police agents that they had better not draw the attention of some others of the force by going into it. Perhaps the members of the police were bribed by O'Donnell and his friends; perhaps they foresaw that in all probability he would be the next man to rise to power.

O'Donnell was forty-five at this time, a member of the family whose name has already appeared often on these pages. He was made a sub-lieutenant when a boy; at nineteen he was a captain; at twenty-four a colonel; at thirty a lieutenant-general. Soon afterwards he was made Count de Lucerna, having forced Cabrera to raise the siege of that place. At one time he was attached to the army of Espartero, and was afterwards made commander-in-chief of the forces that in 1840 were directed against him. When Espartero aimed a blow at Queen Christina's regency, O'Donnell gave in his resignation, which the Queen Mother refused, presenting him at the same time with the *grand cordon* of a Spanish order. Under the regency of Espartero he headed the insurrection at Pampeluna to re-establish the authority of the ex-Queen Regent. From that time till 1848, he remained in France until he was appointed Governor of Cuba. In 1849 Narvaez named him director-general of the infantry, which post he occupied for two years, when on the fall of Narvaez he entered the senate as one of the most active members of the opposition.

While all this ferment was taking place, balls, receptions, *bals masqués*, operas, and all kinds of festivities were going on in Madrid within and without the walls of the palace. As we read of them in the pages of the "Attaché," they make us think of that verse in Scripture: "They did eat, they drank, they married wives, they were given in marriage, until the flood came and destroyed them all."

The court and the capital were not, however, without warning; there was a general impression that some startling events must be near at hand.

"The liberty of the press," says Madame Calderon, "is nothing as compared with the invaluable privilege of liberty of

LEOPOLD O'DONNELL, DUKE OF TETUAN.

the tongue. . . . 'I cannot imagine,' said M. de —— to me, 'how a conspiracy is ever carried through in Spain, for rather than not tell the news, a Spaniard would mention it before the very persons to be conspired against.' 'It is precisely for that reason that these plans succeed,' was the reply. 'At the moment when nobody believes it, and when the government is unprepared for it, a revolt or a revolution breaks out. Everybody had heard of it; but amidst the mass of truth and falsehood, no one could discern fact from fable, and no one felt sure of what was about to occur except those who were positive agents in the affair.'"

At this time court circles and society in general were much excited by the publication of a very violent but well-informed news-sheet, called the "Bat," though its first number appeared without any name. The utmost endeavors of the police could discover neither its editor nor its printer. It was sent to all the ministers, diplomatists, leaders of society, and even to the Queen. The first number attacked the ministry, exposing some of its bargainings, and mentioning by name a high official engaged in such transactions. Its second number attacked the banker Salamanca, who formed one of the ministry, and the Duke of Rianzares, whose known passion was for stock-jobbing. It also accused Queen Christina of receiving forty millions of reals out of a forced loan of one hundred and eighty millions raised by the government to supply its immediate necessities. The third and last number of this mysterious paper attacked the Queen in person, warning her that in the streets her august name could no longer be mentioned without some scornful epithet. Anonymous warnings multiplied; fingers even wrote them in the dust that had settled on the furniture of her palace.

On February 23, 1854, a revolt broke out at Saragossa in the regiment of Cordova, under its colonel Flore. The revolt was put down, and Flore was shot; but it was the first drop of the thunder-shower, the beginning of troubles. It was believed that Flore, who made this premature attempt, had counted on the assistance of other regiments and of General Concha; nay, even on that of General Dulce, commander-in-chief of the Spanish cavalry, the officer who had commanded the halberdiers who had defended the door of their young queen when Leon and Concha sought to carry her off to the camp of O'Donnell.

The non-success of Flore's attempt gave the Sartorius ministry a momentary *prestige*. But on June 28, there was tremendous excitement in Madrid. One of the reports, true, false, or semi-false, that were in circulation, asserted that the whole of the cavalry had revolted with their general, Dulce. The Minister of War, General Blazer, at once sent for his colleagues. Shortly before that, anonymous warnings had reached him that Dulce was in correspondence with discontented members of the opposition. He had at once sent for General Dulce, told him of these warnings, and received such satisfactory assurances that his suspicions were allayed, and the government affected to make light of the reports that came to them from all quarters, that a military insurrection was contemplated, and that General O'Donnell was at its head.

During the period of suspense that preceded the insurrection an attempt had been made to bring about a coalition between the Moderado and Progresista parties. Both, whatever their differences, desired the downfall of the Sartorius ministry, reform in the manners and the morals of the court, and that Spain should be governed constitutionally.

The nickname by which the friends of the Sartorius ministry and its Absolutist programme were known, was " Poles " or " Polacos," Sartorius being believed to have had a Polish ancestor.

General Dulce had won for himself many honors, not by political intrigue, but by honorable service and at the point of his sword. He passed for a Progresista, and most of his friends were of that party ; but he had never mixed much in politics, and professionally had served all governments, but in his heart he cherished a strong love of liberty, and detested the ignoble tyranny under which his country groaned. Chief of the whole Spanish cavalry, respected and beloved by officers and men, he was a great acquisition to the insurgent party. The other leaders besides Dulce and O'Donnell were General Messina, an intimate friend of Narvaez, Ros de Olano, a general officer of some repute, and Brigadier Echague, colonel of the Principe Regiment, who had served with distinction in the civil war.

On June 13 a revolt was to have taken place. The garrison of Madrid had been ordered to parade before daybreak for a review outside the city. O'Donnell in disguise was stationed near, intending to discover himself on the arrival of the Principe Regiment. But it failed to appear at the rendezvous, and the intention of the leaders to declare against the government was abandoned for that day.

Some days passed over, and nothing more was heard of the insurrection. O'Donnell furiously reproached Dulce for not having carried out their plan, in spite of the non-arrival of the Principe Regiment. It was then that Dulce was sent for by General Blazer, and it is said that the Duke de Rianzares asked him jestingly if it was true that he intended to shoot the Queen and all her family.

When the revolt broke out on June 28, Madrid, in spite of all these warnings, was taken by surprise. The Queen was at the Escurial — more than twenty miles away. All the ministers but two were absent from the city; these two seemed paralyzed by the news of the revolt, and were utterly helpless. It was thought that no news could reach the Escurial. The insurgents did not know, or had forgotten, that only the day before communication by telegraph had been opened between the Escurial and the capital.

At daybreak on June 28, General Dulce set out with his staff, to try, as it was said, a new saddle just ordered for the cavalry. As he passed General Blazer's house, the War Minister, disquieted by rumors that had reached him, appeared at his window. Dulce called out to him, "Good-morning, General; will you not come with us?" "No, I am too busy." "Well, then, *adios*," said Dulce, and went on his way to the rendezvous.

This time things went well with the insurgents. Generals Ros de Olano and Messina informed the soldiers that they had revolted, and presented to them General O'Donnell in citizen's dress as their commander.

Only one officer refused to join the revolt, and was permitted to retire. Madrid for the first few hours remained strangely quiet. The insurrection was entirely military. The city was declared in a state of siege.

Isabella had been notified by telegraph of what was taking place ; and Sartorius had set out to attend upon her in case she should be in danger. But Isabella was never wanting in courage ; she was even capable of reckless, careless bravery. About eleven o'clock at night, when anxiety in Madrid was at its height, she entered the city to the music of the Royal March, and cries from her escort of " Viva la Reina ! " " She came, covered with dust, but full of courage," said one of the diplomatic corps. The ministry tendered their resignation, but at such a moment she said it would be a mark of weakness to accept it. Before she slept she signed a proclamation depriving Dulce of all honors and offices, and appointing his future trial by a council of war.

The Queen next morning reviewed the troops who were going forth under General Blazer to encounter the insurgents, but she was received without enthusiasm.

Overtures made to the insurgent generals were rejected, and they put forth a document addressed to the Queen, stating the causes that had induced them to take up arms, and their resolution not to lay them down until the Sartorius ministry was dismissed, and the government had " satisfied the exigencies of public opinion, and conformed to the principles of liberty, morality, and justice."

Meantime the other great cities of Spain, hearing the news from Madrid, prepared to join the revolt. On the evening of June 29, news came to the capital that the Queen's troops had been driven in by the rebels. Then came in counter reports, and the next morning came an exultant, but wholly incorrect, despatch from General Blazer : —

" The garrison of Madrid is a model of bravery and enthusiasm. It has destroyed the revolted cavalry, both infantry and artillery receiving a close fire from them, and from the regiment of Vicalvaro. The camp is full of dead bodies, wounded men, and horses. Many prisoners are taken, among them Colonel Garrigo, who commanded the Farnesio regiment of cavalry. The troops have not ceased to cry 'Viva la Reina!' The rebels are dispersing. I have not time for more."

This exultation was premature. " Not only was the news of the dispersion of the insurgents false," says the " Attaché," " but they fought like lions, as indeed did the poor soldiers on the other side, casting themselves into the very mouths of the cannon in their endeavor to take at least one of those formidable engines. They fell like sheep in every direction."

The day did not end without another excitement. When news of the victory arrived, Isabella ordered her carriage, and insisted on going out to meet and thank her troops. But just as she was stepping in, an aide-de-camp galloped into the court with news that her troops had been intercepted by the rebels, and the poor Queen sadly retraced her steps up the grand staircase. The news was false. In the darkness the soldiers in one of General Blazer's regiments had fired on their own friends.

The field of battle at Vicalvaro was only about four or five miles from Madrid, on the road to Aranjuez, where the insurgent generals took up their quarters. In spite of favorable news from the provinces, they were reported to be greatly depressed. The road to the battlefield being free from troops, the beauty and fashion of Madrid drove out to see the scene. Though in the course of four days much had been cleared away, and the dead bodies removed, there were still many traces of the bloody affray. There were dead horses lying on the field, saddles broken and blackened, pieces of clothing and soldiers' caps matted with blood. Fifty-eight wounded men had been carried to the hospital, among them Colonel Garrigo, who had commanded one of the revolted regiments, and one of his officers.

There was great sympathy felt for Garrigo, whose death as a traitor seemed sure. His family sought an audience with the Queen. They wept together, and Isabella promised them the life of the husband and father whom they came to save. Subsequently a letter of grateful thanks to the Queen was written by Madame Garrigo. Here are some passages from it which tell the story : —

" Your Majesty, by an act of innate and unequalled clemency, has calmed the grief of a desolate family, has dried up their tears, and has averted from them an incalculable tissue of misfortunes. One word pronounced by your Majesty has raised them to joy in the very midst of their grief and despair.

" Nor is this all, Madam, that they owe to your Majesty. Even before this was done they saw tears flow from your Majesty's eyes, caused by participation in their grief. Your Majesty then lavished upon an unfortunate family the most tender and touching consolatior.s, and made them conceive the grateful hope that their misfortune might not be consummated ; and the value of such kindness, Madam, the deep impression which it leaves on the hearts of those capable of appreciating it, can only be conceived by one who, like her who addresses your Majesty, has obtained such signal favors."

Poor Isabella ! Such genuine goodness of heart, such acts of clemency, which often cost her a struggle with her ministers, go far to cover up the faults which she committed. As Narvaez once said of her, " the wonder was, not that she should have inherited the vices of her ancestors, but rather that she should have so many good qualities which were all her own."

# CHAPTER XVI.

## THE EXPULSION OF CHRISTINA.

AFTER the affair of June 28, 1854, Madrid remained for two weeks extraordinarily quiet, expecting news from the provinces. The insurgents had marched toward Andalusia, followed by General Blazer with his army drawn in part from the garrison of Madrid.

The diplomatic corps waited on the Queen at the palace to congratulate her on the result of the engagement at Vicalvaro. She received them in her dressing-gown, — a breach of etiquette of which she had frequently been guilty in former days, till it was put a stop to with some peremptoriness by Narvaez. Two solemn services were also held in the Church of Atocha, by the orders, and at the expense, of the Queen, — one for the repose of the souls of all those who fell at Vicalvaro ; the other for the peace and prosperity of the kingdom and the cure of the wounded.

Meantime, negotiations were going on between the insurgent chiefs and the Progresista party, at whose head stood General Espartero, who had now lived seven years in retirement.

News from the provinces at last poured into the capital. Catalonia was in revolt, the Captain-General himself heading the insurgents in Barcelona. The Basque provinces and Aragon were roused. Regiments refused to obey the orders of General Blazer, and went over to the insurgents.

When this news reached Madrid, Sartorius and his Cabinet resigned. The Queen formed a new ministry, with General Cordova as President of the Council, but there was a great deal of agitation in the capital. A bull-fight had been announced to be held that day; but the spectators turned it into a political demonstration, calling upon the band to play Riego's Hymn, which had not for eleven years been heard in public. After nightfall the crowds in the streets grew more and more excited; cries were heard of " Viva O'Donnell ! " " Viva la Libertad ! " " Death to San Luis ! " " Death to the thief Christina ! "

The first place attacked was the department of the Prime Minister, opposite the post-office, in which it was thought some of the late ministers had taken refuge. A great bonfire was lighted before the office of the minister in the Puerto del Sol. The door was at last broken by an infuriated street mob with hammers and axes, and the crowd rushed in like a torrent, overpowering the guard.

Then all over Madrid insurgents began to attack places where they expected to find arms. The houses of San Luis and one of his colleagues were forced open and sacked. Tables, beds, chairs, paintings, mirrors, and all else that came to hand were flung into the street, and committed to the flames. Similar scenes took place at the house of the banker Salamanca, but not until his wife and children had been able to escape, while one of his friends and a brave young Englishman held the rioters at bay. Many valuable paintings were thus lost, which the Spanish Monte Cristo had been accumulating for years.

Still more formidable was the mob that rushed to the palace of Queen Christina, who had just recovered from a dangerous attack of measles. It was defended for some time by the royal guard, but then the mob put forward a crowd of infuriated females to drive back the soldiers, who did not like to fire point-blank upon women ; and the same scenes of devastation were repeated. The Queen Mother had taken refuge in her daughter's palace. Some of her servants, entering with the mob, saved valuable papers ; and her waiting maid, disguised as a peasant woman, unlocked a cabinet in the chamber of her mistress, emptied her diamonds into her apron, and carried them in safety through the crowd.

For three days and nights this rioting continued. Cordova

could not form a ministry, but one was got together under the Duke de Rivas, who appointed Colonel Garrigo, now recovered from his wound, to be head of all the cavalry in Madrid. By the close of the day on the 18th of July the mob had gradually overpowered the soldiers, and on the 19th the excitement in the streets increased. Pucheta, a bullfighter, was put forward as a leader, and he used his position to extort money for safe-conducts furnished to prominent persons obnoxious to his followers; in this way he got fifty thousand reals from Arana, the Queen's favorite, the sum being advanced by the French Embassy.

An attempt was made to restore order, by forming a Junta, under the Presidency of General San Miguel, — a body which announced itself as " A Junta for the safety, armament, and defence of Madrid, whose object is to give a successful direction to the popular movement, to economize blood, and to save the institutions trampled on by the most barbarous and unheard of tyranny."

San Miguel was an old man, but a brave one. He succeeded in gaining some little ascendancy over the rioters, but was baffled by the band under the bull-fighter Pucheta.

The few newspapers that made their appearance during those days of insurrection added fuel to the flames of revolution.

One instructed the people as to the uses of barricades. " The barricade," it wrote, " is a majestic castle, a superb fortress, on whose towers waves the flag of liberty, of honor, and of the laws."

Another announced that a Cortes would soon be convoked to decide three important questions : —

Is it expedient that the House of Bourbon should continue?

Is it expedient that Dom Pedro of Braganza should be called to govern constitutionally on the Spanish throne?

Is it expedient that the Peninsula should be constituted into a republic, or are we to give ourselves up to Montemolin?

The Sartorius ministers took refuge in the embassies, or in the palace. He himself was in hiding under the roof of the French ambassador. If he and Christina had fallen into the hands of the mob, they would have been lynched to a certainty. The insurgents showed little feeling of hostility to General Molins, or to General Blazer; and to Calderon de la Barca none. Their houses were left unplundered, while the property of the other ministers was ruthlessly destroyed.

Don Enrique de Bourbon, the cousin and brother-in-law of the Queen, seems to have been rather popular with the mob. The Junta revoked his decree of banishment.

The Queen, finding that no ministry she could form in Madrid had any chance of general support or authority, telegraphed to General Espartero, who was living in his country home at Logroño, on the borders of the Basque provinces. On July 24, a messenger from him arrived in Madrid bringing the conditions on which he was willing to return to the service of his sovereign. The envoy was General Salazar. The exact terms on which Espartero consented to come to the Queen's aid are not known, but one of them was the dismissal of all the *camarilla*.

"General Salazar had no doubt expected to find the Queen in the depths of despair, trembling for her throne if not for her life; but she, more accustomed to insurrections than he was, laughed and chattered until the worthy man, whose morals were better than his manners, losing all patience at what he considered an exhibition of criminal levity, turned upon her and administered a rebuke so sternly indignant that John Knox's noted speech is mildly courteous by the side of it. Her open immorality, he said, was a disgrace not only to her sex, but to her country. Callous as she was, this roused the Queen, who angrily ordered him from her presence, telling him that no one had ever dared to address such language to her before. Salazar replied quietly, 'I have no doubt of it. It is not often that truth is spoken in this place,' and held his ground.

"The Queen, realizing her helplessness, had a violent attack of hysterics, when the King, who, though not present, was within ear-shot, came forward, and requested the envoy to postpone the discussion. The General then retired, saying he would return in the evening." [1]

When Isabella recovered she was furious at the outrage, and declared that rather than accept aid from Espartero, who had sent her such a messenger, she would abdicate ; and in spite of threats from her mother, and persuasions from her husband, she sent for the diplomatic corps, to whom she might announce her intention. The French ambassador arrived first ; when he heard for what reason he was summoned, and that she intended to leave Madrid the next morning, he merely remarked, " Of course your Majesty will have to leave the Infanta behind."

This altered the whole question. Isabella was a devoted mother. She could not leave her child. Resolved not to do things by halves, she then, with almost childish recklessness, put forth a manifesto, in which she declared her perfect sympathy with the views of Espartero, and went so far as to thank the insurgents of Madrid for the zeal with which they had fought against her during the week of insurrection.

Meantime, that the people might be employed during the days that must elapse before the arrival of Espartero, they were set to work to strengthen and adorn the two hundred and eighty barricades that obstructed the streets of the capital. Flags and streamers floated upon all of them, and upon nearly every one was raised a platform covered with colored cloth, on which was displayed a portrait of Espartero. These portraits, hideous caricatures for the most part, were objects almost of adoration with the people. After nightfall lights were placed around them, and sometimes other portraits were set beside them, — O'Donnell's, Dulce's, and, in a few instances, the Queen's. Music of some kind, from military bands down to solo performances on a tinkling guitar, was played before the barricades, in front of which the people assembled in crowds. The revolution, serious enough at first, had been turned into a festival.

[1] This extract is from the " Gentleman's Magazine," but the story is told substantially the same in other places.

20

At last the ex-Regent Espartero came, and his entry into Madrid was a triumph. He was too warm-hearted a man not to feel touched at this reception by the people, and tears stood in his eyes as he stretched out his arms to the populace. He was driven to the palace, and reascended the grand staircase which he had descended in disgrace eleven years before. His stay in the palace was short; but as he left it the Queen, King, and little Infanta came out upon the balcony, hoping to be cheered by the spectators, but the mob was cold.

Next day arrived O'Donnell. He went to the house of Espartero, where a great crowd had assembled to see the two heroes. They came on to the balcony, clasping each other in a fraternal embrace. Times were changed since O'Donnell had marched forth, eleven years before, to fight Espartero.

Madrid soon began to wear a different aspect. Confidence returned, and the barricades were pulled down. Some difficulty had been anticipated about disarming the population; but an offer on the part of the government to buy every weapon that should be delivered up, soon brought in a great store of muskets, carbines, and blunderbusses, to say nothing of fancy firearms brought forth from rich men's armories.

The ministry which Espartero formed did not at first give universal satisfaction. Among its Liberal members there were some Moderados, but soon its prompt and judicious measures won men's good opinion.

Its first and greatest difficulty was how to dispose of Queen Christina. On this point the people would not give way. They were inexorable. Armed men beset the city gates and surrounded the palace, to make sure that she should not depart in disguise until she had rendered an account of her stewardship and refunded at least part of her plunder.

" I saw her during those days," says Madame Calderon. " I found her nearly alone in an inner apartment of the palace, while the execrations of the multitude were borne towards her in yells that drowned all other sounds. She stood at the window, calmly surveying the destruction of her palace. No tears were in her eyes, — not a cloud upon her brow. She stood serene and calm, though thinner and paler than before the dangerous illness from which she had hardly recovered. Whatever her feelings may have been, she crushed them back into the inmost recesses of her heart. She talked calmly of the events that had occurred, without anger, without bitterness. One of her ladies spoke of the possibility of her effecting her escape in disguise. 'I will leave Madrid as a queen,' she said calmly, 'or I will remain here.'"

Two of her daughters had departed in disguise under the escort of a trusty friend, for Portugal. The youngest was about to be sent in the same way to Bayonne.

Espartero had responded to the popular clamor, indeed the insistence of the people, that the Queen Mother, the arch-peculator, should not escape, but must stay and be tried for her plunderings, with the assurance that Doña Maria Christina de Bourbon should not leave the city " *neither by night, nor by day, — nor depart furtively.*" But the people were suspicious, and kept strict watch both for her and the ex-ministers. Not only was the word of Espartero pledged that Queen Christina should not escape by stealth, but she herself could not be persuaded to attempt it.

Yet something had to be done, and that speedily. The palace continued in a state of siege so long as the Queen Mother remained in it.

I have said nothing of the two armies, — the one under O'Donnell and Dulce, the other under General Blazer. The former was advancing into Andalusia, closely pursued by Blazer, who had not yet come up with it, when news was received of the events in Madrid. Blazer turned over his troops to his second in command, and disappeared into exile. O'Donnell gave his up to Dulce, and returned to Madrid to fraternize with his former antagonist and co-hero, Espartero.

Espartero was now sixty-two; O'Donnell forty-five. The one had always acted with the Progresista party, though he had sternly repressed the Revolutionists. O'Donnell had been a Moderado, who had turned against the Absolutists.

As among the various constitutions of Spain it was hard to decide which of them it was best for a constitutional government to act under, a Constituent Cortes was called to settle the question.

To Espartero, Duke of Vittoria, was tendered the Presidency of the Union Club; and his acceptance of that position was considered a proof that he would consent to the trial of the Queen Mother before the Cortes, as that was the measure to which the Union Club was most strongly pledged. O'Donnell, it is said, was of opinion that justice ought to be done upon "the thievish Queen," as she was popularly called by the subjects of her daughter, but Espartero saw all the impolicy of bringing her to trial. He preferred to take the risks which his assumption of all responsibility for her escape would entail on him. He made his plans so that the matter should be arranged in such a manner as would to a certain extent enable him to keep the "word of his promise," that neither by day nor by night should she furtively escape from the capital.

Very early on the morning of August 28, two months after the breaking out of the insurrection, a travelling carriage with four horses drove into the courtyard of the palace. It drew up at the grand staircase and two companies of the Farnesio regiment which had fought on the insurgent side in the affray of Vicalvaro, entered the gates at the same moment as if to serve as an escort to the carriage. These troops were commanded by their former colonel, now General Garrigo, who was now to give Queen Isabella the first proof of his devotion and gratitude. Within the palace was Queen Isabella, wrapped in a dressing-gown, her hair in disorder. Her eyes were red with weeping, and she had evidently passed a sleepless night. She had little cause to love her mother; but her affectionate nature made her cling to her in this hour of peril, for there were many chances that Christina before she passed the city gates would be in the hands of her enemies. Christina herself was in a travelling dress,

pale, calm, and without a tear. Isabella sobbed convulsively. The little Princess, sleepy and wondering, cried
because her mother cried so bitterly. The King was in
uniform, looking anxious and troubled; the Duke de Rianzares made a strong effort to appear composed, but was
evidently full of uneasiness. The ministers and generals,
who had passed the night in the palace, so as to be on
hand, stood by in full uniform.

As Queen Isabella, half fainting, sank on a sofa, loosening
her grasp upon her mother, whom she had tightly held, Christina took the moment to escape from her embrace. She left
the room with a firm step, Espartero walking down the grand
staircase by her side, General O'Donnell following. Christina
bade them adieu in an indifferent tone, and inquired politely
for their wives. Espartero handed her into the travelling
carriage; the Duke de Rianzares stepped in after her. The
postilions cracked their whips. Garrigo rode up to the side
of the carriage, and looked like a man who, whatever the
danger, would be faithful to the trust his Queen had placed
in him. The carriage drove out of the enclosure of the
palace, and took the road to Portugal.

By nine o'clock the news of Queen Christina's escape had
circulated through the capital. The people were furious.
Nothing less than the great popularity of Espartero could
have borne the strain. Had not that woman, whom he had
once before let loose, been the mother of mischief during her
exile when she lived in the Rue de Courcelles? In the excitement of the moment there were even cries of "Down
with the government!" "Death to O'Donnell!" and even
"Death to Espartero!"

The two generals faced the storm. They appeared together on the balcony of Espartero's house, again locked in
each other's arms. They addressed the crowd with praises
and persuasions, and at length prevailed upon them to disperse. But still the streets resounded with the cry, "Bring
back Christina!" "Down with all the ministers, except
Espartero!"

Meantime Christina, unmolested, pursued her rapid journey.

Public excitement finally calmed down, though a rude shock had been given to Espartero's popularity; but he and his Cabinet had conducted themselves with patience and energy, and had saved themselves and their country from a great and permanent disgrace.

To complete the story, I copy another page from the " Attaché," or rather from Madame Calderon de la Barca, on whose testimony, as she was an eye-witness of what went on in the palace, I have depended for these particulars : —

" All the ministers fled in disguise, more or less complete. Fair hair was dyed black, bushy whiskers and fierce mustachios fell under the edge of the razor. If the *diable boiteux* could have unroofed certain houses where members of the late Cabinet lay *perdus*, his companion might have imagined that the fallen statesmen were preparing themselves for attendance at a masked ball. He would have seen San Luis divesting himself of mustache and whiskers, and appearing with a closely shaven countenance, and hair like the raven's wing; Calderon de la Barca changing his gray hair to jet black, Molins and Collantes laying low their mustachios and cherished whiskers, and all arraying themselves in habiliments forming as great a contrast as possible to the brilliant uniforms in which they were wont to meet the public eye. San Luis, acting the part of a valet, was jolted across the Pyrenees in the *rotonde* of a diligence. Calderon de la Barca, saved by the generosity of a French gentleman, performed the part of a wine merchant of Bordeaux till he had crossed the Bidassoa; and the rest, like stout swimmers, all reached port. The vessel wrecked, the cargo lost, but the crew saved."

# CHAPTER XVII.

## THE FLIGHT OF ISABELLA.

THE so-called revolutions in Spain were not like revolutions in other countries. They were episodes in the great revolution going on from 1808 to 1873, — which may be going on even now. In other lands the word means an uprising of popular feeling, whose strength enables it to get the upper hand; or it is an attempt made by force by the Executive, which brings about some great political change, and it is then called a *coup d'état*. The multiplied "revolutions" in Spain had little or nothing to do with public sentiment. They were changes of ministry, brought about by some violent convulsion. The nation had little part in them; they were the work of factions. The uprising of 1868 was, however, a real revolution, for which the years that followed the uprising of 1854 had been years of preparation.

The success of the mixed rising of Progresistas and Moderados related in the last chapter placed Espartero the Progresista, and O'Donnell the Moderado, at the head of the government. Espartero became President of the Council; O'Donnell chose for himself the post of War Minister, and thus had the whole military power of the nation in his hands; Escosura was Minister of the Interior.

It soon became a wonder how the Queen could ever have done without Espartero. She seemed to lean on him. She sent for him at all hours. On slight pretexts she called him away from important business, or from the hordes of importunate office-seekers who infested his anterooms, imploring him to use his influence not only in bestowing high offices, rewards for public services, and compensations for sufferings, but expecting him to obtain for his petitioners petty appointments in the royal household, such as that of Remover of Grease-spots from the Queen's furniture.

But matters of vital importance confronted the new administration. How was a rupture to be avoided with the United States, whose sympathies were roused for Cuba? Above all, how was the national purse to be refilled?

The story of Spain's troubles with the United States in 1853 and 1854, the embassy of Mr. Pierre Soulé, the filibustering expedition of Lopez, and the affair of the Black Warrior, I will relate in my last chapter.

In Madrid the first feeling, after the change of government had been successfully accomplished, was one of general rejoicing. Feasting took the place of fighting. Then came the return of the troops that, under Dulce and O'Donnell, had fought on June 28 the battle of Vicalvaro.

O'Donnell, a week later, issued a proclamation, short, pithy, and explicit, calculated to satisfy the Liberal party. It promised the Spanish nation the benefits of the representative system, for which it had shed so much blood and made so many sacrifices. It said : —

" We desire the preservation of the throne, but without the *camarilla*, which dishonors it; the rigorous enforcement of the fundamental laws, improving them, especially those of elections and the press; a diminution of taxation, founded on strict economy, and also respect to seniority and merit in the military and naval services. We desire to give the towns the local independence necessary to preserve and to increase their own interests, and as a guarantee of these things we desire a national militia. . . . We 'devote our swords to the national will, and will sheathe them only when it is accomplished."

Who would have suspected that O'Donnell, never a Liberal at heart, was simply taking advantage of the direction in which the tide was flowing, to serve his own purposes?

Espartero enjoyed the public confidence. His honesty and disinterestedness had never been denied, even by his greatest enemies, who knew that he remained poor after opportunities a tithe of which had sufficed others to amass enormous fortunes. He had been living, since his return to Spain in 1847, on his estate at Logroño, and had taken no part, direct or indirect, in events that had since happened; but his name seemed to represent, certainly better than that of O'Donnell, the popular feeling at the back of them.

O'Donnell, who was the right arm of the rebellion, could not but acquiesce in Espartero's being placed at its head. The Queen could hardly in six weeks have transformed into a prime minister the man who had incited revolt against her in her army. So he was well content to accept the war office, which put all military power into his hands.

There were many who thought that Espartero and O'Donnell, though they fraternized and embraced each other in public, could never work together in the same Cabinet, and that O'Donnell, having the harder, coarser, stronger nature of the two, was the one most likely to get rid of his rival. He himself saw that there could not long be harmony between the Queen, ultra-Catholic and capricious, — a woman who always confounded political questions with her personal likings, subject besides to the influence of a *camarilla*, clerical and absolutist in the extreme, — and a general who, so to speak, was born of the people.

Without loss of time O'Donnell laid down his plans to gain the entire confidence of Isabella, and, as the first means to that end, he became her lover. He was a man of handsome person, of undoubted talents, and he plied her assiduously with flatteries. Arana had been sent away by Espartero, and O'Donnell used every means to interest her in himself and in his abilities. Before long she had arrived at the conclusion that there was but one man who could save Spain and restore her to her former position, — and that man was O'Donnell.

The ministry took care to do nothing that might justly provoke hostility on the part of the strong church party; but with all its caution it could not refuse religious toleration to non-Catholics, though the clause introduced on that subject into its revision of the Constitution was quite as much a threat as a concession.

" The nation binds itself to maintain and to protect the observance and the ministers of the Catholic Religion, professed by the Spaniards; but no Spaniard nor stranger shall be prosecuted for his opinions or beliefs, so long as he shall not manifest them in acts contrary to religion."

The fall of the Sartorius ministry left seven million pounds sterling ($35,000,000) deficiency in the Treasury, and not as many pence in the coffers of the State for the immediate and pressing necessities of government. With difficulty, and only by the aid of the San Fernando bank, the finance minister obtained a loan of about fifty thousand pounds ($250,000) secured on colonial revenues. But so small a sum could not last long. Economy is not to be effected on an important scale at a moment's notice.

The financial situation was so bad, owing to the dishonesty and rapacity of the deposed government, that it was evident to all that *something* must be done to fill the Treasury. A few Spaniards — very few — hinted at a remedy through the sale of Cuba. The United States at that time were holding out money for its purchase, but Spanish pride could not brook a bargain which would deprive Spain of the brightest jewel in her crown.

The only other expedient that seemed practicable was the sale of lands held in *mortmain ;* that is, lands unalienable, lands that could not be sold, bequeathed, exchanged, or in any way diverted from the original purpose of the testator; lands that, however long that testator had been dead, were still, as it were, held in his dead hand. But many of these lands had been bequeathed to the clergy, to benevolent institutions, and to convents. There was the danger.

The Cortes, under the pressure of necessity, passed a law authorizing the government to sell these lands, but Isabella persistently refused to sign it. She said that her confessor told her that if she did so she would imperil her eternal salvation. All the eloquence of Espartero was helpless against her inflexible resolution. The other ministers tried their powers of reasoning and persuasion, and were equally unsuccessful.

The agitation at court was extreme. There was even some talk of carrying the Queen off to the Basque provinces, where, relying on the Catholic element, which was all-powerful, she might defy her ministers and the Cortes, even at the cost of civil war.

On the other hand, the threats of the Liberals were so alarming that Isabella at last gave way; but she wrote at the same time a piteous letter of apology to the Pope, assuring him that she would take the earliest opportunity of undoing what nothing but the force of pressure could have induced her to do.

Another act on the part of Espartero, which, however necessary, she could not but consider arbitrary, helped to widen the "little rift" opening between them. The *camarilla* had been expelled from the palace. The oldest servants were dismissed. The Queen, although she took leave of them with tears, was submissive, but the King was furious. He talked even of fighting in defence of his household.

Sister Patrocinio had returned to court after a temporary seclusion at Talavera. She possessed the greatest influence over the mind of the Queen. It would be hard to call her a deceiver. We rather gather from what is told of her that she was possessed of hypnotic power. As for her *stigmata* (the signs of our Saviour's wounds imprinted on her flesh), there have been instances when those marks appeared on the bodies of highly nervous persons under great religious excitement; but those of Sister Patrocinio, when she was forced to submit to medical advice, entirely disappeared.

However this may be, she exercised an extraordinary influence at court, and several times the whole political power of Spain was in her hands. "Ministers were obliged to come to terms with her. She was the main cause of the Queen's resistance to the liberal measures which all her ministers, even the most conservative, found it necessary to urge upon her, — measures strongly backed by the worldly wisdom of Queen Christina." Much money was expended upon Sister Patrocinio. A superb convent was built for her.

Narvaez, when he came into power, courted her favor, and bore candles in her processions.

Poor Isabella ! Her Catholicism bordered more closely on idolatry than on actual religion. Her confessor was Father Claret, whom she made Archbishop of Cuba, but there was also at court, and high in the confidence of the Queen, Father Cyril, Archbishop of Toledo, who had been formerly confessor to King Ferdinand, but was removed from that office by Russian influence in 1815, the Russian minister having thought his counsels dangerously reactionary. In face and character Father Cyril was thought to be like the great inquisitors of the Middle Ages. He was the counsellor heard on all political occasions of importance ; but, as he got his instructions in the main from Pio Nono and Cardinal Antonelli, they were less narrow and less dangerous than the advice of ignorant fanatics like Father Claret and Sister Patrocinio.

The political union between Progresistas and Moderados lasted about two years. Then O'Donnell, who felt sure that another political convulsion was at hand, and that he could turn it to his own advantage, privately selected a ministry that would suit himself when he should have become prime minister and have got rid of Espartero.

It was July, 1856. The air was full of rumors. Riots broke out in various large towns in different parts of the country. They were suppressed by O'Donnell; but the heads of the Progresista party, believing they had cause for distrust, sent the Minister of the Interior, Escosura, to report on the causes of discontent in the provinces.

Escosura, on his return to Madrid, had an audience with the Queen, who assured him, with apparent sincerity, that she was fully satisfied with all her ministers, and had no desire for any change in her Cabinet. Yet Isabella, even in dissimulation, could not be reticent or prudent. She had not brought that art to such perfection as her grandfather had done. She chanced to say, while assuring Escosura of the confidence she placed in himself, that she had not the same confidence in all his colleagues. Did she allude to

O'Donnell? Did she mean Espartero? Escosura endeavored to make her say more, but she was silent.

He repeated this conversation to Espartero; but the old
general placed full confidence in the Queen's attachment to
himself. He told Escosura that only a few days before the
Queen had said to him, with a most charming smile : " My
dear Duke, if it came to choosing between you and General
O'Donnell there could not be a shadow of doubt as to the
choice I should make."

Not long after this at a cabinet council some words arose
between O'Donnell and Escosura, and Escosura exclaimed
that it was very evident that they could not work together
in the same Cabinet. " Well, then," said O'Donnell, " we
will both resign." After further discussion, they proceeded to the palace, accompanied by Espartero; and as
is often the case in Spain, to the great astonishment of foreigners, men who have quarrelled bitterly in the Cortes or
elsewhere in public meet socially in the most friendly fashion ; so O'Donnell and Escosura walked arm in arm like old
friends, as indeed they had been from their childhood.
Espartero and his colleagues entered the palace together,
Espartero full of confidence, Escosura feeling certain that
the Queen was about to betray him.

Espartero told the Queen that in a cabinet council there
had been a dispute between the Minister of War and the
Minister of the Interior, that he had tried in vain to reconcile them, and that he believed a few words from her Majesty would have better success ; but if either should leave
the Cabinet he himself would go with him. Espartero had
felt sure that she had but to soothe O'Donnell, and that the
dispute would be at once arranged. " But," says the writer
in the " New Review," from whom I take this narrative, " he
did not know that the Queen and O'Donnell understood
each other, and were playing their parts in a little comedy
which was to end in his dismissal."

O'Donnell said coldly that he would not stay in the Cabinet with Escosura, and that her Majesty must choose between them. " Well, then," said the Queen, " I accept the
resignation of Señor Escosura."

Espartero, although he had been warned, could hardly believe that the Queen meant to forsake him. "If you go," he said to Escosura, "we will go together." "But O'Donnell will not abandon me!" cried the Queen; and going up to him, " *You* will not abandon me!" she said with great fervency.

Thus fell Espartero; and there were riots throughout the country when the affair was known. But O'Donnell's triumph was complete, and for a moment he felt himself master of Spain.

Not long after this, when the Queen found that O'Donnell, uninfluenced by her bidding or persuasions, would not revoke the law concerning lands held in mortmain, which she had signed with such reluctance, she began to intrigue for the return of an Absolutist ministry.

O'Donnell yielded to her so far as to get his Cabinet to sanction the repeal of the law when it related to the property of the clergy, but further the Cabinet could not be brought into the Queen's views. O'Donnell then tried to move the Queen, and at last threatened to resign, telling her he was sure that she desired to replace him by General Narvaez. The Queen with tears implored him not to leave her, and assured him she had no thought of replacing him by any one. A week later she refused to sign a paper that he brought her, and he gave in his resignation. She accepted it. He left her in anger, and before night Narvaez, Duke of Valencia, had got together an Absolutist administration.

The next day he issued decrees for the restoration of the estates of Queen Christina, and revocation of the laws relating to mortmain.

Narvaez, like O'Donnell, was devoted heart and soul to Isabella, but to him she was the Queen, and not the woman. He was a soldier, brusque and unceremonious; a man who loved to drink the cup of pleasure, and to lead a fast life in the society of dissipated men and women; but he was loyalty itself to the Queen. She was the one ideal in his life, and when she marred that ideal by the irregularities of her conduct he was furious against her lovers.

He was an Andalusian, short, powerfully built, with a

high forehead and prominent eyes, — a man full of energy and resolution. Moreover, he disdained all pettiness and trickery in his administration ; and it came to pass that during the two years he governed Spain there was more or less peace and prosperity. His was the only government that allied itself with the *camarilla*. The court indeed intrigued against him, making ready for the time when Absolutism *pur et simple* could have full sway ; but there was less public corruption than there had been under other rulers, and there was a marked advance throughout Spain in material improvements and in modern progress. Steam, electricity, and facilities for travel placed her on a line with other countries. Industry of all kinds received a stimulus, order was protected by an improved police, and there were greater facilities for education.

On November 28, 1857, while Narvaez was at the head of affairs, the Prince of the Asturias (afterwards Alfonso XII.) was born. All supporters of the Crown rejoiced at the birth of a male heir. It seemed to give a pledge of security to the dynasty, and to restore the mother for a time to the place which she had forfeited in the hearts of her people.

But Carlos Luis de Bourbon, Count de Montemolin, was making preparations for another Carlist rising, which should dispute the succession with the newborn babe.

He had learned craft, if not wisdom, by his failure in 1849. Every aid was welcomed. The old advisers of his father and himself were thrown aside. He professed himself prepared to come to terms with the Spanish people, and to govern constitutionally. This change of base lost him the hearty support of many of the elder Carlists, who, like Cabrera, declined to draw their swords this time in his cause.

Among his new adherents were Ortega and Morales. The former had long been a leader in the Progresista party, but he was converted into a Carlist by intercourse with the intriguing, unscrupulous Infanta Carlota, wife of Don Francesco di Paula, sister of Queen Christina, and mother of Don Francisco, the husband of the Queen. She had bitterly

quarrelled with Christina, and now, in confidential intercourse with Ortega, revealed to him her secrets, amongst
them much that had taken place at Ferdinand's death-bed,
which so excited Ortega's indignation and awakened his
sympathies, that he went over, heart and soul, to the Carlist
cause.

In Paris he entered into relations with the Carlist princes,
and on his return to Spain asked O'Donnell, then Minister
of War, to give him some important military post. O'Donnell, well pleased to secure the services of a prominent
Progresista leader, offered him the captain-generalship of
the Balearic Isles.

Ortega excused to himself the treachery he contemplated
by saying that he should break his sword and retire into
private life as soon as the cause of Charles VI. had gained
the victory, fully assured that he had done a deed of justice
and patriotism. He should also use his best endeavors, he
said, to induce Count Montemolin "not to establish an
absolute monarchy, but to allow the voice of the country
in the direction of affairs."

From his government in the Balearic Isles he urged on
the projected rising. Morales thought out the political programme, and drew up a manifesto so liberal that he doubted
whether the Count de Montemolin could be induced to sign
it. But the Count made no objection whatever. Perhaps
he looked upon it in the same light as his uncle Ferdinand
had looked on similar liberal promises. The existence of
this document was kept a profound secret. Its promulgation was reserved until the Count should have achieved successes in Spain, and, as that moment never arrived, it was
never given to the world. Every copy that General Dulce
could get hold of was afterwards destroyed. It is said to
have denied that Don Carlos would wish to re-establish an
absolute monarchy, and to have proposed a whole series of
reforms, which, could they have been carried out, would
have converted Spain into a Utopia.

The conspiracy went on ripening for three years, and its
secrets were kept faithfully. We are told that many Spanish

grandees were in the plot, and that in their private chapels, oaths of fidelity to Carlos VI. were taken before the crucifix, on the Gospels, held by priests in their sacerdotal robes.

The Count de Montemolin with a few followers was to join Ortega in Majorca, and in the month of March, 1859, they were to be landed on the coast of Valencia. But at the last moment blunders arose, which disconcerted their plans, and aroused suspicion.

On March 20, Don Carlos Luis, Count de Montemolin, left Paris for Marseilles. He was accompanied by his brother Don Fernando, his secretary Elio, Morales, two other officers, and a valet. They took passage on a steamer bound for the African coast, which touched at Palma, the chief town of Majorca. There Ortega had got together a little fleet of transports, a body of 3600 Spanish soldiers, and four pieces of artillery. But the soldiers were ignorant of the service on which they were to be employed, and the officers themselves were far from being all Carlists.

On Palm Sunday, April 1, the expedition reached a small port near the mouth of the river Ebro, called San Carlos de la Rapita. The troops were disembarked, and they began their march toward the city of Valencia. The Alcalde of La Rapita had been told that a review was to be held near his village, but what he saw induced him to believe that this was false, and he sent warning to the authorities in his district. The troops began also to be in doubt. At the first halting-place, while Ortega was breakfasting in a cottage, their officers conferred together, and appointed a commission to inform the General that if he was really marching against the government, they would not follow him. Then a shout arose among them, " Long live the Queen ! " Almost all the soldiers joined the cry, while only a few subalterns and non-commissioned officers cheered the Captain-General.

Don Carlos, in a carriage, was ahead of his army. Suddenly Ortega dashed past at full gallop, crying, " Turn into a side road ! All is lost ! " The carriage, and those who attended it, turned off into an olive wood, and when night fell the party dispersed. Don Carlos, his brother, and a servant took refuge in a peasant's cottage, where they lived for eighteen days, almost perishing for want of food, as they dared not send out to obtain provisions. Before dawn on the eighteenth day, a party of the government soldiers entered the cottage. Don Carlos came forward, and said: "Gentlemen, we are in your hands. I am Count Montemolin, this gentleman is my brother, and this is a confidential servant. We will go with you where you will."

Their imprisonment would have embarrassed the government. The conspiracy was so widespread that it was impossible to punish everybody. It was decided to pardon all. Don Carlos and his brother Fernando renounced by solemn declaration all the rights that they professed to have to the Spanish crown, and they wrote letters to their cousin Isabella, entreating her to draw a veil over the past and to permit them to retire to Austria, where they would live "quietly in retirement, by the domestic hearth."

Isabella was always ready to show mercy, and she exerted herself eagerly on her cousins' behalf. They and Elio, their secretary, were put on board a government ship and landed in France.

Ortega was the only victim. He had been captured in his flight, taken to Tortosa, and there shot.

In 1859 occurred also a war with Morocco. The Sultan of that country had taken advantage of the disturbed state of Spain to oppress and even to attack the Spanish settlements. O'Donnell in person took command of a considerable army. Early in the year 1860 he fought the battle of Tetuan, from which he obtained his title. His victory was followed by the Treaty of Tetuan, by which the Sultan promised to pay Spain an indemnity of twenty million piastres, to give her permission to make a commercial station at Santa Cruz de Mar Pequeta, and to allow her a missionary establishment at Fez, such as she had already at Tangier. But as money for the indemnity was not forthcoming, control of the customs was made over to the Spanish Government for a term of years.

In 1861, when we of the United States were busy with

our Civil War, the Emperor Napoleon thought he perceived a chance to interfere in the affairs of the New World, without giving rise to controversy on the subject of the Monroe doctrine. He proposed to England and Spain to send their fleets with his to demand from President Juarez of Mexico redress of the grievances of the foreign holders of Mexican bonds. As Spain was an impenitent sinner in this respect from a date more remote than that of the Mexican republic, it seems a little strange to find her in the position of an outraged creditor, demanding redress for her subjects by force of arms. However, the combined fleets sailed for the Mexican coast, the expedition being under command of the Spanish general Prim, who was the senior general. President Juarez offered to make reasonable terms, and to assure future payments. An agreement was drawn up at a place called La Soledad, signed by the Mexican authorities and the Spanish, French, and English commanders. This agreement, when the document was sent to Europe, proved satisfactory to the governments of Spain and England, but by no means so to the French Emperor. The English and Spanish fleets withdrew; but Napoleon, unwilling to neglect the chance of making, as he said, the Latin races as powerful as the Anglo-Saxon race in the New World, declared war against President Juarez, sent Maximilian to raise a throne in Mexico, and we all know the melancholy result.[1]

While these affairs were reflecting credit upon Spanish arms abroad, discontent was increasing in the provinces. The Republican party was gaining strength, the members of which styled themselves Democrats. A general feeling prevailed that something must be done to change the dynasty ; that no mere change of ministers would serve. But who could be called to the throne? The country was decidedly unfavorable to what was called the Iberian Union ; that is, the consolidation of the crowns of Spain and Portugal. The Duke de Montpensier was hardly more popular than when

[1] The story of Maximilian is told at some length in " France in the Nineteenth Century."

in the early days of his marriage the Spanish populace used to hoot every bull that in the arena showed no spirit with the yell *Fuero Montpensier!* Don Enrique, brother of the King, was hot-headed, and accused of irreligion. He had some supporters, for he professed liberal ideas, but then — he was a Bourbon. Had there been any man ready to take the place that seemed to be waiting for him, — any man who could have awakened national enthusiasm, — the fury of the factions would have been calmed for a moment; he would have been hailed with acclamations; but then, it was necessary that he should not be a foreigner.

In 1858 O'Donnell had been succeeded by Narvaez. A few years later Gonsalez Bravo, the ex-journalist, succeeded him. He governed according to the ideas of the court and the *camarilla*. Since Ferdinand declared himself an Absolute King, there had been no such complete disregard of the Constitution.

When the Revolution broke out in September, 1868 (the Revolution of Disgust, some people have called it), O'Donnell and Narvaez were both dead. The former had been laden with all the honors that his queen could bestow. It was said that his stars, crosses, and ribbons might have filled a wheelbarrow. He had no children, and his title of Duke of Tetuan descended to his nephew. Narvaez died in April, 1868, at Madrid, just before the revolution.

The chief mover in the new conspiracy which was to overthrow the dynasty was Olozaga; with him was associated General Dulce. Dulce had been Captain-General of Cuba, and had recently brought back with him a wife possessed of immense wealth; but affluence did not diminish his taste for conspiracy and power. Hand in hand with Dulce was his friend General Prim, not long returned from his Mexican expedition. It is said that he had bitter personal hatred of the Queen; for that once when she had been cajoling him and expressing her hope that, as her faithful adherent, he would form a ministry, he caught sight of her in a mirror as he quitted her presence, making behind his back a grimace at him. There was another man now bitterly and personally the Queen's enemy who joined heartily in the conspiracy.

*MARSHAL PRIM.*

This was General Serrano, Field Marshal in the Spanish army, and Duke de la Torre. At first Olozaga hesitated to approach him on the subject; but he received the proposal heartily, and thenceforward the conspiracy made rapid progress. Serrano was beloved by his subordinates, as he was by nearly all who knew him.

The plot was deeply laid and well organized, and the secret was well kept. Soon a new element was introduced into it. The navy of Spain had never before taken part in an insurrection; now it was to lead the van.

Gonzales Bravo, then prime minister, though disturbed in mind and suspicious that something was on foot, had no knowledge that would have enabled him to grasp the threads of the conspiracy. He, however, arrested on suspicion a few generals, and sent them into exile, — to the Canaries, to Majorca, and the Philippine Isles; but the ramifications of the conspiracy were too extensive, and the need of change too urgent, to cause the idea of a revolt to be set aside. "It seemed as if, even without chiefs, the event must have come to pass by a spontaneous rising of the nation."

As it was, nothing failed. Prim and other leading conspirators assembled at Cadiz; and at dawn on the morning of September 19, 1868, the inhabitants of that beautiful, highly revolutionary city were startled from their sleep by the firing of salutes and by bands playing Riego's Hymn, which had not been heard for long years upon the shores of Spain. Then they beheld an imposing line of men-of-war assembled before their houses, bunting flying and sailors cheering, to celebrate the deposition of an execrated dynasty, and the inauguration, it was hoped, of a better state of things. Prim was on board the flagship; when he landed and showed himself in the streets, men thronged around to hug him and to grasp his hands, while the women kissed him with transport, and with cries of " How young! how handsome!" — though he was no longer in the prime of life. But "blessings on his bonny face " followed him from the lips of old and young.

This was followed on the same day by what is called the *Pronunciamento* of Cadiz, — a document which set forth the causes of disaffection in the country: fundamental laws trampled under foot; elections perverted by intimidation and bribery; personal freedom dependent on the arbitrary will of magistrates; communal freedom extinct; the exhaustion of the Treasury through extravagance and peculation; the press silenced; education committed solely to ecclesiastics; patents of nobility shamelessly lavished upon favorites; corruption, in short, throughout every branch of the administration.

This document was signed by Serrano (Duke de la Torre), Prim, Dulce, Topete, admiral of the fleet, and other men of known patriotism and great influence. A Provisional Government was formed, and Marshal Serrano placed at its head.

Isabella at that time was at San Sebastian for sea-bathing, with the King, her children, her court, her lover Marfori (an opera-singer, raised lately to the Spanish peerage by the title of Marquis de Loja), and her confessor, Father Claret, Archbishop of Cuba. Marfori had also been made Intendant of the Palace, — an office usually bestowed on men of rank or distinction.

When news of the rising at Cadiz reached Madrid, Gonsalez Bravo fled, with an instinct that the situation was desperate, and that all was over. General Manuel Concha, who, for a short time after the flight of Gonsalez Bravo and the other ministers, concentrated in his own person such government as the country still possessed, telegraphed to the Queen, urging her to return with all speed to her capital. "Your Majesty may safely come," he said, "*but without your Intendant.*" Salamanca, the financier, also waited on the Queen, to urge her return upon the same conditions. It is said that Isabella in her excitement came near maltreating him as no queen since Elizabeth Tudor had ventured to deal with unpalatable advisers.

Three generals held out for the cause of Isabella, while the whole country was against her; these were Pavia, Pezuela, and Calonge. They collected what troops they could, and marched against Prim and Dulce. They were defeated at the battle of the Bridge of Alcolea, not far from the city of Cordova, and the Queen's cause was utterly lost. Seeing this, Don José Concha followed Gonsalez Bravo into exile; leaving in his place his brother, Don Manuel Concha, Marquis of Duero, who was military captain of Old Castile. He in his turn flung the reins of government to two men, Señor Madoz and General Jovellar; but the latter resigned his appointment to Ros de Olano, his superior officer.

Meantime, Isabella at San Sebastian watched with an anxious heart the progress of the revolution. She and those about her could see no hope at last, save in the intervention of the French Emperor, who might, it was thought, be moved by the intercessions of his wife, Isabella's former subject, Eugénie de Montijo.

The French court was then at Biarritz, near the Spanish frontier. It is said that Isabella, in disguise, and almost unattended, went by night to seek an interview with the French Emperor and Empress, but no supplications could move Napoleon. He could not afford to commit so grave an error as would have been an armed intervention in the affairs of Spain.

A letter was published on October 4, 1868, in one of the French journals, containing a graphic account of what took place at Biarritz when the Queen of Spain and her party, the day after her clandestine visit to the Emperor, crossed the frontier. The Emperor had politely intimated by telegraph to Isabella that she had better take up her residence at Pau.

" It is one o'clock. The Queen is at the station of St. Jean de Luz. The Emperor and Empress arrive at the Biarritz station. The Emperor walks alone upon the platform with head bent, and plunged in thought. . . . The departure from St. Jean de Luz is signalled, and soon after the especial train entered the Biarritz station. The Queen was alone on the balcony of the saloon carriage. The King stood at the door of the saloon. Marfori stood behind the Queen, pompous, and wearing over his black coat the broad ribbon of the Order of Charles III.

" At the moment when the Emperor advanced to offer his

hand to the Queen, the express train from Paris to Madrid thundered up, bearing exiles now returning to their country, and from it were heard to proceed cries most insulting to the Queen, the loudest being *Fuera !* (Out with her !)

"At those cries the Emperor made a step backward, and tears gushed from the eyes of the Queen, who got out, as well as the King, her children, the high personages of her suite, Father Claret, and the inevitable Marfori.

"After having shaken hands with the Emperor, and kissed the Empress, they all four — the Emperor, the Empress, the Queen, and the King — entered the first-class waiting-room. Nobody else entered. Nobody heard what was there said.

"The interview lasted twenty minutes. At last the Queen made a movement towards the door; and they all four advanced. At that moment a Spanish general who stood beside me exclaimed in Spanish, 'We have nothing left but to depart,' showing that up to the last moment hopes had been cherished of the intervention of the Emperor.

"The parting was brief, silent, and mournful. The Emperor was unmoved; the Empress hardly restrained her tears; the Prince Imperial looked astonished. The Queen endeavored, but in vain, to smile. The little King fidgeted about to hide his emotion. The suite stood aghast. The Queen got into the carriage again; then the King, the Prince of the Asturias, whom the Emperor had kissed, and the royal children. . . . I never was present at a funeral where the grief of the mourners was more profound. It was the funeral procession of a dynasty two hundred years old, which had breathed its last sigh in the Biarritz station. The signal is given. The train is put in motion. Everybody bows; and all is over."

It is said that the Prince Imperial, watching the departure of the train, said to his father, "Papa, what is meant by going into exile?" and that his father answered sadly, "My child, perhaps some day you will know."

# CHAPTER XVIII.

## AMADEO.

THE revolution of 1868 had been prepared with rare forethought and skill; but its leaders seem never to have asked themselves, What next? The Bourbons having been expelled, what form of government shall we propose to succeed them?

It seems to have been in the minds of the leaders who signed the manifesto at Cadiz that a constitutional monarchy was the government most suited to Spain. But no leader dared openly to proclaim his views. A republican party was now strong throughout the country, and as to choice among the eight candidates named for the vacant throne, the leaders of the revolution found themselves divided.

The eight candidates were as follows: (1) The Duke of Madrid, grandson of Don Carlos, *soi-disant* Charles V.; (2) little Alfonso, Prince of the Asturias, the son of Isabella; (3) Prince Leopold of Hohenzollern; (4) Amadeo, Duke of Aosta, second son of Victor Emmanuel; (5) the Duke de Montpensier, husband of Doña Luisa Fernanda, Isabella's sister; (6) King Ferdinand of Portugal, whose successful regency during his son's minority had terminated when Pedro V. came of age. Numbers 7 and 8 were Espartero, the ex-Regent; and Don Enrique de Bourbon, Duke of Seville.

Of these, the three Bourbons were, by the common feeling of the country, set aside as unavailable; there remained the three foreign princes, Espartero, and Montpensier. The crown was refused by all these except Montpensier. But before it could be settled whether a throne or a Presidential chair was to be offered, it was necessary to decide on some sort of Provisional Government. Madoz and his colleague kept Madrid quiet ; and the Provincial Juntas, with more or less success, appear to have maintained order in the provinces. It seemed as if the nation were holding its breath, awaiting events ; since, to borrow a vulgarism from schoolboys and stump orators, no one knew "who he was to hurrah for."

A ministry was formed with Serrano as President of the Council, Prim as Minister of War, Topete of the Navy, Lorenzana Minister of Foreign Affairs ; Figuerola as Finance Minister, Sagasta as Minister of the Interior, and Zorilla as Minister of Commerce. I name them because they were at that time prominent young men, and some of them are political leaders at the present day.

Their first duty was to summon a Cortes, which met early in 1869 ; and the question at once submitted to the deputies was, "What form of government shall be established in Spain ? "

This question was answered by loud and various shouts, which proved the divided feelings of the Assembly. "Constitutional Monarchy ! " "Democratic Monarchy ! " "The Republic ! " "A Federal Republic ! " To a committee of fifteen which included no avowed Republicans was committed the task of drawing up a Constitution. The restoration of a monarchical form of government, with constitutional guarantees, was the leading feature of this document. It established freedom of conscience, substituted the sovereignty of the people for the principle of legitimacy, and established a Senate and a Council of State, to act in conjunction with the House of Representatives. A strong Republican party, both within and without the Cortes, opposed its adoption ; but by a majority of the deputies, on June 2, 1869, it was signed upon ornamented parchments, each deputy being presented with a gold and ivory penholder, set with brilliants, in acknowledgment of his signature. One deputy had proposed that it should be signed with eagles' quills. The public received the promulgation of this constitution without enthusiasm.

Marshal Serrano was named regent until authority should be assumed by a suitable sovereign; but the task of king-making was especially confided to General Prim, his colleague. Prim's favorite candidate was Prince Leopold of Hohenzollern, brother of Prince Charles of Roumania, who had governed his principality wisely and well. Prince Leopold had every qualification for making a good sovereign; and Prim not only thought that an infusion of northern blood into the royal race would be of great advantage, but that a closer *rapprochement* of Spain to the rest of Europe, through an alliance with Germany, was a point in its favor. For two centuries Spain's relations with the rest of Europe had been almost solely through France. Even while she had fought Napoleon, she had been becoming Frenchified. Her Constitution of Cadiz had been founded upon French ideas. It seemed as if it might be a good thing to introduce a little German stability into her institutions as a counterpoise. Prim was therefore empowered to offer the Spanish throne to Prince Leopold of Hohenzollern, grand-nephew of William, King of Prussia. Prim probably little foresaw that he was throwing a lighted match into a powder magazine when he made his offer to this young prince, who was little known at that day to the public. But the moment the Emperor Napoleon III. heard of it, his alarm and indignation knew no bounds. He desired his minister at the court of Berlin to inform the King of Prussia that if he did not forbid his young relation to accept the crown of Spain, it would be a "cause of war" with his empire. King William, irritated by the tone assumed by the French sovereign, replied, somewhat curtly, that it was no affair of his; that he left it to Prince Leopold to accept or to decline the Spanish crown. We cannot here go into the origin of the Franco-Prussian War, which I have related at some length in "France in the Nineteenth Century;" it is sufficient to say in this connection that the young man's father refused the honor for his son, who, when he made in after years a visit incognito to the Spanish capital, is reported to have expressed his great satisfaction that he had not been made the King of Spain.

Espartero, the old hermit of Logroño, stubbornly refused any proposal in his favor. His health was too weak, and his age too great, he said, for the cares of government.

The next most popular candidate was Ferdinand of Coburg, the widowed husband of the Queen of Portugal, Maria da Gloria. He had governed Portugal admirably as regent during the minority of his son, so there was a United Iberian party in Spain which strongly favored his election, but King Ferdinand was not to be persuaded to abandon private life for an uneasy crown. He had married a young New England lady of German descent (not morganatically, but *legally*, as may be seen in the Almanach de Gotha). She had created an earthly paradise on the heights of Cintra, and Ferdinand was not disposed to quit the peace and rest of such a home. Besides he knew well that the antecedents of his wife, who had sung as *prima donna* in European opera-houses, would make her position very embarrassing if he placed her in the conspicuous position she must occupy as wife of a Spanish king. He therefore refused persistently.

The Duke de Montpensier was considered by foreign onlookers to be far the most eligible candidate upon the list, but he was very unpopular with the Spanish people. His very virtues were unpopular. He gave large sums in charity, but that did not prevent his being considered mean and *bourgeois* for selling grapes and olives from his estate near Seville. Then, too, a great misfortune which happened to him in March, 1870, while it increased his popularity with certain classes, may have impaired his chances for selection. The story is too long to be told in this place with full particulars. It may be read in Mr. Hay's "Castilian Days." We must accept an abridged version. Don Enrique de Bourbon, son of Don Francesco de Paula, brother of King Francisco, cousin and brother-in-law to the Queen, was a man of considerable parts and courage, but notoriously a scatterbrain. He had been on bad terms with his family for years, and when his chance of marrying his cousin Queen Isabella was put an end to by the intrigues of Queen Christina and Louis Philippe, he married a subject, Doña Helena de Cordova.

She died in 1863, and he remained a widower. His hatred
to the House of Orleans, and especially to his rival, Prince
Antoine de Montpensier, was intense. In 1868 he was
posing as another Égalité, — a Republican leader. He had
dropped his title of Duke of Seville, and called himself only
a citizen. He was the counterpart of the turbulent and
better known Plon-plon, Prince Napoleon, son of Jerome
Bonaparte. In the winter of 1869–70 he learned that
the Duke de Montpensier had come to Madrid. It was a
hard winter ; the poor were suffering for want of bread ; and
daily distributions of food were made from the Duke's palace,
without, however, greatly increasing his popularity even
among the recipients of his charity.

Don Enrique could not brook even the tepid good-will that
his wealthy cousin seemed to be gaining in the capital. He
resolved to put upon him an affront which, according to the
code of Spanish honor, could only be wiped out by blood.
He thought Montpensier a man lacking in courage ; for such
had been the popular opinion of his character. He therefore wrote and published an extraordinary manifesto, to
express his contempt for the Duke personally, and ended
by calling him a " bloated French pastry-cook."

It would have served his turn had Montpensier taken no
notice of these absurd words. But as soon as the paper
came into the Duke's hands, he sent his aide-de-camp to Don
Enrique to ask if it was genuine. The Infante replied by
signing a copy of the document, and handing it to the messenger. At once Montpensier selected his seconds, and sent
his challenge. His seconds were not chosen from among
his own personal and political friends. One was General
Alamines, the bosom friend of Prim, who had been always
hostile to the Orleans candidature ; the other was General
Cordova, of high military reputation.

Enrique, on the contrary, could get no men of character
and rank to act as his seconds, so he had at last to choose
them among Republican deputies, who, before they agreed
to act, signed a paper declaring themselves not in the least
responsible for the acts or opinions of their principal.

The duel took place on a morning in March, on a desolate sandy plain a few miles from the city. Don Enrique gained the choice of pistols, choice of ground, and the first shot. The first three shots all missed. With the fourth Montpensier broke his opponent's pistol. Then the veteran generals wished to end the duel, but Enrique and his seconds insisted upon fighting to the bitter end. They stood up for a third round. Enrique, who had been wounded by a splinter from his broken pistol, was a little nervous. He fired and missed. Montpensier fired, and his opponent fell, with blood oozing from his temple. Montpensier, some say, swooned; at any rate he turned so faint that he had to be supported by a surgeon from the ground.

It is etiquette in Madrid for seconds to deny all knowledge of a duel, and if it ends fatally friends of the parties and the press attribute the catastrophe to an accident; so the gentlemen who witnessed this affair went before the magistrates and testified upon their honor and conscience (the generals with their hands upon their swords) that the death of Don Enrique de Bourbon was a pure accident; that he and his dear cousin Montpensier had been trying some new pistols when one of them accidentally went off, and the bullet lodged in the head of Don Enrique, causing his untimely end.

Thus seven of the eight candidates for the throne of Spain were disposed of before the autumn of 1870. Prince Leopold, King Ferdinand, and Espartero had declined. Enrique, who had never had much chance, was dead. The Count de Montemolin and Alfonso were considered out of the question; Montpensier was under a cloud. There remained Amadeo, Duke d'Aosta. As soon as the proposition was made to him, he too declined, and it required much persuasion from his father to make him accept the offered throne. Prim was earnestly in his favor. Admiral Topete, who early in 1868 had been charged to carry the whole Montpensier family on his flagship into exile, was as earnestly in favor of Montpensier. He had learned to admire him and to trust him during their brief voyage. But Prim's candidate triumphed. On November 16, 1870, one hundred and ninety-one votes in the Cortes, out of three hundred and eleven, elected Amadeo of Savoy constitutional king of Spain. Montpensier and his duchess had only twenty-eight votes, Espartero had eight, Alfonso two, the Federal Republic sixty, and one was given for a republic after the French plan.

Prim had entered the army a mere lad in 1834, and fought for the Constitution and Queen Isabella. He became in time a lieutenant-general, Count de Reus, and a grandee of Spain; but he was destitute of the arts of a politician, though he had led several insurrections, and had sat for many sessions in the Cortes, where he distinguished himself as a fluent speaker, and a man intrepid in debate. When sent to Mexico in 1862, he withstood flatteries from the Emperor Napoleon, who professed himself his personal friend, and when he discovered the Emperor's real designs with regard to Mexico, he told him plainly : —

" It will be easy for your Majesty to conduct Prince Maximilian to the capital, and to crown him king; but his kingdom will find in the country no other support than that of the Conservative chiefs, who never dreamed of establishing a monarchy when they were in power, but who would fain do so now when they are dispersed, vanquished, and emigrant. A few rich men will also accept a foreign monarch supported by your Majesty's soldiers; but that monarch will have nothing to sustain him upon the day when that support shall be withdrawn."

At the time of the election of Amadeo, Prim was the foremost man in Spain. Serrano, indeed, was nominally the first, but Prim was the favorite of the multitude, and shared with Serrano popularity in the army. The twenty-eight votes given to Montpensier by the Cortes destroyed the political influence of Topete; and Dulce with ten thousand Spanish soldiers had been sent away to Cuba, to make head against an insurrection that broke out in 1868, and lasted for ten years.

It was Marshal Prim who was the Warwick of the Spanish Revolution; the more he knew of Amadeo, the more he was pleased and satisfied with his choice, and doubtless he believed that Amadeo would reign and that he himself would govern. But after the new King had left Italy and before he landed at Barcelona, an event occurred, mysterious and horrible, which sent a shock to many hearts in many lands. On the evening of December 27, as Prim stepped out of the Cortes to enter his carriage, which was waiting in a side street to drive him to the Ministry of War, he found a cab standing by the sidewalk, and at the same moment another cab driving up, as if by accident, blocked the narrow way. In an instant men stepped from behind the cab that was standing in the street, and fired through the window of General Prim's carriage. Several shots were discharged. No face of the murderers was seen in the darkness, though it was said that a voice was heard crying : " Do you recognize us? Have we not kept our word?" But no one to this day knows who killed Marshal Prim. Though mortally wounded, he did not die instantly, but lingered a day or two, and met his fate with the courage he had shown on the battlefield, glad to the end that the chief work of his life had been successfully accomplished. " I am dying, — but the King is coming !" were his last words.

It was a melancholy arrival. When the King came he drove at once to the Church of Atocha to gaze on the face of his dead friend lying in his coffin. In that church Prim now sleeps beneath a monument of bronze, beside the tomb of General Narvaez.

In spite of the name which was at once fastened on Amadeo, — the Intrusive King (*El Rey Intruso*), — he seemed to acquire in Madrid a certain popularity. He looked well ; he bore himself gracefully ; he was affable and friendly ; he reviewed his troops with the soldierly air befitting a son of the House of Savoy. He knew how to return the salutations of assembled crowds, and showed great interest in the customs of his new country. But he had much to contend against. First, and emphatically *foremost*, he was a foreigner ; an Italian, who of all foreigners is in Spain the most despised. He belonged to a family then at odds with the Papacy. His father was excommunicate ; and his election had brought dissension among the very leaders who had prepared the way for him to ascend the throne. Serrano and Topete passed over to the opposition, and the usual succession of ministerial changes ensued.

De Amicis, the Italian traveller who tells so charmingly all that befell him in various lands, was in Spain at this period. He one day endeavored, in conversation with a *caballero* whom he met at Burgos, to gain some insight into the state of parties in Spain. I give the story in his own words, presuming that the information imparted to De Amicis will be sufficient for my readers. De Amicis says : —

" This man was the first Spaniard who fully explained the political situation to me. ' It can be described in two words,' he said ; ' there are five principal parties, — the Absolutists, the Moderates, the Conservatives, the Radicals, and the Republicans. These are subdivided . . . until there are twenty-two parties already formed, or in process of formation. Add to these those who desire a republic with Amadeo for president ; the partisans of the Queen ; the partisans of Montpensier ; those who are Republicans on condition that Cuba be retained ; those who are Republicans on condition that Cuba be given up ; those who have not yet renounced Prince Leopold ; those who wish for a union with Portugal, — and you will have thirty parties. As for their leaders, Sagasta inclines towards the Unionists ; Zorilla towards Republicans ; Serrano is disposed to join the Moderates ; the Moderates, if they had the chance, would join hands with the Absolutists, who, in their turn, are disposed to coalesce with the Republicans, who would be glad to join the Radicals to blow up Sagasta, who is too conservative for the Democratic Progresistas, and too liberal for the Unionists, who are afraid of the Federal Republicans, who place no confidence in the Radicals, who are always vacillating between the Democrats and the followers of Sagasta. Have I given you a clear idea of the situation ? ' ' As clear as amber,' I answered ironically, and with a shudder."

Amadeo was proclaimed King on January 2, 1871 ; he abdicated in February, 1873. He spent the first year of his reign chiefly in Madrid, where he was joined in the spring by his wife, Doña Vittoria, a lady of a princely Italian family, though not of royal birth ; one son had already been

22

born to them, the first grandchild of Victor Emmanuel. He was christened Emmanuele Filiberto, and made Duke of Puglia. In 1895, he married the beautiful Princess Hélène of Orleans ; and, should the Prince of Naples have no children, he or his sons may some day mount the Italian throne.

The life that Amadeo led as King of Spain was wholly at variance with the court etiquette of the past. He rose at dawn, and walked about the palace gardens, or extended his stroll into the city. Spaniards habitually turn night into day, and the upper classes of society are rarely astir in the early hours. " He seems resolved to be shot, at any cost," was the frequent remark made by the Madrilenos. Once he was shot at, soon after his arrival, but he was then in his carriage. He daily received his ministers, heard their reports, and discussed public affairs. Twice a week he met them in council. He gave daily audience to all sorts and conditions of men and women, and listened to their innumerable demands. The Queen, too, gave audience when her health, which was very delicate, permitted her to do so. To her lot fell deeds of charity. She gave away every month a hundred thousand francs, besides liberal donations to hospitals and asylums. She founded several Children's Nurseries, where working women might leave their little ones to be cared for while they went forth for the labors of the day. The Sisters of Charity received from her, besides, thirty thousand francs a month, with which to succor those whose position in life forbade their having recourse to public charity. Sometimes she stole away *incognita* to hear mass at a quiet little church in the neighborhood of the palace.

"Poor young things!" said Queen Isabella, when she heard that they did not occupy the great state apartments in their palace ; "they can't have room to turn round!"

Ministers might remonstrate against the King's rides on horseback, attended only by a groom, and grandees of the old court circle might declare that he was trailing the majesty of the throne of San Fernando through the mud of the streets ; but the Spaniards in general, however unwilling they might be to be ruled over by a foreigner, did justice to his bravery, and to all their animadversions never failed to add, "So far as courage goes, there is nothing to say against him."

It was considered unpatriotic to be satisfied with a foreign sovereign. Even when Amadeo reviewed his troops, they received him coldly, and the man who raised his hat to him in the street was liable to be taunted by his friends for his politeness.

In vain the young King endeavored to conform to Spanish customs. In vain he patronized bull-fights, and flung his card-case full of bank-notes to the successful *torero.*

He was at all times reluctant to change his ministers, nevertheless such changes were forced upon him more than once during his short reign. In the early summer of 1872, the ministers in power — Serrano, Sagasta, and their colleagues — lost heart, and proposed to the King to ameliorate the situation by a *coup d'état.* It was only by parliamentary manœuvring that Sagasta had avoided a vote of censure in the Cortes for tampering with the elections, and that the Minister of Finance had filled up the deficit, though at the cost of a serious blow to the credit of the State. The Carlists, who had been temporarily put down by Serrano, were again in arms and active; the Treasury was again in difficulties; and the Cortes, though so far as possible packed to support the government, showed an inclination to disobey. The Conservative ministry was at its wits' end. It declared that it had not sufficient power, and formally proposed to the King to suspend the Constitution, to proclaim the kingdom under martial law, dismiss the Cortes, and leave the country to be kept quiet by the army, until they could establish a better state of things. They did not doubt the acceptance of this proposal by the King, harassed as he was on all sides by factious opposition, but they met with an unexpected obstacle. A son of the House of Savoy rules always according to the traditions of his dynasty. The family policy is to support, at all hazards, the fundamental laws. After a brief interval for reflection, Amadeo summoned his ministers, and asked them one by one whether they advised the suspension of Constitutional guarantees; then finding them all agreed, he told them in plain terms that he would sooner resign his throne; that the Constitution was the pact with his people under which he held his crown, and that under no circumstances whatever would he violate his oath. If a *coup d'état* was necessary to the safety of the monarchy, then the monarchy must fall.

The ministers, in extreme wrath and surprise, offered their resignations, which were coldly accepted, and the King sent at once for Zorilla, the leader of the Radical party. Zorilla at first refused. Believing the King thoroughly conservative, he had resolved to abandon public life, but he was so impressed by this evidence of his loyalty that he agreed to resume power.

A free Cortes was called, and asked to vote measures for the reduction of expenses and for new taxes; the National Guard was to be embodied as a counterpoise to the army, and the government was to face the difficulties of its position with only its legal powers.

The new ministers advised a Royal Progress, that the personal appearance of Amadeo among his subjects might remove their prejudices against him. It had been carefully circulated that the "intrusive King" was humpbacked, had only one eye, could not speak a word of Spanish; that he travelled surrounded only by Italians; was a drunkard and a libertine.

He set out, therefore, and first visited the ports on the Bay of Biscay, — the stronghold of the Carlists who were in arms in Catalonia. He visited Bilbao, Gijon, and Oviedo, and was received everywhere with wreaths, flags, illuminations, and deputations, but without popular enthusiasm. That enthusiasm increased, however, as he became personally known; and in Biscay peasants ran from their work in the fields as he passed, to kneel upon the wayside in the presence of their lord.

The year before, he had visited Saragossa, where he was received by the Alcalde with a speech that made some stir in Spain. This gentleman, Don José Mariné, was a strict Republican; and his address was to the following effect:

"We do not recognize you as king; but however you may come here we will not murder you, because heroes like the inhabitants of Saragossa do not murder by treachery; and if you will be brave and treat us as you ought to do, we may possibly consent to support you as President of the Republic."

At the conclusion of this speech the King smiled and pressed the hand of the Alcalde, to the great surprise of all present. He subsequently asked Don José Mariné to dinner, which that functionary refused, on the ground that he could not receive favors from royalty.

From Saragossa Amadeo went to Logroño. There for the first time he met the venerable Espartero. As soon as they saw each other, they ran together. The General sought the hand of the King, the King opened his arms, and the crowd gave a shout of joy. "Your Majesty," said the illustrious soldier, in a husky voice, "the people welcome you with patriotic enthusiasm, because they see in their young monarch the firmest support of the liberty and independence of their country, and are sure that if by any misfortune our enemies were to cause us trouble, your Majesty, at the head of the army and the citizen militia, would overwhelm and rout them. My broken health did not allow me to go to Madrid, to felicitate your Majesty and your August Consort upon your establishment upon the throne of Ferdinand. To-day I do so, and I repeat that I will serve faithfully the person of your Majesty as King of Spain, chosen by the will of the nation. Your Majesty, I have in this city a modest home, and I offer it to you, and entreat you to honor it by your presence."

"In these simple words," says De Amicis, "the King was greeted by the oldest, the best beloved, and most renowned of his subjects."

But after a few months of trial the Zorilla ministry, which came into power in July, 1872, was found as incompetent to satisfy the factions as the Conservative ministry under Serrano. It was a Radical ministry, but the word "radical" has not, in Spain, the same meaning that is attached to it by English politicians. It would rather mean "reformer."

Amadeo, who had four times refused the crown of Spain, although at last, in obedience to the wishes of his father, he accepted it, found it impossible to govern constitutionally. His life had been attempted; his Queen was continually insulted by the wives of the grandees, who refused to grace her court, while their carriages crowded round the military prison where some young officers of rank were confined for refusing to take the oath of allegiance to a foreigner. One change of Cabinet after another had failed to produce men enlightened, unselfish, and patriotic enough to control a country in which both Republicanism and Carlism were making great strides. "Spain for the Spaniards! Out with the Savoyard!" was the popular cry. The Spaniards disliked their young King's very virtues. The name of the "inoffensive Italian" was applied to him as a term of reproach. He struggled faithfully for two years against the disadvantages of his situation, and when he found that the most liberal ministry could not make head against the factions, and that perhaps what his ministers had told him in July was true, that nothing would bring order out of chaos but a temporary despotism, he resolved to do what he had said he would in such a case, and he resigned the crown.

He had sent his wife to the south of Spain, ostensibly to benefit her failing health, but principally that she might be conveniently near the frontier of Portugal. On the 11th of February, 1873, he quietly took his seat in a railway carriage, joined his wife, and together they crossed the frontier of Portugal. "A republic succeeded the monarchy as quietly as one sentinel succeeds another." Along their route the royal pair were received with demonstrations of respect; indeed, there was a large party in Spain who wished that Amadeo would have remained to be President of the Republic.

We must now turn to the third Carlist war, undertaken by Carlos VII., son of Don Juan, who was the second son of Carlos VI., the second Pretender to the Spanish throne. Carlos V. had failed; his son Carlos VI. (the Count de Montemolin) had failed; now Carlos VII., Duke of Madrid, was to try his chances, which were rendered more favorable because the Republicans, in their anxiety to get rid of their "intrusive" King, were coalescing with the Carlists, to a certain extent, in the elections.

The Count de Montemolin, as we have seen, when on April 23, 1860, he and his brother were made prisoners on the coast of Valencia, at San Carlos de la Rapita, renounced his claims to the throne of Spain, together with his brother, Don Fernando. But his other brother, Don Juan, had no part in this renunciation. As soon as the Count de Montemolin arrived safely in England, his first act was to endeavor to annul his renunciation. He said that it was null and void, having been made when he was not a free agent, but in the power of his enemies.

Don Juan instantly objected to the retraction of the renunciation. He sent his remonstrance to Madrid to be laid before the Cortes (who declined to read it) and he wrote also to his cousin, Queen Isabella.

The persistency of Don Juan in maintaining the rights which he held had been given him by the renunciation of his elder brother, led to a sharp family quarrel; in the course of which Don Carlos addressed a letter to the Count de Chambord on the subject, as head of the House of Bourbon. The Count de Chambord, who was the soul of honor and honesty, a man who gave up a crown because he would not dissemble his real feelings or falsify his pledges, replied that in his opinion the renunciation of April, 1860, had been an act of weakness; but as for the retraction, he refrained from describing it as it deserved, doubting as he did if a single priest or layman could be found in the Legitimist party capable of advising such a step, or encouraging an act of such dubious morality.

Not many weeks after this Don Carlos and Don Fernando went to pay a visit to their relative the Marchesa di Lucchesi-Palli, ex-Duchess of Berry. There Don Fernando became suddenly ill with typhoid fever, and on the morning of January 1, 1861, he died.

Five days later the Count de Montemolin and his wife

went back to Trieste. They were both much affected by Don Fernando's unexpected death, and both felt unwell. Next day the Count took to his bed, and three days afterwards he died. His death was followed by that of his wife. They were childless, and Don Juan and his two sons remained sole representatives of the direct line of succession to the Spanish throne.

Don Juan, like his cousin Don Enrique de Bourbon, had put forth pronounced liberal views, which made him unacceptable to the Carlist party not only in politics, but religion. He was bitterly reproached for his opinions by his stepmother and aunt, the widow of the first Don Carlos, who declared that the motive that had impelled the Count de Montemolin to annul his renunciation of the crown of Spain was that he felt that so wrong-headed a brother was unfit to mount the Spanish throne.

One afternoon in March, 1848, at the very moment when Louis Philippe as Mr. William Smith was seeking an asylum in England, a post-chaise containing a lady and gentleman drove up to a small hotel in the little Austrian town of Laybach. The weather was so cold, the lady so faint and weary, that they could not go on to Vienna that night, but were glad to find a room in the little tavern. Before daylight a little boy (Don Carlos, Charles VII.) came into the world; for the gentleman was the Infante, Don Juan, and the lady was his wife, Doña Maria Beatrix of Modena. They had been living in Venice, and were hurrying on to Vienna when thus stopped at Laybach. Before they were ready to resume their journey, a revolution had forced the Austrian royal family to fly from their capital. The young pair and their first-born proceeded therefore to England, where a year later a second boy, Don Alfonso, was born.

The conduct of Don Juan was so eccentric that his wife left him, returning with her children to her brother's court at Modena, whence, when Modena became part of the kingdom of northern Italy, she retired to Prague, where the education of her boys was carefully superintended by an old ecclesiastic. In 1863 she went to Venice, where her kinsfolk, the Count and Countess de Chambord, were then living. There too was the Duchesse de Berry with her husband, the Marquis Lucchesi-Palli, and her daughter, the Duchess of Parma. The children of these families were very intimate, and very happy together. Don Carlos fell in love after a boyish fashion with young Margherita of Parma. The match was approved by their families; and when old enough they were married in the chapel at Frohsdorf, the residence in Styria of the Count de Chambord.

After the abdication of Isabella, Don Juan renounced his pretensions to the throne of Spain in favor of his son, Don Carlos, who considered that the time was ripe for a fresh rising in the interest of legitimacy. He was an enthusiast in Spanish history, and had collected materials for writing the life of King Jaime of Arragon, the Conquistador.

Don Carlos was good-looking, over the middle height, and had regular features, not unlike those of his ancestors, the Spanish Bourbons; that is, the lower part of his face was rather heavy, but he had fine black eyes and a thick black mustache. His wife was small and fair, with a face that had a very pleasing expression.

In order to embarrass the government of Amadeo, the Republican deputies voted with the Carlist deputies in the Cortes, until after the abdication of Amadeo, when the latter were withdrawn, and a premature rising in Catalonia took place, which was put down without much difficulty by Marshal Serrano. In vain Don Carlos, or, as he now called himself, Charles VII., published proclamations containing liberal opinions and liberal promises; those opposed to him believed that he would re-establish the Inquisition with some fierce monk at the head of it; that he would be guided in State affairs by clerical influence and by his confessor, and so on. He endeavored to correct these ideas by public proclamations, and to laugh at them in private, but they were fixed in the minds both of Spaniards and of foreigners.

During frequent visits to London and Paris, the Prince (calling himself the Duke of Madrid) had opportunities of conferring not only with his own partisans, but with Spaniards of all political creeds, and seems to have produced on those with whom he conversed a favorable impression. On one occasion while in Paris, shortly before the Franco-Prussian War, he and his wife attended some races in the Bois de Boulogne, at which the Emperor and Empress and Queen Isabella were also present. When the Queen saw her cousins, she advanced toward them, her natural kindliness prompting her to greet them in an almost affectionate manner. The Emperor, noticing that the Queen's advances were received with embarrassment, stepped forward, and with the tact and good-nature which distinguished him, joined the group, and after some moments' conversation offered his arm to the Queen, bowed to the Duke and Duchess, and led her back to her own seat.

Don Carlos in person joined the rising that in 1872 was put down by Marshal Serrano, and issued an appeal to the Spanish people ; but his adherents in the Basque provinces were indifferently supplied with arms and ammunition, and without arms and ammunition enthusiasm was useless. Such arms as they had had served them in former wars, and were no match for Chassepots and Minie rifles. Their uniform, when they had any, consisted of the cast-off clothing of French *gardes mobiles*, which their agents had contrived to pick up at Bayonne or other places on the French frontier. For some time they kept up a desultory warfare, but dispersed after their defeat by Serrano at Orosquieta, which their leaders considered a proof of complete discomfiture, and a terrible blow. Worse than that, the daring of their Prince was thenceforward doubted by his soldiers. He had proclaimed before the engagement that he would " shoot the first man who stood before him in the fight," and " that he had come to Spain to seek a throne or a grave." But he was not seen during the engagement, and after it was over he mysteriously disappeared.

He gave proofs of courage afterwards, however ; but the year 1872 closed with his cause thrown into confusion, and himself under a cloud.

# CHAPTER XIX.

### THE REPUBLIC.   THE THIRD CARLIST WAR.

IMMEDIATELY after the abdication of Amadeo, the Republic was proclaimed in the Cortes by two hundred and forty-eight votes against thirty-four. The cry of 1868 — "Out with the Bourbons!" — had given place to *Al fin los hemos logrado!* — "At last we have got it!" They had a republic; but what kind of a republic? Was it to be a united centralized republic, or a Federal republic? Statesmen and men of experience all declared for the former, but the body of the people were resolved on federation. Meantime, until that question and others in connection with it could be settled, it was necessary to appoint a provisional government. Serrano was placed at its head. Before six months had passed, he was forced to take refuge in the English Embassy, and, under English protection, make his way to safety. Zorilla, who was never a violent politician, had to escape into Portugal in order to save himself from the fury of his associates; Admiral Topete found himself imprisoned by those whom his *pronunciamento* at Cadiz in 1868 had raised to power; Figuerola, who had tried in Amadeo's time to put some order into the finances, was arrested in the street, imprisoned in the offices where he had lately sat as minister, and was then dragged, amid the hootings and howlings of the populace, to a common prison; while Figueras, after abandoning the ministerial post, to which the Cortes, only forty-eight hours before, had elected him, disappeared as suddenly from public view as O'Donnell had done in the spring of 1854. He had been heard to say before the downfall of Amadeo that the first thing he should do if the Republic were proclaimed, would be to take his place in a railroad carriage for France. He had also tendered unpalatable advice to his countrymen ; namely, " that the first condition of a republic was the establishment of order."

When news reached Barcelona of the abdication of Amadeo, and the proclamation of a republic in the capital, people were at first stunned by the suddenness of such an event. Even the ultra-liberals of Barcelona manifested but little of the animation and enthusiasm that the news of the proclamation of a republic might have been expected to call forth among them. Then the different factions of the party proceeded to meet and to take counsel. Clubs were formed, meetings were held, processions and manifestations took place in the streets ; and it was soon made clear that the determination of the Republicans of Barcelona was to offer the most strenuous and uncompromising hostility to the Cortes, should it show the slightest hesitation in accepting their peremptory demand for a *Federal* republic. As it was in Barcelona, so it was in other large cities. All Spain was in a ferment ; and our own experience for a few months in every four years will enable us to judge what must have been the state of an excitable population, trained up in revolutions, during the twenty-three months that ensued of disorder and anarchy.

At first sight it may seem to us, who live under a Federal Republican form of government, that there was no reason why a Federal republic should not have succeeded in Spain. The provinces had long had municipal privileges and juntas of their own. The people of the provinces were separated from each other by character, prejudices, and social customs ; and politically they were all alive, ready to form local juntas and to render them obedience. But the statesmen of Spain and all her generals dreaded Federalism as dangerous to the very existence of the country. They said that Navarre and Biscay would probably make use of their Federal independ- ence to call in Don Carlos ; that Catalonia might elect to become a dependency of France, and Andalusia an agrarian commune ; that religious war might break out in the Castiles, and that the South might set up a Mediterranean republic. Under a Federal republic what would become of the National Debt? What of the credit that wise Spaniards were so anxious to re-establish? The fleet would disappear if there was no central government to pay it and provide for it, and the army would be abolished, for all Federalists were hostile to conscription. Spain, as modern history had known it, would be replaced by a knot of republics, — possibly as happy as the Swiss Cantons, but more probably as quarrelsome as the republics into which the viceroyalties of Spanish South America had been divided.

Thus argued statesmen trained to public life, particularly that most earnest Republican leader, Olozaga; and the Provisional Government sought to induce the Cortes to declare for unity. But this took the heart out of the rank and file of the Republicans. The masses hoped that local freedom might benefit their own condition, might relieve them from military service, prevent military punishment for every trivial act of riot, and place authority for the re-establishment of order in the hands of a local police.

Under these circumstances the marvel was that in January, 1873, the Republic was accepted all over Spain without bloodshed. Men were so taken by surprise that no one knew what else to propose on the spur of the moment.

On June 11, the Provisional Government was summarily dispersed, and a dictatorship *ad interim* was offered to Pi y Margall, a highly respectable archæologist, lawyer, and man of learning. He resigned it in five weeks, finding the task of government too hard for him; Nicolas Salmeron succeeded Margall. He was a University professor, who soon followed the example of his predecessor. Next came Emilio Castelar, the Republican leader, a brilliant orator, a delightful writer, a man of sense, conscience, and experience, who long took a prominent part in public affairs. He stood face to face with four difficulties when he was raised to power, — the Army, the Church, the finances, and the spirit of the ultra-Democratic (or *Intransigente*) party. These proved too much for him.

On January 3, 1875, a party of soldiers, commanded by General Pavia, entered the Cortes, fired over the heads of the deputies, and commanded them to disperse. This demonstration — a victory for the army — was followed by a provisional dictatorship under Marshal Serrano.

We will here leave the state of parties in the capital, and turn to the Carlist war, Navarre, Catalonia, and the Basque provinces.

In May, 1872, the official journals at Madrid had congratulated the country that in the province of Gerona there remained nothing of the Carlist faction but some paltry bands under guerilla leaders, like Savalls and some others, who traversed the country, swiftly flying, and avoiding all encounters with the government troops. But Savalls was a trained soldier. From the time he was sixteen he had served in the armies of Don Carlos; and when the Carlist cause collapsed in 1849, he offered his services to Pio Nono, and fought in Italy as one of the Papal Zouaves.

When in 1870 Rome fell before General Cadorna and the troops of Victor Emmanuel, Savalls took the first opportunity of writing to a friend whom he knew to be in the confidence of the chiefs of the Carlist party: "As his Holiness no longer needs my services, let the King know that I am in Nice, and that I await his orders. I cherish the hope to be one of the first to raise the royal standard in Catalonia, and I shall be found to die sword in hand in the good cause, as my father died before me."

When news reached him, early in 1872, that the Duke of Madrid (Charles VII.) projected another rising, he went privately to Rome, to obtain the blessing of the Pope, and then without delay found his way back to his native province of Gerona, and unfurled the royal flag of him whom he looked upon as his legitimate sovereign. The Spanish Government sent two armies to the north, one to the Basque provinces, which defeated the Carlists at Orosquieta. That battle was followed by the Convention of Amorovieta and the disappearance of the Pretender; the other army was sent into Catalonia, where Savalls and his lieutenants were not disheartened;

*EMILIO CASTELAR.*

they continued the war with such success that a deputy in the Cortes, by no means favorable to their cause, declared that "the real Captain-General of the principality of Catalonia was Francisco Savalls."

On one occasion, when surrounded by government troops led by an experienced general, he imitated the tactics of Mina in similar circumstances. He called his men together and proposed to them to disperse singly, by goat-paths, through the mountains; consequently, when day dawned and the troops from Madrid prepared for the attack, no enemy was to be found.

In the autumn of 1873 the Duke of Madrid returned to his followers, and war again broke out in the Basque provinces.

After the proclamation of the Republic the government troops became greatly disorganized. Their chief generals were summarily dismissed, and a large part of their officers were discontented. The Republican army in Catalonia became little better than an armed mob. Savalls took heart, and was encouraged by the arrival at his headquarters of Don Alfonso, the brother of the Pretender, who himself about the same time made his appearance among his followers in north-western Spain, where his army was besieging the city of Bilbao.

The first attempt of the Prince had been met and completely put down by General Serrano in the last months of Amadeo's reign, but a partisan warfare had been still kept up in the mountains, besides the more formidable raids of Savalls in Catalonia, — a province always ready to rebel against any government established in Castile.

In February, 1873, the date of the abdication of Amadeo, not seven thousand men of the Spanish army were available to crush the rising revolution.

Forty years before this time Sarsfield had written to his government that they must give him an army of thirty thousand men, adding, "Civil war is like a spark, which, if you do not put it out at once, will lead to a conflagration."

Small as the force of the Republic was, it was divided into several columns. One under General Loma, nicknamed "the indefatigable," did everything that could be done under the circumstances to embarrass the enemy and to protect the small towns (all of them more or less fortified) scattered through Biscay, Navarre, and Guipuscoa. But neither side had any fixed plan of campaign, or any definite object.

In March, 1873, the new government sent a fresh general, Noavilas, with a larger force under his command, and orders to make a speedy end of the insurrection. But Noavilas found his task harder than he expected, and soon sent in his resignation.

In July, Don Carlos (it is easier to call him thus than King, Pretender, or Duke of Madrid) returned to Spain and assumed command of his army, about sixteen thousand men. He had two excellent generals in Northern Spain, Ollo and Dorregaray. On the first of August he made his appearance in Biscay, and visited Guernica, where the great oak under whose branches the Lords of Biscay swore to maintain their people's local privileges had stood for centuries, until it was cut down by the French during their invasion. On the spot where it had been he swore, as his ancestors had done before him, to maintain those ancient privileges.

Don Carlos was at that time twenty-five years old, and had three children, — two daughters and Don Jaime, his son. His wife, Doña Margherita, he left at Bayonne, where she occupied herself in obtaining and forwarding to the front hospital supplies.

General Elio, now seventy-four years old, a descendant of the governor murdered in 1822 at Valencia, had been with the Count de Montemolin in 1859, and was made by the third Don Carlos his minister of war. He was the prince's chief adviser. Other Carlist commanders besides Ollo and Dorregaray were Lizzaraga, Mendiry, and Velasco; and in addition to these were the guerilla chiefs, Savalls, Tristany, Santa Cruz, and others.

At the time Don Carlos joined his army, Bilbao and Portugalete, at the mouth of the river on which Bilbao stands, were besieged by Velasco. His force was not large, but his men had worked so diligently with pick and spade that the mountains around seemed almost impregnable.

Marshal Serrano, who had appointed himself commander-in-chief in the Basque provinces, attacked the fortified heights that commanded the city. The mountains around Bilbao are full of iron ore, worked by English companies, who had given employment to numerous men and women. To the latter was committed the heavy task of carrying the ore to vessels, and their strength and industry made a great impression upon English travellers.

For three days Marshal Serrano attacked the fortified positions on these iron mountains with very little success, though his troops showed great courage. The Carlists, however, retired after losing two of their best generals and about two thousand men, in what was called the battle of Somorrostro. The siege of Bilbao, which had been some time in progress, was then raised, to the great joy of its inhabitants, who had sustained for weeks a terrible bombardment. Marshal Manuel Concha, Marquis of Duero, had succeeded in making a détour and attacking the investing army on the other side. General Martinez Campos distinguished himself on this occasion, and the republican army entered Bilbao on the second of May.

"The entrance to Bilbao on that day," says Mr. Furley, an Englishman who was with the armies in the interest of the Red Cross, "presented a most gay and animated appearance. The temporary gates had been opened, and streams of people were pouring out to enjoy the liberty of which they had been so long deprived, or to inspect the state of property in the neighborhood belonging to themselves or their friends. . . . Almost every house bore marks of the bombardment. . . . The windows of the principal buildings were boarded up and filled with sand bags, barricades remained untouched, wooden boardings in some streets formed a covered way to protect pedestrians from the enemy's sharpshooters; temporary gates, trenches, and improvised batteries had quite changed the aspect of some parts of the town. One kind of protection against bullets and shell-splinters was quite new to me, but it was evidently very effective. All the windows of the Bank of Bilbao were covered with bullock-hides, and as these were uncut, and the hair was still upon them, the building bore a very barbaric and original appearance."

Here, too, is a description of the little church of San Pedro Abanto, on one of the heights that had commanded the city : —

"The church was knocked out of all shape; the arches were cut down close to the capitals of the pillars, and one side of the tower had fallen. Figures of saints were lying scattered about amongst tons of stone, and tiles, and charred wooden beams. Over the remains of the altar was standing a gaudily colored figure of the Virgin, pressing her hands upon her breast, as if appealing for mercy."

Don Carlos and his army, after this check, retired in good order to Durango. As we have seen already, his forces in Catalonia, Navarre, and Valencia, now nominally under his brother Don Alfonso, were making progress. His troops in those provinces, though not well organized, amounted in all to about thirty-five thousand men.

Marshal Serrano, being compelled by political events to return to Madrid, left Marshal Concha in command of the Republican army of the North, to carry out a plan of advancing on Estella, a little town in the interior, not fortified, but so surrounded with rocks, cliffs, and mountains that it had never been taken by an enemy. It was a place of importance, as it was a point where several great roads met, and was a sort of centre to the Carlist military operations.

General Manuel Concha's great difficulty was to obtain reinforcements and supplies. The government at Madrid, notwithstanding its desire to end the war, which was ruining the northern and eastern provinces of Spain, could not send the men and money which it was incessantly urged by its generals to furnish. The weather had been bad, the march of Concha's troops was slow, and the Carlists, under Dorregaray, had time to throw up earthworks on important heights commanding the town of Estella.

On June 25, 1874, began the battle of Abazuza, so called from a little village near the town which was the chief object of attack. The battle lasted for three days. On the last Mendiry, one of the Carlist generals, ordered his men in ambush to lie low till the troops of Martinez Campos were at point-blank range, then, as they climbed the steep and slippery ascent, breathless, and with difficulty, they were received with a terrible fire. Three times, encouraged by their officers, the men, who were mostly young recruits, advanced, but were three times repulsed by an unseen enemy. Then Mendiry called upon his Navarrese to charge, and they drove before them the discomfited troops of the Republic. Marshal Concha, seeing this, collected a small body of his reserves, and was hastening to retrieve the disaster, when a ball struck him in the breast. This completed the rout. Echague, to whom the command fell, ordered a retreat. It was a complete victory for the Carlists. They lost about five hundred men, while the loss of the Republicans was one hundred and twenty-one officers and fifteen hundred and forty-two men, including prisoners. But the greatest loss the Republican cause sustained was that of Marshal Manuel de la Concha, the Marquis of Duero. He was born in one of the colonies. In 1824 he entered the royal bodyguard of Ferdinand, and had taken part in every military movement since that day, to say nothing of political agitations. He had retired into private life when Serrano, a few weeks before his death, called upon him for assistance. After he was struck he was carried into a peasant's cottage, where two hours later, in a small room surrounded with little comfort and no luxury, he expired. His body was carried to Madrid, where a magnificent funeral was given him.

In Mr. Furley's book we have a curious picture of what goes on behind the scenes on the day of a battle. The inhabitants of Estella had all quitted the town ; most of them had sought refuge upon a neighboring mountain, where two or three small hamlets were clustered together. They took with them their beds and bedding, tables and chairs, food and tobacco, their flocks and their mules, leaving the town bare of everything that might have served the enemy. From the heights on which they took refuge, they watched the battle ; and the moment they saw the enemy in retreat, they flocked back, bringing their goods with them. " The wonder was," says Mr. Furley, " how so much could have been removed in so short a time."

But the saddest part of the story is to come. Marshal Concha had declared war without quarter and without pity, so that little mercy was shown on either side during the engagement. A hundred and ninety-two Republicans fell into their enemy's hands, and three days after the battle these were brought before a council of war and condemned to be shot. They were taken near two burning villages, and were accused of incendiarism.

" The people of the ruined villages," says Mr. Furley, " clamored for their execution, and there is no doubt that, if they had not been well guarded, the public would have taken the law into their own hands. Scarcely any one could be found who did not approve this sentence. (I am glad to say that amongst the exceptions were some of my French friends, who declared that nothing would induce them to stay another day in the Carlist army, if such a butchery were perpetrated.) It was useless to attempt argument, and equally so to speak of the impression that would be created throughout Europe, if such wholesale murders were committed. Even at headquarters it was generally asserted that the whole number would be shot. Thank God, such a cruel massacre was averted ! . . . I can bear testimony to the fact that Don Carlos was of a merciful disposition, and he has always been averse to carrying out the extreme sentence of military law. Often, against the advice of his generals, has he interposed to save life. There were many persons, therefore, who were anxious that these prisoners should be executed before he arrived. A commutation of the sentence was received at the last moment, whilst the poor fellows were being confessed by the priests, and instead of a hundred and ninety-two men being ruthlessly butchered in cold blood, thirteen were selected for death ; namely, a captain, a sergeant-major, two corporals, and nine privates. Against these, it is said, there were specific charges that could be supported by evidence. It is reported that Don Carlos sent a messenger to stay execution even in the case of these thirteen men, but he arrived too late."

Five days after the battle Don Carlos and his wife Doña Margherita joined the army. General Dorregaray and his staff went out to meet them, and the villagers, amidst the ruins of their houses, gave them an enthusiastic welcome, with cries of " Long live the King ! Death to the prisoners ! "

There is little space here to tell of the triumphal procession that welcomed the sovereigns to Estella. Foremost in it were the four giants who belong as much to the history of Estella as Gog and Magog do to the city of London. They were from fifteen to twenty feet high. One represented a king dressed in blue robes, another his queen dressed in pink; the remaining two were giants black as paint could paint them; their robes were gorgeous, and on their heads were crowns made of feathers. Attended by esquires, who cleared their way with bladders attached to sticks, they danced up the street in a sedate sort of way, heading a procession composed of military bands, generals, municipal officers, priests, and young girls who called themselves Queen Margherita's bodyguard. Under a white silk canopy, with silver poles, borne by four men in purple mantles, came Don Carlos and Doña Margherita. It was the day of their great triumph; none other succeeded it. Both seemed affected by the warmth of their reception, especially the Duchess, who had never before witnessed the intensity of Navarrese loyalty; and she and her husband must for that moment have indeed felt themselves to be King and Queen of Navarre. The next day both visited the hospitals, and nothing could have been more gracious and sympathetic than the kindness they showed to the sick and wounded, — to the Republicans as well as to the Carlist soldiers.

Zabala, the Minister of War at Madrid, took command of the Army of the North, which had lost its chief in Marshal Concha. Zabala's first care was to call out reserves, and to restore spirit and discipline. The Spanish soldier deteriorates in inaction, and loses heart under defeat. The new general withdrew his troops to the Ebro, and remained on the defensive. But in August the Carlists resumed operations; and on the whole they seem to have met with success, until the Republican Moriones, burning to avenge the defeat at Abazuza, gained some slight advantages, after which both armies in the North seemed to give up all idea of assuming the offensive. That of the Republicans limited its efforts to attempts to revictual towns besieged by the Carlists, while the latter contented themselves with making raids.

In Madrid during this month of August, 1874, Marshal Serrano, the dictator, achieved a great political success. His government was recognized by all the European powers except Russia; but what his army needed was a chief whose attention, undistracted by politics, might be solely directed to military affairs.

In Navarre Pampeluna was in the hands of the Republicans, but so closely invested by the Carlists that neutrals desiring to enter it had to obtain passes to go through the Carlist lines. No letters, newspapers, or telegrams from the outside world reached it for months. Savalls and other guerilla chiefs scoured the country, raised contributions, requisitioned horses, and retired to secure camps in mountain strongholds.

The Republican forces in the east were commanded by General Pavia, who by his invasion of the Cortes, eight months before, had brought about the dictatorship of Marshal Serrano. A new man became prominent in the army at this period, Lopez Dominguez, whom I mention because he has since obtained some political prominence.

Early in September there was a ministerial crisis in Madrid, and General Zabala not only relinquished his portfolio as Minister of War, but his position as general-in-chief of the army. As such he was succeeded by General Laserna, a good officer, but the appointment created great discontent in the army. Officers and soldiers alike thought it ought to have been given to General Moriones, and their attachment to the cause of the Republic, which had been never very strong, was greatly shaken.

About the same time — that is, toward the close of the year 1874 — discouragement began also to weaken the Carlist army. It had met with success in almost all its encounters with the troops of the government, yet the situation of affairs was not really changed. Notwithstanding the proverbial fidelity of the volunteers from the Basque provinces, signs of disaffection appeared in their ranks. The cause of Don Carlos began to decline.

For two years war had desolated the northern part of Spain, and the country was very much exhausted. The recognition of Marshal Serrano's government by the Powers made it probable that a blockade would be strictly enforced, and that arms and supplies would find their way with difficulty to Don Carlos and his army. That army felt the need of field artillery and cavalry; but, like the army opposed to it, what it needed *most* was an energetic commander, capable of opening the road for Don Carlos to enter his capital. Appeals were made to General Cabrera, but he could no longer be persuaded to give personal support to the Carlist cause.

Dorregaray also at this time sent in his resignation, giving ill health as his reason for doing so. His place was supplied by General Mendiry; but the army considered that Dorregaray had fallen out of favor with Don Carlos, and was much dissatisfied. Many valuable officers sent in their resignations; while among the men desertions became frequent, and many even repaired to the *indulto;* that is, to stations where amnesty was offered by the Republican Government.

A further complication in military affairs arose from the abrupt dismissal of General Pavia, whose forces were opposing those of the brother of Don Carlos, Don Alfonso, in Catalonia. The order to turn over his command to General Jovellar was so curt and peremptory that his honor as an officer forbade him to retain his post even for a day, although he had just completed plans by which he felt confident of getting the main army of the enemy into his hands.

Don Alfonso having escaped this danger, thanks to the abrupt action of the war office at Madrid, retired to the mountains, whence his guerilla bands made raids through Valencia, Murcia, Granada, and even came within a few hours' march of Madrid. The chief who most distinguished himself in these expeditions was Lozano, who had once been an officer in the regular army. His especial object in his raids was to destroy railroad stations, break up lines of railway, and cut down telegraph wires. Here is one of his orders : —

IN THE NAME OF GOD, COUNTRY, AND KING.

Every employé at any station on this line who continues his work shall be shot after he has confessed and received the last sacraments. If trains, after this notice, continue to run, the stations and all else, including the rolling stock, shall be utterly demolished.

May God give you long life !

MIGUEL LOZANO,
*Chief of Brigade.*

ALPERA, September 17, 1874.

These barbarous orders were followed in many instances by their execution. At one place four employés were shot ; in many the stations were burned. Two trains were set on fire, and then run into each other. It is only fair to say, however, that the passengers were suffered to alight before this was done.

At last, about a month after the order I have quoted, a Republican colonel with a small force surprised Lozano and his band, killed many, took some prisoners, and dispersed the rest. Lozano, while attempting to seek refuge in the mountains, was again intercepted, and the remains of his band dispersed. Tearing off his uniform, and accompanied by two or three of his former staff, Lozano crossed the mountains, and boarded at some way station a train for Cordova. But he was recognized by a Frenchman in the employ of the railway, who had not forgotten the murder of his comrades a few days before. Lozano was arrested, turned over to the military authorities, and shot.

Another famous guerilla chief, who operated in Guipuscoa, was Santa Cruz, the curate of Hernialde. His adventures, exploits, and escapes would be thrilling material for an historical novel. He operated more as a brigand than an officer, not acknowledging any authority, though fighting in the cause of the Carlist King. Some attempts were made by Don Carlos to bring him to order, and even to arrest and court-martial him. At last, after much difficulty, and many complaints on the part of the Carlist Junta of the injury done to the cause by his excesses, he was forced to submit to superior authority.

Jovellar, having succeeded Pavia as commander-in-chief, had some success in Catalonia which discouraged Don Alfonso, who was already out of favor with his royal brother. He threw up his command, and issued the following order of the day to his soldiers : —

" I leave you with the approbation of the King. I trust you will continue the struggle with hope and courage until the day of triumph, which God will assuredly grant you in return for your heroic sacrifices."

He and his wife succeeded in making their way unmolested into France, whence they retired to Austria.

Meantime Don Carlos, judging that it was imperative that something important should be effected in the Basque provinces, laid siege to Irun, a little town on the Spanish bank of the Bidassoa. The Spanish Government attached great importance to the possession of Irun ; and as Don Carlos had no fleet, and it could not be invested on the river-side, they sent troops to its relief by water. But those troops were largely composed of civil volunteers, recently recruited, who burned and plundered with the ferocity of bashi-bazouks. Before a stop could be put to their excesses, all the beautiful dairy farms which covered the rich valley of the Bidassoa were set on fire, — an act which did great injury to the reputation of the Republican army.

Repulsed from Irun, Don Carlos laid siege to St. Sebastian and Hernani, which lies so near to it as to be almost its suburb. Erecting a battery on a neighboring hill, the Carlists opened fire on the town, to which the inhabitants replied by dragging a cannon to the top of the church tower and firing from the belfry.

At the close of the autumn of 1874 the Republican generals were busy reorganizing their forces. Serrano quitted Madrid, and joined the northern army. He knew that he left behind him at the seat of government elements of dissatisfaction that might result in revolution, but he knew also that some brilliant military success could alone satisfy the people and confirm his power. Suddenly news reached him of a *pronunciamento* at Madrid, on the last day of the year 1874, and that the Prince of the Asturias, son of Isabella, had been proclaimed King of Spain by the title of Alfonso XII. Both the Army of the North and the Army of the Centre " pronounced " at once for the young King. Serrano, whose legal title had for a year past been Chief of the Executive Power, made no attempt to oppose the movement which deprived him of his dictatorship. He gave in his adhesion to the new government, left Spain, and passed over into France.

During the last week of December, 1874, General Martinez Campos, in accordance with the principal chiefs of the Alfonsist party in Madrid, had left the capital and gone into Valencia to induce the Army of the Centre, commanded by Jovellar, to declare for the Prince of the Asturias. He had complete success, and communicated by telegraph with other divisions of the army.

In vain the ministry at Madrid issued proclamations against Martinez Campos and Jovellar, who, they said, had raised a seditious banner in the face of the enemy. But the army in the capital proved to be of one mind with the armies in the provinces, and Serrano, instead of " pronouncing " against Alfonso, had accepted the situation. A new ministry was at once formed with Canovas di Castillo as President of the Council.

Madrid and the principal cities in the provinces acquiesced in the change without a murmur ; the people seemed as pleased at the return of the Bourbons as they were six years before to get rid of Isabella.

# CHAPTER XX.

THE Republic had fallen. It had lasted only two years, and had gone through five changes of administration : the Provisional Government, under the ministry of Serrano ; the chief executiveship of Margall ; that of Salmeron ; that of Castelar ; and lastly the virtual dictatorship of Serrano.

A few words may be said concerning its existence [1] before we go on to the story of the close of the Carlist war and the reign of the new King, Alfonso.

"Some races of men are formed to flourish under institutions that would be the despair of others," said M. de Custine, writing about Spain in 1832. "Spanish peasants, even under the miserable government of their Austrian and Bourbon rulers, were probably the happiest in Europe. Their few wants were fully supplied. They had no aspirations. They were not conscious of oppression. All classes met one another socially with courtesy and punctilio. Inequality of degree was not felt in ordinary intercourse."

While the rest of the world was being transformed by the ideas of the French Revolution, Spain was a country of another century. "*En faisant deux cent lieues,*" says M. de Custine, "*on pouvait reculer de trois cent ans.*"

Then came events related in the earlier chapters of this book, and propaganda found its way cautiously into the upper classes of Spain and into the maritime cities. "The spirit of propagandism is the desire to impose our own will upon

---

[1] I am indebted to an article on "Spain a Democratic Nation," by Emilio Castelar, published in a number of the "Forum," in the summer of 1891. We could have no higher authority on such a subject than Señor Castelar. — E. W. L.

others, — the impatience of superior minds to do good, which in many cases only stirs up evil. Every century has its own chief leading idea. That of the first half of the nineteenth century was to attach too much importance to the exterior forms of political life."

M. de Custine says, also with truth, that no nation in Europe at the beginning of this century was better prepared for democratic institutions than Spain; yet no nation was so loyal to its kings and so submissive to its clergy. We have seen how the Basque provinces and Navarre clung to their ancient privileges; and they have succeeded in retaining them to the present day. The Basques, under their "lord," the King of Spain, form what is virtually a little republic, and manage their own affairs in their own way. "This right is secured to them by a compromise with the general government, by which they pay annually about $300,000 as an equivalent for all taxation; in consideration of which they have complete civil and municipal administration, and are free from the intrusions of the public tax-gatherer. Whatever revenue is to be raised is collected by themselves; and this is managed in such a way by indirect taxation that the people do not feel it, and the burthen of government falls lightly on these hardy mountaineers."

People can live happily under a despotism so long as they do not attempt to resist it. When they do, and the iron heel begins to trample them, revolutionary horrors ensue. It was oppression from the nobles, the land-owners, and local tyrants in France, not oppression directly from the court, that galled the rural population of that country during the last century. The *people* were not eager to rise against the King's government; it was the nobles and men of cultivation in the middle class who felt themselves oppressed, and started the Revolution.

Señor Castelar says that revolution began in the fifteenth century with the Renaissance, and that while other nations were going through its preliminary stages, Spain remained stationary, occupied with her great mission of planting Christianity in the New World. In Spain, according to Señor

Castelar, the war waged by the Bourbon kings against the Jesuits was the first step in modern revolution. " It taught that if kings could expel priests, peoples might expel kings."

It is very hard to speak of revolutions in Spain as proceeding from *the nation ;* the " nation is composed of many races, besides being divided into a rural and an urban population : with the former the leading idea was loyalty ; with the other, political emancipation. The feeling common to both was a keen hatred to foreigners." It is amusing to find Señor Castelar, in common with his countrymen, ignoring the assistance of the English armies under Wellington in the Peninsular War. He says : —

" In opposing Napoleon the Great, who threatened with his legions the existence of Spain, we re-established, not only the independent existence of our country, but liberty and law as well. . . . Our fight with Bonaparte for independence can hardly be equalled in the future. The most depressed of nations at that time, — without treasure, without an army or a navy ; sold and betrayed by her kings ; her doors wide open to the invader in whom she believed she would find a brother, but in whom she found only an enemy ; her fortresses occupied by treason and perfidy, and her capital held by a garrison of invaders, — Spain confronted the greatest captain the ages had ever known, having nothing with which to oppose him but fragile houses, naked breasts, women's curses, pikes cut from trees, flames from the hearth, stones from the road, and what was left of a decimated population."

These are eloquent words, and these are the sentiments of the whole Spanish people in our own day. " Alone I did it, — I ! " We may find them in any Spanish oration, or on any Spanish page of history ; but contemporary official correspondence tells another tale. Señor Castelar continues :

" Spain nevertheless succeeded in terrifying Murat at Madrid ; in driving Moncey back from Valencia ; in defeating Dupont at Baylen ; in disarming Lefebvre at Balmaceda ; in disconcerting Napoleon himself at Chamartin ; in stopping Ney at San Payo ; in expelling Soult from Galicia ; in compelling Massena to leave Salamanca, — in eclipsing the marshals styled by Europe the planets of the sun of battles."

One would suppose from such boasts that Wellington had never been born ; that no British warships had kept guard over the coasts of Spain ; that no English soldier had ever set foot in the Peninsula.

But the concluding words in Señor Castelar's burst of patriotic enthusiasm are more just. He extols his country-men for —

"Sustaining sieges like those of Saragossa and Gerona, for holding mountain passes resembling those of Thermopylæ, for raising armed corps like those of Mina and Merino, for sup-plementing the most scientific tactics by a popular warfare whose successes were incomprehensible to the very men who employed it, because they were inspirations of genius."

Señor Castelar is more interesting, if less eloquent, and speaks more to the point and purpose of this chapter when he, the great Spanish Liberal leader of the present day, tells us of his own position under the Republic, and in the re-actionary revolution. The quotation will be a long one, but it is valuable. My readers must accept it as the best exposi-tion of the past, present, and future attitude of Republican statesmen in Spain.

"The generation to which I belong," he says, "turned in anger against the hypocritical absolutism of Isabella. . . . As a consequence of the partial failures that followed our first attempts, we went into exile, and saw our names inscribed on death-warrants. Spain fell again into absolutism. But this reaction served only in the long run to demolish the throne. The intensity of reactionary violence finally uprooted the mon-archy, — an institution which had lasted since the time of Augustus, the oldest of all our institutions, except the munici-palities, and much older than the Church, which did not have full sway over our people till the seventh century of the Chris-tian era. In the midst of revolution we cast forth the germs of new ideas. . . . In order to sow so much, and to put ourselves, in a short time of incessant creation, on a level with the foremost nations, we were forced to exhaust our strength. . . . Among the various forms of government that might be deduced from the principle of national sovereignty, we looked for anchors for our liberties, and, lo! we could not find them. The democratic monarchy and the radical republic failed in this work of carrying out the new ideas, and another reaction came. On December 30, 1874, we saw a dynasty similar to the one we had expelled on September 30, 1868, restored, in the person of Alfonso XII. As soon as the dynasty returned to the throne, I went back to exile; but this time it was a voluntary exile.

"Then I took counsel with myself, and I resolved to restore all we had lost by that reaction. To do this, I realized that it was necessary to change our methods. During the revolution we had acquired a revolutionary temperament; it behooved us to throw off that temperament, and to accommodate ourselves to a slower but surer method, — that of evolution. Revolutions are like wars, after all, and in wars we can forge heroic warriors; but we cannot educate good citizens endowed with that juridic conscience and respect for law that the moderate and legal exercise of liberty demands. . . .

"Thus I declared that in politics I placed law and order above all else. And, having said this, I added that, while bound by restrictive laws, I intended to work for liberal laws. . . . I acknowledged that laws should be improved, but in a lawful manner. I said that in order to define ourselves we ought to limit ourselves, never going beyond what was possible and demanded by our great social aspirations.

"I spoke thus in the first parliament of the restoration, which I entered as a deputy from Barcelona. Of all the historic Republicans I was the only one who had reached so high a place. When I first rose to speak within that hostile body, the flight of an insect could have been heard. All listened with attention. I told them that I, shipwrecked by civil discord, finding unfriendly shores wherever I turned my eyes, accused no one in my misfortune, but on the contrary, appealing to all by my teaching and my example, proposed to restore *without violence* the democratic principles that seemed crushed under the overwhelming weight of the restoration.

"Nearly fifteen years[1] have passed since I uttered those words, and what I then promised has been accomplished."

All obstacles to the accession of Alfonso XII. having disappeared, he embarked at Marseilles on the 7th of January, 1875, and with a little squadron as his escort, set sail for Barcelona. From Barcelona he continued his voyage to Valencia, and thence took the railroad to Madrid, making his

[1] 1891.

solemn entry into his capital on the 14th of January. He was received with the utmost enthusiasm.

He had no sooner reached Madrid than he announced his intention of going at once to the seat of war. The soldiers of the Army of the North had declared for him at once. His cause had been espoused more heartily by soldiers than civilians. Marshal Serrano had prepared all things for an advance ; and the presence of the young sovereign would, it was thought, reanimate the troops, many of whom were mere recruits who had been severely tried by the inclemency of the season, and by inaction.

Alfonso XII. quitted Madrid five days after he had made his public entry, and went to take nominal command of his Army of the North.

It had been thought that the accession of a new king of the House of Bourbon would have weakened the cause of Don Carlos, and have brought back many valuable officers to their old flag. But it was not so. Don Carlos and all members of the Bourbon family who were fighting in his name protested vehemently against the bestowal of the crown on the son of Isabella.

Meantime the Carlist troops, too few and too ill provided to undertake offensive operations on a large scale, were employed with pick and spade in strengthening their positions, and awaited with great confidence the coming of the storm.

Dorregaray, whose health had been restored (or who had become reconciled to the Pretender), returned from France, and took once more command of the Carlist Army of the Centre. He issued proclamations, forbidding, under pain of death, any railroad employé to assist in running trains on the roads that led from Madrid to Valencia, Alicante, or Saragossa. The train by which Alfonso reached his capital was escorted by two other trains filled with troops, and all stations on the route were occupied by government soldiers. Similar precautions protected the King a week later when he travelled to the North, until, having reached the seat of war, he went forward on horseback. General

*KING ALFONSO XII.*

Jovellar, who had taken an active part in proclaiming the young King, accompanied him, as well as Laserna, to whom was confided the chief direction of offensive operations.

When Alfonso reached headquarters he made an effort to effect a reconciliation with his rebellious subjects by issuing two proclamations, one to his soldiers, the other to the Navarrese. "Soldiers," he said, "I appeal to your forbearance and your energy, not now that you may win new glory, but to obtain peace." And to the people of Navarre he said: "Before opening the campaign I offer you peace. Listen to the friendly voice of your King. I am a Constitutional king, and I will ever remain so; yet I represent the monarchical principle, to which your fathers swore to be faithful."

No effect was produced by these proclamations, and war was resumed. The first thing to be done was to revictual Pampeluna, which was closely invested by a small force of Carlists, who hoped to reduce it by famine, as they had no siege guns. Moriones succeeded in throwing succors into the town, whose garrison and whose inhabitants were decimated by hunger, cold, and typhoid fever.

Leaving part of his army in Pampeluna, Moriones marched with the rest to rejoin the main division of the army under the King himself and the Commander-in-Chief, which was again advancing to attack Estella.

In the attempt upon that town recorded in the last chapter, the Republican army attacked, while that of Don Carlos stood on the defensive. This time the positions were reversed. Don Carlos, against the advice of his generals, insisted on attacking Alfonso's troops, and so gaining a success which might offset the relief of Pampeluna.

He succeeded. Estella, which had never been taken, again escaped. The army of Alfonso retired, after suffering a check in what was called the battle of Lucar. In this battle the young King received his "baptism of fire," one of his staff being struck dead at his side. But his generals, when they saw that failure might be apprehended, insisted on his return to Madrid. He did return, but in spite of all

24

persuasions he first visited Pampeluna and several towns on the Ebro. The train which bore him back to his capital was fired into, in spite of all precautions, by a party of guerillas, but he reached Madrid in safety, the second week in February.

The campaign closed with losses and successes on both sides. The King's troops had indeed taken possession of Navarre, and of Pampeluna, its capital, but they had been foiled at Estella, and had by no means accomplished what had been expected of them when the campaign opened. It was determined by the government to wait until the spring before recommencing offensive operations, and meantime to strengthen their hold on the country already in their power. Laserna was made aide-de-camp and adviser of the King; while his post of Commander-in-Chief of the Army of the North was given to Quesada, a brave and prudent soldier who had distinguished himself in Morocco under O'Donnell in 1859.

About this time — that is to say, in March, 1875 — an event occurred which caused general surprise. Cabrera, who had refused to join the Carlist cause, gave in his adhesion to that of Alfonso, and endeavored to effect a reconciliation. He published a manifesto exhorting his old companions-in-arms to follow his example, at the same time proposing an arrangement for putting an end to the civil war by giving very liberal concessions to the Carlists.

But though Cabrera had many friends in the Carlist ranks and had long kept up with them cordial relations, his attempt at a pacification founded on the Convention that in 1839 had put an end to the Seven Years' War, not only brought no officers over to the standard of Alfonso, but inspired them solemnly to renew their oath of fidelity to Don Carlos on March 10 at Bergara. At the same time Don Carlos issued a proclamation depriving Cabrera of all titles and dignities, and threatening him with a court-martial (which meant death) if he were taken prisoner.

It is needless to follow the petty operations of both armies in the ensuing campaign. Martinez Campos received full powers from Madrid to effect the pacification of Catalonia. He was opposed by Dorregaray, the best general in the service of Don Carlos, and was very much worried by bands of guerillas under Savalls. On the side of Alfonso, but under the command of Martinez Campos as General-in-Chief, were Generals Jovellar and Weyler.

In August, while Jovellar was actively pursuing Dorregaray, Martinez Campos laid siege to the town and citadel of Seo d'Urgel, which in every war had been a Carlist stronghold. Lizzaraga, who commanded the garrison, offered to surrender, when reduced to extremity, if he might march out with his garrison. The Alfonsist general declined this offer, and gave him twenty-four hours for deliberation. At the end of that time Lizzaraga capitulated without conditions, but to the astonishment of everybody he obtained the honors of war. This favor was more than an acknowledgment of the bravery which during the siege had distinguished the Carlist troops and their commander; it was giving to the Carlists belligerent rights. For the honors of war and exchange of prisoners were by the laws of war not accorded to rebels, except by especial convention.

On August 29, 1875, the garrison of Seo d'Urgel, headed by the Bishop of the place, marched out of the town, laid down their arms, and were forwarded to Barcelona. Lizzaraga was paroled, and received a safe-conduct to France.

Don Carlos, seeing that Catalonia was almost lost, conceived a plan of marching on Madrid, but it was never accomplished; and by the end of November, the Carlist army in Catalonia had ceased to exist. Some of the men were made prisoners; some had retired to their homes; some had joined the force still under the command of Don Carlos in the neighborhood of San Sebastian. The principal guerilla chiefs, Savalls and others, had passed over into France; and Martinez Campos wrote to the government at Madrid: —

" I have the satisfaction of announcing to you that not one band of the enemy remains in arms in Catalonia. . . . The war has been on our part a war of courage, legs, and privations; in all these the soldiers have behaved admirably. . . . I wish also to observe to your Excellency that I have not bribed or purchased a single guerilla leader, and that arms alone have terminated this war."

Peace was hailed with satisfaction by the inhabitants of Catalonia, especially those engaged in manufactures; for three years their towns had never felt secure, either from surprise by the troops of one party, or from requisitions by the other. By the pacification of Catalonia forty thousand tried soldiers were left free to join Quesada, who was in the North opposing the Pretender.

About this time a war with the United States on the question of Cuba was considered probable; and Don Carlos sent an aide-de-camp to Madrid to make to his cousin Alfonso an extraordinary proposal. It was that they should join their forces and fight the United States as their common enemy; after which, each commander should be free to maintain his rights to the Spanish throne. No answer was returned to this proposal.

In Navarre the Alfonsist army had a brilliant little success in the vicinity of Pampeluna, and then under Martinez Campos it once more advanced to take Estella. On the 18th of February, 1876, while the surrounding mountains were covered with snow, General Rivera and the Alfonsist troops entered unopposed the gallant little city.

The great struggle was, however, along the banks of the Bidassoa, and the shores of the Bay of Biscay. But the armies of Alfonso were closing round the Carlists, ever pushing them nearer to the French frontier, whose proximity was too great a temptation to be resisted by disheartened volunteers. Many passed over the mountains into safety.

In the middle of winter Alfonso XII. arrived at Bergara, and was received in silence. Bergara (or Vergara) had long been the most helpful and most faithful place in all the Carlist country, and now, by its devotion to the third Don Carlos, seemed to endeavor to make atonement for having been the place where the Convention signed by Maroto with Espartero in 1839 had sent the first Don Carlos into exile.

The Carlist forces had been so completely swept out of Biscay that Alfonso XII. made a triumphal march through cities that but recently had been held or bombarded by the enemy. His reception was enthusiastic, but he did not linger long to be fêted and to receive honors ; he put himself at the head of his men, and determined to complete his victory. But as he marched onward he found no enemy to oppose him. Don Carlos had become convinced that his cause was lost, and, protected by a few squadrons of faithful troops, had passed over the French frontier. From a little town in the upper part of Navarre, near the pass of Roncesvalles, he sent word to the French General commanding a small army of observation that it was his intention to enter France ; and he asked that the officers of his staff might be permitted to retain their horses.

He was received in France with punctilious courtesy, but it was evident that his presence was not desired in that country. A special train conveyed the ex-King Charles VII. (thenceforward Duke of Madrid) to Boulogne, whence he crossed over to England.

Don Carlos is at present residing in Venice. His amiable wife, Margherita of Parma, his early love, died some years since, and he remarried with a lady of the princely House of Rohan, who is said to give herself rather more royal airs than she is entitled to by her position. The Count de Chambord left by will much valuable property to Don Carlos as head of the House of Bourbon. He is said to have renounced his rights as King of Spain and *France* in favor of his son Jaime, who may now be considered the Bourbon Legitimist heir to both thrones, setting aside the law which, in 1713, barred the claim of Spanish Bourbons to be French kings. One of Don Carlos' daughters, the Infanta Elvira, made a recent scandal in Italy. The other remains as yet unmarried.

Don Carlos, when he left his troops, absolved them from their oath of allegiance ; but in his manifesto to the Spanish nation he strongly insisted on "the rights" for which he had fought for four years. "My banner," he said, "will stay furled until God shall announce for Catholic and monarchical Spain that the day of her redemption has arrived, — a day that cannot but be decreed by Providence as a reward for your many sacrifices."

Thus the civil war terminated two and twenty years ago. The Constitutional Government had made no engagements, and was at liberty to show either clemency or severity to the late rebels. It had a free hand in pacifying the conquered provinces, while at the same time it took measures to suppress risings for the future, and to protect the inhabitants of the country, exhausted by this long struggle, from future criminal attempts to upset a stable government.

# CHAPTER XXI.

## ALFONSO XII., HIS WIDOW, AND HIS SON.

WE pass now to a period when Spain enjoyed compara-
tive rest and quiet, — a period in which there are
fewer events to record than in our previous chapters. "Happy
the people whose annals are blank in history books," was said
truly by Montesquieu and quoted by Carlyle. Spain on the
accession of Alfonso was like a patient lying exhausted, after
having passed through the stages of some dread disease,
yet gathering strength from the quiet produced by mere
exhaustion.

Alfonso, son of Isabella, was born on November 28, 1857,
so that he was a boy eleven years of age when he accompanied his mother in her flight to Biarritz and Pau. I have
said already that Isabella, with all her faults, was not only an
affectionate but a very sensible mother. The first years of
Alfonso's life had been passed under the care of Madame
Calderon de la Barca; when Queen Isabella took up her
residence in Paris, he was sent, as Louis Philippe's sons had
been, to a Lycée, or public school. He saw Paris in its
state of excitement on the eve of the Franco-Prussian war,
and the Parisians used often to see him in the Bois de Boulogne, driving his pretty pair of ponies. But when France
became more troubled, he was sent to continue his education
in Vienna. He felt his separation from his sisters very
much, and from his little cousin Mercedes (daughter of his
aunt Luisa and the Duke de Montpensier).

After two years of study in Austria his tutor, Count Morphy,
went with him to England, where he again met the Prince
Imperial, now, like himself, an exile, and they became

attached friends.  The Prince Imperial was a pupil at the Military College at Woolwich ; the Prince of the Asturias was sent to a similar training school at Sandhurst.

The English climate did not seem to suit Alfonso, who was constitutionally consumptive, but he had not to endure it long.  Don Antonio Canovas del Castillo had exercised a very important influence upon his education.  By Canovas' advice liberal ideas were substituted for the Clerical and Absolutist ideas of his mother.  For some time during the interregnum that followed the abdication of Amadeo, Canovas secretly carried on a widespread propaganda in favor of Don Alfonso, whilst different forms of government were on trial at Madrid ; and at the close of 1874 he saw that the moment had come to strike.  To use the words of a French writer, " During the two years that followed the abdication of Amadeo, the Spaniards flattered themselves that their Ship of State had got into port, and had cast anchor under the flag of the Republic ; on the contrary, she had dragged her anchors, and gone forth into the tempest again."

It was Canovas who urged the Spanish nobility to send an address to Alfonso on his birthday in the autumn of 1874, and he himself wrote the answer of Don Alfonso to that address.  A few months later, on the last day of the same year, Alfonso was proclaimed King, not by the Cortes, but by the Spanish soldiers ; and Canovas became Prime Minister of what was called the Conciliation Cabinet.  It is said that when the telegram announcing to Isabella that her son was proclaimed King of Spain reached her, she flew to the bedside of her boy, who was at the time passing a few days with her in Paris, and throwing herself on her knees beside his bed, she begged to kiss his hand as the first and most devoted of his subjects.  Alfonso sleepily put out the hand demanded of him, and fell asleep again.  But the next day all was bustle.  He had to make preparations for his journey to Spain, and, above all, to be provided with a captain-general's uniform.  So hastily was this done that the hat was forgotten, and he reached Barcelona with only the college

his aunt Luisa Fernanda de Borbon, was named Maria de las Mercedes, — Our Lady of Mercy. She was now about eighteen. Alfonso had been the bosom friend of her beloved brother and playfellow, Don Ferdinand, and had seen much of Mercedes when as a little boy in France he was almost daily with his cousins. From a very early age he had declared that little Mercedes and no other should be his wife.

The Montpensier children had been strictly and carefully brought up, and Mercedes must have been one of the race of child-angels. She was sent when about fifteen to the School of the Sacré Cœur near Paris ; and a very interesting article describing her school-days, written by one of her school-fellows, was published in " Scribner's Magazine " in 1878.

Several ladies were proposed by the ministers of Alfonso as his bride, but his heart clung to Mercedes. It was represented to him that she would not be acceptable to the Spanish nation ; that her father, the Duke de Montpensier, was not popular ; that she in short was *afrancesada*, — but he was firmly resolved to marry his beloved cousin.

According to Spanish court etiquette there was no possible chance for any word in private passing between the lovers, but they understood and trusted each other. The lady at the head of Alfonso's court was his widowed sister, Doña Maria del Pilar, who had married a nobleman of Naples, and was now, as her brother's presumptive heiress, Princess of the Asturias. The lady in waiting on the Princess was her dear friend and ex-gouvernante, Madame Calderon de la Barca. The Princess and this lady sympathized in the young people's affection. They contrived a country party, at which Mercedes was present. Alfonso manœuvred to separate his cousin and Madame Calderon from the rest, and getting them into a carriage whispered in German to Mercedes, " Let them say what they will, I will marry none but you." She laid her finger on her lips and looked up at him archly ; that was all.

Finding the King determined, his ministers and his parliament gave way. Ten happy days the lovers spent at Seville, seeing each other daily. Mercedes was with her parents. Alfonso and his sister were lodged in the Alcazar, "where," says Madame Calderon, "I thought I should have died of the cold, but I heard no complaint from the lovers."

Who does not love a lover? All Spain grew interested in the story. As Mercedes came to be known, she endeared herself to her people.

The wedding took place in January, 1878. All Madrid was festive and sympathetic. The wedding presents were superb. Queen Victoria sent a splendid bracelet of diamonds to the bride. The Prince of Wales sent a scimitar, in a sheath studded with jewels, to the bridegroom. The Emperor of Morocco sent Arab horses.

The procession to the church was very splendid, and the young King and Queen returned together in a carriage panelled with glass, and drawn by eight milk-white horses. The whole city was hung with rich tapestries and displayed everywhere the royal colors of Spain, crimson and gold.

Of course there were bull-fights to celebrate the occasion. Before the combats of the day began the *matadors* rode as knights in a splendid procession round the arena, the *picadors* attending them as pages. It may have taken considerable nerve for Mercedes to sit with composure through the spectacle; but it was part of her royal duty, and she did not shrink from it.

She was married on the twenty-third of January; she had five brief months of unclouded happiness, and then came the end. She was prostrated by gastric fever.

We bow to the Love and the Wisdom that sends such catastrophes; and yet I can never think of Mercedes' death without remembering the lines of Coleridge : —

> "Besides, — what grieved us most, — we knew
> They had no need of such as you
> In the place where you were going.
> On earth are angels all too few,
> While Heaven is overflowing."

Between husband and wife there had been love, — deep, simple, and sincere. The warm, generous disposition of

Alfonso and the calm, serene, confiding character of his bride, animated, however, by a natural bright mirthfulness, seemed to promise a long life of domestic happiness; for Mercedes had the *mens sana in corpore sano.* Spain had witnessed little married happiness among her rulers.

She died, sweet, loving, and beloved Mercedes, with all the world so bright about her, on June 25, 1878.

To the last her husband hung over her bed, calling upon her name, "Mercedes! Mercedes mia!" To the last her eyes were turned on him with love. He said to one who saw him a few days after her death, that for him there was no consolation, but that he would do his duty.

From the windows of his palace he watched the funeral train departing for the royal burial-place at the Escurial. Long after it had left he remained steadily looking in the direction it had taken.

Here is a sonnet written by Lord Rosslyn, who was appointed ambassador extraordinary by Queen Victoria to the court of Spain on the occasion of the marriage.

"It was written," says its author, "with tears."

> "Mercedes mia! turn thine eyes away;
>   I have no power to grant thy longing prayer;
>   Their mute appeal is more than I can bear.
> Could I but snatch thee from Death's cruel sway
> God knows how gladly I would give this day
>   My life for thine. For whom have I to care
>   When thou art gone? The darkness of despair
> Clouds all my heart with terror and dismay.
>   Mercedes mia! I am brave once more!
>   Turn thy dear eyes on me until they close
>   Forever. I will look love into thine
> Till death arrests their sight. What! is all o'er?
>   Then farewell hope, and farewell sweet repose.
>   Now duty's rugged path be only mine!"

And soon, alas! for Alfonso, came the bitter day when duty to his people called on him to make a second marriage.

In Queen Victoria's journal, seventeen years before, she wrote, as she recorded the death of King Pedro of Portugal, who not long before had lost his beloved wife Stephanie, "Dear, loving, pure-souled Pedro! At least he was spared that sorrow of knowing it incumbent on him to make a second marriage."

But all Spain felt that the land must have if possible a prince to mount his father's throne. So one of the ladies who at first had been proposed for Alfonso was chosen, the Archduchess Maria Christina, niece of Francis Joseph, the Emperor of Austria. She was tall, fair, sensible, and well educated.

She was married by proxy to Alfonso in the summer of 1879, and came as queen into his kingdom. Their first child, a little daughter, was named Mercedes, a touching tribute to the memory of her whose loss could never be forgotten.

In 1879 the ministry of Canovas fell in consequence of disturbances in Cuba, but he was recalled the next year, when he held power only a short time, being defeated in the Cortes on some financial question. He for the third time assumed office, in January, 1884. Certain reactionary measures brought forward by this Cabinet roused the Republicans, who threatened revolution.

Nevertheless, as time went on Alfonso endeared himself more and more to his people. Whatever might befall himself as a sovereign, he would be always *faithful to his duty*. Two painful events occurred to him during his reign : one was a severe carriage accident as he was passing with his family in one large *char à banc* over some high mountain on a summer tour, when the carriage was overturned, and his beloved sister, the widowed Princess of the Asturias, was painfully injured.

The other was that he made a trip to Germany to visit the Emperor, and when at Berlin accepted the honorary colonelcy of a Prussian regiment. Passing through Paris, on his way back to Madrid, he was set upon by the Parisian mob, and hooted and insulted, as one who had shown sympathy with the Prussians. President Grévy was obliged to make the most profuse apologies ; but the Parisian world in general declared that the wrath of the mob had been stirred up by the indiscretions of his son-in-law, M. Wilson.

The ex-Queen Isabella returned to Spain, but has taken no part in politics ; nor would she be permitted to do so.

Her daughter, Maria del Pilar, is still a widow; the Princess Maria Paz married a prince of Bavaria; the Princess Eulalia was united to Prince Antoine, son of the Duke de Montpensier. She represented the court of Spain in London at Queen Victoria's Jubilee in 1887, and in Chicago in 1893, at the World's Fair.

When cholera broke out in southern Spain in 1885, Alfonso hastened to the scene of suffering, and did all he could to establish proper hospitals, provide medical attendants, asylums for orphans, and food for the starving. His self-devotion on this occasion endeared him still more to his subjects. In him they had a king of *their own*, — a Spanish king, — whom for the first time for generations they could reverence and love.

But his doom had gone forth. His constitution was consumptive, and after his return from the cholera districts in southern Spain, the disease rapidly developed itself. He died at Madrid, November 25, 1885, his wife Christina tenderly attending on him to the last, and receiving his last sigh ere he went to rejoin Mercedes.

When his funeral was over, Queen Christina found herself alone; and never was any human being more desolate.

Alfonso with all his merits had not always been to her a faithful husband; and at one time she was so moved by scandals whispered about in society at Madrid, that she gathered up, as it were, the two little princesses, her children, and returned indignantly to her own country, and to her father's protection. But Alfonso at once went to seek her and reclaim her, to explain all that could be explained, and for the rest to plead repentance and implore her pardon. He was forgiven, and the remainder of their married life was affectionate and happy.

After his death her position might be described as truly pitiful. She had never established herself in the hearts of the Spanish people. To them she was a foreigner; even her husband's sisters thought her cold. Besides, her position was not defined. Though a queen, she was not a sovereign. She was only the widow of a Spanish king. She had two daughters, but it was still hoped that she might have a son. There were a few days of painful suspense throughout the country; then her very helplessness appealed to the hearts of the Spanish deputies, and she was chosen Queen Regent of Spain during the minority of Mercedes, her daughter, or, as was earnestly hoped, during the minority of a Spanish prince, her son.

When she took the oath to be faithful to her duties as Queen Regent, the Cortes presented a touching scene. She stood in deep mourning among men most of whom were clad in brilliant uniforms, and in a low voice, in profound stillness, swore to hold sacred the rights and liberties of the Spanish nation. The sight of her, so young, so lately widowed, so helpless and alone, moved all in the assembly. She conquered their hearts and the hearts of the Spanish people. " From that moment," says one who tells the story, " she was a sovereign indeed, with a loyal people round her."

Canovas, head of the Conservative party, was premier when Alfonso died; but he knew that his administration was extremely unpopular, and he most nobly advised the Queen Regent to call upon Sagasta, the Liberal leader, to form a ministry. He told her that a Sagasta Cabinet was the only one that could rule Spain at that time, but that he himself would not hesitate to combat such a cabinet, if it showed anti-monarchical tendencies.

The Cabinet formed by Sagasta included men of several parties; it secured large majorities in the Cortes and brought forward and passed several popular measures, but questions of finance were its stone of stumbling.

Meantime, on May 17, 1886, ministers and other high officials were summoned to the palace. As they waited, a faint cry was heard; and the Prime Minister, Sagasta, emerged, with a beaming smile, from the Queen's chamber, exclaiming, " Viva el Rey!" Little Alfonso XIII. was born! He had no father, as other royal Infantes had had, to present him to the assembled dignitaries on a golden salver. That office was performed by a chamberlain. But great was the joy throughout his kingdom. From the hour

*KING ALFONSO XIII.*

he was born he was King of Spain, and all official documents are put forth in his name. His mother has always taken delight in presenting him to his subjects. When he was only a few months old, the army in Madrid passed in review before him, and never did a little prince receive more tender maternal care, or a more princely education. He is rather a delicate child, and it may earnestly be hoped that he has not inherited the consumptive tendency of his father. That tendency, however, if it is his, may be counteracted by judicious nurture.

And Christina herself, with a face that is always somewhat sad, but that appeals to other hearts by an expression better than beauty, — a tender, a beseeching look, that comes only to those who have experienced a great sorrow, — is now honored and beloved by her son's people. When in the King's infancy she first presented herself in public with the child in her arms, the feeling of all who saw them was expressed at the time by Castelar, "Spaniards cannot fight against a woman, or against a child in his cradle."

The Queen cares little for display, though she is constantly obliged to pose as Queen Regent in public, giving brilliant receptions and audiences to foreign ministers; but her taste is for a quiet life, and her happiness in the care of her children.

About a year after the King's death a revolution, or rather a mutiny, was attempted. It was to have broken out in the barracks at Madrid. At its head was General Villacampa, who probably hoped, like generals who had headed revolts in the days of Isabella, to rise by that means to honors, wealth, and power. His designs were, however, discovered, and the *pronunciamento* nipped in the bud. The soldiers who were to have joined it were caught in their beds, dressed in their uniforms, all ready to sally into the streets and "pronounce," it is not very clear for what. Six officers were sentenced to be shot; but within twenty-four hours of the fatal moment, the daughter of Villacampa procured the commutation of their sentence, and they were exiled to the coast of Africa.

25

The affair, however, brought the ministry into disrepute, and led to much angry discussion and to some brilliant speeches in the Cortes. Sagasta ended a speech which a politician of the time held to have been *inspired*, with a picture of the widowed Queen drawing to her all hearts by the dignity with which she bore her great sorrow, and carrying in her arms the young life that was the hope of Spain.

During the regency of Queen Maria Christina there have been five principal parties in Spain, — the Conservatives led by Canovas ; the Liberals led by Sagasta ; the Federalist Republicans, by Pi y Margall ; the Unionist Republicans, whose chief is Salmeron, and the still lingering Carlist party at whose head is the Marquis de Cerralbo.

It is remarkable that all these leaders, with the exception of the last, are professional men, without titles, men who have risen from the people. Each of these parties has its malcontents, especially the Carlist faction, which has in its ranks a Don Ramon Nocedal, an ambitious dreamer, who has announced himself as an apostle of ultra-clericalism and ultra-absolutism ; and who has roused to fanaticism many of the poor mountaineers of Navarre, Biscay, and Guipuscoa. He preaches that Liberalism is the greatest evil upon earth, — far worse than adultery, robbery, and murder. In all this he places himself in antagonism with Pope Leo XIII., who appreciates the exertions of the Union Catholic party.

The first parliamentary struggle under the regency was one between the Ultramontanes and the Liberals, the former struggling for old-fashioned exclusive Catholicism, the other for liberty of worship. A compromise was effected, which pleased no one. Under the Republic the legality of civil marriages had been admitted. But as a concession to the Clerical party this permission was repealed, so that the children of Protestants married in Spain lost their legitimacy. This was a sore grievance, but happily is now removed.

Canovas once described the state of political parties in Spain as follows : —

" There are at the extremes of the political arena two *intransigeant* (irreconcilable) parties, — the Carlists in the rural districts, the Socialists and advanced Republicans in the large cities. Between these there is the great mass of the nation, who remain calm and resigned, whether Sagasta or I direct the affairs of the monarchy. It is not the mode of government, but the manners and customs of a country, that influence its elections. Abroad, people do not understand the necessary and preponderating rôle which the royal prerogative plays with us."

That is to say, that whereas in England a change of ministry is always the result of the loss of a working majority in Parliament, in Spain (as with us in the United States) a change in the Cabinet is more often the result of the Constitutional intervention of the executive or the sovereign.

All men agree that the Queen Regent has been remarkable for the tact with which hitherto she has rallied all parties in support of the throne of the little King.[1]

In 1889 a measure was carried that Castelar had much at heart, and Spain obtained the doubtful blessing of universal suffrage. Whether the good sense of the body of the people is sufficient to overbalance the influence of the ignorant and the turbulent remains to be decided.

The main difficulties of Spain lie in her present struggle with her colonial possessions, and in the state of her finances. Canovas was a protectionist, but there is a considerable free-trade party. In former times Spanish politics were regarded by politicians as means to advance their private ends. Now all the great leaders are men of integrity, who never dip their hands into the public purse ; but probably among their underlings there may be much to be desired.

[1] Among all the confusion of Spanish politics, the whirlwind of rejoicing, lamentation, intrigue, religion, corruption, collective patriotism, and individual grabbing, there is one noble figure which prominently stands out in vivid contrast, a model of virtue and enviable tact. Her Majesty, the Queen Regent, notwithstanding her foreign birth, knows exactly how to do the right thing at the right moment with exquisite taste. She has won by her charitableness the adoration of the masses; by her gracious sympathy the love of the middle classes ; and by her clear comprehension of all that is traditionally Spanish, the esteem and admiration of the aristocracy. — JOHN FOREMAN, *National Review*, July, 1897.

The head of one branch of the Liberal party is General Martinez Campos. He was imprisoned after the fall of Amadeo because he refused to recognize the Republic, but was shortly after released, and, as we have seen, played a great part both in the pacification of Catalonia and the restoration of the monarchy.

A writer on Spanish statesmen in the "Leisure Hour Magazine" said of him in 1892 : —

"Intrusted with supreme command in Cuba, he succeeded in an incredibly short space of time, partly by military, partly by diplomatic tactics, in putting an end to the disorders which had lasted in the island for seven years. He also endeavored to impress on the home government, but in vain, the necessity for giving way to the financial and political aspirations of Cuba. Prime minister for a brief period, he afterwards became governor of Madrid; which charge he resigned in 1888, on a question of etiquette. He subsequently differed from Sagasta on the subject of army reform, and has since at times opposed him in the Senate."

But the Spanish politician upon whom all eyes are turned, both in his own and other countries, is Emilio Castelar. At present (1897) he has retired from public life, and is devoting himself to literary work, which at no time in his career has he wholly neglected. He writes weekly articles, chiefly on the social and political condition of Spain, in the "España Moderna," but he also writes articles on foreign literature, and books on foreign countries as well as on his native land. Above all his gifts, however, stands that of oratory.

He was for a brief period head of the government under the Republic; more than once he has seemed to hold in his hands the destinies of bleeding and distracted Spain. He lives plainly in Madrid in second-story apartments, where his sister keeps house for him. His rooms are filled with gifts and offerings from his friends and admirers, but he is willing to accept no public tribute. He and Canovas were old and dear friends; and though one was a Conservative prime minister, and the other a Republican chief, their practical views on politics were so nearly alike that any slight differences of opinion only lent salt to their conversation.

Though an earnest advocate of religious toleration, Castelar never neglects the observances of his church, and shows deep religious feeling in his writings. In this it is greatly to be regretted that his followers are few. In Spain, at the present day, there is a marked absence of real religion. The enlightened classes have emancipated themselves from the priests, and at the same time from their belief in the essential truths of Christianity; while the peasantry seem to combine irreligion with superstition. There are a few devout persons who have formed themselves into the " New Christian Church " in Spain, and of course there is Protestant propaganda; but Spanish character and traditions are opposed to Protestantism. Spaniards never will become Christians after the American or English models ; and it may be doubted if they will ever go back as a nation to anything like the form of Christianity they have repudiated and outgrown. Probably if one of our prominent American cardinals were made Archbishop of Toledo he would find himself very little in sympathy with his flock or his surroundings.

Up to a few years since, education was at a very low ebb in Spain. In 1870, out of a population of almost seventeen millions, only four millions could read and write. But now, though far behind other countries, by reason of her civil wars, her national pride and prejudices, and her mixed races, Spain feels the wave of progress. Let us hope she will feel it in the right way.

In conclusion permit me to borrow an extract from a recent article in the " España Moderna " by Castelar, the man most qualified to reveal to us the very heart of Spain :

"Spain constitutes, notwithstanding the survival after her revolutions of an historical monarchy and an official church, the most democratic state possible in a monarchical form, — if by democracy we understand the exercise of individual rights; of a jury system which places the administration of justice in the hands of the people; and of universal suffrage. . . . This may not altogether fulfil the lofty ideals of many a democrat, who, having paid dearly for adherence to his abstract conceptions, cannot satisfy his generous ambitions with anything less than the radical Republic. . . . I am one of those who had dreamed of those gains for the benefit of my country. But when we turn the eyes of our memory to the sad realities of the past and compare them with the realities of the present, we see what may be accomplished by steady progress without the fulfilment of Utopian dreams and unrealizable ideals. Those who have seen an almost absolute monarchy may to-day see a democratic monarchy. Those who once scarcely dared to express their thoughts, to-day can write whatever they think proper. Those who were once called a party of outlaws now see opened before them the Cortes and the government. Those who were excluded from the Universities for proclaiming free thought and the proper standards of science, to-day have the right to teach what they think and believe. Those who once saw an intolerant Church united to an almost absolute State, crushing every expansion of the soul, to-day have no limit set to the expression of their thoughts. Those who once felt their hearts stirred with indignation against slavery and the markets where human beings were sold and bought, as in Nineveh and Babylon, now know that to-day there is not one slave under the Spanish flag. We may indeed feel well content with the work of the past forty years."

# CHAPTER XXII.

## CUBA.

ON October 28, 1492, Columbus landed on the shores of Cuba, the Pearl of the Antilles, — the "Pearl in the mud," as it is now sometimes termed by Cuban writers.[1]

The word Antilles, now applied to all the islands of the West Indian Archipelago (except the Bahamas), was more especially given to the four largest ones, — Cuba, Hayti, Porto Rico, and Jamaica. It was probably derived from Antilla, the name given by Carthaginian voyagers to some unknown land lying west of the Azores in the Atlantic and mentioned by Aristotle. As an island, Antilla was laid down on maps by geographers in the Middle Ages.

Columbus described Cuba as the most beautiful land that man had ever laid eyes on. Its shape is often compared to that of a lizard. Cuba is smaller than the State of New York, and less than half the size of Italy. Its greatest length is seven hundred and sixty miles, its breadth at the widest part is one hundred and thirty-five miles, its average breadth about thirty miles. It has numerous and splendid harbors. A chain of mountains — the Sierra Maestra — runs like a backbone through the whole length of the island; and short rivers from either side of it water the fertile lowlands and run into the sea. Cuba is said to have in the ocean surrounding it seven hundred and thirty islands, little and big; but the only one of any importance is the Isle of Pines, the favorite resort of pirates from the days of the old bucca-

---

[1] I am indebted largely in the early pages of this chapter to the Supplement, by Louis Edward Levy, appended to the American translation of " Cuba and the Cubans " by Don Raimondo Cabrera (1896).

neers in the sixteenth century to those of Jean Lafitte, who distinguished himself as a volunteer in the defence of New Orleans. The mountains are full of gold, silver, iron, copper, and loadstone. The island has also coal, petroleum, and beautiful marbles. These mineral treasures have been little disturbed by man and lie waiting for peace, labor, enterprise, and capital.

The hot season — or rainy season — in Cuba lasts from April to October; the Cuban dry season corresponds to our late autumn, winter, and early spring.

The island has had many names. Columbus called it Juana, in compliment to Prince Juan, only son of Ferdinand and Isabella, whose white marble effigy, representing him clothed partly in his student's gown and partly in the war gear of a knight, may be seen by any traveller in Spain, on his tomb in the church at Avila. Fernandina was subsequently its name, so called after Prince Juan's bereaved father; Saint James was honored next, and the island was called Santiago; the Holy Mother superseded the Saint, and for a while it was named Ave Maria; but the Spaniards, bewildered by such an excess of nomenclature, fell back on what they conceived to have been the native name, Cubana-can, which means the place where gold is found, — namely, in the interior. The island was partially colonized by Columbus and his son; but as soon as the colonists had acquired any riches they became the prey of adventurers and buccaneers. About sixty years after the discovery of the island the native race had almost disappeared, but Havana had been built, and was becoming a flourishing city.

Charles V. sent a royal governor to the colony, and Havana became the commercial centre of Spanish America, the halting place of the galleons that bore silver from Mexico, and gold from Honduras, to Spain. Under the last of the Austrian kings of that country restrictions were placed upon colonial commerce which almost destroyed legitimate traffic, and trade fell into the hands of smugglers.

Those were the palmy days of the buccaneers.

" From being merely contraband traders in constant conflict with the Spanish officials on land and water, they soon grew to be a powerful body of freebooters who preyed mainly upon Spanish commerce. They gradually attained to the position of a hireling navy, and aided the French in 1641 at Tortuga, and the English in the occupation of Jamaica."

The Treaty of Utrecht in 1713, which secured the throne of Spain to French princes of the House of Bourbon, brought a new era to Cuba. Tobacco began to be cultivated. Up to that period the contributions of the island to the Spanish Exchequer had been through the price paid by traders in Seville and Cadiz for commercial privileges; but in 1717 tobacco became a monopoly of the government, and that attachment of the inhabitants to the Spanish crown which gave Cuba the name of " the ever-faithful island " received a shock from which it has never recovered.

In 1762 war broke out between Spain and Great Britain. The English took Havana after a siege of two months, and secured an immense booty. In return they opened the port to foreign commerce, and although a few months later (February, 1763) they restored their conquest to Spain in exchange for Florida, their brief stay on the island proved of permanent importance, for the Spanish Government found it practically impossible to restore the old restrictions upon trade.

In 1777 Cuba was given an independent colonial government, under a Captain-General, who surrounded himself with office-holders from Spain, and from that date began the race hatred which lies at the bottom of all Cuban troubles to the present day. We have seen in our chapter on the South American colonies how the Creoles — that is, white men born on South American soil — were debarred from all offices under the Colonial Government, and were treated as an inferior race. The children of Peninsulars, — that is, of Spaniards born on Spanish soil, — if born in South America, Mexico, or Cuba became Creoles, and were under the ban. Many were men well educated, — who had travelled or studied abroad, — were wealthy planters or traders; but nothing effaced the radical difference between them and Spain-born Spaniards. Roughly speaking, from that day to this the true Spaniard has been an Absolutist in politics, the Creole an insurgent or revolutionary. I shall have more to say on this subject, but it is sufficient here to point it out in its beginning.

The first captains-general of Cuba seem to have consulted its material interests; and in that connection they protected the slave-trade. They succeeded in keeping the negro population quiet, while all was riot, rebellion, and bloodshed in the neighboring island of San Domingo.

In 1799 King Charles IV. of Spain made the Marquis of Someruelos captain-general. He was in power when the events recorded in the earlier chapters of this book took place at Bayonne and Aranjuez.

The Spanish half of San Domingo had been ceded to France in 1795; and the race war in that island between whites and blacks "benefited Cuba, through the large immigration of white settlers, who were driven from San Domingo. The number of these who took refuge in Cuba during the decade ending with 1808 has been calculated at fully thirty thousand. They settled mainly in the eastern districts of the island, and contributed greatly to the development of that section. They introduced the culture of the coffee plant, which rapidly grew into a large element of colonial commerce." The cession of Louisiana to France and subsequently to the United States also brought several thousand Spanish settlers to Cuba.

When news, in 1808, reached Cuba of the proceedings in Spain, and of the captivity of King Ferdinand at Valençay, the colonists with one accord refused to recognize the government of King Joseph, and stood by their Captain-General, who acknowledged the authority of the Provisional Junta at Seville; while his people endeavored by contributions of money and supplies to aid their countrymen who were struggling against the French invasion.

The Provisional Junta at Seville proclaimed equal rights for all Spaniards, home-born or Creole, and the hopes of the colonists rose high. But, as we know, when the constituent Cortes met in Cadiz and required deputies to represent the colonies, they were obliged to appoint as deputies men who were within their reach ; and the thirty-four deputies intrusted with the interests of the Spanish-American colonies were traders of Seville and Cadiz, who thought only of their own advantage, and not of the hopes and expectations of those they were supposed to represent. The Cortes placed restrictions upon colonial commerce, which the Captain-General of Cuba took the responsibility of modifying. But on the South American Continent no government official espoused the interests of his people. Revolution broke out in Buenos Ayres in 1809, spread to Peru the same year, and was carried on by Bolivar in the northern provinces in 1810. Meantime, the commotions in South America brought many Spaniards to Cuba, thereby considerably augmenting the Spanish-born Spanish race in that colony.

In the Cortes that framed the Constitution of 1812, a motion was made in favor of the gradual abolition of slavery. This measure was vehemently opposed by the Cuban deputies, and was rejected. But news of what had taken place reached not only the masters, but the slaves in Cuba, and led to a brief negro insurrection, which was vigorously put down, and its leader, José Aponto, was executed.

During the sway of the Provisional Government at Cadiz, another captain-general was sent to Cuba, who proclaimed the new Constitution with some modifications. The civil and military powers of the government were separated in Cuba, and the island was divided into three intendancies, each ruled over by a civil governor, subject to the authority of the Captain-General. That officer occupied himself chiefly with military affairs until the return of Ferdinand to power, when he received orders to abrogate the new order of things in Cuba, and to restore the ancient *régime*.

During the administration of the next Captain-General, Cienfuegos, the slavery question agitated the colony. It was in 1817 that England paid Spain two million dollars as compensation for the loss of revenue she might experience by the suppression of the slave-trade ; and a few years later Portugal received for the like reason one million five hundred thousand dollars. Suppression of the slave-trade was violently opposed in Cuba ; and though King Ferdinand made promises to England and received her money, the importation of slaves went on more vigorously than before, and Cuba became the slave-mart for all the slaveholding countries in the Western world.

The citizens of the United States had many claims against the Spanish Government which were settled by the cession of Florida (which had been given back to Spain by the Treaty of Paris in 1783) to the United States in 1819 ; and in the same year Cienfuegos, who had exerted himself to promote the general interests of the colony, was succeeded by a governor sent out to lend aid and support to the military expedition then preparing to start from the Isle de Leon to suppress revolution in the South American provinces. We know already how that expedition fared, how the soldiers revolted, re-established the Constitution of 1812, and destroyed King Ferdinand's " absolute " authority.

The news of what had taken place in Spain produced great disorders in Cuba. The governor, however, followed the current of events in the mother country, recognized the authority of the new government, released all political prisoners, once more proclaimed the Constitution of 1812 ; and Cuba prepared to send deputies over seas to the Spanish Cortes.

The liberal tendencies of the Exaltado party in Cuba seemed so revolutionary that liberal-minded men, sent out from Spain to be governors of the island, endeavored to put some curb upon them. This roused great indignation among the Cubans, and secret societies began their work in the island. The zealous supporters of the Constitution of 1812 were mostly Creoles ; the Spanish-born part of the population was for the King's absolute sovereignty. Thus opinions were divided in Cuba pretty much as they were in the mother country, except that there were no Carlists in the island. The breach between the parties was widened by measures that affected their private interests, — one party favoring the opening of the ports to foreign trade, the other insisting that their commercial prosperity needed the restriction of trade as formerly to ports of the mother country.

The reaction that followed the invasion of Spain by the French under the Duc d'Angoulême, put an end to the hopes of the Cubans for a Liberal government, and they began to think of revolution. The design of the Holy Alliance and of King Ferdinand was to make Cuba a base of operations against the revolted provinces of Spanish America which had established their independence as republics. This design, as we know, was opposed by Mr. Canning, and led to that sentence in the message of President Monroe on December 2, 1823, which was the foundation of the American system of policy popularly known as the Monroe doctrine.

The feeling between the Creoles and the Peninsulars in Cuba became more and more embittered. The Peninsulars had of course with them the Church and the government officeholders. The Creole party was divided on the vexed question of slavery. The Spanish American republics, when they proclaimed independence, had freed their slaves. In Cuba there was some talk of seeking annexation with the United States ; but our Southern States opposed annexation without slavery, while the Northern States refused their consent to such an increase of strength to the slaveholding power in Congress as would be made by the admission of one or more Cuban slave States.

Owing to the political excitement in the island, a royal decree conferred on the Captain-General power to put the country under martial law, and at the same time a Military Executive Commission was appointed for the summary trial, sentence, and execution of political prisoners.

Agitation and conspiracy continued to disturb the tranquillity of the island, and the antislavery controversy became an element of discord in every Cuban city. By way of distracting the attention of the turbulent, the Captain-General in August, 1828, organized a military expedition against

Mexico, which failed ignominiously. To this Captain-General, Marshal Vives, despotic powers had been intrusted to meet extraordinary circumstances ; but these powers have been continued to his successors up to the present time.

When the Queen Regent Christina succeeded Ferdinand, and proclaimed herself a constitutional ruler, she did not extend her nominal constitutionalism to Cuba. On the contrary she sent out a certain Don Miguel Tacon, who exceeded all former governors in severity, and arbitrarily exercised his unlimited powers.

Former chapters have dwelt sufficiently on the depletion of the Spanish Treasury and the greed of Queen Christina. But in 1836, during the administration of Tacon, occurred a little piece of secret history not known at the time to any but the three or four actors engaged in the plot. It was a scheme to sell to France the turbulent and troublesome island which had ceased to be " ever-faithful" to the rule of Spain. Queen Christina commissioned M. Aguado, the Spanish banker in Paris, to request a very private interview with Prince Talleyrand. The message sent by Aguado to the Prince of the old Diplomatists was couched in most mysterious terms, hinting at dark combinations which, if successful, would bring fortune to those engaged in the negotiation ; and if not, must remain a secret never suspected by the rest of the world.

The Spanish envoy sent to Paris on this business was Señor Campuzano. He had accepted the commission with great reluctance, being heartily ashamed of lending his assistance to wrench the brightest jewel from the Spanish crown. But Queen Christina was involved in what she held to be pecuniary difficulties, and insisted that Señor Campuzano must undertake her mission.

A meeting took place between Campuzano, Prince Talleyrand, Aguado, and the Prince's secretary. Campuzano said afterwards that he had undertaken the office for fear it should be seized upon by one of the Queen's favorites, who, without faith or loyalty, would seek nothing but the pecuniary advantage he might derive from the successful transfer of gigantic sums. During the reading of the secret agreement to be signed by the King of France, the Queen Regent of Spain, and their respective ministers, the unfortunate Campuzano is described by Talleyrand's secretary, who told what then took place, as having been deeply affected. The proposition was so monstrous, so rascally, so base, that as he read it, he struck a heavy blow on the table and muttered a curse.

Queen Christina in this document proposed, for a consideration of thirty million reals, to hand over to Louis Philippe the island of Cuba; and the Philippine Islands and Porto Rico for ten million more. The conspirators were in the greatest dread of Lord Palmerston, and this dread guided Aguado in the instigation of the manner in which the measure was to be submitted to the King.

A loan of course would be needed to meet the purchase, and this was to be floated on the Paris Bourse. Out of this loan the great banker would receive large commissions. One million francs was to be offered to Prince Talleyrand, and three hundred thousand was to be distributed as bribes and commissions to other people.

A few days later the parties met in the King's cabinet which overlooked the gardens of the Tuileries, to sign the contract. Campuzano was nervous almost beyond control. The article respecting Cuba hardly provoked any discussion, but when it came to the one on the Philippine Isles the case became more difficult. Louis Philippe seemed to see the opportunity for making a bargain. He remarked that the cession of the Philippine Isles to France would be so obnoxious to England that diplomatic complications, if not a declaration of war, might be the result. He therefore demanded a reduction on the price placed on the Philippine Islands, and pushing the contract across the table to Campuzano, exclaimed imperatively, " The reduction of price *must* be accepted. The terms are too onerous. Seven millions of reals is my offer, or else the contract must be thrown into the fire."

Talleyrand was about to speak. He had stretched forth his hand to take up the paper, when Campuzano, starting up with such force that his chair fell, leaned over the table, seized the contract, crumpled it together in his hands, and, looking full in the King's face, said : "Your Majesty is right. The contract is worthless, only fit to be thrown into the fire." With that he flung the paper on the blazing logs, beating it down with the tongs until nothing remained of it but blackened fragments. So ended the first proposition for the sale of Cuba, — the sale of Cuba to France.

Meantime the furies seemed to be let loose on the unhappy island, which might possibly have been happier under French rule than under the Spanish crown ; for the rancor and hatred with which Spanish officials regarded the Creoles increased, and bitterness in proportion poisoned the Cubans' hearts, as the iron entered into their souls.

The years that followed have been termed " the period of conspiracies " in Cuba ; in Spain it was a period of political disorganization.

At this time a project of annexing Cuba began to be widely discussed in the United States, and President Polk opened some negotiations for the purchase of the island, not by secret conspiracy, but through the American minister at Madrid.

Meantime General Lopez, a Venezuelan by birth, who had fought in the Spanish army against Spanish-American rebels, came to Cuba, held some office under government, and married a Cuban lady. Thenceforward he took the part of the Creoles against the Spanish Government, attempted an insurrection, fled to the United States, and identified himself with other Cuban conspirators who had their headquarters in New York. In 1850 he landed in Cuba with six hundred men. But the expedition was unsuccessful. Lopez and his followers retired to America, and the next year undertook another expedition. The second in command of these filibusters was Colonel Crittenden of Kentucky. Their landing was opposed by a large force of Spaniards, and after defending themselves bravely, those left alive surrendered. Lopez was garroted, and fifty of his men were shot.

In 1853 President Pierce sent Mr. Pierre Soulé to Madrid as United States minister. Up to that time the ministers who had occupied that post had been men of high character and qualifications. Washington Irving had been succeeded by Judge Saunders of North Carolina (father of Mrs. Bradley Johnson, a lady widely known throughout the South for her activity during the war period, her bravery, her large charity, and her many accomplishments) ; but the appointment of Mr. Soulé, a Frenchman by birth, exiled in his youth from his own country as a conspirator against the French Bourbons, was considered by many a highly inappropriate selection. Not long before he sailed, he made a speech in public, lauding Lopez, and expressing his hostility to the Spanish Government in a manner that could not but have been most offensive to Spain. Why the court at Madrid did not refuse to receive him it is hard to understand ; he made his appearance at Madrid, however, as the representative of his adopted country, and was received with politeness in the diplomatic circle. Not long after his arrival, he with his wife and son attended a fancy ball given by Admiral Turgot, the French ambassador. The ball was in honor of the Empress Eugénie, whose sister had married the Duke of Alva. In the course of the evening the Duke happened to remark that Mrs. Soulé, who was clad in green velvet, looked like Mary of Burgundy. It was a perfectly innocent remark, but it was overheard by her son, and led to two duels. Young Soulé challenged the Duke of Alva. The latter disclaimed any intention of being rude to Mrs. Soulé, but the duel took place nevertheless, and society in Madrid congratulated itself that no one had been hurt and that the affair was over. Not so, however. Mr. Soulé the next day addressed the following letter to the French ambassador : —

Monsieur le Marquis, — The difference which has arisen between the Duke of Alva and my son took place in your *salons*. It was at your house, where I and my family were invited guests, and on the occasion of a fête of which the Duke of Alva might consider himself in some measure the hero, that

26

the latter insulted Madame Soulé, without anything having hitherto happened to exonerate us from the bond of good fellowship which that circumstance causes to weigh upon you. It is even positively asserted that the insulting expression made use of by the Duke of Alva first proceeded from your mouth. That being the case, Monsieur le Marquis, I have a right to go to the true source which placed swords in the hands of the Duke of Alva and of my son, to make it mine as far as you are concerned, and to demand personally a satisfaction which you cannot refuse me. Mr. Perry, an American citizen and my friend, is charged to receive your reply. I have the honor to be, Monsieur le Marquis, your very humble servant,

PIERRE SOULÉ,
*Citizen of the United States.*

December 17, 1853.

They fought the next morning with pistols. Admiral Turgot received a ball in his knee, which made him lame possibly for life and for a long period impaired his health; while the affair by no means improved Mr. Soulé's position at Madrid in the diplomatic circle.

Soulé had serious matters besides this private quarrel on his hands. In addition to the proposition he was charged to make on the part of Mr. Pierce for the acquisition of Cuba, the affair of the "Black Warrior" took place about two months after the duel. The "Black Warrior" was one of a line of regular traders between Havana and New York. She was entered at the custom-house, and on her manifest, as being in ballast; but a searcher from the custom-house found that she was laden with cotton. She had nearly a thousand bales of cotton on board; and her captain and owners, who had not, according to law, "declared" the cotton, might have been fined four hundred dollars for each bale. The Captain-General Pezuela hesitated, however, to impose so large a fine, and offered to compromise for six thousand dollars, including all costs and charges. The consignees protested that there was no fraudulent intention on their part in the matter; that cotton was not an article needed in Cuba, and was not to be landed there; that the "Black Warrior" and her consort traded between Mobile and New York, and merely

touched at Havana to take in passengers. In short, that the
"Black Warrior" had been in the habit of entering the Cuban
port with a manifest representing her to be in ballast, as she
was bound to New York, and carried no cargo for Cuba.

Relations between the United States and Spain were
strained as regarded Cuba. The affair of the "Black Warrior"
was taken up by our people as a great wrong which must
look for redress through Congress. Mr. Soulé demanded
an indemnity of three hundred thousand dollars, and the
dismissal of all the Cuban authorities who had been concerned in the proceedings. Calderon de la Barca was
minister of state in the Sartorius ministry at Madrid at that
time, and it is said that he was very much bullied by Mr.
Soulé. Mr. Pierce too took a very high tone on the subject
in his message to Congress; but when the Sartorius ministry
fell in July, 1854, as we have seen in a former chapter, the
matter was pacifically arranged with their successors. It
led, however, to what was called the Ostend Manifesto, in
which three ministers of the United States — envoys to
England, France, and Spain — protested to the powers of
Europe that the possession of Cuba by a foreign country was
a menace to the peace of the United States; and it was proposed that Spain should be offered the alternative of taking
two hundred million dollars for her sovereignty over Cuba,
or of having it taken from her by force. This was on the
eve of the election of Mr. Buchanan, who, having signed the
Ostend Manifesto as the United States ambassador to England, might have been disposed, when President, to follow
up the affair, had it not been for the outbreak of our Civil
War.

Lersundi, who had been one of a cabinet in Madrid whose
arbitrary and absolute proceedings prepared the way for the
outbreak of 1854, was sent to Cuba in 1857; but his tyranny
provoked such complaints that he was replaced by Marshal
Concha after a brief sway. Concha made a good governor,
and the island would have prospered under him, had it not
been for the tariff regulations which restricted commerce with
foreign countries, and the enormous weight of taxes imposed

upon the Cubans by the necessities or the extravagance of Spain.

"But," says the editor of the American translation of "Cuba and the Cubans," by Raimondo Cabrera, "the effects of these ill-advised measures were minimized during the period of the American Civil War, by the moderating sway of two able and liberal-minded governors, Francisco Serrano and Domingo Dulce, who ruled successively from 1860 to 1865."

The abolition of slavery in the United States stimulated revolutionary movements in Cuba. The more moderate Liberals demanded a revision of the laws under which Spain governed the island, but all projects of reform proved abortive from the start. The Creoles of Cuba required that measures should be inaugurated for the gradual extinction of slavery. The Peninsulars, or Spanish race, the men most interested in sugar-planting and coffee estates, opposed it.

In 1868 General Dulce, who had married a rich Cuban lady, and had identified himself with the Creole party in Cuba, went back to Spain and was prominent in the revolution which ended in the flight of Isabella; but before this revolution took place Lersundi had another brief reign in Cuba, under the Gonzales Bravo ministry. He increased the taxes and provoked general discontent, especially in the eastern and central provinces of the island.

In October, 1868, Carlos Manuel de Céspedes, a Creole by birth, but at one time in his youth a conspirator in Spain, started the cry for independence on his own plantation at Yara, at the head of a band of his own slaves whom he had manumitted, and about one hundred and forty other poorly armed followers. This was the beginning of a war which lasted ten years, chiefly in the eastern and central parts of Cuba, — a war which cost Spain eight thousand officers, two hundred thousand privates, and three hundred million dollars; besides as much more lost to its Cuban sympathizers by destruction. A republic was proclaimed, and Céspedes was made its President. His *rule*, if such it could be called, lasted three years; at the end of that time discord among his followers caused his deposition. But those who led the

movement found it hard to agree on his successor, so Cisneros, Marquis de Santa Lucia, was made Provisional President. Céspedes went into retirement, but was surprised by
the enemy, wounded, escaped, but died of his wounds,
homeless, starving, and abandoned. "He was," says Mr.
Levy, "a man of exceptional ability, unselfishly devoted to
the cause he professed." His deposition caused widespread
disaffection in the Cuban ranks, and for a season the insurrection was brought practically to a close.

As we know already, one of the revolutionary measures
while Spain was for a brief season a republic was the raising
of volunteer battalions, or home guards. These in Spain
were the despair of generals, who could not enforce discipline
among them, or restrain them from burning and destroying.
It was these national guards who set fire to dairy farms in
the valley of the Bidassoa. But in Cuba their work was in
the cities, which they were supposed to defend ; and their
behavior was like that of brigands. They made and unmade
their own officers, and they actually deported Captain-
General Dulce to Spain, because they considered him too
lenient toward the insurgents. The Republic, to satisfy
them, sent out a governor of sterner stuff, named Balmaceda.
He did nothing of any importance against the insurgents,
who carried on, among their mountains in the eastern and
central provinces, the same guerilla warfare that we have seen
already so baffling to regular troops in Spain.

But if Balmaceda and the volunteers could do nothing
against the bands of insurgent Creoles, negroes, and mulattoes, they terrorized the cities, and many anecdotes are told
of their excesses.

In 1870, when a performance was to be given at the theatre in Havana, the proceeds of which, it was whispered,
would be forwarded to the insurgents, the volunteers fired
on the audience as they were leaving the playhouse, killing
and wounding many persons.

In November of that year, forty-three boys, students in
the University of Havana, were arrested on the charge that
one of them had defaced a glass plate at the cemetery, in a

vault which contained the remains of a volunteer. The boys were acquitted by a court-martial composed of Spanish officers, but the volunteers demanded of Balmaceda a new trial, before a court-martial composed of *their own officers.* The governor acceded to only part of their demand; otherwise the whole forty-three boys would no doubt have been shot; but a mixed court of regular and volunteer officers sentenced eight of them to death, and thirty-one to imprisonment. The execution was made an occasion of fête by the volunteers. The government cowered under their dominion.

On a former occasion a number of schoolboys were arrested for having broken in a game of ball the glass of a picture of Queen Isabella; and a medical commission was appointed to report whether any fragment of glass had wounded the counterfeit presentment of her Majesty in a vital part, as in that case the offence would have been high treason.

From 1870 to 1878, Cuba had eight captains-general, — Dulce, Lopez-Pinto, Pieltan, Caballero de Rosas, Balmaceda, Jovellar, Concha, and Martinez Campos. During Pieltan's administration in 1873, an American steamer, the "Virginius," with supplies of men and arms for the insurgents, was captured by the Spaniards. Fifty-three of those on board were instantly executed, including the captain; and the hundred and two survivors would have been similarly disposed of had not help come from an unexpected quarter.

"The incident," says Mr. Halstead, "is one gleam of light in this dark chapter. The British steamer 'Niobe,' Captain Sir Lampton Lorraine, ran in to Santiago, where the executions were taking place, at full speed from Jamaica, starting in such a hurry that she left some of her crew behind; the captain was landed in Cuba before his ship was anchored, and demanded that the massacre should be stopped. He claimed to represent the United States as well as England, it is said, and he even threatened to bombard the city. His vigor caused the suspension of the sentences still remaining to be executed, and the lives of the prisoners not already put to death were saved. On his way home Sir Lampton Lorraine stopped at New York, where he was invited to hold a reception, which he declined; but by way of saying to him, 'You are a brick,' a silver brick from Nevada was presented to him, bearing this inscription, ' Blood is thicker than water.' For some reason, not clear, the House of Representatives laid a resolution of thanks to Sir Lampton on the table."

Captain Joseph Fry, commander of the " Virginius," wrote a manly and pathetic letter to his wife the night before his execution. Mr. Halstead will pardon me if I extract this also from his pages : —

On Board the Spanish Man-of-War "Tornado,"
Santiago de Cuba, November 6, '73.

Dear, Dear Dita, — When I left you I had no idea that we should never meet again in this world; but it seems strange to me that I should to-night and on Anne's birthday be calmly seated on a beautiful moonlight night in a most beautiful bay in Cuba to take my last leave of you, my own dear sweet wife! and with the thought of your own bitter anguish, — my only regret at leaving.

I have been tried to-day, and the president of the court-martial asked the favor of embracing me at parting, and clasped me to his heart. I have shaken hands with each of my judges, and the secretary of the court and the interpreter have promised me as an especial favor to attend my execution, which will, I am told, be within a few hours after my sentence is pronounced.

I am told my death will be painless. In short, I have had a very cheerful and pleasant chat about my funeral, to which I shall go a few hours from now; how soon I cannot say yet. It is curious to see how I make friends. Poor Bambetta[1] pronounced me a gentleman, and he was the brightest and bravest creature I ever saw.

The priest who gave me communion on board this morning put a double scapular around my neck and a medal which he intends to wear himself. A young Spanish officer brought me a bright new silk badge with the Blessed Virgin stamped upon it, to wear to my execution for him, and a handsome cross in some fair lady's handiwork. They are to be kept as relics of

[1] A Cuban rebel general, a passenger on board the "Virginius," who with three other generals had been at once shot.

me. He embraced me affectionately in his room with tears in his eyes.

Dear sweetheart, you will be able to bear it for my sake, for I will be with you if God permits. Although I know my hours are short and few, I am not sad. I shall be with you right soon, dear Dita, and you will not be afraid of me. Pray for me, and I will pray with you. There is to be a fearful sacrifice of life, as I think, from the "Virginius," and as I think a needless one, as the poor people are unconscious of crime, and even of their fate up to now. I hope God will forgive me if I am to blame for it.

If you write to President Grant, he will probably order my pay due when I resigned to be paid to you after my death. People will be kinder to you now, dear Dita; at least, I hope so. Do not dread death when it comes to you. It will be God's angel of rest, — remember this. I hope my children will forget their father's harshness, and remember his love and anxiety for them. May they practise regularly their religion, and pray for him always. Tell ——— the last act of my life will be a public profession of my faith and hope in Him of whom we need not be ashamed; and it is not honest to withhold that public acknowledgment from any false modesty or timidity. May God bless and save us all! Sweet, dear, dear Dita, we will soon meet again. Till then adieu for the last time.

Your devoted husband,

JOSEPH FRY.

It was said that these executions were due to the insistence of the volunteers of Santiago. If so, this letter affords another proof that savagery and barbarity in war are more often to be attributed to the passions of civilians than to any instinct of cruelty in those trained to the profession of arms.

In 1873 the Italian patriot Gallenga, better known to the English and American public by his literary name of Mariotti, went to Cuba to report upon the state of things he found there. On his return to England he wrote a small book called "The Pearl of the Antilles," which is the best account of the island from an entirely unprejudiced source that I have found anywhere.

He dwells strongly on the ineradicable race hatred between Creoles and Peninsulars. "No hatred in the world," he says, "can be compared to that of the Cuban for Spain and everything Spanish. To the stranger's eye the split between the races is nowhere apparent; the line of demarcation is not visibly drawn. Under the surface of daily life in the cities, there is a depth of simulation and dissimulation, of spoken and acted lies, not to be fathomed by a stranger on a mere superficial survey. . . . The Spanish settlers own very nearly the mass of the landed property and of the movable wealth of the country. They have largely the trade of Havana in their hands, partly in consequence of their superior thrift and activity, but in a great measure owing to the privileges and monopolies awarded to them by a partial, grasping, and unscrupulous administration."

Possibly a long quotation from Gallenga as to what the war was in Cuba in 1873, will enable us to understand something about the present insurrection : —

" Reports concerning the progress of the troops are forwarded daily from headquarters, and find their way into the papers, as, for example: 'Such a commanding officer has come up with an insurgent band. . . . To attack the rebels and completely rout them was for the heroic Spanish troops one and the same thing. They killed many of them, wounded many more, and took fourteen horses, and one rifle.' In another report we read, 'there were three rebels killed, seven prisoners, one of the latter wounded, three muskets were captured, and sixteen small arms; two able-bodied men surrendered.' And so on daily. . . . The marvel is that such skirmishing should go on from day to day for four years without more decisive results. . . . All allowance made for exaggeration on both sides, there can be little doubt about the ruthless character of these Cuban hostilities. Printed reports of massacre and torture may be wildly exaggerated; but there can be no doubt that there is a vast deal of shooting in cold blood, as indeed is admitted, not without boasting, on either side; and property fares no better than life in the belligerents' hands. I know from the very best authority that in the district of Trinidad de Cuba, one of the oldest settlements in the centre of the island, about two thirds of the sugar and coffee estates, and of the grazing farms, were either destroyed or abandoned, or thrown out of cultivation before the end of 1871. That magnificent valley was turned into a state of desolation from which it will need years of peace to recover. The same has been the fate of many other old settlements in the central districts. Of late the movement has taken another direction, beyond the Trocha, or military cordon which the Spanish troops have established."

A Trocha is an imaginary line, as intangible as the equator, along which the Spanish generals establish troops, and which they draw from time to time in different places, according to military necessity.

Cuba is divided into three intendancies. At one time each had its governor, though all were under the supreme sway of the Captain-General. The western part, which has always been the least insurrectionary, has Havana for its capital. It is the most prosperous division of the island, has numerous sugar factories and flourishing tobacco plantations.

The central province has for its chief city Puerto Principe. Its rural districts have been hardly brought under cultivation, and its dense forests of brushwood are favorable to guerilla warfare. If troops have to advance on the insurgents, they have to cut themselves paths through these entangled woods.

The eastern and broadest part of the island contains the oldest colonies. The valleys had been brought into cultivation, and coffee plantations once clothed the sides of the mountains, nevertheless much of the interior in 1873 was in a state of nature. "What cultivation there was in this region," says Gallenga, "is rapidly disappearing. Many of the land-owners, with such wealth as they have been able to save from the wreck of their estates, have emigrated to the United States, to the western part of the island, to Jamaica, or elsewhere."

The "volunteers" never attempted to encounter the insurgents. They left that duty to the troops from Spain; theirs was to coerce the cities.

In 1870, at the commencement of the Provisional Spanish Republic, the Spanish Cortes passed what is known as the Moret Bill, by which freedom was decreed to every child born of a slave mother after July 4 of that year; also to such slaves

*GENERAL WEYLER.*

as had helped, or would help, the Spanish forces against the insurgents. Under this law freedom was also to be given to every slave as soon as he attained the age of sixty years. But the Spanish authorities in Cuba were slow to publish this law, although slaveholders, seeing the extinction of slavery inevitable, were not unfavorable to it. But the volunteers opposed it bitterly. Two years elapsed before they would suffer any mention of it to be made in Cuban papers, and it was a dead letter until the days of Martinez Campos.

After the Carlist rising in Spain had been put down, and Alfonso XII. (largely through the adhesion of the victorious general Martinez Campos) had been seated on the Spanish throne, Campos, with twenty-five thousand veterans from the Carlist war, was sent to Cuba. Still the insurgents succeeded in constantly eluding the Spaniards when pursued by a large force, or defeating them when they encountered a small one. In 1877 General Jovellar undertook to conduct the war in Cuba; while Campos employed himself in devising some measure of compromise with a view to pacification.

Nine generals, with Garcia (who had succeeded Cisneros as third President of the insurgent republic) at their head, met Campos and a number of his officers in February, 1878, at Zanjon, and there signed a document by which the Cubans gave up their struggle for independence, and Spain conceded the reforms it had refused to grant in 1867.

The "Compromise of Zanjon" consisted of eight articles, of which the principal were: (1) Concession to Cuba of the same privileges enjoyed by Porto Rico; (2) Complete amnesty; (3) Freedom to Asiatic coolies and slaves in the insurgent ranks; (4) No insurgent to be compelled to do military service to the Spanish Government until peace should have been established in the land; (5) The government would lend aid and protection to all desiring to leave the island; (6) Insurgents publicly to lay down their arms; (7) Railroad and steamship facilities to be afforded by the Captain-General to all sections of the insurgent army repairing to the place appointed for the surrender of their arms.

With this "Compromise of Zanjon" General Martinez Campos returned to Madrid and laid before the Cabinet of Canovas his plans for putting into force, by legislation in the Cortes, the reforms that had been promised the insurgents by these articles of capitulation. But Canovas dared not ask the Cortes to confirm the Compromise. He said that that body would feel — and feel *always* — that Spanish honor demanded the complete subjection of Cuba. If General Campos insisted upon laying the Compromise before the Cortes, it must be done on his own responsibility. The result was that Canovas resigned the premiership. General Campos then formed a ministry ; but his Cuban proposals were not cordially supported even by his cabinet, and he was forced to resign. Canovas resumed the task of government, and the promises made at Zanjon were laid aside.

In 1880 some attention was, however, paid to the proposals of Campos, and partial reforms, incomplete and ineffectual, took place.

Since 1880 the Creole Liberals have been divided into two parties, — one for autonomy, the other for independence. The latter is the stronger, having the voices of the reckless and the ignorant on its side.

For sixteen years — that is, from 1879 to 1895 — Cuba was not precisely in a state of insurrection, but it was never quiet. The intense race hatreds were as rancorous as ever. There were brigands in the hills, and on the part of the government ever-increasing exactions and taxation. General Prendergast in 1882 was a Captain-General after the pattern of Balmaceda.

There may be said to be but one point on which Creoles and Peninsulars cordially agree, and that is in hatred and contempt for the lower ranks of Spanish officials. These men are, and always have been, sent from Spain. Their term of office is generally short, and they come out determined to employ their time so as to make their fortunes. "Cuba for the Cubans !" is the popular cry. Since the early days of the sixteenth century, "Cuba for the Spaniards" has been the principle on which the island has been governed.

In 1887 slavery was abolished in Cuba. The measure had been so long expected that it seems to have produced no social convulsion. Nor has any one as yet written much upon the subject. In the insurrection from 1868 to 1878, "the Cuban insurgents were," says Gallenga, "a mere handful of white men with a large following of negroes, who consist mostly of free mulattoes and blacks, though their ranks are occasionally, though not to any great extent, swelled by fugitive slaves." It was remarked, however, that cases of mutiny among the slaves, or of desertion from their masters, were extremely rare.

In the war that is now in progress (1897) the insurgent ranks must be greatly swelled by emancipated slaves. To fight is much easier than to labor. It is the nature of men bred in the tropics to be spasmodically energetic, with long intervals of doing nothing.

Mr. Levy sums up as follows his supplement to the book of Señor Cabrera : —

" The current of Cuban affairs following the peace of Zanjon, and the failure of the Spanish Government to fulfil the spirit of that compact, have been graphically narrated by our author. The efforts of cultivated and patriotic Cubans to maintain their country as an integral part of the Spanish monarchy under a form of home-rule government, have been eloquently set forth by Señor Cabrera, and the anachronism of the conditions which existed when he wrote in 1887 has been forcibly indicated in his work. It was the continuance of these conditions that brought on the armed conflict which began February 24, 1895, and which has now grown to greater proportions than any that has preceded it. It is manifest to every student of modern history that this conflict can have no final ending but in autonomy or independence, and that Cuban independence can have no future."

Independence achieved, a republic set on foot, and what will follow? Lersundi said that Cuba must be either Spanish or African. Lersundi's opinion may go for what it is worth, but there is always a possibility that it might come true.

Can Cuba sustain herself as a republic? — with her race

hatreds ; her domestic broils ; her mongrel population ; her lack of a navy ; her jealous neighbors ; and, above all, with her want of a *past !*

Why have Spanish-American republics been for years the opprobrium of liberty, but because of the nature of the people who inhabit them ? — the dilution of the blood of the proud and boastful Spaniards with that of servile races. Spanish-Americans have crude ideas of freedom, and apparently no capacity for self-government. Any success they have attained in the way of independence has always resulted in the boldest or the bloodiest of them seizing the reins of government and proclaiming himself a dictator.

The conditions have been far more favorable for the success of republicanism in Mexico and the South American republics than they seem now for the future of a Republic in Cuba.

Annexation to the United States ? Could the Cubans, who hate foreigners and foreign rule, desire it, unless as a *pis aller ?* Can any two natures be more alien than the Creole and the Yankee ? Hitherto, when the United States has annexed territory, the acquisition has been preceded by the settlement of a considerable number of born Americans in the country. Cuba has nothing of this kind to form a foundation for American sentiment or institutions.

Can the United States want a million more free blacks to be added to our population ? — or an immense accession to the already too large number of our un-Americanized voters ?

Again, the Creoles and mulattoes have no race antipathy to each other, — no objection to social intercourse, little to miscegenation. How should we accommodate their ideas to those of our people ?

Brigands and lawless bands infest the mountains. The establishment of a regular government will not bring them back to rural labor. They will not turn their swords into plough-shares, or their *machetes* into cane knives. It would take every man of our small American army to hunt them through their coverts. It would be the old war between regulars and guerillas over again, not in the healthy atmosphere of the Basque mountains, but in a climate which would prove as fatal to our own men as it has done to Spanish soldiers.

Spain, it is said, now offers autonomy to Cuba. A large number of intelligent and educated Cubans of social standing earnestly desire that the offer should not be refused. Those who have conversed with Cuban leaders in their camps think that during the first three months of the struggle Cubans would gladly have accepted such an offer, — autonomy, that is to say, with effective guarantees. But now the cry for independence is raised by those who scarcely know what autonomy may mean, and to secure its acceptance would be much more difficult. Autonomy might lead to independence, or in the end to annexation, but first its task would be to do a work of education. "To create a republic," said a Spanish statesman, "we must make republicans;" and republicans need a Past to grow in. They will not spring up in a night in ungenial soil.

Another project has been started which may possibly lead to independence; if the first steps can be taken, Free Cuba must deal with subsequent difficulties as best she can. It is proposed that Cuba should buy herself from Spain, whose monetary difficulties increase with every season; that the payment of the price offered shall be met by a lien upon the customs, and revenue from the customs be placed in charge of the United States. Whether Cuba will have much produce to export, or much money to pay for foreign imports for some years to come, may be doubted.

But we will not here discuss these questions; my business is simply to relate events. And a few brief words upon Spain's present wars must close both this chapter and this volume.

All accounts from the seat of war, whether Spanish or insurgent, may be held to be unreliable. We can judge how the war stands only by its results, and these results seem in the present year (1897) to favor the Cubans.

News derived from the insurgent camps reaches the *junta* of Free Cuba, which has its headquarters in New York, *via* Key West and Tampa; Spanish accounts come to us by way of steamers from Havana. In both cases the Father of Lies might have acted as reporter.

The present war commenced in February, 1895. No one, I think, has told us the immediate exciting cause of the outbreak. Cubans had apparently made up their minds to begin another war, and they waited for the close of the rainy season. " Since the failure of Martinez Campos to procure the fulfilment of the promises of constitutional reform made in 1878 at Zanjon, the island," says the Hon. H. Howard, an Englishman who spent five weeks with the insurgents in 1896, " had been nursing itself for the present insurrection."

" The war in Cuba," says Mr. Murat Halstead, " is the second and enlarged edition of that which raged from 1868 to 1878, originating in the same grievances of the Cubans and the same abuses of government by the Spaniards. The ten years' war was of like character with this in the conduct of hostilities, and the leading men in both wars are the same. There were the roving bands of insurgents and pursuing columns of Spaniards then as now; the same strong Spanish lines across the island, the same deadly skirmishing and deadlier fevers, the same deplorable incidents, exasperation, and exhaustion. Martinez Campos and Maximo Gomez were the great figures at the close of that war, as they were at the beginning of this; but there is one change always to be considered, that the area of strife is extended. Then but three of the six provinces were partially laid waste; now the whole extent of the island is devastated. There is about the same proportion of forces now as then. Both armies have in numbers been multiplied by three, and the insurgents have gained in confidence and in readiness to apply the torch. Then they were comparatively conservative in dealing with the plantations they occupied ; now, when they traverse the lands which are the sources of wealth, they become destroyers, until we may assume — indeed, we cannot do otherwise — that the sugar and tobacco crops are at an end while the war lasts, and the whole country is frightfully impoverished."

The object of this destruction is not the ruin of once wealthy owners; it is not even to assist the operations of war, but to prevent effectually the crushing of the sugar-cane throughout Cuba, and so to hinder Spain from getting any financial assistance from the island.

As soon as news of the fresh outbreak in 1895 reached Spain, Martinez Campos, "the Pacificator," who had closed the previous war, was sent to put down the rebellion. But the struggle gradually assumed far greater proportions than he had imagined possible. " He began by so far recognizing the Cubans as belligerents, not rebels, as to endeavor on his own part to carry on the war in a civilized way; but his enemies charged that his tenderness in dealing with the rebels was the great fault that filled the insurgent ranks. That, however, was injustice to a competent soldier. There is a great deal of intense political feeling in Havana, and soon all the politicians, except a few Moderates, were against him. Then he was recalled, and his successor, General Weyler, who had put down a revolt in the Philippine Isles in 1889, is believed by all Cubans to have been indebted for his appointment to his reputation for severity. Now Campos does not deserve his good name for benignity, nor Weyler the fulness of his fame for brutality and barbarism."

The prominent leaders on the side of the insurgents were Maximo Gomez, the Maceos, and Calixto Garcia. Gomez and Garcia are elderly men, and held in the war of 1868 the same military position that they hold now. When that war ended Gomez retired to his little farm in San Domingo, a town in Puerto Principe, one of the central provinces. Garcia left Cuba after the compromise at Zanjon; but his return when the present war commenced was hailed with rapture by his countrymen, who, well aware that they had not among them many generals of experience and capacity, received him as an accession of great importance to their cause.

The Maceos, Antonio and José, were the mulatto sons of a planter in one of the central provinces of the island. All accounts of the present war in Cuba, even the private letters

27

of young Southern gentlemen who have joined the insurgents, speak in warm terms of the Maceos, and especially of Antonio.

"General Antonio Maceo," says the Englishman I have quoted, " is the moving spirit of the whole revolt. He is a tall, broad-shouldered mulatto, with a reputation for reckless bravery and a good knowledge of Cuban warfare, gained during the last insurrection. He is the hero of the Cubans, and the terror of the Spanish soldiery, a volcano of energy, with a charming manner, a kindly disposition, and eyes which are perpetually smiling through a pair of gold-rimmed eye-glasses."

During the insurrection of 1868–78 the war was never carried into the province of Pinar del Rio. That province forms the western extremity of the island; it was covered with sugar plantations and sugar factories; it was the abode of men of wealth, and its capital is the city of Havana; but at the close of 1896 Gomez and Maceo concerted a joint movement. They were to pass with separate bands into the western part of the island. Maceo flanked Havana, crossed the Trocha, carried devastation through the rich province of Pinar del Rio, and threatened for some weeks the brilliant city of Havana. "War," says Mr. Halstead, "has roared and flamed at her gates : even her milk and water supplies have been threatened; her vegetable gardens have been robbed by rebels; and the writer has seen, half an hour from the great city, the flag of the rebellion flying from a hilltop."

Castelar, in the "España Moderna," wrote a paper on the death of Antonio Maceo. His article makes us forcibly realize how tenaciously Spain still clings to "the ever faithful isle," since even the Spanish Republican leader feels it to be a point of honor to crush those revolutionists who would throw off the oppression of the mother country.

Maceo, with his own army, composed largely of negro soldiers, entered Pinar del Rio with torch and sword. The narrowness of the island in its western part was favorable to the establishment of a Trocha. Maceo planned to recross this Trocha with a small part of his force, make a swift march on Havana, create a panic, and by this success obtain possibly from the United States a recognition of belligerency.

He took few men with him ; the main body of his troops he left behind, and those he gathered on his way were inexperienced and undisciplined. On their first encounter with the Spaniards they fled panic-stricken ; only the most valiant and resolute remained with their leader.

" If the negroes whom the General commanded," says Castelar, " had been his daring comrades of the past, he would have been able to direct them from the rear, but he had to place himself in the van in order to stimulate and encourage them. Thus, compelled by imperative necessity to fight hand to hand, he could not maintain the guard about his person which is indispensable for a safe command."

There were only three or four of his own people with him when he was killed, and the manner of his death remains a mystery.

When the news that he had fallen reached Havana, the most indecent demonstrations of joy took place. General Weyler put a stop to such public rejoicings. Perhaps he remembered the kind treatment accorded by Maceo to wounded Spanish prisoners ; perhaps he believed the story which, whether true or not, had wide circulation in Cuba, that at Bayamo, an engagement that took place between Spaniards and Cubans in the early days of the insurrection, Maceo, perceiving General Campos in the fight, pointed him out to his men and told them not to kill him, as he made war honorably.

Here is a letter which, after the same battle, Maceo addressed to General Campos : —

DEAR SIR, — Anxious to give careful and efficient attendance to the wounded Spanish soldiers that your troops have left behind upon the battlefield, I have ordered that they be lodged in the houses of the Cuban families that live nearest the battleground, until you send for them. With my assurance that the forces you may send to escort them back will not meet with any hostile demonstration from my soldiers, I have the honor to be, sir,                Yours respectfully,

ANTONIO MACEO.

The general impression abroad, however, is that the insurrection is being sustained by bands of savages, undisciplined and half-armed guerillas, outcasts from Cuban society, and negroes who carry on a marauding warfare of rapine and murder.

Mr. Howard in 1896, when he spent five weeks with the Cuban insurgents, tells us that —

" In the whole island there were some twenty-five thousand insurgents under arms, all, both infantry and cavalry, carrying the *machete* [1] as a side arm, and a rifle of one kind or another, usually a Remington. . . . With an increased supply of arms the insurgents in the field could be very largely increased. . . . Everywhere in camp discipline was strictly maintained, guard was regularly kept, and orders had to be carried out to the letter. In their drill the insurgents cut a most ridiculous figure, but drilled they were, and that generally twice a day, by Spanish deserters. . . . The cavalry were much better in hand than the infantry, and those I saw manœuvred with tolerable ease. . . . The rank and file of the rebels in the east are black, but farther west they are almost exclusively white, and a negro there is an exception. . . . In Maceo's army a few of the officers were black, but usually they were Cubans. The staff of General José Maceo was largely composed of the sons of wealthy Cuban planters, of doctors, and other professional men, many of them educated in America and speaking excellent French and English. . . . Almost every Cuban on the island is in sympathy with the insurrection. Nothing is more false than to suppose that only those who have nothing to lose, favor the revolt. Rich and poor, educated and uneducated, even the children born in Cuba of Spanish parents, — all are against Spain."

Perplexing as the affairs of Cuba are, and hopeless as outsiders feel it to be that Spain can hold the island, she has another problem as difficult to solve in the Philippine Isles, a few words concerning which ought to conclude this chapter.

The Philippine Isles, of which there are several groups, are said to consist of fourteen hundred volcanic islands, or

---

[1] The large knife of the country, which in time of peace serves to cut the sugar-cane.

islets; of which many are uninhabited, and others only partially known. The principal island is Luzon, and its capital, Manila, is an important station for trade between the West and the East Indies. The island raises hemp, tobacco, opium, and some sugar and coffee. Its resident white population, exclusive of monks and missionaries, is very small, though during the revolutionary years in Spain, generals, colonels, and civilians who had incurred the displeasure of any existing administration were transported in numbers to the Philippine Isles. They did not settle there, however; the next turn of the wheel of Fortune was sure to bring them back to Spain.

The islands were discovered in 1521 by Magellan, who was killed shortly after by some of the natives. The group was named after Philip II., and his spirit seems to have lingered in the islands, for the present difficulty has its origin, it is said, in the inquisitorial tyranny of the Spanish ecclesiastics. They have been ever lenient to all the sins of their converts, except heresy and rebellion against their own authority, to enforce which they have had recourse to the secular arm.

In 1823 the *mestizos*, or half-breeds, and the Creoles made an attempt to obtain a Liberal government; but the insurrection was put down by the Spaniards, who employed in this service a force formed of converted natives. In the present revolt the natives seem to have taken part on the other side. Up to 1842 the Spanish commercial policy with respect to the Philippines was the same as that in Cuba. All foreign ships were excluded from the ports of the islands, and one ship only once a year was allowed to trade between Manila and Acapulco. Now the ports are open to foreign commerce, but heavy protective duties are imposed on foreign commodities imported in foreign vessels.

The government is placed in the hands of a captain-general, whose powers are unlimited; but he is assisted by the advice of a Junta, consisting of the principal persons, military, civil, and ecclesiastical, in the island. The wild tribes of the interior of the island of Luzon did not acknowledge

Spanish supremacy until the year 1829. The converted natives and *mestizos*, though nominally Roman Catholics, have a strong reluctance to part with their heathen observances and superstitions. It is this that has led to what they consider ecclesiastical oppression, and has caused the savagery shown to captured priests and monks in the present conflict. There are many Chinese on the island, both native Chinese and Chinese *mestizos*. The European population, — not over eight or nine thousand, — comprises very few European women; while the number of half-breeds (natives crossed by Chinese, Japanese, or whites) is very great. It is these men who wish to free themselves from the civil oppression of Spain; while the native population, converted and heathen, resist ecclesiastical authority.

A Jesuit Father, writing shortly before the year 1890, thus expresses his opinion of the politico-economical results that may be looked for from alliances between white men and native women : —

"These unions have given us a querulous, discontented population of half-castes, who sooner or later will bring about a distracted state of society, and occupy the whole force of the government to stamp out the seeds of discord."

# POSTSCRIPT.

WHILE the earlier pages of this book were going through the press, the civilized world was startled by news that on Sunday, August 8, Señor Canovas del Castillo, prime minister of Spain, had been assassinated by an Italian anarchist, who at first gave his name as Rinaldi, later as Golli, and was subsequently identified as one Anglolillo. Señor Canovas had gone to the baths at Santa Agueda, a health resort in the north of Spain. He had just returned with his wife from mass, and was sitting in a public gallery reading a newspaper, when the murderer approached and fired three shots directly at him. All these shots took effect; the murdered premier lived afterwards barely an hour.

The assassin declared that he had no personal motive, either of enmity or animosity; but that he acted as the agent of a band of Anarchists who had decreed the death of the prime minister in revenge for the execution of certain Anarchist conspirators who a year before threw a bomb into a religious procession at Barcelona, which killed and wounded many harmless, helpless persons. " I have avenged my friends and brothers at Montjuich!" was the first exclamation of the murderer. He had been expelled from Italy for conspiracy and crime, and coming to Spain affiliated himself with the secret societies, whose hotbed is Barcelona.

Señor Canovas had been a prominent figure in public life for over forty years. In 1865, before the flight (or expulsion) of Isabella, he was a member of one of the temporary cabinets of the period, and he then showed a disposition to establish a liberal policy in colonial matters. We have seen how active a part he took, not only in the movement which led to the proclamation of King Alfonso XII., in 1873, but in the training and education of that young prince. On the accession of Alfonso, he became his trusted friend and counsellor, and after the young King's death he held the same position with the Queen Regent. From 1874 till 1884 he was alternately in and out of office. On Alfonso's death, in 1885, he was at once reappointed premier. When Sagasta was in office Canovas for a short time lent his support to the Progresista party. He soon, however, joined the opposition, and did not again enter the

Cabinet until 1890. He was then in power for two years, when he resigned; but in 1895 he was called back to conduct the troublous affairs of Spain, and remained in office until his death, though he had more than once offered his resignation. He was a man of strong will and obstinate determination; an orator and debater of great power, and a statesman well skilled in diplomacy. Personally he was honest and high-minded, quiet and virtuous in his private life, and inclined to literary pursuits. His historical writings are numerous and of great value.

The Queen Regent appointed General Azcarraga, who was Minister of War under Canovas, and his personal friend, to hold his place until it should be filled by a more permanent appointment. General Azcarraga has since been confirmed in his position. " There seems no doubt," says the " Outlook " of New York, August 28, 1897, " that he will continue to carry on his predecessor's policy, which is, as relates to Cuba, marked by the fixed intention of conquering the insurgents. After the assassination of Canovas there was a general hope among Spanish Liberals that Sagasta might be called to the premiership; and should the leadership of Azcarraga prove a failure, this may possibly be yet the case. It is well known that Sagasta has earnestly advocated a policy of conciliation with Cuba, and of home-rule for the Cubans. The chief difficulty in making such a policy practicable is that the Cuban insurgents show not the slightest disposition to accept anything but complete and absolute independence. The same difficulty stands in the way of the much talked of friendly interference by the United States with Spain. There is at present no reason whatever to believe that the Cuban leaders will even consider anything short of complete freedom from Spanish rule; any form of local autonomy which can be suggested would, they say, be easily perverted by Spain in actual practice, and of Spanish promises Cuba in the past has had too much experience to trust them again."

# INDEX.

# INDEX.

———◆———